Lawrence of Arabia

An Encyclopedia

Stephen E. Tabachnick

GREENWOOD PRESS
Westport, Connecticut • London

Library of Congress Cataloging-in-Publication Data

Tabachnick, Stephen Ely.
    Lawrence of Arabia : an encyclopedia / Stephen E. Tabachnick.
        p.   cm.
    Includes bibliographical references and index.
    ISBN 0-313-30561-7
       1. Lawrence, T. E. (Thomas Edward), 1888–1935—Encyclopedias.   I. Title.
  D568.4.T33   2004
  940.4′15′092—dc22   2004003574

British Library Cataloguing in Publication Data is available.

Library of Congress Catalog Card Number: 2004003574
ISBN: 0-313-30561-7

First published in 2004

Greenwood Press, 88 Post Road West, Westport, CT 06881
An imprint of Greenwood Publishing Group, Inc.
www.greenwood.com

Printed in the United States of America

The paper used in this book complies with the
Permanent Paper Standard issued by the National
Information Standards Organization (Z39.48–1984).

10 9 8 7 6 5 4 3 2 1

Contents

Alphabetical List of Entries

Preface

This first-ever Lawrence of Arabia encyclopedia is intended to serve the needs of everyone, from novices to aficionados, with an interest in T. E. Lawrence and the subjects associated with him. Because these subjects range from the history and politics of the Middle East in the World War I period to biblical archaeology, medieval castle-building, modern literature, and modern mechanical work, the scope of this book is necessarily very broad. What differentiates it from standard biographical, political, or historical encyclopedias of the Middle East or Great Britain in the twentieth century is that in every case the criterion for a subject's inclusion in the present volume is that it relates to Lawrence in a direct and important manner, whether because of his own interest in that subject, his influence upon it, or because it helps illuminate his life and work. So someone who looks up William Henry Hudson, for instance, will find not only the standard information that he was a British novelist, naturalist, travel writer, and the author of *Green Mansions* but also that Lawrence was a great admirer of Hudson's work and that his library at his Clouds Hill cottage included many of Hudson's books. Similarly, a reader looking up the Sykes-Picot Agreement, which laid out a plan for the division of the post–World War I Middle East between Britain, France, and Russia, will discover not only the basic ideas in this famous document but what Lawrence thought about them.

Even with this criterion in mind, an encyclopedia that would include every person, event, book, article, and idea associated in any way with Lawrence or his influence would run to many thousands of pages. That is because he was involved in so many activities and made important and sometimes unrecognized contributions to them. For instance, while many people have read *Seven Pillars of Wisdom* and have seen the David Lean film about Lawrence's desert campaign against the Turks during World War I, few know that he made an important contribution to biblical archaeology or that he is one of the best translators of Homer's *Odyssey*. Even fewer, perhaps, know that he loved motorcycles and airplanes far more than he did camels and that he also had a role in testing a possible prototype of what would become the PT boat of World War II. If Lawrence's multiple professional attainments were not reason enough to consider him an important facet of culture in the first third of the twentieth century, there is also the fact that he had a very complex and attractive personality that has proved perennially intriguing to journalists and writers of all kinds. Partially as a result of his own personality and exploits and partially because the British and American public needed a hero after the bloody impersonality of World

War I, he became one of the first media celebrities of the century, with hundreds of newspaper articles and well over 50 biographies to date devoted to his story. The demands of both time and economy dictated that I would have to make decisions about what was and was not important or essential enough to be included in this book. I have chosen to include only the most prominent and influential of his works, acts, and thoughts as well as the most influential aspects of things in which he had a hand. Inevitably, my choices will not satisfy everyone. However, I want to stress that I see this encyclopedia as an ongoing project that I will continue to augment and modify over time as more and more evidence and opinion become available.

The structure of the encyclopedia is straightforward: standard alphabetical order. Middle Eastern names and places, with few exceptions, are spelled as Lawrence himself spelled them in *Seven Pillars of Wisdom,* so the reader will find it easy to move from that book to this one, or vice versa. I also have followed the practice of *Seven Pillars of Wisdom* in another area, again with the convenience of the reader of both that book and this one in mind: as is done in the index to *Seven Pillars,* I have listed all Arab names under the first name when the first name was known. For instance, **Feisal ibn Hussein** is listed that way and not under **Ibn Hussein, Feisal,** or **Hussein, Feisal ibn.** References to the text of *Seven Pillars* are given in terms of chapter rather than page numbers, so readers may look up those references in any of the many available editions of *Seven Pillars.* Western names often are listed in fuller detail than Lawrence listed them in his index. I have tried to supply birth and death dates for all biographical entries, but as the reader will see, I have been unable to do so for many of the Arab personalities. With the Western figures, this information has been more consistent because it is more available, but here too I sometimes have been unable to supply one or both of these dates. I hope that I have been able to detail concisely the connections existing between Lawrence and the items in this book, which was my main purpose. There are numerous cross-references indicated by boldface type, and because two cross-referenced entries usually provide more information than one, I urge the reader to make use of these references.

A work such as this is of necessity largely synthetic, made up of facts gleaned from many sources, in the first place from Lawrence's works themselves, particularly *Seven Pillars of Wisdom, The Mint,* and his many letters. The second important source is the accumulated work of writers in the Lawrence field over almost the whole of the past century and the beginning of the twenty-first. Starting in 1919 with Lowell Thomas's slide show and book, *With Lawrence in Arabia* (1924), many biographers have been drawn to tell Lawrence's story. Of these earlier works, particularly notable is Richard Aldington's *Lawrence of Arabia: A Biographical Enquiry* (1955), a debunking of the Lawrence myth created by Lowell Thomas. Beginning in 1962 with the release of the David Lean film and then the discovery of new archival and interview material in 1968 by London *Times* journalists Phillip Knightley and Colin Simpson, a new impetus for interest in the field emerged, and soon academics joined the journalists and popular writers in tackling the Lawrence story. These academics now regularly turn out dissertations, articles, and books devoted to all aspects of Lawrence's life and career, be they military, political, literary, or personal.

They have established many facts and filled in the outline of a career that has always appeared mysterious in several respects, although less so now than before they did their excellent work. Among these academic Lawrence colleagues, I particularly want to indicate my reliance for the checking of facts (in addition to Lawrence's works themselves and histories of the period) on John Mack's Pulitzer Prize–winning biography *A Prince of Our Disorder,* on the manifold volumes of J. M. Wilson including particularly his *Lawrence of Arabia: The Authorized Biography* and his edition of the 1922 Oxford text of *Seven Pillars of Wisdom,* and on the second edition of Philip O'Brien's massive Besterman Prize–winning *T. E. Lawrence: A Bibliography.* For accuracy of facts and depth of research, these works tower above all other recent secondary materials in the Lawrence field. The collections of letters edited by David Garnett, Malcolm Brown, Harold Orlans, and Jeremy, Nicole, and Peter Wilson also have been very important for me. Among older biographers, the works of Lowell Thomas, Robert Graves, and Liddell Hart are especially notable not for their accuracy, but for their psychological insights because the biographers themselves knew Lawrence personally. Similarly, the volumes *T. E. Lawrence by His Friends* and *Letters to T. E. Lawrence,* both edited by Lawrence's brother A. W. Lawrence, contain essential eyewitness testimony. With regard to scholarship on World War I in general, I particularly want to acknowledge my indebtedness to Stephen Pope and Elizabeth-Anne Wheal's superb *Dictionary of the First World War* and to Philip J. Haythornthwaite for his equally outstanding *World War One Sourcebook.* For General Allenby's campaign, which was parallel to Lawrence's, I have found A. P. Wavell's *The Palestine Campaigns* the most useful of several sources. For Middle East politics of the period, George Antonius's *The Arab Awakening* and the *Political Dictionary of the Middle East,* edited by Yaacov Shimoni and Evyatar Levine, have been especially useful sources. For biographies, I have used many standard works, including the *Dictionary of National Biography, Who's Who,* and the Larousse *Dictionary of British History,* as well as the biographies that are listed in the entries and in the bibliography at the end of this volume. All of the above sources have been supplemented by numerous specialized studies and memoirs, to which references can also be found in the entries themselves as well as in the bibliography. I also want to note the advantages of the Internet, which has brought the catalogs of many English and American libraries and archives—for instance the British, Bodleian, and Harvard University Libraries—within easy reach. I am grateful to Dr. Philip O'Brien, Mr. Jacob Rosen, and Mr. St. John Armitage for answering my questions and to Dr. David Jacobson and Ms. Felicity Cobbing of the Palestine Exploration Fund, Mr. Alan Jutzi of the Huntington Library, and the staffs of the Australian War Memorial, Corbis, and the Library of Congress for help with the photos. I thank Ms. Tanya Broadbent for her maps. Any error of fact or incorrect representation of another person's viewpoint is of course entirely my responsibility. I have done my very best to minimize such errors and can only hope that I have succeeded in doing so.

Many Lawrence topics, including for instance the importance of his role in the Arab Revolt (and the importance of the Arab Revolt itself), why he joined the Royal Air Force as a private after he had been a colonel in the army, the nature of his sexuality, and whether or not he romanticized terrorism, remain controversial, and I have tried to give voice to opposing viewpoints on all such issues. Readers with a deeper interest in these various perspectives or in pursuing a given topic may consult the source references in many of the entries and in the bibliography. Publication information for articles cited in the entries is given in full in the entries themselves, while full publication information for books cited is given in the bibliography. My intention throughout this work has been, in the most accessible and convenient way possible, to help open the reader's mind to a fascinating, complex, controversial, and perennially relevant subject, not to try to close it. No one, least of all I who have studied Lawrence off and on for 30 years, would claim to know all of the answers to the Lawrence controversies and mysteries, especially when there is fundamental disagreement about certain basic events reported in *Seven Pillars of Wisdom,* such as the Deraa incident and the Tafas massacre. Ideally, this book will serve as a gateway to the appreciation of Lawrence and his Middle East because his period and, I venture to suggest, his life itself, have remained strangely important for an understanding of our own period and lives.

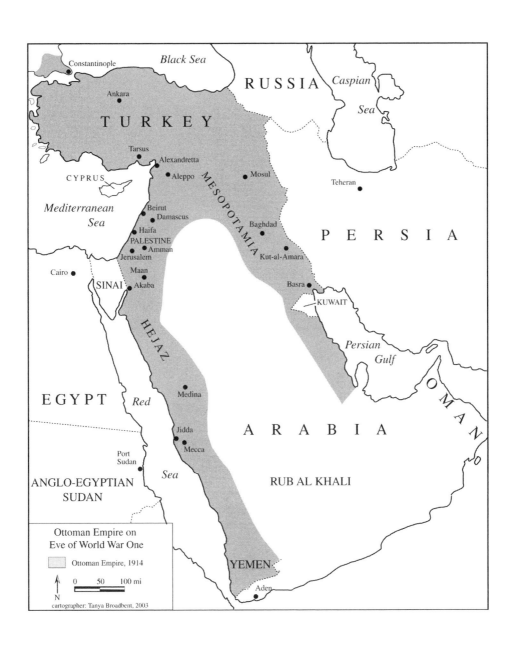

Black Sea

RUSSIA

Caspian
Sea

Constantinople

Ankara

TURKEY

Tarsus

Alexandretta

Aleppo

Mosul

MESOPOTAMIA

Teheran

CYPRUS

PERSIA

Mediterranean
Sea

Beirut
Damascus

Baghdad

Haifa
PALESTINE
Amman
Jerusalem

Kut-al-Amara

Cairo

Maan

Basra

SINAI

Akaba

KUWAIT

Persian
Gulf

HEJAZ

EGYPT

Red

Medina

OMAN

Port
Sudan

Jidda

Mecca

Sea

ANGLO-EGYPTIAN
SUDAN

ARABIA

RUB AL KHALI

YEMEN

Aden

Ottoman Empire on
Eve of World War One

Ottoman Empire, 1914

0   50   100 mi

N

cartographer: Tanya Broadbent, 2003

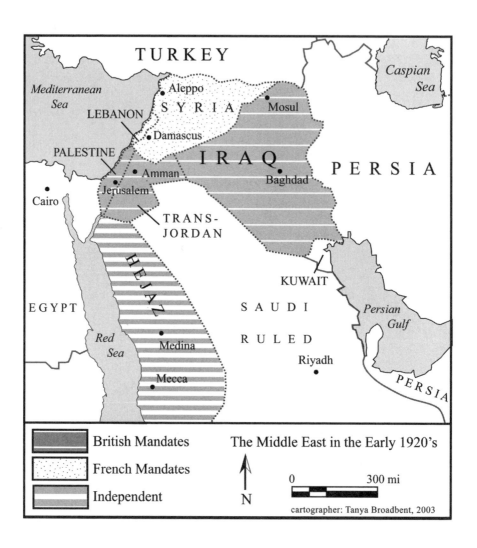

The Middle East in the Early 1920's

Legend:
- British Mandates
- French Mandates
- Independent

0 — 300 mi

N

cartographer: Tanya Broadbent, 2003

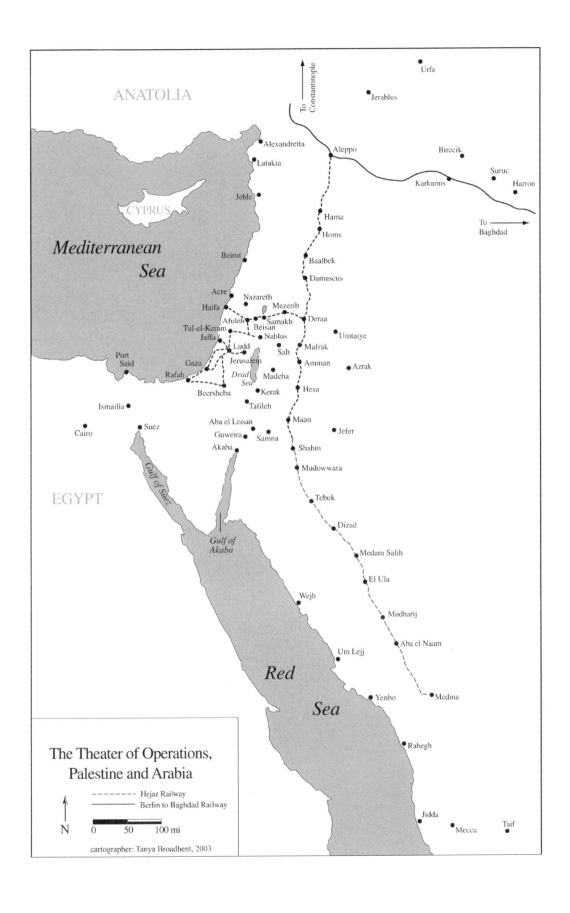

ANATOLIA

Urfa

Jerablus

Alexandretta

Aleppo

Birecik

Latakia

Suruc

Harron

Karkamis

To Constantinople

Jeble

CYPRUS

Hama

To Baghdad

Mediterranean Sea

Homs

Beirut

Baalbek

Damascus

Acre

Nazareth

Mezerib

Haifa

Deraa

Afuleh

Samakh

Umtaiye

Tul-el-Keram

Beisan

Jaffa

Nablus

Mafrak

Ludd

Salt

Amman

Azrak

Port Said

Gaza

Jerusalem

Rafah

Dead Sea

Madeba

Hesa

Beersheba

Kerak

Tafileh

Ismailia

Aba el Lissan

Maan

Jefer

Cairo

Suez

Guweira

Samna

Akaba

Shahm

EGYPT

Gulf of Suez

Mudowwara

Tebuk

Dizad

Gulf of Akaba

Medain Salih

El Ula

Wejh

Mudharij

Aba el Naam

Red Sea

Um Lejj

Yenbo

Medina

Rabegh

The Theater of Operations, Palestine and Arabia

- - - Hejaz Railway
——— Berlin to Baghdad Railway

N

0   50   100 mi

Jidda

Taif

Mecca

cartographer: Tanya Broadbent, 2003

Introduction:
Leonardo of Arabia

This book presents an encyclopedic approach to an encyclopedic man. Lawrence legitimately may be compared even to the polymathic Leonardo da Vinci. Most people know Lawrence of Arabia as the Peter O'Toole character in the David Lean film, leading a revolt of the Arabs against the Turks during World War I. What they may not know is that T. E. Lawrence did more things well than almost anyone else of his period. In archaeology, intelligence, guerrilla warfare, diplomacy, writing, translating, and mechanical work he made important, lasting contributions. Lawrence also was extraordinarily self-doubting and fragmented, composed of many different and contradictory compartments. He was a man of action and a quiet intellectual; politically, he was for the Arabs as well as for the British; he liked publicity and hated it; he wrote very well but always doubted the value of his writing; he wanted to tell the truth about his personal life but could not quite bring himself to do so; and he was drawn to sexuality but repressed it. His self-criticism allowed him no rest, and his life largely consisted of a search for a unity and peace of mind that he never quite found. Not surprisingly, such a complex person also has meant many different things to different people at different times. The resulting images have been expressed, for instance, in the form of Lowell Thomas's early 1920s slide show that hyped Lawrence as a complete hero; in the Richard Aldington 1954–55 exposé that accused him of being anti-British, pro-Arab, and a liar; in the David Lean film of 1962 whose script by Robert Bolt shows him conflicted between his British and Arab identities; and in the Knightley and Simpson 1969 biography that accuses him of imperialism. And the arguments continue right into the present generation of biographers including John Mack, J. M. Wilson, Lawrence James, Michael Asher, and Harold Orlans. Not only are there questions about Lawrence's position on imperialism, but also about many other issues that hang over his life and career: Was his influence in the Middle East beneficial or destructive? Why did he join the Royal Air Force as a private after he retired from the army as a colonel? Was he a truthful autobiographer? Was he a homosexual? The personal questions are no less relevant to an assessment of Lawrence than are the public ones, because as biographer John Mack has pointed out, in Lawrence's case personal neuroses were translated into public achievement. Along with a great deal of factual information, this encyclopedia offers summaries of opinion on these issues within individual entries. Because the approximately eight hundred entries form separate pieces of the puzzle known as Lawrence of Arabia, I will now try to pull together the pieces of this very unusual and diverse person's life and work in one coherent narrative. Perhaps, at this time of overt conflict between the West and the Islamic world, we can find something in Lawrence's life and career that might benefit us in our contact with the Middle East. In any case, his biography forms an amazing tale.

Lawrence was born on August 16, 1888, to parents who were not married and whose natures were very different. His father, Thomas Robert Tighe Chapman, an Anglo-Irish landowner, abandoned a wife and four daughters on his estate in County Westmeath to run off with the girls' young governess, Sarah Junner, whom he set up in an apartment in Dublin. While in Dublin, she gave birth to one child, Montagu Robert. When Sarah was discovered by the family butler in a grocery store calling herself "Mrs. Chapman," and the real Mrs. Chapman refused to give Thomas a divorce, Thomas and Sarah ran off to Wales and assumed the name Lawrence. There Thomas Edward was born, the second of what were to be five sons; he understandably felt little allegiance to the name Lawrence and later adopted Ross and then Shaw in its place. Restless moves to Scotland, where Sarah's family was from, and venues around the English Channel, including a stay in Dinard, a small French town on the Normandy coast, finally ended when the family settled in Oxford. Lawrence's father, Thomas, never had to work because he continued to collect some income from his estate. He taught the boys the gentlemanly skills of sailing and shooting and even photography, all of which would be immensely valuable to Lawrence later on in his many careers. But no longer ostensibly the lord of a manor, Thomas Robert was a smaller person socially than he had been in Ireland, while Sarah became increasingly religiously rigid and a repressive monitor of her sons' sexuality because of her own transgression. She found great comfort in the saying that God hated the sin but loved the sinner. The family attended an Evangelical church, and Lawrence derived an excellent and later very useful knowledge of the Bible, if little religious belief, from his church attendance. Eventually the truth about the parents' relationship seeped through to the boys, who in staid late Victorian England had to live with the explosive secret of their parents' unorthodox union. It is tempting to deduce from this background an explanation of some of Lawrence's later behavior, and many of his biographers have done so. Deprivation of his own aristocratic inheritance may have especially suited him to work with kings and emirs in the Middle East in order to gain what he saw as their (and vicariously his own) rightful inheritance, as Kathryn Tidrick has claimed; keeping secrets early on made him a natural for intelligence work and may have accustomed him to sometimes telling more or less than the truth, as Richard Aldington has claimed; and his admitted self-divisions, especially in terms of an internal battle between sexual expression and repression, has been attributed to his parents' consciousness that they were living in sin. One possible result is that he never married or, according to him, performed the sexual act, outside of a flagellation compulsion toward the end of his life, a compulsion that may (or may not) be seen as punishment for any expression of sexuality or sexual desire. Of course, his brother A. W. Lawrence, coming from the same background, led a perfectly normal married life and was a distinguished professor of archaeology, so one does not want to press psychology too far. However, each child will be differently affected by circumstances, and it may be that A. W. simply adapted to the circumstances of his parents better than T. E. did.

His parents' personal circumstances certainly did not stop Lawrence from benefiting to the utmost from his presence in Oxford. He attended the Oxford High School for Boys from 1896 to 1907, in the process becoming an expert brass rubber, a voracious reader (especially of medieval literature and of William Morris's neomedieval fantasies), and an adventurous explorer of Oxford and its hidden pathways. In 1907 he entered Oxford University, where he came to the attention of D. G. Hogarth, keeper of the Ashmolean Museum. Hogarth encouraged Lawrence's interest in archaeology, Arabic, and the Middle East, and his influence had an effect. After several summers spent bicycling through France observing medieval military architecture, Lawrence decided to write a thesis reflecting that interest, but with a Middle Eastern flavor. He was now ready to embark on his first adventure: a tour on foot through 1,000 miles during the broiling Middle Eastern summer of 1909, all by himself, in the course of which he studied and beautifully sketched the features of 36 Crusader castles. Not surprisingly, the resulting honors thesis received a first, the highest possible grade at Oxford, and Lawrence's tutor was so pleased with Lawrence's work that he gave a party in his honor. This innovative and deeply researched thesis presents the view that the Crusader castle builders were influenced only by Western designs, not by Eastern ones as other authorities at the time held. While we now see the influence upon the castles as coming from both East and West, Lawrence's thesis remains respected and is often cited in the field, even in the present day. Several editions of it are currently in print under the title *Crusader Castles;* needless to say, this is not the usual fate of a B.A. honors thesis.

Several months after his graduation in 1910, Lawrence went to work for Hogarth at a dig that Hogarth was directing at Jerablus, Syria, the site of Carchemish, the ancient viceregal city of the Hittites. Lawrence remained at this dig from 1911 to 1914 (with time off for vacations) and later described those years as the best time of his life. He had a close friendship with a young Arab named Dahoum, who is thought on good evidence to be the "S. A." of *Seven Pillars of Wisdom*'s introductory poem, which speaks of giving the Arabs freedom as an expression of love for "S. A." C. Leonard Woolley, one of Lawrence's colleagues at the site and later famous for his discovery of Ur of the Chaldees, implies that Lawrence's friendship with Dahoum was a homosexual relationship. This view has been upheld by some critics, notably Jeffrey Meyers, who sees Lawrence as someone drawn to homosexuality, and Daniel Wolfe, who presents him as an outright homosexual. Both views have been strongly denied by Lawrence's official biographer, J. M. Wilson, who claims that Lawrence had a repressed sexual nature and never committed any sexual act voluntarily; it is also denied by psychologist and Lawrence biographer John Mack. In any case, Lawrence's friendship with Dahoum, whom he also brought home to Oxford with him one summer along with the dig's foreman, Hamoudi, helped make this a wonderful time for Lawrence. He was free from worries and responsibilities and living in an exotic environment that had begun to fascinate him. Lawrence enjoyed rigging up all kinds of small tools and appliances, photographing finds, and supervising workers, all the while improving his Arabic. Moreover, Hogarth and Woolley were two of the leading archaeologists of the early twentieth century, and Lawrence learned an enormous amount from them, making this an important period of apprenticeship in an intellectually exciting locale. Lawrence is given credit for contributions in the volumes resulting from the dig, *Carchemish: Report on the Excavations at Djerabis on Behalf of the British Museum,* and the dig itself was considered very important for future British study of the Hittites, who were important contemporaries of the Hebrews in the time of kings David and Solomon.

But Lawrence's work during this period started edging away from archaeology proper and into intelligence—a precursor of the tasks that he would soon perform during World War I. A telegram in December 1913 summoned Lawrence and Woolley to a meeting in Beersheba, then in Palestine, with Capt. Stewart Newcombe of the Royal Engineers. They were to participate in a six-week survey of the northern Sinai and the southern Negev deserts, straddling the border between Turkish-dominated Palestine and British-controlled Egypt. The survey team had received Turkish permission to explore Nabataean and Byzantine ruins for the Palestine Exploration Fund, and that is what Lawrence and Woolley, at least, did. There were many archaeological sites to survey. The team would not have much time to go over biblical ruins, which lay far below the surface, but the Nabataean and Byzantine layers were easily accessible. The Nabataeans, who had been conquered by the Romans, were the engineers of great dams and water systems, while the Byzantines, who had followed the Romans, built great churches and other structures on the foundations of the older Nabataean cities. These Nabataean-Byzantine cities and their magnificent churches were ultimately destroyed by the newly Islamic Arabs in the seventh century C.E., leaving many shards and ruined stone buildings on the surface. But the real purpose of the Wilderness of Zin survey, as it came to be called, was to explore Turkish defenses in southern Palestine about only 100 miles from the Suez Canal. The British were understandably nervous about protecting the canal, their lifeline to India, as the winds of World War I began to stir and Turkey and Germany began making overtures to one another. Lawrence's and Woolley's archaeological work supplied cover for the military survey, which was conducted by Newcombe and the other military members of the survey team.

Beersheba, the dusty center of Turkish administration in the desert area, about 150 miles north of the Suez Canal, would become the first town conquered by the British in Palestine in World War I, which is partially a testimony to how well the military team performed its topographical work. Lawrence and Woolley devoted themselves to the study of ruins on this trip, but it is worth noting that the Red Sea port Akaba, which Lawrence visited during this survey and from which he was expelled by the Turks because it was outside the official survey area, became the site of his greatest military triumph during the war as well.

Even during this brief, six-week survey, Woolley and Lawrence accomplished a great deal. They completed the best plan ever of the ruined city of Shivta, about 35 miles south of Beersheba, and also came to the conclusion that the climate of the desert had not changed since biblical times. This view is now accepted by modern archaeologists. In addition, they identified Negev pottery, unique to the region. Even more impressively, the pair made an important contribution to biblical archaeology by correctly identifying Ain el Qudeirat in the northern Sinai as the probable site of Kadesh Barnea, where the Israelites sojourned, rather than Ain Kadeis, which had previously been thought to be the site. This identification, in which Lawrence had a substantial role, has been accepted by contemporary archaeologists. In the course of this survey, Lawrence also daringly investigated the ruins, possibly built by Saladin in 1170 C.E., on the Isle de Graye, now known as the Coral Island and Jezirat Faroun, some seven miles below Akaba and half a mile from the eastern Red Sea coast, by going through the sometimes shark-infested Red Sea waters on an improvised raft.

Soon after Lawrence returned from the Wilderness of Zin survey, Newcombe in June 1914 sent him and Woolley, this time alone, on a definite spying expedition along the track of the Berlin-to-Baghdad Railway, which the Germans were building through the Amanus Mountains near the Carchemish site. From a disgruntled Italian engineer they succeeded in securing all of the blueprints.

When World War I broke out in August 1914, both Lawrence and Woolley were in England. They were instructed to publish their archaeological report on the survey quickly in order to provide cover for the military spying mission that had taken place. *The Wilderness of Zin,* still highly valued in archaeological circles and with the equal participation of both men in its thinking, writing, and preparation, appeared in 1915.

In the fall of 1914, Lawrence began serving with the Geographical Section of the general staff in London, but by December he was sent to join military intelligence in Cairo. There the story recounted in his important, brilliantly well-written, and exciting memoir, *Seven Pillars of Wisdom,* begins. In Cairo, Lawrence at first made maps, debriefed spies, and helped prepare a handbook of the Turkish army, as part of a group that included C. Leonard Woolley and that was directed by Stewart Newcombe. Overseeing Newcombe was the head of military intelligence, Gilbert Clayton. Clearly his superiors had a very high regard for young Captain Lawrence, because during this period he and Aubrey Herbert, another Middle East expert from Cairo intelligence, were secretly sent to bribe Khalil Pasha, a Turkish commander, whose army surrounded 10,000 British troops under Gen. Charles Vere Ferrers Townshend at the Mesopotamian town of Kut-al-Amara. Lawrence and Herbert unsuccessfully offered Khalil one million and then two million pounds sterling to let the British go. With Townshend's surrender on April 29, 1916, the British suffered the second of their two most decisive defeats in the Eastern war, the first having been the catastrophic campaign in Gallipoli, which had begun with a failure by the British navy to breach the Turkish defenses of the Dardanelle Straits, then continued with a static, meaningless campaign that saw the British mired in trenches and unable to advance against the Turks on the heights above them, and that finally ended with the evacuation of British forces in January 1916. Lawrence witnessed similar bumbling and disorder on the Mesopotamian front and wrote a scathing report about it, for which he was never forgiven by the Indian army, which was responsible for that theater.

Things were somewhat better for the British on the Sinai and Palestine front at this early stage of the war, but far from ideal. In February 1915, the Turks attempted a daring attack on the Suez Canal, which was repulsed, but they continued cross-border harassment raids on British forces in Sinai and even attempted a second raid in force in April 1916, which got as far as Romani, about 20 miles east of the Suez Canal, before being repelled. In response to these attempts, the British bolstered their forces on the Sinai-Palestine border. They built a supply route across Sinai, including an extensive railway line and roads as well as a water pipeline, in order to support a substantial forward base at the town of El Arish, close to the border.

In late 1916, Lawrence was able to transfer from military intelligence to the Arab Bureau, a section of the intelligence service devoted exclusively to Arab affairs and especially to the revolt of the sharif of Mecca and his sons against the Turks. The British were happy about this revolt by the guardian of the holy city of Mecca, which was openly proclaimed on June 5 after the sharif received promises of British support. The pro-British sharif's opposition to the Turks ensured that Turkey would not be able to enlist broad Muslim support by calling for a religious war against the British in Arabia, Palestine, Syria, and Mesopotamia and because the sharif's positive attitude toward the British also would reassure the large and potentially restive Muslim minority in India. In the Arab Bureau, Lawrence worked with a like-minded set of men, including D. G. Hogarth and Aubrey Herbert (who had accompanied him on the trip to Mesopotamia). They were dedicated to supporting the Arab Revolt and reducing French influence in order to produce a situation of British dominance in the Middle East after the war. While still working in military intelligence, Lawrence suggested the publication of a secret newsletter, which came to be named *The Arab Bulletin* and was implemented under the editorship of Hogarth, with many contributions from Lawrence. Now available in a reproduced edition, its four volumes make fascinating reading even today and cover such subjects as attempted coups in Constantinople, military events in the Hejaz, and even Muslim opinion in Singapore about the Arab Revolt.

But in the late summer and fall of 1916, Sharif Hussein's revolt began to founder, and the British faced the problem of how to support it. They were reluctant to send troops from Egypt because of the possible need for them on the western front and hesitant even about sending supplies. Instead, they sent Lawrence along with Ronald Storrs to assess the situation and report on it. The background of the Arab Revolt and Lawrence's own work in Cairo are detailed in the introduction of *Seven Pillars of Wisdom,* which is followed by 10 books, or major sections, each of which tells of another of the revolt's phases.

We learn of Lawrence's first trip to Arabia, including his assessment of the sharif and his four sons, Ali, Abdullah, Feisal, and Zeid, and his view that Feisal was the best person to lead the revolt. The writing at first has the tone of a light-hearted travel diary, reflecting the excitement of Lawrence's first trip to Arabia and his lack of personal involvement. Then we read of Lawrence's appointment as Feisal's adviser and his adoption of guerrilla tactics and railway attacks as the best methods to advance the revolt. Feisal, with the help of the British navy, is able to move his base from Yenbo farther up the Red Sea coast to Wejh. We follow, especially in the famous chapter 33, the evolution of Lawrence's guerrilla strategy, which consists of a way to win the war with a minimum of fighting: no frontal assaults, but instead hit and run attacks that harass the Turks (who under commander Fahkri Pasha managed to hold the city of Medina with around 10,000 men until the end of the war) and demolitions of the Turks' Hejaz Railway line, which they constantly were forced to repair. According to

Lawrence's strategy, these activities would be accompanied by preaching to the Arab tribes to enlist their support and to make the whole territory hostile to the Turks. He tested his theories with some success and, with the newly won support of Auda abu Tayi, a major Beduin chief, prepared a plan to attack Akaba, the town at the northern end of the Red Sea coast from which he had been unceremoniously expelled during the Wilderness of Zin survey.

Lawrence then details the 600-mile march and successful attack that culminated, in July 1917, in the taking of Akaba from the inland side, where the Turks never expected an attack. Lawrence also briefly mentions the daring ride he took with only a few companions when he left the march on Akaba for a short period. In the course of that ride, he conferred with Ali Riza Pasha Rikabi, a Turkish administrator in Damascus who was secretly aiding the Arabs, and also assessed support for the Arab Revolt and Feisal in Syria.

The victory at Akaba closed the Arabian war and moved the conflict north into the area of Transjordan and Syria as the Arab forces became a useful British ally by diverting Turkish resources from the Palestine front. Lawrence's announcement of his capture of this city was particularly welcome because in Palestine up until this time the situation was not very positive for the British. Two major attacks on Gaza from the British base at El Arish in March and April 1917 failed miserably, with high casualties. Gen. Archibald Murray was forced to move aside for Gen. Edmund Allenby, fresh from the western front in Europe, who would infuse new spirit and innovation into the campaign. The military impetus emanating from Allenby as well as Lawrence's own successes, as he organized Akaba as the new base of the Arab Revolt forces, spurred him on to more raiding attacks. With the new importance of the Arab forces, however, Lawrence moved from the position of freely acting adviser in a remote theater of operations to an officer under direct British command, and the mood of his writing grows troubled as his responsibilities and need to coordinate closely with the British army increase.

Lawrence and his campaign suffered some harsh reversals of fortune, too. A raid on the Yarmuk bridges, far to the north, which was intended to aid Allenby by blocking Turkish supplies from coming into Palestine by rail, failed after great exertion when one of Lawrence's men made a noise, alerting the Turkish guards. Worse, on November 20, 1917, during a reconnaissance of the city of Deraa, Lawrence was captured by the Turks, tortured, and raped; this is described in ambiguous but still horrifying terms in chapter 80, which remains in many ways at the center of *Seven Pillars of Wisdom*. Fortunately, Lawrence was able to escape and, amazingly, soon found himself triumphantly standing by Allenby's side in Jerusalem, which Allenby captured in December 1917.

Jerusalem had been taken with a relatively conventional series of attacks against demoralized Turkish forces, from which many soldiers had deserted. The reason for the Turks' demoralization was that in October 1917, farther south, Allenby had broken into Palestine from Sinai via a brilliant feint. Instead of attacking Gaza directly, as Murray had done so unsuccessfully, Allenby decided to attack the weaker Turkish defenses at Beersheba, 30 miles to the east. His intelligence chief, the ruthless Richard Meinertzhagen, had prepared a false set of plans showing that an attack was coming on Gaza. He had then ridden close enough to the Turkish line there to get himself chased and shot at and had deliberately dropped the previously bloodstained and faked set of plans. The Turks, thinking the false plans true, shifted their 24-mile-long line toward Gaza, leaving Beersheba exposed. One of the last great cavalry charges, by two Australian light horse regiments, seized the city in one day, and Allenby then proceeded to encircle Gaza, from which the Turkish troops hastily withdrew. His follow-up capture of Jerusalem was an important psychological turning point, and Lawrence called it the high point of the entire war for him, showing how memories of his early biblical training remained planted within him.

In January 1918 Lawrence received the Distinguished Service Order for his performance in routing the Turks at the battle of Tafileh, southwest of the Dead Sea. This triumph, however, turned to despair by February, when the Emir Zeid, to whom Lawrence had entrusted gold to be used to purchase the tribes' allegiance during Allenby's projected spring 1918 offensive, told Lawrence that he had spent all of the money. For the first time, Lawrence wanted to quit the Arab movement altogether, but Allenby himself sent him back to Feisal's forces.

Then came a waiting period, during which the Arab forces cut the railroad between Maan and Mudowwara, further isolating the Turkish garrison at Medina. But an offensive of Allenby's against Salt and Amman failed, in part because the Beni Sakhr Beduin, who had said they would support the offensive, did not do so. The Turks also recaptured Tafileh from the Arab forces under Sharif Nasir. But Allenby surprised Lawrence by giving Feisal's army 2,000 camels so they could take part in the major offensive that was now moved back to autumn 1918.

Even in June of that year, when the war was moving toward its inevitable conclusion, Lawrence learned that Feisal had been secretly negotiating a separate peace with the Turks. This was not entirely unexpected by Lawrence, for the Arabs for their part had learned that the British had already agreed, in the Sykes-Picot Agreement, that the French, not the Arabs, were to receive control of Syria in the event of a victory. Feisal's hoped-for independent Arab state in Syria was therefore stillborn, even as the Arabs were fighting for it. Lawrence dealt with both of these situations by assuring Feisal that Britain always kept her word and by secretly hoping that even if Britain did not intend to keep her word to the Arabs the revolt would be so successful that the British would, in the end, have to reward them with at least semi-independence—an Arab state under a British mandate. In *Seven Pillars of Wisdom,* he testifies to the shame that this two-faced situation gave him, because while fighting for a British victory he also had become deeply sympathetic to the Arabs' hopes for independence from foreign rulers after hundreds of years under the Turks. This conflicted situation of dual loyalties accounts for a good deal of the personal tension that comes through in Lawrence's account of himself in *Seven Pillars.* Lawrence also had to deal with the fate of his servant Dahoum, the "S.A." or Salim Achmed of the *Seven Pillars* introductory poem, whom he had employed as a spy behind enemy lines but who died of typhus around September 1918.

In the last part of *Seven Pillars of Wisdom,* Lawrence details the brilliant preparations for Allenby's final offensive and the actions that Lawrence and the Arabs took in support of those preparations. Because of his success by deception at Beersheba, Allenby again decided on a subterfuge to cap his campaign. A false camp of thousands of surplus tents from Egypt and false horses made of canvas was set up near Jericho, in Transjordan, and Allenby ordered the movement of as many noncombatant troops as possible and the dragging of sleds by mules over roads near that camp to raise dust and to make it appear that a huge force was assembling. Moreover, the air force put lots of planes in the air over the Jericho area. The Arabs were to help by creating as many attacks and diversions in adjacent areas as possible. All of this would convince the Turks, Allenby hoped, that an attack would be aimed across the Jordan River at Amman. Instead, Allenby's attack would come in Palestine itself, farther to the west.

In its final sections, *Seven Pillars of Wisdom* details how Lawrence, aided by British and Arab forces, carried out their part of the diversion plan. Lawrence's forces cut the rail lines around Deraa and isolated it, thus leading the Turks to believe that the attack would come in the east. Then, on September 19, Allenby attacked with 57,000 infantry, 12,000 cavalry, and 540 guns (in addition to another 36,000 troops in reserve) during this Megiddo or Armageddon offensive (because Armageddon, the final battle of all, is supposed to take place in Megiddo, according to the Bible). The ground offensive was aided by Airco DH9 bombers and Bristol Fighters. The surprise broke Turkish resistance—consisting of only 29,000 troops, 3,000 cavalry, 400 guns, and no airplanes to speak of—in Palestine completely, sending the Turkish Eighth Army into complete retreat and disorder. Allenby now followed up with genuine attacks on Amman, on Deraa, on Nablus, and on Kuneitra, with General Chetwode forcing the Turkish Seventh Army back with his cavalry. By September 24, 1918, thousands of Turkish soldiers were captured.

For the Arab forces, events now moved very quickly. Lawrence found himself first in Deraa, the scene of his earlier torment when captured; then in the village of Tafas, where a massacre perpetrated on townspeople by some troops of the Turkish Fourth Army was followed by a massacre of Turkish prisoners by the Arabs (which Lawrence says was by his order, but this has been questioned); and finally in Damascus itself, which the Arabs were allowed to enter first already on October 1, 1918, as a gesture of goodwill by the British and for whose civilian control Lawrence found himself responsible. He first worked to establish governmental authority for Feisal by eliminating any rivals for power and establishing civil order. At the Turkish military hospital, Lawrence confronted rotting corpses and half-dead, abandoned men. He did his best to have it cleaned up but was slapped in the face by a British officer who mistakenly thought that Lawrence had been responsible for the hospital for some time and had simply not kept it hygienic. Lawrence accepted the slap as fitting payment for a job—advising the Arab Revolt—that had involved too many compromises, brutalities, and concealments as well as personal humiliation and a loss of control at Tafas (if he indeed ordered no prisoners to be taken, possibly as revenge for his own torture at Deraa). When Allenby sent him home, Lawrence was relieved to be leaving the war behind, but he was surprised to feel sorry that his great, if demanding, adventure was all over. *Seven Pillars of Wisdom* closes on a mixed note of military triumph and personal doubt. But whatever personal defeats Lawrence felt he experienced, his campaign has become a model of guerrilla thinking and influenced the conduct of armies around the world during World War II and in many of the small wars that followed it, including Vietnam. Even today, Lawrence's dictum that propaganda among civilians is essential to military success may profitably be applied to the case of U.S. forces in Iraq.

After the war, Lawrence played a colorful role at the 1919 Paris Peace Conference, serving as Feisal's adviser and trying his best to help him gain control of Syria. Dressed in a kaffiyeh, or Arab headdress, and using his fluency in French as well as Arabic, Lawrence was a striking figure at the conference. Yet it was all for nought, because at that conference and again at the San Remo conference of April 1920, the French were given mandatory control of the country.

Lawrence also began writing *Seven Pillars of Wisdom* in Paris in January 1919, losing one draft and taking it through several more until 1926, when his sumptuously produced subscriber's edition was published for a select group of approximately 200 purchasers. In the course of writing this book, he had to relive painful experiences and suffer through the strains of writing. He suffered further pain, this time physical, in April 1919 when he broke his collarbone in an air crash in Rome while on his way to retrieve his notebooks in Cairo so he could use them while writing his book.

In March 1919 a far-reaching event occurred when American journalist Lowell Thomas, who had visited Lawrence briefly during the Arab campaign, began a lecture and slide show about Allenby and Lawrence in New York. When during that summer Lawrence returned home to England from the Paris Conference, he found himself fast becoming a national hero because of this show, which also was performed in Covent Garden. This intoxicating multimedia extravaganza featuring slides, music, and incense established Lawrence as one of the first celebrities of the twentieth century, with all of the attendant problems and pleasures. He enjoyed (although he denied it) being seen as a hero and came to the see the show five times, albeit surreptitiously. But simultaneously, he was aware that his political work on behalf of Feisal was in jeopardy, because while Feisal was tentatively ruling in Iraq the French were insisting upon exercising their mandatory rights. Lawrence also came to resent bitterly the lack of privacy that attends celebrity. In addition to these developments, he had to contend with the fact that two of his brothers had been killed on the western front, and that his father had died in April 1919 during the great influenza epidemic. That left only his mother, him, Montagu Robert Lawrence, and A. W. Lawrence remaining of his original seven-member family.

In January 1921 Lawrence, until then living on a scholarship at All Souls College, Oxford, where he was not much in residence but performed many pranks and also met Robert Graves, became an adviser to Winston Churchill in the Colonial Office. He saw his role as trying to set things right in the Middle East. Feisal had been expelled by the French after the battle of Meissaloun, which took place on July 24, 1920, after ruling in Syria for about two years, and Lawrence wanted to make good on the promises that he himself had made to Feisal during the war. So at the Cairo Conference of 1921, he supported the recommendation that Feisal be made king of Iraq and his brother Abdullah confirmed as king of Transjordan. With this solution, Lawrence felt that his wartime promise to the Arabs had been fulfilled, if not in Syria. He served until July 1922, also doing his best to establish Abdullah's rule and trying to conciliate the difficult old sharif of Mecca, who finally was driven from Arabia by Ibn Saud in 1924 and in 1925 went into exile in Cyprus and in Transjordan.

Lawrence's next career move was startling: though he was a colonel upon retirement from the army, he decided to join the Royal Air Force as a simple airman, the equivalent of private, under the name John Hume Ross to conceal his identity. Why he was willing to submit himself to the inevitable humiliation of basic training is not clear to this day. Some of his friends, like Robert Graves and Wyndham Lewis, thought it a surrender of his intellect, and Lawrence may well have wanted to become less self-conscious and less burdened with responsibilities by becoming involved in mundane activities in a lowly position in the military hierarchy. Some biographers have ascribed Lawrence's decision to his desire to lead a monastic existence free of the responsibility for earning a living in the "real" world; still others have said that he needed the discipline of the R.A.F. to hold himself together. In any case, he enjoyed the romance of flying and was relatively happy in the R.A.F. But when the newspapers discovered that the famous Colonel Lawrence who was lionized in the Lowell Thomas show was serving as a private, he was discharged.

This occurred in January 1923, and a month later he enlisted in the Tank Corps under the pseudonym of T. E. Shaw, a name that may owe something to his friendship with G. B. and Charlotte Shaw. In the Tank Corps, the recruits were of a lower order than those in the R.A.F., and barracks life was correspondingly rocky. Moreover, Lawrence had no particular liking for tanks. He was very unhappy during this period and even approached suicide. Another reason for his depressive state was first revealed by journalists Phillip Knightley and Colin Simpson in their biography of 1969, *The Secret Lives of Lawrence of Arabia.* From 1923 until his death in 1935, he had himself whipped, at varying intervals, by a young Scotsman, John Bruce, whom he tricked into this arrangement with a false tale of a rich uncle who demanded this punishment of Lawrence. He could not seem to free himself from this obsession and obviously derived a certain satisfaction from it. The contrast between his self-knowledge and his external heroic image, similar to Dorian Gray's knowledge of his decaying portrait and his own outward innocence in Oscar Wilde's novel, must have further increased the mental pressure on him, and he seems to have foreshadowed the feelings of many celebrities in this respect. Even his austere cottage at Clouds Hill, not far from the Bovington Tank Corps base, filled with books and phonograph records, did not offer him enough privacy, and he once even attacked a reporter who had disturbed his peace. After repeated pleas from powerful friends, Lawrence was allowed to reenlist in the R.A.F. in August 1925, ending a particularly difficult period for him.

Although he never mentioned his flagellation obsession to anyone, Lawrence did write about his difficulties in becoming part of his R.A.F. unit. *The Mint,* which was composed between 1922 and 1928 but not published until his death in 1935, tells of his experience in the R.A.F. Depot from August to December 1922. It consists of three parts. In the first, "The Raw Material," Lawrence reveals his nervousness from the time he waited outside the R.A.F. recruiting station through his eventual acceptance in the service. His detailed statement of all of the humiliations of drill, fatigue duty, and his officers' personalities, including that of his wounded commanding officer, who is shown in a very harsh light, expresses typical resentment over basic training. The only unanswered question is why Lawrence willingly volunteered for this treatment, especially given his attainment of much higher rank during the war. The next section, "In the Mill," shows how the men are formed into a unit, but despite his attempt to integrate himself with the other men, he admits to being odd man out, which is not surprising given his history and age. The final section, "Service," however, reveals a Lawrence who has found unity and peace at the R.A.F. Cadet College: he has stopped thinking too much, is free of heavy responsibilities, and actually feels a complete part of his unit. Lawrence, who always wanted what Oxford philosopher F. H. Bradley saw as the unity beyond thought, seems to have finally achieved it in his feeling that he was no longer separate from the men or from nature. This is a happy conclusion indeed to the perilous self-division he felt during the war period, even though Lawrence cannot be said to have been completely happy, given the continuation of his flagellation problem.

During his Tank Corps and R.A.F. period, Lawrence not only became a good mechanic, but continued his cultural work. He translated Adrien le Corbeau's tale of the growth of a redwood tree, *The Forest Giant,* from French into elegant English. The publication of the limited 1926 subscriber's edition of *Seven Pillars of Wisdom* made him famous among writers and book collectors, while its abridgement, *Revolt in the Desert,* created a sensation among the general public when it was published in 1927. Prices of each of the approximately 200 copies of the subscriber's edition that were printed now regularly reach $100,000 or more; it is one of the twentieth-century books most sought by collectors.

From 1927 to 1929, Lawrence served in India, where he had continued his intellectual as well as his mechanical work. He began transforming Homer's *Odyssey* into one of the best prose translations in English. He also added a typically unique introduction criticizing Homer both as a man and as a writer. In January 1929, Lawrence was ordered back from India when the newspapers began to speak of him as if he were a spy rather than a simple clerk and mechanic. On his arrival, he was whisked off the troopship from a side away from the reporters' cameras, creating even more of a sensation. In March 1929 he began his service at an R.A.F. seaplane base. Here, with Wing Commander Sydney Smith and his wife, Clare Sydney Smith, Lawrence enjoyed a friendly relationship and satisfying work. Clare Smith wrote the memoir *The Golden Reign* about this period, and her title describes Lawrence's feeling about it. He helped prepare for the important Schneider Cup seaplane race. He enjoyed overhauling a Biscayne Baby speedboat, a gift from an English millionaire, and taking the boat, which he shared with Commander Smith, out on excursions. He also learned to fly a Gypsy Moth light plane.

In 1931, he witnessed a terrible seaplane crash in Plymouth Sound near the base, and, while six men drowned, he helped save six men by directing the rescue operations and diving into the water himself. As a result, he became dedicated to the use of fast boats for rescue purposes and was assigned to help design such a boat at the Hubert Scott-Paine shipyard in Hythe near Southampton. For the rest of his R.A.F. career, which was to last until 1935, Lawrence worked on the testing of this boat, the 200 Class Seaplane Tender, and even wrote a maintenance manual for it. He seems to have found genuine satisfaction in the mechanical phase of his career, and in retrospect one can see that this interest runs like a thread through his entire life. As a boy he had repaired his own bicycle; in Carchemish he was adept at rigging up all kinds of things; during the Arab campaign he improved his Ford's ability to withstand desert heat by coming up with a thermostatic device; he advised George Brough on improvements to the Brough motorcycles when he became a motorcycle enthusiast after the war; and he even wrote about a science fictional piece of machinery upon the request of Laura Riding and Robert Graves for their novel *No Decency Left* (which was published under the pseudonym Barbara Rich). He retired from the R.A.F. in early 1935.

He retained his love of speed despite his retirement, and it was because of a motorcycle crash that he died, on May 19, 1935, after having been injured six days earlier when swerving to avoid hitting a delivery boy on a bicycle. His pall bearers included some of the most famous names in England, such as Winston Churchill and his wife; painter Augustus John, who had created one of the best Lawrence portraits; his publisher Jonathan Cape; and one of his biographers, the military historian Liddell Hart, among many other notables. Clouds Hill has since become a site of pilgrimage and a permanent display site, testimony to the religious position that Lawrence seems to fill for some people. As often happens in the case of outstanding people, his death became the source of many completely unfounded myths—that he had been deliberately murdered, for instance, or that he had committed suicide.

Lawrence's roles as mechanic and motorcycle enthusiast were just the latest of many transformations. In each of the fields that he touched, he was outstanding, and it is difficult to name one other individual who did so many things so well and also was so involved with a nodal point in history—in his case, the birth of the modern Middle East. Moreover, because of the brilliantly written classic *Seven Pillars of Wisdom* even more than because of Lowell Thomas's show or the David Lean/Robert Bolt film, Lawrence's fame has spilled over from his century to the twenty-first and is likely to outlast it.

Lawrence's greatest book seems to have permanently captured a sense of the West's problematic relationship with the Middle East, and Lawrence's perplexities seem to represent those of many Westerners who deal with that thorny area of the world, while his decisions continue to influence present events. Lawrence was instrumental in putting King Hussein's family on the thrones of Jordan and Iraq. They continue to rule Jordan but were ousted from Iraq by a coup in 1958, thus eventually clearing the way for Saddam Hussein's brutal dictatorship. The late King Hussein of Jordan's brother Hassan has been suggested as a possible regent for Iraq. The ghost of Lawrence still lingers in the Middle East, as it does whenever the Israelis and Palestinians start to consider a peace proposal. It was Lawrence, after all, who got Chaim Weizmann and Feisal to sign a treaty of agreement in 1919, the first such agreement ever between the Zionist and Arab national movements.

Elie Kedourie has accused Lawrence of glamorizing terrorism, and this is a serious charge now that terrorism has become a worry for the entire world. For their part, the Arabs have gone from hero worship of him during the revolt to branding him an imperialist. Lawrence also has defenders, such as John Mack and J. M. Wilson, who see him as a liberator. Whatever disagreements we may have over Lawrence's roles and lessons (and these are likely to continue forever), the salient point is that he remains in the public eye in both the West and the Middle East now no less than in the past. An excerpt from *Seven Pillars of Wisdom* is now included in the *Longman Anthology of British Literature,* a testimony to Lawrence's acceptance by the academic literary establishment. His *Odyssey* translation is acknowledged to be one of the very best prose translations of that work. His strategic theories, his special intelligence gathering, and his campaign are studied at war colleges around the world. His technological ideas helped create the PT boat. Lawrence himself never seemed to believe in his own worth. But, it seems, we do. Hence this encyclopedia, which is intended to enable the reader to find his or her own position on a fascinating subject that seems never to lose relevance and excitement.

Chronology

1888   Birth of T. E. Lawrence on August 16, at Tremadoc, Wales, to parents who are not married and who have assumed the name Lawrence.

1907   Lawrence graduates from City of Oxford High School for Boys.

1910   Lawrence graduates from Oxford University with First Class Honors in Modern History for his B.A. thesis on "The Influence of the Crusades on European Military Architecture—to the End of the XIIth Century."

1911   Works on a dig at Carchemish, Syria, under D. G. Hogarth and C. Leonard Woolley. Writes *Diary of a Journey across the Euphrates.* Translates *Two Arabic Folk Tales.*

1914   Takes part in the Wilderness of Zin survey. Finishes work at Carchemish.

1914   World War I begins. Lawrence joins Geographical Section, War Office; then is sent to Intelligence Department in Cairo, Egypt.

1915   *The Wilderness of Zin,* coauthored with Woolley, published. Lawrence's brothers Frank and Will are killed fighting in France.

1916   Arab Bureau formed. Lawrence sent to rescue British troops surrounded at Kut-al-Amara by bribing Turkish general. Lawrence joins Arab Bureau and contributes to intelligence newsletter, *The Arab Bulletin,* which he also had suggested. Lawrence sent to assess situation of the sharif of Mecca's forces and is sent back to join the Emir Feisal's forces in the field.

1917   Allenby's conquest of Beersheba and Gaza. Lawrence's secret ride behind enemy lines; his capture of Akaba; his torture at Deraa. He joins Allenby in conquered Jerusalem.

1918   Capture of Damascus by Lawrence's and British forces. Returns to Britain. World War I armistice declared.

1919   Participates in Paris Peace Conference as Feisal's adviser. Lawrence is injured in plane crash in Rome. Feisal starts ruling in Syria. Lowell Thomas starts lecture and slide show. Lawrence's father dies of influenza.

1920   Finishes year as fellow at All Souls College, Oxford. Feisal expelled from Syria by French General Gouraud after Battle of Meissaloun.

1921   Participates in Cairo Conference, which confirmed Abdullah on throne of Transjordan and Feisal on throne of Iraq, as adviser to Winston Churchill in Colonial Office.

1922   Oxford text of *Seven Pillars of Wisdom* printed. Lawrence joins Royal Air Force under the name John Hume Ross.

1923   Lawrence is discharged from Royal Air Force and joins Tank Corps under the name T. E. Shaw. Lawrence begins renting cottage at Clouds Hill. The flagellation sessions with John Bruce begin.

1924   Ibn Saud unites Arabia, defeating Ibn Rashid dynasty in the north and Hussein dynasty in the Hejaz. Lawrence publishes his translation of Adrien Le Corbeau's *La Gigantesque* (*The Forest Giant*).

1925   Lawrence is permitted to rejoin the Royal Air Force. Sharif Hussein of Mecca goes into exile in Cyprus.

1926   Lawrence privately publishes the subscriber's edition of *Seven Pillars of Wisdom.*

1927   Lawrence publishes *Revolt in the Desert,* an abridgment of *Seven Pillars of Wisdom* with the introspective passages removed.

1928   Lawrence completes *The Mint.*

1932   Lawrence completes "A Handbook to the 37½ Foot Motor Boats of the 200 Class."

1935   Lawrence retires from the Royal Air Force. He is fatally injured in a motorcycle accident on May 13 and dies on May 19. He is buried on May 21 at Moreton cemetery.

A

Aaronsohn, Aaron (1876–1919)

A brilliant agronomist who discovered wild wheat in **Palestine,** and a fervent Zionist, Aaronsohn founded NILI, an organization of Jews in Palestine that spied for the British during **World War I.** NILI is an acronym for *nezach Yisrael lo yishaker,* "the strength of Israel will not lie," from 1 Samuel 15:29 in the Hebrew Bible. Aaronsohn worked with **Leonard Woolley** and then **Gilbert Clayton** in British Intelligence in **Cairo** and became friendly with **Gen. Edmund Allenby.** He met Lawrence several times there starting in February 1917. At first they did not get along because Aaronsohn felt that Lawrence was insufficiently supportive of **Zionism,** but Lawrence's support of Zionism grew, and they worked together at the **Peace Conference** until Aaronsohn's death in a plane crash in May 1919. See Anita Engle, *The NILI Spies.*

Aaronsohn, Sarah (1890–1917)

Director of the pro-British Jewish spy network NILI's operations in **Palestine** while her brother **Aaron Aaronsohn** worked in British general headquarters in **Cairo.** After a NILI carrier pigeon was intercepted by the Turks, they began investigations. She committed suicide to avoid betraying the group while being tortured. She was once thought to be the "S. A." of *Seven Pillars of Wisdom,* but it is unlikely that she and Lawrence ever met, and most authorities now believe that "S. A." was Salim Achmed, or **Dahoum,** Lawrence's Arab servant. See Anita Engle, *The NILI Spies.*

Aba el Lissan

Turkish garrison of about 500 troops at an oasis in the Nagb el Shtar (in present day Jordan), overcome by Lawrence's forces on July 2, 1917, en route to their attack on **Akaba,** about 50 miles to the south, as recounted in chapter 53 of *Seven Pillars of Wisdom.* The Turks later recaptured the site, but in December 1917 they abandoned it under Arab pressure, and it became a base for the Arab forces.

Aba el Naam Station

Hejaz Railway station about 50 miles north of **Medina** with a garrison of around 400 Turkish troops. On March 29, 1917, Lawrence blew up a train near here, as he tells us in chapter 34 of *Seven Pillars of Wisdom.*

Abd el Kader el Abdu, Sheikh

Feisal ibn Hussein's representative at the **Yenbo** base of the Arab forces. Lawrence mentions his efficiency in handling stores in chapter 17 of *Seven Pillars of Wisdom.*

Abd el Kader el Jesairi, Emir (died 1918)

Traitorous companion on the **Yarmuk Valley Bridges** expedition who deserted Lawrence and **Sharif Ali ibn el Hussein** and went over to the Turks with their plans, forcing them to attack the nearest and most dangerous bridge, at Tell el Shehab. Lawrence claimed that he was later identified by the Bey during the **Deraa incident** because of Abd el Kader's description of him. Abd el Kader's brother Mohammed Said claimed that he was left in charge of the government in Damascus by the retreating Turks, but the pair had changed sides and had taken provisional control of the government for the Arabs. They were removed by Lawrence, despite their offers of cooperation with **Feisal** (*Seven Pillars of Wisdom,* chapter 119). Of Algerian extraction, Abd el Kader opposed British and especially French involvement in the Arab movement because of his pronounced Islamicism, as Lawrence explains in chapter 70.

Abdul Aziz el Masri (1878–1965)

Egyptian colonel in the Turkish army and an early member of the **Young Turk** movement. When Arab independence did not follow the Young Turk revolution of 1908, he initiated the secret **Al Ahd Society.** Arrested and sentenced to death by the Turks, he was nevertheless allowed to leave for **Egypt** owing to British pressure. Following the **McMahon-Hussein Correspondence** promising Arab independence, he joined the **Arab Revolt** in 1916 as chief of staff of the sharifian army, but was removed in 1917 owing to his inability to work smoothly with **Sharif Hussein** or

with the British. He remained pro-German and anti-British during both **World War I** and World War II.

Abdul-Hamid II, Sultan (1842–1919)

Ruler of the Ottoman Empire from 1876 to 1909, when he was finally deposed by the **Young Turks,** who carried out a revolution in 1908. He kept **Sharif Hussein** a prisoner in Constantinople for almost 18 years because he feared Hussein's potential for leading the **Hejaz** region of **Arabia** to break away from Turkish rule. Hussein was allowed to go back to the Hejaz and assume the role of sharif of **Mecca** by the Young Turks in 1909, as Lawrence explains in chapter 5 of *Seven Pillars of Wisdom.* An autocratic and conservative ruler, Abdul-Hamid was nevertheless responsible for initiating modernization projects, including the **Hejaz Railway.** He also instituted the close relations between Turkey and Germany that came to full fruition during **World War I.**

Abdullah el Nahabi

Member of Lawrence's bodyguard. "Nahabi" means "robber," and Abdullah was a stylishly dressed but reckless outlaw whom Lawrence accepted as an attendant, as related in chapter 83 of *Seven Pillars of Wisdom.* Despite his negative demeanor toward people, he was exceptionally kind to animals.

Abdullah ibn Hussein, Emir (1882–1951)

Second son of **Sharif Hussein** of **Mecca,** Abdullah accompanied his father into exile in Constantinople in 1891, becoming active in Arab nationalist circles there. He returned to Mecca with his father after the **Young Turk** revolution of 1908 and later

Emir Abdullah I, Feisal's brother, seated during the Cairo Conference of 1921. Photo by A. Reid. Courtesy of the Palestine Exploration Fund.

became deputy for Mecca in the Ottoman parliament. In 1914, on his way back to Arabia through **Cairo,** he spoke to British administrators **Kitchener** and **Storrs** about a possible revolt against the Turks. Lawrence felt that Abdullah's talents were political rather than military, and during the **Arab Revolt** he served as foreign minister to his father. After **Feisal** had been deposed from the throne of **Syria** by the French in July 1920, Abdullah arrived in **Amman** in March 1921 with an army but was kept from invading Syria by the British, who instead offered him the throne of **Transjordan,** which was then separated from the rest of **Palestine** as a result of the **Cairo Conference** of 1921. He ruled there as king until he was assassinated on July 20, 1951, by a Palestinian Arab who opposed his contacts with Israel and with Britain. See R. Bidwell, ed., *Arabian Personalities of the Early Twentieth Century*.

Abu Tayi Beduin

A branch of the **Howeitat tribe** based around **Maan,** now in Jordan. Their sheikh during the **Arab Revolt** was **Auda abu Tayi,** an epic personality.

Afghanistan

When Lawrence served in the **Royal Air Force** near **Karachi** and then in **Miranshah** in what is now Pakistan in 1927–29, British newspapers falsely claimed that he was spying in the Punjab and in Afghanistan. This publicity eventually led to his recall to England. Lawrence felt that the Soviets, following their czarist predecessors, had designs on Afghanistan, but he was never in that country himself despite his desire to see it.

Ageyl

Not a tribe, but mercenary camel riders of north Arabia, paid for a certain period of service. When one of the Ageyl was killed by **Hamed the Moor,** Lawrence was forced to execute him to prevent a feud between the Ageyl and the Moroccans in the Arab army. Ageyl corpsmen were in Lawrence's personal bodyguard, and he noted their elegant dress in chapter 74 of *Seven Pillars of Wisdom.*

Aircraft

Upon the outbreak of the **Arab Revolt,** the Ottoman Air Service's No. 3 Squadron, consisting of German-made Pfalz II monoplanes, was sent from the Caucasus front to the **Hejaz.** In response, the British supplied four B.E.2 aircraft under Major Ross in November 1916. But the B.E.2 was a slow (70 miles per hour) reconnaissance aircraft and its only armaments were the pilot's own light weapons and handheld bombs. *Seven Pillars of Wisdom* mentions the use of a Handley-Page bomber and Bristol fighters from 1917 on. Two Handley-Page 100s took part in the **Palestine** campaign. With a crew of four, 16–112-pound bombs, and a wingspan of 100 feet, this was a very large plane for the period and flew at a slow 85 miles per hour. The Bristol F-2b, which was equipped with two or three .303 inch machine guns, flew 110 miles per hour and was one of the best planes of the war. It redressed the balance between the British and the Turkish planes. The Ottoman Air Service had German AEG C-type biplanes, with a maximum speed of 95 miles per hour, two machine guns, and a maximum bomb load of 198 pounds. The Germans and Turks also used single-seat Fokker and two-seat Aviatik and Albatros CI aircraft. The Fokkers were equipped with interrupter gear, which enabled their machine guns to fire through the propeller. In chapter 61 of *Seven Pillars of Wisdom,* Lawrence reports that his men were bombed every day by a Turkish plane without any casualties when they were at **Guweira** in November 1917, and he claims negligible effect from most Turkish air efforts. In chapter 60, he describes a successful British raid on one day in August 1917, when the Turkish garrisons at **Maan** and **Aba el Lissan** were hit by British aircraft stationed at Kuntilla. After the war, on May 17, 1919, Lawrence suffered a broken collarbone in an air crash while on his way from the **Peace Conference** in **Paris** to **Egypt.** This did not diminish his love of flying, as his enlistment in the **Royal Air Force** after the war proves. During his stint in the air force, Lawrence studied aerial photography at the R.A.F. School of Photography at **Farnborough,** helped prepare for the **Schneider Trophy** seaplane race, and learned to fly a Gypsy Moth himself. *See* J. Lloyd, *Aircraft of World War One;* L. W. Sutherland, *Aces and Kings,* which, despite an inaccurate chapter on Lawrence, has descriptions of the planes used in his campaign; M. Sharpe, *Biplanes, Triplanes, and Seaplanes;* and **A. P. Wavell,** *The Palestine Campaigns.*

Airships

In 1929, Lawrence suggested to **Sir Hugh Trenchard,** marshal of the **Royal Air Force,** a crossing of the **Rub al Khali,** or Empty Quarter, of Arabia by a new airship (the R.100 or R.101) on its trial flight; but his idea was rejected, and **Bertram Thomas** and then **St. John Philby** did it by camel.

Ais, Wadi

A valley of oases and villages beginning near **Yenbo,** which is on the **Red Sea** coast, and running about 60 miles north of **Medina.** From this valley, **Abdullah ibn Hussein**'s force could threaten the Turks at Medina and also receive supplies from the sea at Yenbo. Lawrence claimed that it was at Abdullah's camp at Abu Markha in this valley that Lawrence, suffering from a bout of dysentery and malaria that lasted from approximately March 15 to 26, 1917, devised the guerrilla strategy related in chapter 33 of *Seven Pillars of Wisdom.*

Akaba

Town at the northern tip of the **Red Sea,** now part of Jordan. Lawrence first visited Akaba in 1914 with **Dahoum** during the **Wilderness of Zin** expedition. On July 6, 1917, he returned as the town's conqueror, after having conceived and executed an arduous 600-mile desert march from **Wejh** with the assistance of **Sharif Nasir** and **Auda abu Tayi** and his **Beduin** tribe. The Turks had anticipated only an attack from the sea, so Lawrence's land attack, his most important success of the war, took them completely by surprise, as related in chapter 54 of *Seven Pillars of Wisdom.*

Al Ahd Society (The "Pact" Society)

A secret organization composed of Mesopotamian officers in the Turkish army initiated by **Abdul Aziz el Masri** and others in 1913 to work for the cause of Arab independence. It was more pro-British than the **Al Fatat Society.** In 1915, in response to the society's (and the Al Fatat Society's) request, **Sharif Hussein** cautiously sent his son **Feisal** to act as a liaison with both societies; during the four weeks Feisal remained in Damascus from March 26, 1915, he established contact with both of them. The organizations produced the **Damascus Protocol** stating the conditions under which they would aid the British; these included Arab independence and the abolition of special privileges for foreigners. But the societies were decimated by the Turks before they could openly rebel. See *Seven Pillars of Wisdom,* chapters 4 and 5; **G. Antonius,** *The Arab Awakening;* and E. Tauber, *The Arab Movements in World War I* for more information.

Al Fatat Society (The "Young Arab" Society)

This secret society was founded in **Paris** in 1911 by seven Muslim students, according to **George Antonius,** and held a conference there in 1913. Its purpose was to work for Arab independence from the Turks. **Feisal,** sent by his father **Sharif Hussein,** was initiated into the society in Damascus in spring 1915. During the war, the Al Fatat Society decided to support the British if guarantees of Arab independence were forthcoming. **Jemal Pasha** however got wind of the society's plans, and when Feisal revisited Damascus in 1916 ready to plot revolt, he was forced to witness the executions of many of his friends in the society and another, **Al Ahd,** which was comprised of Arab officers in the Turkish army. One of the factors impelling Feisal to take a leading role in the **Arab Revolt** against Turkey was this experience, as described in chapter 5 of *Seven Pillars of Wisdom.* Antonius criticizes the account of some of the events involving these societies given in *Seven Pillars of Wisdom.* See G. Antonius, *The Arab Awakening,* and E. Tauber, *The Arab Movements in World War I.*

Aldington, Richard (1892–1962)

British novelist and biographer. Shell-shocked and gassed during **World War I,** Aldington in his novels *Death of a Hero* (1929) and *The Colonel's Daughter* (1931) attacked a British establishment that he held responsible for the war. He extended this criticism to Lawrence in his scathing *Lawrence of Arabia: A Biographical Enquiry* (1955; French edition 1954), accusing him of hypocrisy, falsehood, neurosis, and undeserved fame. While Aldington emphasized psychological factors in Lawrence's life (including the first revelation of his illegitimacy in English) and discovered genuine discrepancies in Lawrence's account of the **Arab Revolt,** he wrote without access to archival material. Therefore, Aldington's work, while of lasting importance as a skeptical view of Lawrence, cannot be considered a balanced, fully documented assessment. There were attempts to prevent Aldington's book from getting published, and when it appeared, it generated bitter criticism from Lawrence's defenders; the controversy continues to some extent to this day. Fred Crawford's *Richard Aldington and Lawrence of Arabia* (1998) is a full-length treatment of the Aldington episode presented from Aldington's point of view. S. E. Tabachnick and Christopher Matheson's *Images of Lawrence* provides a concise summary of Aldington's viewpoint.

Aldridge, James (born 1918)

Author of *Heroes of the Empty View* (1954), which contains a fictionalized account of Lawrence under the name of Gordon or Gordion.

Aleppo

The largest city in **Syria** in Lawrence's day, and one of the seven great cities of the Middle East about which Lawrence in the pre–**World War I** years proposed to write a book that he never wrote. Lawrence liked its cosmopolitanism and its citadel. Aleppo, some 200 miles north of Damascus, was the last Syrian city to be captured from the Turks at the end of **Allenby**'s Middle Eastern campaign. Although Lawrence departed from the Middle East soon after the capture of Damascus on October 1 and took no part in subsequent military action, **Feisal**'s forces were the first Allied units to enter Aleppo and had it in their possession by October 26, 1918.

Alexandretta

Now known as Iskunderun, Turkey. Because of its importance to Turkish supply routes, it was advocated as the site of a proposed Allied landing by Lawrence and others when he was a member of the **Cairo Military Intelligence Department** in 1915, but this idea was rejected, partially because of French opposition. Lawrence claimed to **Liddell Hart** that he was the originator of this plan, but that has been disputed by **John Mack.**

Alexandria

The second-largest city in **Egypt,** founded by Alexander the Great in 332 B.C.E. Lawrence claimed that he had slept on the ship docks here, perhaps when he was sent to work with archaeologist **Flinders Petrie** near **Cairo** in 1912. He was a guest of **Sir Reginald Wingate** at the British Residency in Alexandria in 1917, and in 1925 praised **E. M. Forster**'s guidebook to the city, which remains famous because in ancient times it housed a great library.

Ali

The true name of Lawrence's servant, who volunteered for service during the first week of the **Akaba** march. He is the "Daud" of the Daud and **Farraj** couple in *Seven Pillars of Wisdom* and died in March 1918 of cold, leaving his homosexual partner Farraj (real name Othman) desolate as related in chapter 92 of *Seven Pillars of Wisdom.*

Ali ibn Hussein, Emir (1878–1935)

Eldest and favorite son of **Sharif Hussein** of Mecca. Lawrence considered Ali a possible leader of the **Arab Revolt** as described in chapter 10 of *Seven Pillars of Wisdom,* but preferred **Feisal.** Consumptive, scholarly, and sensitive, Ali, with his own force of 7,000 men, was yet capable of taking vigorous military action as described in chapter 21 of *Seven Pillars of Wisdom.* He ruled **Hejaz** for 10 days in 1924 but was overcome by **Ibn Saud** and went into exile in December 1925 after trying unsuccessfully to continue to rule under him. He spent the rest of his life at Feisal's court in **Iraq.** His son Abd-ul-Ilah was regent of Iraq from 1939 to 1953, and King Feisal II of Iraq (1935–58) was his grandson. See Robin Bidwell, ed., *Arabian Personalities of the Early Twentieth Century;* Shimoni and Levine, *Political Dictionary of the Middle East in the Twentieth Century.*

Ali ibn el Hussein, Sharif (of Modhig)

Spirited leader of the Harith tribe who accompanied **Feisal** from the start of the revolt against the Turks. In chapter 79 of *Seven Pillars of Wisdom,* Lawrence gives a highly favorable portrait of Ali, and in chapter 81, Lawrence compares his and Ali's leave-taking, including their exchange of clothes with one another, to that of David and Jonathan in the Bible. In the 1962 film *Lawrence of Arabia,* Ali is played by Omar Sharif.

Ali Riza Pasha Rikabi (1866–1942)

General officer commanding Damascus under the Turks but always secretly loyal to the Arabs. He deserted to the British when the Turks began to retreat in late September 1918, and was appointed military governor of Damascus by **Feisal** and then by **Gen. Edmund Allenby,** who subsequently demoted him. In January 1915, Ali Riza, a leading member of the **Al Ahd Society,** proposed to **Sharif Hussein** a rebellion of Arab officers in Damascus against the Turks, and he remained clandestinely loyal to the **Arab Revolt** after that (*Seven Pillars of Wisdom,* chapter 5). Lawrence met with him outside Damascus during his secret ride behind Turkish lines in June 1917, informing him that Feisal would advance to **Syria** in stages and telling him that the Arab soldiers serving in the Turkish army should be encouraged to desert and to join Feisal's forces in **Akaba** and that the time was not yet ripe for an uprising in the city. See **G. Antonius,** *The Arab Awakening* (pp. 221–22).

All Souls College, Oxford

Although Lawrence failed to receive a research fellowship at All Souls in 1910, he

Gen. Edmund Allenby enters Jerusalem on foot on December 11, 1917, as a gesture of respect after the city surrendered a few days earlier. Photo by Underwood and Underwood. Courtesy of the Library of Congress.

was given one in 1919. This was good for seven years and included lodging in the college, but Lawrence did not spend much time there and gave up his rooms in 1922. He wrote *Seven Pillars of Wisdom* during this time mainly in an attic owned by architect **Herbert Baker** in Barton Street, Westminster. During his residence at All Souls, he met **Robert Graves,** compiled his poetry anthology *Minorities,* and indulged in pranks, such as ringing the bell that he had taken from Tell Shahm station in the quadrangle, and flying the **Hejaz** flag from the college pinnacle.

Allenby, Gen. Sir Edmund Henry Hynman, 1st Viscount (1861–1936)

Commander of the 3rd Army during the Battle of Arras (1917) on the western front, Allenby did not get along with his superior, Field-Marshal Haig, and so was made commander of the British Expeditionary Forces in **Egypt.** Using deception, high mobility, and overwhelming force, he captured **Beersheba** on October 31, 1917, entered **Jerusalem** on December 9, 1917, and took **Damascus, Aleppo,** and **Beirut** in late 1918, thus recouping early British failures under **Sir Archibald Murray** and proving himself one of the best generals of **World War I.** Lawrence greatly admired the leadership of Allenby as he makes clear in chapter 56 and several other chapters in *Seven Pillars of Wisdom.* Allenby became high commissioner in Egypt from 1919 to 1925, and he was lionized in **Lowell Thomas**'s show, "With Allenby in Palestine and Lawrence in Arabia." See Raymond Savage, *Allenby of Armageddon;* **A. P. Wavell,** *The Palestine Campaigns* and *Allenby;* Philip Haythornthwaite, *The World War I Source Book;* and Matthew Hughes, *Allenby and British Strategy in the Middle East, 1917–1919.*

Altounyan, Ernest Huie Riddall (1889–1962)

Poet, author of *Ornament of Honor* (1937), a long poem about Lawrence. The poem was written in **Aleppo** within six months of Lawrence's death. It has three "movements": "Prelude," "Fugue," and "Finale." The Fugue section consists of 119 sonnets. Altounyan was the son of an Armenian surgeon who hosted Lawrence in Aleppo during his prewar archeological work in **Carchemish,** and for whom Lawrence felt deep friendship (Garnett, *Letters,* p. 760). While Altounyan's poem praises Lawrence highly, Lawrence felt that the style of this poem was too difficult for most readers, as he wrote Altounyan himself on April 7, 1934 (Garnett, *Letters,* p. 794).

American Mission

Consisting of a system of Presbyterian schools in Constantinople, **Syria,** and Asia Minor, this mission was the source of reformist ideas, which may have served as the impetus behind the **Young Turk** revolution of 1908. In August 1909 Lawrence stayed for a few days at the school in Jebail, **Lebanon,** where he was welcomed by Miss D. Holmes, the principal. Lawrence varied in his opinion of the mission, sometimes seeing its influence as positive and sometimes as negative, because he could not wholeheartedly subscribe to its role in Westernizing the Arabs.

Amery, Leopold Stennett (1873–1955)

First lord of the admiralty who offered Lawrence a coastguard station or a lighthouse position after he had been expelled from the **Royal Air Force** in 1923. Lawrence rejected this as too remote a posting.

Amman

Now the capital of Jordan, but in 1914 a small town originally settled by **Circassians** in the 19th century and located on the site of the biblical Rabbat Ammon (Hellenistic Philadelphia). **General Allenby**'s failure in a raid near Amman in March 1918, as described in chapter 93 of *Seven Pillars of Wisdom,* almost caused **Feisal** to consider joining the Turks, and Lawrence strove to buttress Feisal's resolve to remain loyal to the British. It was captured during Allenby's final offensive on September 25, 1918, by **General E.W.C. Chaytor**'s force after a strong battle with the Turkish rear guard. In 1921 it became the capital city of **Abdullah ibn Hussein,** Feisal's brother and the new ruler of **Transjordan,** whom Lawrence advised during his **Colonial Office** service.

Aneyza Tribes

A large grouping of Arabian and Syrian **Beduin** tribes, several of which, including the **Rualla,** the Aida, the Fuqara, and the Wuld Suleiman, supplied men for the sharifian forces.

Anglo-French Declaration

A statement made in November 1918 by the British and French governments for the purpose of calming Arab nationalists to the effect that they sought only to help the inhabitants of **Syria** and **Mesopotamia** toward self-government. This followed an agreement between **Lloyd George** and **Clemenceau** according to which France recognized Britain's control of the **Mosul** area of Mesopotamia and of **Palestine,** while Britain acquiesced to French control of **Lebanon** and **Syria.** Lawrence opposed this declaration as he did the **Sykes-Picot Agreement** and indicated as much in a letter of September 8, 1919, to the London *Times.*

"Antiquarian and a Geologist in Hants, An"

This article, which appeared in the *Oxford High School Magazine* (1:5, March 1904), is signed "L.ii" (indicating that Lawrence was the second child born in his family) and includes many architectural and natural observations made during a family bicycle trip in Hampshire.

Antonius, George (1892–1942)

Arab author of Greek Orthodox extraction. His *The Arab Awakening* (1938) is a sympathetic, detailed, and authoritative account of the origins of Arab nationalism that challenges Lawrence's claim to have devised the plan to take **Akaba** from the

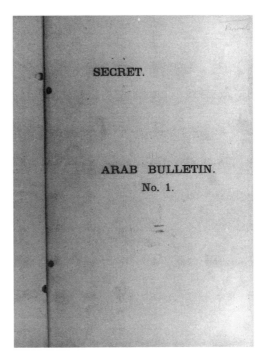

The cover of the first issue of the *Arab Bulletin,* the secret intelligence newsletter that was published by the Arab Bureau in Cairo from 1916 to 1919. Courtesy of the Huntington Library.

land side, crediting **Auda abu Tayi** with it instead, and challenges some of Lawrence's statements about early twentieth-century Arab nationalist movements.

ANZAC

See **Australians and New Zealanders**

Arab Bulletin

Secret **Arab Bureau** intelligence newsletter, founded at the urging of Lawrence, who edited its first number (June 6, 1916). It was printed by the Egyptian Government Press and appeared at weekly intervals for most of its existence. Owing to its excellent contributors, including **Alfred Parker** and **Gertrude Bell** among others, it continued to supply high-quality intelligence about the Arab movement and other Middle Eastern developments to British lead-

The Savoy Hotel, Cairo, served as the headquarters of the British forces in Egypt during World War I. Courtesy of the Australian War Memorial.

ers in **Cairo** under the editorships of **D. G. Hogarth,** then **Kinahan Cornwallis,** and finally **Herbert Garland.** It ceased publication with issue number 114 of August 30, 1919, but was reprinted in 1986 by Archive Editions of Gerrards Cross, Buckinghamshire, England, and still makes fascinating reading.

Arab Bureau

First conceived by **Mark Sykes,** this secret office was established in **Cairo** under **Gilbert Clayton** in early 1916 for the purpose of gathering political intelligence and assisting the **Arab Revolt.** Its offices consisted of a few rooms in the Savoy Hotel. The deputy director of the Arab Bureau was **D. G. Hogarth,** who began his work on March 26, 1916. Lawrence joined it in October 1916. Other members and affili-

ates included at various times **Kinahan Cornwallis,** William Davenport, **Pierce C. Joyce,** George A. **Lloyd,** and **Alfred Parker,** among others. In the Bureau's last days in 1919, its director was **Herbert Garland,** who had assisted Lawrence by training the sharifian forces in explosives. In chapters 6 and 7 of *Seven Pillars of Wisdom,* Lawrence gives a colorful account of the Arab Bureau and of his own involvement in it. For a full account of the Bureau's activities, see Bruce Westrate, *The Arab Bureau: British Policy in the Middle East, 1916–1920.*

Arab Revolt

Beginning in **Mecca** on June 5, 1916, the revolt of **Sharif Hussein** and his sons **Ali, Abdullah, Feisal,** and **Zeid** against the Turks was prepared for by the **McMahon-**

Hussein Correspondence, which discussed the extent of Arab independence after the war. The British (and to a much lesser extent the French Military Mission to the Hejaz) supplied money (reaching some 200,000 pounds sterling a month), provisions, armaments, naval support, and advisers, including Lawrence. At first, progress was slow (Medina was never taken during the war, largely because of Fakhri Pasha's spirited defense), but the Arab forces (at first consisting of an indeterminate number of irregulars, never totaling more than several thousand at one event but drawn from a pool of tens of thousands), under Feisal's and Lawrence's leadership (including Lawrence's development of an appropriate guerrilla strategy, as outlined in chapter 33 of *Seven Pillars of Wisdom*), constantly disrupted the Hejaz Railway and harassed the Turks. After Lawrence's conquest of Akaba on July 6, 1917, the Arab forces (which numbered 70,000 regulars and irregulars by the end of the war), became the right wing of Allenby's army in Palestine, entering Damascus in October 1918. Feisal, however, was evicted from Syria by the French under Gen. Henri Joseph Gouraud in 1920, and Sharif Hussein lost Arabia to Ibn Saud in 1924, so in spite of its military success the Arab Revolt ended in political failure. However, as Lawrence notes in chapter 47 of *Seven Pillars of Wisdom,* Britain tried to stand behind its promises to the Hussein family by installing Feisal as ruler of Iraq in 1921 and confirming Abdullah as emir of Transjordan in the same year. *See also* "Evolution of a Revolt, The."

Arabic Language

By his own admission, Lawrence's knowledge of Arabic was far from perfect. George Antonius confirms this self-estimate, calling into question Lawrence's accent and diction. In preparation for his 1909 thesis trip, Lawrence consulted Professor David Margoliouth of Oxford University and studied with the Rev. Nasar Odeh, and in 1911 he studied for two months at the American Mission School in Jebail, where his teacher was Fareedah el Akle. He also improved his Arabic during his time at Carchemish, when he was helped by his servant Dahoum. In 1937, his translation of *Two Arabic Folk Tales*, possibly a student exercise dating from the prewar period, was published. In *T. E. Lawrence to His Biographers Robert Graves & Liddell Hart,* Lawrence says that he knew some colloquial grammar before he went to Carchemish and that there he added about 4,000 words of vocabulary to his knowledge. Then, during his two wartime years in Cairo he barely spoke Arabic at all and so had to begin again in a new dialect when he joined Feisal. By the end of the war, Lawrence says, he knew some 12,000 words, which sounds impressive but was not enough for a genuine command of the language. Lawrence also claimed that he never heard a single Englishman who knew Arabic well enough to pass for an Arab.

Archaeology

Lawrence started to rub brasses in his early teens and avidly read the works of Sir Henry Austin Layard, the nineteenth-century archaeologist of Mesopotamia. He and his friend C.F.C. Beeson contributed small items to the Ashmolean Museum in their teens, and when at Oxford University Lawrence wrote his honors thesis on Crusader castles. Lawrence considered his time during the Carchemish Hittite dig, following his graduation from Oxford in 1910 with first-class honors, the happiest of his life and thought of resuming an archaeological career after the war. As an archaeologist, Lawrence's strongest achievements were his noting of Western features, such as keeps, at Saone and other

Crusader castles; his helping salvage objects from cemeteries near Carchemish and his noticing Parthian period graves there; his successful attempt, with **C. L. Woolley,** to locate the Biblical **Kadesh Barnea** at Ain el Qudeirat in the Sinai desert; and his work, also with Woolley, on the Nabataean-Byzantine cities in the Negev desert, including the conclusion that the climate had not changed since biblical times. *See also* **"The Influence of the Crusades on European Military Architecture—To the End of the XIIth Century";** *Carchemish: A Report on the Excavations at Djerabis*; *The Wilderness of Zin.* For more information, see Rupert Chapman, "Lawrence as Archaeologist," *Journal of the T. E. Lawrence Society* 1:1 (Spring 1991): 21–29, and S. E. Tabachnick, "Lawrence of Arabia as Archaeologist," *Biblical Archaeology Review* 23:5 (Sept./Oct. 1997): 40–47, 70–71.

Arendt, Hannah (1906–75)

German-born American political philosopher, who in her *Origins of Totalitarianism* (1951) stated that Lawrence was one of the most decent people ever to undertake secret politics.

Aristophanes (257?–180? B.C.E.)

Greek comic dramatist. Aristophanes was one of Lawrence's favorite authors during the war and immediate postwar period, the others being **William Morris, Charles M. Doughty, Sir Thomas Malory,** and some of the poets in his 1915 edition of *The Oxford Book of English Verse.* During breaks in the Arab campaign, he read Aristophanes's *Peace* in the original Greek, in an 1835 edition now held in the **Houghton Library, Harvard.**

Armenians

During **World War I,** well over one million Armenians died as a result of Turkish policies as formulated by the **Young Turk** triumvirate of **Talat Pasha, Jemal Pasha,** and **Enver Pasha.** In chapter 4 of *Seven Pillars of Wisdom,* Lawrence writes sympathetically of the Armenians' plight under the Turks, claiming that the example of their oppression and the failure of the Armenian leadership to prevent it helped galvanize Arab nationalism. See **John Mack,** "Lawrence and the Armenians," *Ararat* 21 (Summer 1980): 2–8.

Armor

Lawrence's interest in armor grew out of his interest in the Middle Ages and continued from his teenage **brass rubbing** enthusiasm through his later years. Lawrence shared this enthusiasm with his school friend **C.F.C. Beeson,** and discussed it with **Charles J. ffoulkes,** who taught armor at **Oxford University** during Lawrence's time there. Lawrence had a personally inscribed copy of ffoulkes's *Armour and Weapons* (1909) in his library at the time of his death. In the motto on the cover of some editions of *Seven Pillars of Wisdom,* Lawrence refers to a sword, which is also a pun on the name of his comrade-in-arms **Feisal,** which means a downward sword stroke in Arabic, as Lawrence explains in chapter 19.

Armored Cars

The first armored cars, developed before 1914, were simply civilian vehicles with armor plating added to them. British forces were particularly involved in the use of armored cars, having begun policing their colonies with them. The British usually employed Rolls-Royces for heavy work and other British and American cars, with or without armor plating, for light transport. The use of armored cars during the **Arab Revolt,** given the relative mobility of the action compared to the Western front, is considered particularly far-sighted and exemplary. In *Seven Pillars of Wisdom,* Lawrence mentions Rolls-Royce, Talbot, and Ford cars on several occasions. The Penguin edition includes a photo of a Rolls-Royce tender, and S. E. Tabachnick and Christopher Matheson's *Images of Lawrence* contains additional photos of Rolls-Royce tenders and one of a Crossley car, with Lawrence in or near them. The Ford and Crossley cars were for light transport of supplies or in the case of the Ford Model T Patrol car, which was equipped with a Lewis machine gun, for raiding. The Rolls cars, however, were the main models used for fighting. One of the Rolls cars shown in *Images of Lawrence* (p. 126), although the year is 1917, appears to be a 1914 "Admiralty pattern" model which was based on a Silver Ghost chassis, weighed 3.5 tons, had an engine of 40 or 50 horsepower, and had a machine gun in a revolving turret. Compared to camel raiding, Lawrence considered the use of armored cars luxury fighting, and it is clear that he enjoyed zipping across the desert in them. To **Robert Graves,** Lawrence wrote that he had fought in approximately 50 armored-car engagements and that he had evolved a special method of using the cars (*T. E. Lawrence to His Biographers Robert Graves & Liddell Hart,* p. 1:129). He especially valued his unit's five Rolls-Royces, stating that each car in the desert was worth many men in military value. In chapter 108, he details how his driver S. C. Rolls temporarily repaired a spring that had broken while they were under threat by the Turks, thus saving the valuable vehicle, a Blue Mist. Owing to its own strength as well as the skill of the temporary repair, the vehicle was able to go on for three weeks and enter **Damascus.** In his essay in **A. W. Lawrence**'s *T. E. Lawrence by His Friends,* Rolls comments that Lawrence chose armored cars when camels were no longer fast enough for a rapidly developing campaign. Rolls also explains that Lawrence had a passion for speed and reached as high as 70 miles per hour on flat surfaces, and that he encouraged races between the cars, and sat next to Rolls, urging him on. Moreover, Rolls recalls that, at the Nagab, a mountain range 100 miles from **Guweira,** his car had to negotiate some 13 sharp turns on a very steep incline with no margin for error because precipices loomed. Rolls himself, with bleeding hands, wondered how the Rolls was able to pass over rough country full of boulders, but so it did. In chapter 117, Lawrence mentions German machine gunners who managed to repulse several Arab attacks while grouped around three cars; these might have been Daimler or Mercedes cars, but Lawrence gives no indication. A small number of tanks were used in the British assaults on Gaza, but not in Lawrence's area of the war. See S. C. Rolls, *Steel Chariots in the Desert* and B. T. White, *Tanks and Other Armored Fighting Vehicles 1900 to 1918.*

Artillery

The artillery in use during **Feisal**'s campaign was at first limited to some captured Turkish guns. By November 1916, the sharifian forces had 23 mostly obsolete pieces, including 5-inch howitzers and 10-pound field pieces, and four 20-year-old Krupps mountain guns (with a range of only 3,000 yards) sent from the British army in **Egypt,** all of which were outranged by the weapons in the hands of the Turks. **Commandant Cousse,** the French liaison to the sharifians following the departure of **Colonel Brémond,** supplied four Schneider quick-firing mountain guns, which, eventually combined with some captured weapons, such as 7.5-inch Skoda mountain howitzers, helped redress the balance. (A photo of such a gun can be found in **J. M. Wilson,** *T. E. Lawrence,* p. 71). However, Lawrence doubted the military usefulness of artillery to the Arabs, who were engaged in a hit-and-run guerrilla campaign, seeing it as of morale-building value only, as he explains in chapter 15 of *Seven Pillars of Wisdom.* The Arabs were aided by British naval artillery and landing parties, which were responsible, early in the revolt, for the successful defense of **Yenbo** and for the capture of **Wejh** from the Turks.

Ashmolean Museum, Oxford

Britain's oldest public museum. Lawrence began his archaeological career while still in his teens by contributing small finds of his own from sixteenth- and seventeenth-century **Oxford** to this great museum of ancient and modern art and archaeology. During his university years, he came to the notice of **D. G. Hogarth,** keeper of the museum, who became his mentor and subsequently his senior colleague during a dig at **Carchemish** and in the **Arab Bureau.** The museum now houses some brass rubbings made by Lawrence, as well as some artifacts from his Arabian adventures, including his Arab dagger and robe.

Astor, Viscountess Nancy (1879–1964)

American-born Conservative member of Parliament from Plymouth (1919–45) and the first woman member in the House of Commons. From their first meeting in 1929, she and Lawrence became friends and correspondents.

Ataturk

See **Kemal Pasha, Mustapha**

Ateiba Tribe

Emir Abdullah ibn Hussein's force at **Wadi Ais** in 1917 included about 3,000 warriors, most of whom were **Ateiba Beduin.** Lawrence felt that they were inferior to the **Harb** and **Juheina** as fighters.

Athens, Greece

In December 1910, on his way to the dig at **Carchemish, Syria,** Lawrence first visited Athens briefly, enjoying the Acropolis. In August 1915, he was sent from **Cairo** to improve communication with the Levant branch of British Intelligence and stayed almost a week without having the opportunity to visit any historical sites. He visited again in 1919 on his way to Cairo by plane and was also able to explore the Aegean islands. *See also* **Greece.**

Athlit

Site on the Mediterranean coast south of Haifa. Lawrence visited the ruins of Chateau Pellerin there in the summer of 1909 during his research on Crusader castles. Between 1910 and 1914, **Aaron Aaronsohn** built at Athlit an agricultural station, which served as the center for the Jewish organization NILI's spying activities against the Turks during **World War I.** NILI is an acronym for *nezach Yisrael lo yishaker,* "the strength of Israel will not lie," from 1 Samuel 15:29 in the Hebrew Bible.

Auda abu Tayi, Sheikh (circa 1870–1924)

Head of the **Abu Tayi Beduin,** Auda joined **Feisal**'s movement in early 1917

Australian soldiers patrolling along the Dead Sea in two Ford cars equipped with Lewis guns. Courtesy of the Australian War Memorial.

and helped the Arab forces take **Akaba.** In chapter 38 of *Seven Pillars of Wisdom,* Lawrence portrays him as an epic figure. However, shortly after the Akaba victory, Auda was in treasonable correspondence with the Turks, and Lawrence had to purchase his loyalty to the British and to Feisal, as related in chapter 57. Thereafter he remained loyal and entered **Damascus** at Lawrence's side.

Auden, W. H. (1907–73)

Important mid-century poet. Lawrence was reading Auden's work in 1933 when it was new, and in 1934 expressed to **C. Day-Lewis** his appreciation of it. He never met the young poet, who, however, used him as the model for the character Ransom in his play *The Ascent of F.6* (1937), written with Christopher Isherwood.

Australians and New Zealanders

Australian and New Zealand units of the British army played a major role in the **Palestine** campaign, taking part in all important engagements, including the captures of **Beersheba, Jerusalem,** and **Damascus.** Lawrence mentions an Australian Sergeant Major Yells, who was called "Lewis" after the Lewis guns in whose use he trained the Arabs. Yells displayed a tendency toward quick, willing action that Lawrence saw as typical of Australian troops, as described in chapter 60 of *Seven Pillars of Wisdom.* **Gen. Henry G. Chauvel,** commander of the Australian troops during the capture of **Damascus,** disputed Lawrence's account that the Arabs had entered the city first, claiming that honor for the Australians. The acronym for the

Australians and New Zealanders was ANZAC—Australian and New Zealand Army Corps. There are **World War I** military cemeteries containing many Australian and New Zealander graves in Beersheba and Jerusalem. The Australian films *Gallipoli* and *The Light Horsemen* (about the capture of Beersheba) portray the roles of these soldiers in the eastern theater of the war. For a full account, see H. S. Gullett, *The Australian Imperial Force in Sinai and Palestine, 1914–1918,* and **A. P. Wavell,** *The Palestine Campaigns.*

Autogiro

A science fiction vehicle the description of which was invented by Lawrence at the request of **Robert Graves** and **Laura Riding** for use in their novel *No Decency Left* (1932), published under the pseudonym Barbara Rich.

Azrak

An oasis about 65 miles east of **Amman,** in what is now Jordan. Azrak is the site of a ruined castle built by the Mamelukes and dating to the thirteenth century but founded on Roman ruins. This was one of Lawrence's favorite places, as described in chapters 75, 79, and 105 of *Seven Pillars of Wisdom.*

B

Baalbek

Site, about 50 miles northwest of Damascus, of an attack by Lawrence in June 1917, during his secret trip behind Turkish lines. With a party of **Aneyza Beduin,** he damaged a small bridge near the **Hejaz Railway** station at Ras Baalbek. Lawrence does not give more than a brief mention of this trip in chapter 48 of *Seven Pillars of Wisdom,* but its details, including the Baalbek raid, can be found in his secret report to **Gilbert Clayton** (Garnett, *Letters,* pp. 225–30).

Bair

Site, now in central Jordan, of **Ghassanid** ruins and wells—some of which had been destroyed by the Turks—where Lawrence rested for a week in June 1917 during the march to **Akaba.** At Bair on August 15, 1918, his 30th birthday, on the way toward Damascus with the **Howeitat** and the **Imperial Camel Corps,** Lawrence embarked on a self-examination, the results of which are revealed in chapter 103 of *Seven Pillars of Wisdom.*

Baker, Sir Herbert (1862–1946)

A leading architect and friend of Lawrence, who starting in 1919 allowed Lawrence to use spartan rooms in the attic of his office at 14 Barton Street, Westminster, to write the second and third drafts of *Seven Pillars of Wisdom,* and later, after Lawrence's return in 1929 from his tour of duty in **India,** to continue work on his *Odyssey* translation.

Baldwin, Stanley, 1st Earl (1867–1947)

Prime Minister of England, 1923–24, 1924–29, and 1935–37. **John Buchan** and **George Bernard Shaw** appealed to Baldwin in 1925 to allow Lawrence back into the **Royal Air Force** over the objections of **Samuel Hoare,** the secretary of state for air, stressing the possibility of Lawrence's suicide if this request were not granted. Lawrence remained grateful to Baldwin for acceding to his request. In 1930, when Baldwin was about to be installed as chancellor of the University of St. Andrews, he wanted Lawrence to receive an honorary doctorate. Lawrence however never accepted it, owing to his fear of being evicted from the R.A.F. because of the publicity that might result.

Balfour Declaration

British government declaration made by Foreign Secretary Arthur J. Balfour on November 2, 1917, to the Zionist Organization via Lord Rothschild, viewing with favor the establishment of a national home for the Jewish people in **Palestine.** In chapter 101 of *Seven Pillars of Wisdom,* Lawrence states that this declaration promised something equivocal to the **Jews,** just as the **McMahon-Hussein Correspondence** promised something equivocal to the Arabs, which the **Sykes-Picot Agreement** seemed to retract.

Bank of England

In 1928, the architect **Sir Herbert Baker,** working on the bank's offices, succeeded in securing for Lawrence the offer of a job as night watchman if he wished to retire from military service. Lawrence, however, was happy in the **Royal Air Force** and was not interested in this proposal. In 1934, Lawrence was offered the post of secretary for the bank but rejected it.

Barker, Sir Ernest (1874–1960)

A fellow of St. John's College who tutored Lawrence on the Crusades when he was at **Oxford University. A. W. Lawrence**'s collection, *T. E. Lawrence by His Friends,* contains Barker's memoir of Lawrence, including his high praise of Lawrence's honors thesis on Crusader castles.

Barrie, Sir James M. (1860–1937)

Dramatist, author of *Peter Pan.* Lawrence met him on several occasions beginning in the early 1920s, but he did not respect Barrie's artistry. In 1930 Barrie, under the influence of **Stanley Baldwin,** who was to be installed as chancellor of the University of St. Andrews, unsuccessfully tried to persuade Lawrence to accept an honorary doctorate there.

Barrow, Gen. Sir George de Symons (1864–1959)

Commander of the 4th Cavalry Division of the Desert Mounted Corps given responsibility by **Gen. Edmund Allenby** for the thrust, in September 1918 during the war's final offensive, from the Jordan River to **Deraa.** In his *The Fire of Life* (1942), Barrow disputes Lawrence's account of their meeting in Deraa and other claims made in chapter 117 of *Seven Pillars of Wisdom.*

Bartholemew, Gen. Sir William Henry (1877–1962)

Gen. Edmund Allenby's chief of staff, responsible for planning the British army's movement from **Jerusalem** to **Damascus.** Lawrence describes him positively in chapter 97 of *Seven Pillars of Wisdom* as being thorough, responsible, and friendly.

"Bastion, The"

An essay published by Lawrence and **C.F.C. Beeson** in the *Oxford High School Magazine* 3:5 (February 1906), describing the remains of a fortified turret dating from the eleventh century standing in the school playground. It is available in *The T. E. Lawrence Society Journal* 3:1 (Summer 1993): 8–10. *See also* **"Playground Cricket"** and **"Playground Football."**

Baxter, Dr. Frank Condie (1896–1982)

University of Southern California professor and educational teleseries host who began collecting Lawrence materials in the 1920s. In 1968 he published an *Annotated Check-List* of his collection.

Beach, Col. W. H.

Head of Military Intelligence, Indian Army Expeditionary Force "D," **Mesopo-**

tamia, who accompanied Lawrence and **Aubrey Herbert** in spring 1916 on their unsuccessful mission to bribe **Khalil Pasha,** then besieging **General Townshend**'s division at **Kut-al-Amara.**

Beauforte-Greenwood, Fl. Lt. W.E.G. (born 1878)

Head of the **Royal Air Force** Marine Equipment Branch, who in 1931 requested that Lawrence test the new **R.A.F. 200 Class boat.** He also consulted Lawrence about the design for two armor-plated target boats based on the 200 class.

Beaumont, Tom W. (1898–1991)

Hejaz Armoured Car Company machine gunner serving under Lawrence during the later days of the **Arab Revolt,** who claimed that Lawrence's servant **Dahoum** was "S. A." and that Lawrence told him in September 1918 that Dahoum was dying of typhoid behind Turkish lines. This testimony can be found in **Knightley** and **Simpson,** *The Secret Lives of Lawrence of Arabia* (p. 186).

Beduin

Tribesmen of Arabia and Syria, still nomadic in Lawrence's day, who made up the bulk of the **Arab Revolt**'s irregulars. Like many Anglo-Arabian travelers before him, Lawrence preferred the Beduin to the Arabs of the towns, seeing in the Beduin aristocratic and heroic warrior traditions. However, he was also aware of the difficulty of molding them into modern fighting roles, particularly with regard to their fear of artillery, as he explains in chapter 15 of *Seven Pillars of Wisdom.* He enlisted many tribes and tribal leaders with the rhetoric he records in chapter 74 and with the promise of payment. *See also* the various tribes, including the **Abu Tayi, Aneyza, Beni Sakhr, Howeitat, Rualla.**

Beersheba

Biblical site known especially for Abraham's "well of the oath," where he made a covenant with God (Gen. 21: 22–32). The modern town was a center for Beduin established by the Turks around 1907 and had a population of around 800 in 1917. It was the first town in **Palestine** captured by **General Allenby,** on October 31, 1917, following a brilliant deception of the Turks by **Col. Richard Meinertzhagen,** who deliberately lost a false set of deployment plans, as related in chapter 69 of *Seven Pillars of Wisdom,* and one of the campaign's great cavalry charges, by two regiments of Australian light horse. Lawrence was in Beersheba first in January 1914 during the **Wilderness of Zin** expedition and then several times during the **Arab Revolt** itself. The modern town, now Beersheva, Israel, has a cemetery for fallen **World War I** Australian and British soldiers and an obelisk commemorating Allenby's victory. See H. S. Gullett, *The Australian Imperial Force in Sinai and Palestine, 1914–1918* and **A. P. Wavell,** *The Palestine Campaigns.* The Australian film *The Light Horsemen* (1988), directed by Simon Wincer, while not shot on location, convincingly depicts the battle for Beersheba.

Beeson, Cyril F. C. (1889–1975)

Lawrence's school friend, nicknamed Scroggs, with whom he went on archaeological expeditions around Oxford when young. *See* **Archaeology.** See Beeson's piece in **A. W. Lawrence**'s collection *T. E. Lawrence by His Friends.*

Australian Light Horsemen round up Turkish prisoners in Beersheba, which they had captured on October 31, 1917, with one of the campaign's great cavalry charges. Photo by Joseph Harley Graves. Courtesy of the Palestine Exploration Fund.

Beirut

On October 3, 1918, before the arrival of British forces on October 8, **Feisal** sent **Shukri Pasha el-Ayoubi** to hoist the Arab movement's flag and declare an Arab government in Beirut, which caused trouble with the French, who anticipated control of all of **Syria,** including the coast, after the war. Lawrence denied that he had anything to do with this flag-raising. He was in Beirut himself only during the prewar period: for about two weeks during his 1909 Crusader castles walking tour, and again during his **Carchemish** period, when he visited poet **James Elroy Flecker,** then British vice-consul. In 1913, he wrote his mother that he had helped smuggle rifles to the British consulate at Beirut (Brown, *Selected Letters,* p. 47).

Bell, Charles Francis (1871–1966)

Keeper of the Department of Fine Art at the **Ashmolean Museum,** fellow of Magdalen College, **Oxford,** and trustee of the National Portrait Gallery. Bell was a friendly acquaintance of Lawrence's, especially during the period of his archaeological interest before the war.

Bell, Gertrude Margaret Lowthian (1868–1926)

Archaeologist, translator, intelligence agent, political adviser, and recipient of the Royal Geographical Society's Gold Medal (1912). She described her travels in *The*

Desert and the Sown (1907), *The Thousand and One Churches* (1909), and *The Palace and Mosque at Ukhaidir* (1914). Bell met Lawrence at **Carchemish** in 1911 and predicted that he would become involved in Middle Eastern affairs. She worked with him at the **Arab Bureau,** the **Peace Conference** (1919), and the **Cairo Conference** (1921). Like Lawrence a supporter of the sharifian cause, she was **Feisal**'s adviser in **Iraq** during the last five years of her life, helping to establish it as an independent state, before committing suicide for undisclosed reasons. Lawrence admired her emotional strength but found her lacking in depth. See Janet Wallach, *Desert Queen: The Extraordinary Life of Gertrude Bell, Adventurer, Advisor to Kings, Ally of Lawrence of Arabia.*

Belloc, Joseph Hilaire Pierre (1870–1953)

Essayist, historian, novelist, poet, and member of Parliament (1906–10). Author of *The Path to Rome* (1902), *Cautionary Tales* (1908), and *Cromwell* (1934), among other works. Lawrence felt that Belloc was a writer of talent who rarely produced his best work because of a desire to sell (Garnett, *Letters,* p. 361), and he rejected Belloc's antisemitism (Orlans, *Lawrence of Arabia, Strange Man of Letters,* p. 139).

Beni Atiyeh Tribe

Beduin tribe of northwestern Arabia whose fighting effectiveness was nullified, according to Lawrence, by the inability of its leader Sharif Mohammed Ali el Bedawi.

Beni Sakhr Tribe

Beduin tribe of the Dead Sea area, led by Sheikh Mithgal. In June 1917 during his secret trip behind Turkish lines, Lawrence was almost betrayed to the Turks by Fawaz el Faiz, a prominent Damascene relative of Mithgal's whom he met near Ziza. Luckily Lawrence was informed in time by Fawaz's brother, Nawaf, and managed to escape, as explained in chapter 95 of *Seven Pillars of Wisdom.* The failure of the Beni Sakhr to attack the Turks as planned was partially responsible for the failure of **General Allenby**'s operations around **Salt** in spring 1918, as explained in chapter 95 of *Seven Pillars of Wisdom.*

Béraud-Villars, Jean (died 1979)

French author of *T. E. Lawrence, or The Search for the Absolute* (1955; English version 1958), which claims that Lawrence sacrificed European interests to those of the Arab movement. He was also the author of a 1946 book about the Muslim invasion of Spain.

Berlin–Baghdad Railway

A railroad being built by the Germans through the Amanus Mountains near the **Carchemish** site, run by **D. G. Hogarth,** at which Lawrence was working from 1911 to 1914. Begun in 1902 as part of Germany's Drive to the East policy, the railroad was 1,875 miles long and 90 percent complete at the beginning of **World War I.** A crucial part of the railway, from Adana to **Aleppo,** remained incomplete, thus hampering the Turkish military effort against the British in **Syria** and **Palestine.** In June 1914, before World War I began, Lawrence and **C. L. Woolley** secured the plans for the railway from a disgruntled Italian engineer, as Woolley recounts in his *As I Seem to Remember* (1962). The **Hejaz Railway** was a branch of the Berlin-to-Baghdad railway project.

Billi Tribe

Beduin tribe of northern Arabia, in the area around **Wejh.** Tribal leaders were initially reluctant to join the sharifian cause, but eventually did so as it gained success.

Bir Abbas

Site, about 30 miles southwest of **Medina,** of a victory of **Feisal**'s forces over the Turks in October 1916, a few months after the start of the **Arab Revolt.**

Bir ibn Hassani

Small settlement at the eastern end of Wadi Safra, about 100 miles southwest of **Medina,** where the Arabs repulsed a Turkish reconnaissance patrol in late 1916, and the site of later skirmishing between Arab and Turkish forces, as recounted in chapter 17 of *Seven Pillars of Wisdom.*

Bir Said

Site about 100 miles southwest of **Medina,** where a Turkish force under Ghalib Bey surprised the **Emir Zeid**'s forces in late 1916, almost capturing Zeid himself and scattering his forces, as recounted in chapter 18 of *Seven Pillars of Wisdom.*

Biscuit

The name of a Biscayne Baby speedboat, built by the Purdy Boat Company, that Lawrence and **Wing Commander Sydney Smith** received as a joint gift from eccentric British millionaire Maj. Colin Cooper and that Lawrence restored during his service at **R.A.F. Cattewater** (later R.A.F. Mount Batten) in 1929. It remained at **R.A.F. Felixstowe** when he retired in 1935. *See also* **Boats.**

Blackmur, Richard P. (1904–65)

Noted American literary critic who wrote one of the first serious critiques of *Seven Pillars of Wisdom,* the essay "The Everlasting Effort: A Citation of T. E. Lawrence" in his *The Expense of Greatness* (1940).

Blackwood, Algernon (1869–1951)

British supernatural writer whose *Episodes Before Thirty* (1923), *Dudley and Gilderoy* (1929), and *The Centaur* (1911) Lawrence recommended highly despite his dislike of Blackwood's other works.

Blumenfeld, Ralph David (1864–1948)

London *Daily Express* editor who supported Lawrence's view that a new **Middle East Department** of the British government should be created and who published Lawrence's editorial to that effect in May 1920. In 1922 the *Daily Express,* perhaps at Blumenfeld's initiative, exposed Lawrence's presence in the **Royal Air Force** as an ordinary airman.

Blunt, Lady Anne (1837–1917)

Arabic scholar and Middle Eastern traveler. With her husband **Wilfred Scawen Blunt,** she was the author of *A Pilgrimage to Nejd* (1881) and other works.

Blunt, Wilfred Scawen (1840–1922)

Poet and polemicist. A member of the diplomatic corps from the age of 18, Blunt served in British embassies in Europe and the Mediterranean, including those at **Athens** and Constantinople. In 1875 he visited **Egypt** and then traveled in central Arabia, becoming an ardent anti-imperialist in the process. He was defeated twice when trying to become a member of Parliament and spent two months in prison for championing Irish nationalism. Blunt was the author of *The Future of Islam* (1882), *The Secret History of the British Occupation of Egypt* (1907), and *My Diaries 1884–1914* (1922). With his wife **Lady Anne Blunt,** he translated *The Seven Golden Odes of Pagan Arabia, Also Known as the Moallakat* (1903), which Lawrence greatly valued, and other Arabic works, including *The Celebrated Romance of the Stealing of the Mare* (1892). Blunt supported Lawrence's 1919–1920 newspaper campaign on behalf of **Feisal,** and Lawrence respected him enough to discuss with Blunt Lawrence's own political intentions concerning the Middle East when he became a member of the **Colonial Office** (see Brown, *Selected Letters,* p. 184).

Boats

Lawrence's father taught him to sail, but only in his final six years in the **Royal Air Force** was he able to indulge this interest as a tester, designer, and restorer of boats. In 1931, he was assigned by **Beauforte-Greenwood** to test fast experimental boats. Lawrence had felt the need for a faster launch to tend seaplanes since acquiring his own speedboat, the *Bisquit,* and witnessing the crash of a seaplane at **R.A.F. Cattewater/Mount Batten** in February 1931. In that month, he began work at the **Scott-Paine** shipyard in Southampton, and later wrote **"200 Class Seaplane Tender— Provisional Issue of Notes."** He taught crews how to use this boat and piloted target launches during R.A.F. bombing prac-

tices. He also wrote "Power Boat Hull Reconditioning," an unpublished 79-page manuscript, here. At the end of his life, he may have participated with engineer **Edward Spurr,** who also worked in the Scott-Paine shipyard, in the design of a new kind of speedboat that raised itself off the water, but this boat, named *Empire Day* and dedicated to Lawrence, was not built until 1938, three years after Lawrence's death.

Bodleian Library, Oxford

Lawrence used this famous library when a student, and as if in repayment, on February 22, 1923, he donated the now-priceless 1922 manuscript of *Seven Pillars of Wisdom* to it through its director Dr. Arthur E. Cowley, an expert on the **Hittites,** whom he had known since before the war. This library remains one of the most important Lawrence repositories, with numerous Lawrence manuscript materials and letters. Some of these materials were restricted in access until 2000 but are now part of the regular Lawrence collection, a listing of which may be accessed through OLIS, Oxford University's online library catalog. *See also* **Seven Pillars of Wisdom, Texts of.**

Bols, Gen. Sir Louis (1867–1930)

Gen. Edmund Allenby's chief of staff in France and then during the **Palestine** campaign. Lawrence got on well with him, as described in chapter 69 of *Seven Pillars of Wisdom.* Bols, having served as military governor of **Jerusalem** in 1919–20, protested the appointment of **Herbert Samuel** as high commissioner in Palestine, claiming that this would be unfair to the Arabs, because Samuel was Jewish; this led to a counterprotest by **Richard Meinertzhagen,** who was pro-Jewish.

Bolt, Robert Oxton (1924–95)

Playwright, most famous for *A Man for All Seasons* (1960) and for the screenplay for David Lean's film *Lawrence of Arabia* (1962), for both of which he won awards. His characterization of a Lawrence divided between loyalties and enjoying and yet fearing power is appropriate and true to the text of *Seven Pillars of Wisdom,* making his Lawrence one of the most complex film heroes. Excellent acting by **Peter O'Toole** brings out all of the subtleties in the role, and the other roles are equally well-realized.

Botany

Lawrence liked wild rather than cultivated flowers, mentioning happily that **Clouds Hill** was surrounded by rhododendrons. In *Seven Pillars of Wisdom,* he mentions plants on several occasions. At **Petra** he favorably notes oleanders, ivy, and ferns, and at **Azrak** oasis grass and rustling palm trees. At a Roman ruin in northern **Syria,** he prefers the desert wind, tinged with smell of dried grass, to jessamine, violet, and rose.

Boussard, Léon (born 1908)

Author of *Le Secret du colonel Lawrence* (1946), the first book to reveal Lawrence's illegitimate birth.

Bovington Camp, Dorset

Tank Corps training center to which Lawrence was posted in March 1923 after having successfully lobbied the government to allow him back into military service after his expulsion from the **Royal Air Force,** now under the name **T. E. Shaw.** After basic training, he served as a clerk in the quartermaster's stores for two years here until he returned to the R.A.F. in August 1925. Lawrence was unhappy in the Tanks and even threatened suicide, but his move into his **Clouds Hill** cottage near the camp provided him with some solitude and solace.

Bowra, Sir Maurice Cecil (1898–1971)

Oxford classicist and wit who praised Lawrence's translation of **Homer's** *Odyssey* in a *New Statesman* review of April 8, 1933.

Boyle, Capt. William H. D., 12th Earl of Cork and Orrery (1873–1967)

Captain of the HMS *Suva* and commander of the **Red Sea** Patrol Squadron. Boyle provided artillery and logistical support for the **Arab Revolt,** assembling five warships including the monitor (light river or coastal defense warship) *M.31* and HMS *Dufferin* to discourage a Turkish attack on **Yenbo.** He also helped capture **Wejh** with landing parties before Lawrence and the Arab army arrived, as described in chapters 26 and 27 of *Seven Pillars of Wisdom.* A very professional officer, he disapproved of Lawrence's wearing of Arab dress, as related in chapter 16 of *Seven Pillars of Wisdom.* See Capt. Charles Parnell, "Lawrence of Arabia's Debt to Seapower," *United States Naval Institute Proceeedings* 105 (August 1979): 75–83.

Bradbury, Sgt. W. (born 1901)

Then-corporal Bradbury worked with Lawrence as a mechanic for the R.A.F. 200 boat tests at Plymouth and at the **Scott-Paine** shipyard in the early 1930s and served as a pallbearer at Lawrence's funeral.

Brass Rubbing

One of Lawrence's favorite hobbies during his high school and university years, brass rubbing involves making reproductions of funerary and heraldic brass plates by placing a special white paper over them and rubbing the paper with a waxy pigment. Lawrence taught **C.F.C. Beeson** how to rub brass, and Beeson testifies in his essay in **A. W. Lawrence**'s collection *T. E. Lawrence by His Friends* that at the age of 15 Lawrence had several rubbings of knights prominently displayed on the walls of his bedroom.

Bray, Capt. Norman Napier Evelyn (born 1885)

Indian army officer and commander of Indian machine gunners during Lawrence's failed **Yarmuk Bridges** expedition. Bray was the author of *Shifting Sands* (1934), which criticizes Lawrence's guerrilla strategy, and of a biography of **Colonel Leachman,** *A Paladin of Arabia* (1936).

Brémond, Col. Edouard (born 1868)

Head of the **French Military Mission** in the **Hejaz** from September 1916. Brémond wanted British, French, and colonial troops to land at **Rabegh,** about 100 miles north of **Jidda** on the Arabian **Red Sea** coast, and to participate in the Hejaz campaign in order to ensure a European role in the Middle East at the end of the war. Lawrence wanted only Arabs to conduct the campaign. Lawrence triumphed in this strategic policy dispute because in late 1916 the British did not want to spare troops for the Hejaz, as related in chapter 16 of *Seven Pillars of Wisdom.* Lawrence respected Brémond's military expertise despite this disagreement, but Brémond's memoir *Le Hedjaz dans la Guerre Mondial* (1931) is highly critical of Lawrence.

Bridlington, Yorkshire

Coastal town with a garage of **boats** used in **Royal Air Force** bombing practice. Lawrence worked here, overhauling the boats, from November 1934 until he retired from the R.A.F. and left on February 26, 1935.

British Library

Among this famous library's important Lawrence holdings are his war diaries and his letters to **Charlotte Shaw.** The library also holds a 1922 "Oxford text" of *Seven Pillars of Wisdom* (one of only eight printed), presented by **A. W. Lawrence** and containing corrections by **Edward Garnett** and Winifred Fontana. A list of the library's Lawrence holdings can be accessed online by means of the British Library Public Catalogue. *See also Seven Pillars of Wisdom,* **Texts of.**

British Military Mission to Hejaz

A group of British military advisers dispatched by **Sir Reginald Wingate** in early 1917 under the command of **Col. Stewart Newcombe** to train the Arab forces as regular soldiers. It included **Bray, Garland, Joyce, Vickery,** and others.

British Power Boat Company

Founded in 1927 by **Hubert Scott-Paine** and located in **Hythe,** Southampton, this company designed and built the **200 class seaplane tender** that Lawrence tested at Plymouth and Hythe in 1931 when he was in the **Royal Air Force.** *See also* **Boats.**

Brittany

An area of northwestern **France** through which Lawrence bicycled for about a month in the summer of 1906 studying castle and church design. Lawrence stayed with the **Chaignon family** some of the time and was accompanied by his friend **C.F.C. Beeson** for about two weeks. As a child, he lived in the town of **Dinard** from 1891 to 1896. In all, Lawrence made at least four trips to France from 1906 to 1910, including three bicycle trips in 1906, 1907, and 1908, during which he got as far as the Mediterranean, the Pyrenees, and the Loire. These trips contributed greatly to his study of Crusader castles in the Middle East by giving him examples of contemporaneous castle designs in France.

Brodie, Capt. Samuel H. (born 1886)

Commander of a section of six Talbot armored cars that took part in the actions against Tell Shahm and **Mudowwara** stations, as related in chapters 82 and 94 of *Seven Pillars of Wisdom*. **A. W. Lawrence**'s collection *T. E. Lawrence by His Friends* includes an admiring memoir by Brodie.

Brophy, John (1899–1965)

British author of a novel, *Flesh and Blood* (1931), with a Lawrence figure.

Brough, George (1891–1970)

Nottingham manufacturer of motorcycles from 1910 and from 1921 the maker of the **Brough Superior,** which Lawrence preferred to all other motorcycles. Lawrence corresponded with him and met him in 1925; **A. W. Lawrence**'s collection *T. E. Lawrence by His Friends* includes Brough's memoir of Lawrence.

Brough Superior

Lawrence's favorite motorcycle model, which led to his service colleagues' nick-

name Broughy for him. During his postwar service years he owned seven of these magnificent, largely handmade machines known as "the Rolls-Royce of motorcycles," dying in an accident on the last of these, which he had named *George VII* after its maker **George Brough.** He never rode an eighth, which was on order at the time of his death. Lawrence owned *George VII,* which was manufactured in 1932, for three years and three months. Its model number was S.S. 100, and it had a 1,000 cubic centimeter engine. Lawrence had clocked over 25,000 miles on it before he crashed. He insisted on having his stainless steel gas tank from *George VI* installed on *George VII;* otherwise it was standard. Brough offered Lawrence new models on very favorable terms, so he could use Lawrence's patronage in advertising. A full description of *George VII*'s mechanical specifications can be seen in Paul Marriott and Yvonne Argent, *The Last Days of T. E. Lawrence: A Leaf in the Wind,* pp. 100–101. In chapter 16 of **The Mint,** Lawrence describes his race with an airplane on one of these machines, which he named *Boanerges,* meaning "loud preacher." See Mike Leatherdale, "Lawrence and his Brough Superiors," *Journal of the T. E. Lawrence Society* (Winter 1991–92): 63–96.

Brown, Curtis

See **Savage, Raymond**

Brown, Malcolm

Lawrence researcher, filmmaker, and writer. Brown produced the earliest BBC documentary film on Lawrence, *T. E. Lawrence: 1888–1935,* which was first shown on November 27, 1962. This important film includes interviews with many witnesses of various phases of Lawrence's life. Brown also coproduced, with Julia

Cave, the fine 1986 BBC documentary film *Lawrence and Arabia,* which includes **A. W. Lawrence**'s testimony about Lawrence's flagellation problem as well as testimony by Arabs, including that of **Auda abu Tayi**'s son and scholar **Suleiman Mousa.** Brown went on to edit Lawrence's *Selected Letters* (1988), to coauthor, with Julia Cave, a biography entitled *A Touch of Genius* (1988), and to write another biography, *T. E. Lawrence* (2003). He is also the author of numerous works on **World War I.**

Bruce, John

Tank Corps service companion and Lawrence's paid retainer, who testified that between 1923 and 1935 he had administered seven to nine beatings to Lawrence at Lawrence's own instigation. These claims were published by **Phillip Knightley** and **Colin Simpson** in the London *Sunday Times* on June 23, 1968, and in their *The Secret Lives of Lawrence of Arabia* (1969). While some points in Bruce's testimony have been questioned, documentary corroboration exists in the form of letters (presented in chapter 33 of **John Mack**'s biography *A Prince of Our Disorder,* 1976). Lawrence scholars now accept Bruce's main claim, and they attempt to understand Lawrence's **sexuality.**

Buchan, John, 1st Baron Tweedsmuir (1875–1940)

Imperialist statesman, director of information at British General Headquarters during **World War I,** member of Parliament for the Scottish Universities (1927–35), governor-general of Canada, and author of the thriller *The Thirty-Nine Steps* (1915) and *The Courts of the Morning* (1929), which contains a character, Sandy Arbuthnot, originally based on **Aubrey Herbert,** but who also resembles Lawrence. As he makes clear in his memoir, *Memory-Hold-the-Door* (1940), Buchan regarded Lawrence as a hero, and Lawrence appreciated Buchan's friendship and support, particularly when Lawrence struggled to be allowed to reenlist in the **Royal Air Force.** As director of the Department of Information, Buchan accepted the journalist **Lowell Thomas**'s request, in 1918, to cover the British campaign in **Palestine,** which eventually resulted in worldwide publicity for Lawrence, because they met during Thomas's trip. See Andrew Lownie, "The Friendship of Lawrence and Buchan," *Journal of the T. E. Lawrence Society* (Autumn 1995): 56–67.

Burton, Percy (born 1878)

British impresario responsible for bringing **Lowell Thomas** and his show, first entitled *With Allenby in Palestine,* and then *With Allenby in Palestine, and with Lawrence in Arabia* to **London** in August 1919. See Percy Burton as told to Lowell Thomas, *Adventures among Immortals* (1937).

Burton, Sir Richard Francis (1821–90)

British master linguist, explorer, and travel writer. Lawrence does not mention Burton's *Personal Narrative of a Pilgrimage to Al-Madinah and Meccah* (1855) in *Seven Pillars of Wisdom* or in his letters, but in his letters he criticizes the portrayal of the Arabs in Burton's translation of *The Thousand Nights and a Night* (1885–88); (Garnett, *Letters,* p. 359; **M. R. Lawrence,** *Home Letters,* p. 207). As he told **Robert Graves,** Lawrence apparently felt that Burton was not a worthy literary artist and not particularly admirable as an explorer. For further information, see Fawn Brodie, *The Devil Drives: A Life of Sir Richard F. Burton.*

Buxton, Maj. Robert V. "Robin" (1883–1953)

Commander of an **Imperial Camel Corps** unit of 300 men that worked with Lawrence. In chapter 103 of *Seven Pillars of Wisdom*, Lawrence praises Buxton as an apt leader. After the war, he became Lawrence's bank manager, advising him about the publication of the 1926 edition of *Seven Pillars of Wisdom* (in which Buxton's portrait appears), and about how to manage the earnings from *Revolt in the Desert*.

C

Cabell, James Branch (1879–1958)

American author of *Jurgen: A Comedy of Justice* (1919), a fantasy of disillusionment that Lawrence liked. In his *The Medievalism of Lawrence of Arabia* (pp. 155–63), Malcolm Allen discusses the influence of this work on *Seven Pillars of Wisdom.*

Caemmerer, Gen. Rudolph Von (1845–1911)

German author of *The Development of Strategical Science during the 19th Century* (1905) and other works of military history and thought. Lawrence writes in chapter 33 of *Seven Pillars of Wisdom* that he read Caemmerer while at Oxford, but he was unable to name one of Caemmerer's books when **Liddell Hart** asked him which one he had read. **Richard Aldington** claimed that Lawrence learned of Caemmerer and the other strategists that he mentions prominently in chapter 33 of *Seven Pillars of Wisdom* only from his **Oxford University** tutor, **Reginald Lane Poole,** who participated in a war games club at the time, and that Lawrence never read them.

Cairo

Lawrence worked in the **Cairo Military Intelligence Department** from December 1914, and then at the **Arab Bureau** from November 1916 in the Savoy Hotel here until he joined the **Arab Revolt** in December 1916 as an adviser. In Cairo, he worked from 9 A.M. to 10 P.M. most days, without much chance to see the historic Cairo. In his letters he indicated that he much preferred the prewar dig at **Carchemish** in which he participated to Cairo.

Cairo Conference

A meeting of British diplomats held at Government House, **Cairo,** in March 1921, which Lawrence attended when he served in the **Middle East Department** of the **Colonial Office** under **Winston Churchill.** In addition to Lawrence and Churchill, other attendees included **Gertrude Bell, Sir Percy Cox, Jaafar Pasha, Gen. Geoffrey Salmond, Sir Herbert Samuel, Sir Hugh Trenchard,** and **Maj. Hubert Young.** At this conference, it was decided to give **Feisal,** who had been expelled from **Syria** by the French in 1920, the throne of **Iraq** and to confirm his brother **Abdullah** as ruler of **Transjordan,** leading Lawrence to conclude in a footnote to *Seven Pillars of Wisdom* that England had lived up to its promises to the **Hussein** family. It was also decided, on the urging of Trenchard, who represented the air force, and Lawrence, that as far as possible, air power rather than British troops would be used to enforce Feisal's rule in Iraq. For further information, see

Aaron Klieman, *Foundations of British Policy in the Arab World: The Cairo Conference of 1921.*

Cairo Military Intelligence Department

This unit, new in 1914, replaced the prewar Military Intelligence Office and was headed by then-captain **Stewart Newcombe,** who had conducted the **Wilderness of Zin** survey in early 1914. In addition to Lawrence, it included **Leonard Woolley** as well as **George Lloyd** and **Aubrey Herbert,** both former members of parliament and experts on Turkey. Newcombe reported to then-Lt.-Col. **Gilbert Clayton,** who had served in the prewar organization and who was now head of military and political intelligence in **Egypt.** It collected information, made maps, and considered strategic questions. In addition to the British army in Egypt, it also served the Mediterranean Expeditionary Force, which was sent to **Gallipoli** and **Greece.** Lawrence's primary role was that of map officer, but he performed many other tasks and considered policy questions, such as a possible Allied landing at **Alexandretta,** as well. In November 1916 he succeeded in transferring to the **Arab Bureau,** which had been established in February of that year to foster the sharif of **Mecca'**s revolt against the Turks, as he tells us in chapter 6 of *Seven Pillars of Wisdom.* See **John Mack,** *A Prince of Our Disorder;* Yigal Sheffy, *British Military Intelligence in the Palestine Campaign, 1914–1918;* and Bruce Westrate, *The Arab Bureau: British Policy in the Middle East, 1916–1920.*

Calshot R.A.F. Base

A marine craft training base located on Southampton Water. Lawrence attended meetings here with **R.A.F. Cattewater/ Mount Batten** commanding officer **Sydney Smith** when working on the **Schneider Trophy** seaplane race.

Camels

Lawrence preferred camels, which he praises in chapter 59 of *Seven Pillars of Wisdom,* to **horses,** but he liked **motorcycles** the best of all for riding (on land). In *Seven Pillars of Wisdom,* he details his transition from an awkward, inexperienced camel rider to an experienced professional who was able, by his own account, to travel 1,400 miles in four weeks this way and who would perfect the hit-and-run camel raid. Whether he was able to cover 55 miles in 12 hours as he claims to have done between **Bair** and **Jefer** during the night of November 24–25, 1917, has been questioned by Charles Blackmore, author of *In the Footsteps of Lawrence of Arabia* (1986), who retraced Lawrence's camel journeys. However, Lawrence was clearly a good rider, who was sometimes allowed to ride **Feisal'**s own camel.

Campbell-Thompson, Reginald (1876–1941)

Archaeological expert on Assyria and Persia with whom Lawrence worked at **Carchemish** in early 1911, until Campbell-Thompson was replaced by **Leonard Woolley.**

Cape, Jonathan H. (1879–1960)

Lawrence's publisher. Cape began his own imprint in 1921 after Lawrence approached the Medici Society, where Cape was working, to publish an edition of

Charles M. Doughty's *Arabia Deserta.* Through the good offices of **Edward Garnett,** Cape eventually became the publisher of *Revolt in the Desert* (1927), Lawrence's abridgment of *Seven Pillars of Wisdom,* and after Lawrence's death in 1935, of *Seven Pillars of Wisdom* itself. The Cape imprint still exists, but in 1988 the firm became part of Random House UK, which in 1998 itself became a part of the Bertelsmann publishing group. In 1988, the firm published *Images of Lawrence* by S. E. Tabachnick and **C. Matheson** in honor of Lawrence's birth centenary.

Carchemish

The Hittite viceregal city, located near the village of **Jerablus, Syria,** and dating from the thirteenth to the ninth century B.C.E. From 1911 to 1914, Lawrence helped excavate this city under the direction of **D. G. Hogarth** and **C. Leonard Woolley.** Lawrence's job was to supervise workers, solve mechanical problems, and photograph and copy finds, but he also contributed to research, noticing some interesting graves in a nearby ancient graveyard at **Deve Hüyük,** among other contributions. The team's findings, including those of Lawrence, were published in three volumes entitled *Carchemish: Report on the Excavations at Djerabis,* which were published by the British Museum in 1914, 1921, and 1952. The work done at Carchemish set the direction of future British study of the **Hittites,** and Woolley went on to become famous as the excavator of Ur of the Chaldees. For Lawrence, this was a period of archaeological apprenticeship. He and Woolley also obtained the plans for the **Berlin–Baghdad Railway,** which the Germans were building in the Amanus Mountains close to the Carchemish mound. See S. E. Tabachnick, "Lawrence of Arabia as Archaeologist,"

Biblical Archaeology Review 23:5 (Sept./ Oct. 1997): 40–47, 70–71.

Carchemish: Report on the Excavations at Djerabis on Behalf of the British Museum

The results of the **Hittite** excavation, run by **D. G. Hogarth,** in which Lawrence participated from 1911 to 1914, are described in this three-volume work, which appeared in 1914, 1921, and 1952. Lawrence contributed actual text only to the 1914 volume, but his notes and photographs appear in all of the volumes, and his name appears on the title page of all of the volumes.

Carline, Sydney (1888–1929)

British artist and former **Royal Air Force** pilot, who (with his brother Richard) was sent to the Middle East in 1919 to memorialize the British role in **World War I.** His painting *The Destruction of the Turkish Transport in the Gorge of Wadi Fara, Palestine* (1920) was chosen by Lawrence as one of the illustrations in the 1926 subscriber's edition of *Seven Pillars of Wisdom.* For this picture see **J. M. Wilson,** *T. E. Lawrence* (p. 117). V. M. Thompson, *"Not a Suitable Hobby for an Airman"— T. E. Lawrence as Publisher,* describes the layout of the subscriber's edition. *See* ***Seven Pillars of Wisdom,* Texts of**

Carlow, Viscount (George Lionel Seymour Dawson-Damer) (1907–44)

Friend of Lawrence and founder of the **Corvinus Press,** which posthumously published several of Lawrence's works in fine editions, including *Letters from T. E. Shaw to Viscount Carlow* (1936) and *The Diary of T. E. Lawrence MCMXI* (1937).

Carrington, Charles Edmond (born 1897)

British professor, who under the pseudonym Charles Edmonds wrote an adulatory biography, *T. E. Lawrence* (1935).

Casement, Sir Roger David (1864–1916)

In 1934, Lawrence considered writing a biography of this British diplomat, Irish nationalist, and homosexual who was hanged by the British government in 1916 as a traitor. In that year, Casement was caught landing in **Ireland** from a German submarine to take charge of the Sinn Fein rebellion. Lawrence felt that Casement was a heroic personality (Brown, *Selected Letters,* p. 508).

Catalogue of an Exhibition of Paintings, Pastels, Drawings, and Woodcuts Illustrating Col. T. E. Lawrence's Book "Seven Pillars of Wisdom"

Pamphlet written by Lawrence to accompany the Leicester Galleries' 1921 exhibition of **Eric Kennington**'s Arab portraits, which were used in the 1926 subscriber's edition of *Seven Pillars of Wisdom.* In 1927 the pamphlet was reprinted, minus one paragraph from the 1921 version, with a preface by **G. B. Shaw,** for a more varied Leicester Galleries exhibition of the *Seven Pillars of Wisdom* artwork.

Cattewater R.A.F. Station, later R.A.F. Mount Batten

At this flying-boat base in Plymouth, Lawrence served from 1929 to 1931 under the friendly supervision of **Wing Commander Sydney Smith.** Smith's wife Clare wrote a memoir, *The Golden Reign* (1940), about Lawrence during this relatively happy period of his life.

Caudwell, Christopher (1907–37)

Pseudonym of Christopher St. John Sprigg, a Marxist writer and critic. Caudwell's *Studies in a Dying Culture* includes a chapter claiming Lawrence as a Marxist manqué. Although Lawrence thought Lenin a great man, he had little affinity for Marxism.

Cecil, Lord Edgar Algernon Robert (1864–1958)

Son of three-time British prime minister the Marquess of Salisbury and British parliamentarian, League of Nations advocate, minister of blockade (1916–1918), assistant secretary of state for foreign affairs and **Paris Peace Conference** delegate, who in 1918 sought Lawrence's advice about British policy toward **Syria.**

Chaignon Family

Family in **Dinard, France,** on the Normandy coast, who became friendly with Lawrence's family when they lived there from 1891 to 1894. Lawrence visited the Chaignons during his bicycle excursions to French castles in 1906, 1907, and 1908.

Chambers, A. E. "Jock" (1896–1987)

Lawrence's service companion at **R.A.F. Farnborough** from 1922 and later a friend and visitor to Lawrence's cottage at **Clouds Hill.** His memoir of Lawrence is included in **A. W. Lawrence**'s collection, *T. E. Lawrence by His Friends.*

"Changing East, The"

An article published anonymously by Lawrence in *The Round Table* 10:40 (September 1920) and reprinted in **A. W. Lawrence**'s collection of Lawrence's pieces, *Oriental Assembly.* In it, Lawrence analyzes the reasons for the fall of the Ottoman Empire and attempts to predict possible future directions for the Turks, the Arabs, and the Jews, among other Middle Eastern nations and groups. He feels that nationalism, having been introduced by the West, will remain a potent force, but that the Arabs' lack of unity will cloud their future. He sees a future for newly independent Middle Eastern nations as dominions in the British Empire.

Chapman, Lady Edith (1837–1930)

Born Edith Sarah Hamilton to a landowning family in **County Westmeath, Ireland,** she was a cousin of **Thomas Robert Tighe Chapman,** Lawrence's father. In 1873 she married Chapman, with whom she had four daughters (Eva Jane Louisa, born 1874; Rose Isabel, born 1878; Florence Lina, born 1880; and Mabel Cecele, born 1881). Lady Chapman, who held rigid Evangelical views, had a strict personality out of tune with that of the easygoing Chapman. Around the beginning of 1886, he left her to elope with Sarah Junner, the family governess, with whom he had a child, Lawrence's brother Montagu Robert, in December 1885. Lady Chapman remained in control of **South Hill,** Thomas Robert's house near Killua, until her death. The couple's daughters never married.

Chapman, Sarah

See **Lawrence, Sarah Junner**

Studio photo of Lawrence in Arab robes by Harry Chase, London, 1919. Courtesy of Corbis.

Chapman, Sir Thomas Robert Tighe

See **Lawrence, Sir Thomas Robert Tighe Chapman**

Chartres Cathedral

During a bicycle trip to France in the summer of 1908, Lawrence visited Chartres Cathedral and wrote an ecstatic letter to his mother about it (*The Home Letters,* pp. 80–81). Lawrence considered the cathedral the finest work of the Middle Ages and one of the greatest buildings of all time.

Chase, Harry Alonzo (1883–1935)

Lowell Thomas's cameraman, responsible for many of the most famous photos of Lawrence in Arab dress, most of which

Australian Gen. Harry Chauvel leading his troops during the official entry into Damascus on October 2, 1918. Courtesy of the Australian War Memorial.

were posed in **Akaba** in 1918 and in **London** in 1919. Chase also managed the visuals and effects for Thomas's show about Lawrence, handling three cameras as he did so.

Chastel Pelèrin

See **Athlit**

Chateau Gaillard

French castle at Petit Adelys visited by Lawrence in 1907 and considered by him to be **Richard I**'s masterpiece. In his B.A. thesis, **"The Influence of the Crusades on European Military Architecture—To the End of the XIIth Century,"** Lawrence disputes the idea that this castle was influenced by Eastern designs.

Chauvel, Gen. Sir Henry G. (1865–1945)

Chauvel, an Australian, is considered one of the best modern cavalry leaders for his successes at Romani and **Beersheba,** among other sites during the **Palestine** campaign. Commander of the 1st Light Horse Brigade at **Gallipoli,** of the **ANZAC** Mounted Division from March 1916, of the Desert Column, and from April 1917 on of the Desert Mounted Corps. He came into conflict with Lawrence after the occupation of Damascus when Lawrence wanted **Feisal** to be established as ruler and Chauvel, who had led the British thrust toward Damacus, moved to assert British control with an impressive parade through the city. His report on the campaign for the Australian War Memorial, now in the **Allenby** Papers, St. Anthony's College, **Oxford,** sometimes contradicts Lawrence's account in chapters 119 through 122 of *Seven Pillars of Wisdom.* See **John Mack,** *A Prince of Our Disorder;* **A. P. Wavell,** *The Palestine Campaigns;* H. S. Gullett, *The Australian Imperial Force in Sinai and Palestine, 1914–1918.*

Chaytor, Maj. Gen. Sir Edward W. C. (1868–1939)

New Zealander who followed **Chauvel** as the commander of the **ANZAC** Mounted Division, in which capacity he took part in many decisive actions, including the defeat of the Turkish Fourth Army based at **Amman** in September 1918, opening the way toward the capture of Damascus. Lawrence mentions him in a neutral way in *Seven Pillars of Wisdom.* Chaytor was the commandant of the New Zealand Defence Force from 1919–1924. See **A. P. Wavell,** *The Palestine Campaigns.*

Chetwode, Lt. Gen. Sir Philip W. (1865–1950)

British commander of the Desert Column from December 1916. Chetwode had a reputation from the Burma War of 1892, the Boer War, and the western front, (where he served under **Allenby**) as an excellent cavalry commander. In **Palestine,** he also commanded the XX Corps, which played a major role in the capture of **Jerusalem.** Lawrence mentions him in a neutral manner in *Seven Pillars of Wisdom.* In 1923, Chetwode, now adjutant-general, allowed Lawrence to serve in the Royal Tank Corps after he had been expelled from the **Royal Air Force.** From 1930 to 1935, Chetwode was commander-in-chief of the British forces in **India.** See **A. P. Wavell,** *The Palestine Campaigns.*

China

Montagu Robert, Lawrence's older brother, became a medical missionary in the China Inland Mission in 1921; he was joined by Lawrence's mother in 1923. Lawrence opposed this work, writing to her in 1927 that China must find its own path, without outside influence.

Christianity

Lawrence's family belonged to St. Aldate's Church in **Oxford,** an Evangelical congregation of the Church of England led by **Canon A.M.W. Christopher,** who believed the Bible to be literally true. In Lawrence's home, there were Bible readings before school and on Sundays; Lawrence taught Sunday school on occasion, and his mother and older brother, **Montagu Robert Lawrence,** eventually became missionaries. This strict religious adherence on the part of Lawrence's parents, and especially his mother, was no doubt a form of compensation for the fact that they were never able to marry. Lawrence's interest in the Middle East was sparked by his childhood Bible studies, but perhaps in reaction to his mother's religious obsessiveness, he was not religious after his teens, when he won a prize for religious knowledge. He did not join a church, express religious emotion, or mention Christianity more than tangentially in his works. In chapter 63 of *Seven Pillars of Wisdom,* however, he praises Christianity's emphasis upon humanity and love while attacking the logic and disputation that he thought typical of northern European forms of that religion. Moreover, he felt that the capture of **Jerusalem** was the most impressive point of the war for him, as he says in chapter 80 of *Seven Pillars of Wisdom.* See S. E. Tabachnick, "Lawrence of Arabia as Archaeologist," *Biblical Archaeology*

Review 23:5 (Sept./Oct. 1997): 40–47, 70–71.

Christopher, Canon Alfred M. W. (1820–1913)

Until his retirement in 1905, Christopher was rector of St. Aldate's, the church that Lawrence and his family attended in Oxford, and a leader in the Evangelical movement within the Church of England. *See also* **Christianity.**

Churchill, Sir Winston Leonard Spencer (1874–1965)

Extraordinary British politician, leader, and writer. A soldier against the Mahdi at Omdurman, **Sudan,** in 1898 as a member of the Nile Expeditionary Force, newspaper correspondent during the Boer War, and first lord of the admiralty during the **Gallipoli** failure, Churchill went on to become one of Britain's greatest war leaders as prime minister from 1940 to 1945. He also won the Nobel Prize for Literature in 1953 for his monumental history of World War II. From January to December 1921, Lawrence served under Churchill, who was then colonial secretary, at Churchill's request, working in the **Middle East Department** of the **Colonial Office** and participating in the **Cairo Conference** at which **Feisal** was given the throne of **Iraq** and **Abdullah** was confirmed as ruler of **Transjordan.** Churchill greatly admired Lawrence as a human being and as a writer, and Lawrence reciprocated this admiration. The only dispute between them concerned whether Lenin, as Lawrence held, or Napoleon, who Churchill favored, was the greater man (*T. E. Lawrence to His Biographers Robert Graves & Liddell Hart*, 2: 144). See *Finest Hour,* the journal of the Churchill Centre, 119 (summer 2003). This entire issue is devoted to Lawrence and Churchill.

Circassians

A people of the Caucasus and Middle East. The Circassians in the Caucasus region went from Ottoman to Russian rule in 1829 and rebelled against it until they were defeated in 1864. At that time, many Muslim Circassians immigrated to the Ottoman Empire, which accepted and settled them in Turkey proper as well as in the Arab parts of its empire, although Lawrence mentions feelings of hostility between the Circassians and the Arabs. Even today, the Middle Eastern Circassians retain a distinct culture, although their language has given way to Arabic. In Lawrence's day, Circassian was still spoken among them. In a letter of 1914, Lawrence discusses a violent confrontation between Circassians and Kurds (Garnett, *Letters,* pp. 172–74). In chapter 80 of *Seven Pillars of Wisdom,* Lawrence says that he claimed to be a Circassian when captured at **Deraa,** and that the bey there might have been a Circassian too. This raises a question about Lawrence's account, because if the bey were a Circassian, would he not have spoken a few words of the Circassian language or asked about Circassian customs, to test Lawrence? Yet *Seven Pillars of Wisdom* gives no indication that he did so. For more information, see Shimoni and Levine, *Political Dictionary of the Middle East. See also* **Deraa Incident.**

City of Oxford High School for Boys

The school that Lawrence attended from 1896 to 1907. Lawrence did not like playing contact sports there, but he did well at gymnastics and bicycle racing and contributed articles about **"Playground Cricket," "Playground Football,"** and a fortified eleventh-century turret (**"The Bastion"**), as well as his first piece of published writing (March 1904), an essay entitled **"An**

Antiquarian and a Geologist in Hants [Hampshire]," to the school magazine. According to biographer **J. M. Wilson,** the school had been founded 15 years earlier by the city corporation and **Oxford University** and was attended by 150 largely middle-class, fee-paying students. It was strong in classics and other humanities but weak in science. Lawrence's scores on his senior local examinations in 1907 reflect these strengths to some degree: out of 4,645 candidates, he tied for first in English language and literature, and for third in religious knowledge. He also did well in arithmetic, political economy, and French but badly in Latin, Greek, and mathematics. While at the school, he won several prizes, including one for an essay on **Tennyson.** Generally, he seems to have regarded school as a distraction from his hobbies, such as **brass rubbing** and local **archaeology.** According to biographer **John Mack,** in the 1930s the Lawrence family donated a scholarship to the high school that allowed its needy students to attend Oxford University. See J. M. Wilson, *Lawrence of Arabia;* John Mack, *A Prince of Our Disorder;* and Paul Marriott, *The Young Lawrence of Arabia, 1888–1910;* as well as **A. W. Lawrence**'s collection *T. E. Lawrence by His Friends* for more information.

Clark, John Cosmo (1897–1967)

Son of artist James Clark and friend of artist **Eric Kennington,** who introduced him to Lawrence. John Cosmo Clark produced *Stokes' Gun Class,* which appeared in the 1926 edition of *Seven Pillars of Wisdom,* and a 1922 charcoal of Lawrence, which did not. See **J. M. Wilson,** *T. E. Lawrence,* and V. M. Thompson, *"Not a Suitable Hobby for an Airman"—T. E. Lawrence as Publisher* for more information.

Clausewitz, Karl von (1780–1831)

Prussian general and author of *On War,* which possibly influenced Lawrence's strategic thinking, as he claims in chapter 33 of *Seven Pillars of Wisdom.* Lawrence, however, criticized Clausewitz for lacking human feeling (*T. E. Lawrence to His Biographers Robert Graves & Liddell Hart,* p. 76).

Clayton, Brig. Gen. Sir Gilbert Falkingham (1875–1929)

A colonel until 1916, when he became a brigadier general, Clayton headed the civilian and military branches of British Intelligence in **Cairo** during **World War I** and served as the Cairo representative of **Sir Reginald Wingate,** governor-general of the **Sudan.** Lawrence greatly respected Clayton, who at least once refused to consider his desire to resign from the **Arab Revolt,** as recorded in chapter 91 of *Seven Pillars of Wisdom.* Clayton later published *An Arabian Diary.* Lawrence admired Clayton's administrative courage, detachment, and support of subordinates, as he tells us in chapter 6 of *Seven Pillars of Wisdom.* After Clayton died, Lawrence interested himself in guaranteeing his widow an income (Brown, *Selected Letters,* p. 431).

Clemenceau, Georges (1841–1929)

Prime minister of **France** from 1917 to 1920, he was known for his aggressive pursuit of French war and peace goals, thus maintaining his country's morale right through the end of the war. On September 13, 1919, at the **Peace Conference** in **Paris** (where he survived an assassination attempt), Clemenceau won **Lloyd George**'s

The Greek inscription above the door of Clouds Hill, Lawrence's cottage in Dorset, translates as "Does not care." Courtesy of Dr. Philip O'Brien.

agreement to the British army's evacuation of **Syria,** thus paving the way for France to assume control of the country, in exchange for French recognition of Britain's interests in **Palestine** and in the oil production of the **Mosul** area of **Mesopotamia.** The Lloyd George–Clemenceau Agreement was signed on November 30, 1918. **Feisal** attempted to achieve some understanding with Clemenceau at the end of 1919, which Lawrence saw as hopeful, but in January 1920 Clemenceau lost the election to the more colonialist Millerand regime, and Feisal was driven from Syria by a French army in July 1920, much to the despair of Lawrence, who had always tried to prevent French control of Syria. Lawrence told **Liddell Hart** that, compared to **Lloyd George,** Clemenceau was mediocre, but that he liked him (*T. E. Lawrence to His Biographers Robert Graves & Liddell Hart,* 2: 66, 190). See **George Antonius,** *The Arab Awakening,* and Pope and Wheal, *The Dictionary of the First World War,* for more information.

Clouds Hill

Lawrence's very small two-story cottage at **Moreton,** Dorset, one mile north of Bovington camp, where he was serving when he first rented it in 1923. At that time, it afforded him the quiet and solitude necessary for revising *Seven Pillars of Wisdom,* and he also entertained friends there. In 1929, after his return from **India,** he completed the purchase of the cottage, and in 1933 he renovated it extensively in preparation for his planned retirement there. The inscription above the door, in Greek, translates as "Does Not Care" or "Why worry?" Lawrence is buried in the cemetery at Moreton church. Clouds Hill, which Lawrence loved, is now owned by the National Trust. **A. W. Lawrence**'s collection *T. E. Lawrence by His Friends* contains a catalog of the books and records that were in the Clouds Hill library at the time of his death. See **E. M. Forster,** "Clouds Hill," *Listener* 20:503 (Sept. 1, 1938): 426–27, and the description given in **J. M. Wilson,** *Lawrence of Arabia.*

Clough, Arthur Hugh (1819–61)

Poet and educator. Lawrence read Clough's "Say Not the Struggle Naught Availeth" in his 1915 *Oxford Book of English Verse* at **Umtaiye** on September 18, 1918, and felt that it expressed his confidence in **General Allenby.** Although he felt that the poem was unoriginal, he included it in his own anthology *Minorities,* which has been edited by **J. M. Wilson.**

Cockerell, Sir Sydney (1867–1962)

Director of the Fitzwilliam Museum, Cambridge (1908–37), and literary executor of **William Morris** and **Thomas Hardy.** Lawrence and Cockerell met in 1922 when they were trying to provide financial relief for **Charles M. Doughty,** and Cockerell introduced Lawrence to **G. B.** and **Charlotte Shaw** in March of that year. Because Cockerell had served as secretary to Morris and his Kelmscott Press (1892–98), Lawrence sought his advice about the typography of the 1926 edition of *Seven Pillars of Wisdom.* See **Wilfrid Blunt,** *Cockerell.*

Collins, Michael (1890–1922)

Irish guerrilla fighter and politician. Lawrence met Collins on December 3, 1920, in Whitehall when Collins wanted to sign an agreement with **Lloyd George** guaranteeing only partial independence to **Ireland** but was afraid to do so for fear that the Irish hard-liners under de Valera would denounce him as a traitor. He did sign the treaty and was assassinated on August 22, 1922. Lawrence was rumored to have been offered a position in the Irish Free State army by Collins a month before his assassination. See **Knightley** and **Simpson,** *The Secret Lives of Lawrence of Arabia* (p. 194).

Colonial Office

From February 1921 to July 1922, Lawrence worked in the Colonial Office under John Shuckburgh, having been solicited for the position of political adviser by **Winston Churchill,** the new secretary of state for the colonies. He also worked with **Hubert Young** and **Richard Meinertzhagen,** with whom he had served during the war. During this period, he took part in the **Cairo Conference** of March 1921, at which it was decided to award the throne of **Iraq** to **Feisal** and to confirm **Abdullah** in the rulership of **Transjordan.** These decisions enabled Lawrence to declare in a footnote in chapter 48 of *Seven Pillars of Wisdom* that England had fulfilled its **World War I** promises to the Arabs. Lawrence advised the separation of Transjordan from **Palestine** and the permanent retention of Abdullah as its ruler, and he helped Abdullah with details of his regime. He was less successful, however, in trying to persuade **Sharif Hussein** to work with Britain and to recognize its position in the Middle East. *See also* **Middle East Department.** See Aaron Klieman, "Lawrence as Bureaucrat," in Tabachnick, ed., *The T. E. Lawrence Puzzle,* and Klieman, *Foundations of British Policy in the Middle East: The Cairo Conference of 1921.*

Committee of Union and Progress

A committee, and then a political party, crystallized in 1907 from the various **Young Turks** groups for the purpose of leading a revolution against **Sultan Abdul-**

Hamid II. It succeeded in this aim in July 1908 and completely deposed him in 1909. Unfortunately, the CUP, which was led from 1913 to 1918 by **Enver Pasha, Jemal Pasha, and Talat Pasha,** proved no less dictatorial than the sultan had been in attempting to impose centralized Turkish rule on the subject peoples of the empire, thereby creating in the Arabs the desire to revolt. Moreover, the CUP decided to enter **World War I** on the side of the Germans, thus hastening the end of the Turkish Empire rather than preserving it. See **George Antonius,** *The Arab Awakening;* E. Tauber, *The Arab Movements in World War I;* **J. M. Wilson,** *Lawrence of Arabia;* **John Mack,** *A Prince of Our Disorder;* Feroz Ahmad, *The Young Turks;* and Erik Zurcher, *The Unionist Factor.*

"Confession of Faith"

A work that Lawrence planned in December 1933 but never wrote. Like *The Mint,* it was to deal with his postwar military service, bringing that story beyond about 1926 where *The Mint* ends, but the emphasis would be on the idea of speed on air, land, and sea. All that remains of this work is a poem, reprinted in Garnett's *Letters* (p. 639).

Conrad, Joseph (1857–1924)

Great English writer born in Poland under the name Josef Korzeniowski. Lawrence met Conrad only once, but his letters contain admiring references to Conrad. *Seven Pillars of Wisdom* contains several allusions to Conrad's works, and some literary critics have compared Lawrence's personal struggles in Arabia to those of Conrad's Kurtz in *Heart of Darkness* (1902) and Lord Jim in *Lord Jim* (1900). In 1927, Lawrence wrote that he particularly liked Conrad's *Mirror of the Sea* (1906), *Arrow of Gold* (1919), *Nostromo* (1904), and

some parts of *Rescue* (1920). See S. E. Tabachnick, *T. E. Lawrence;* H. Orlans, *Lawrence of Arabia, Strange Man of Letters;* and J. N. Lockman, *Parallel Captures?: Lord Jim and Lawrence of Arabia* for more information.

Corbel, Mr.

A teacher and a friend of Lawrence's family from the time of their stay in **Dinard, France** (1891–94). Lawrence met him again at the house of the **Chaignon**s during his second summer trip to France in 1907.

Cornwallis, Lt. Col. Sir Kinahan (1883–1959)

Formerly associated with the **Sudan** Civil Service and the Egyptian Ministry of Finance, Cornwallis worked in intelligence from 1914 and was a founding member of the **Arab Bureau,** becoming its director from 1916 to 1918, during which time he also edited most numbers of the *Arab Bulletin.* He was an expert on the Asir region of Arabia (on the **Red Sea** coast, between **Yemen** and the **Hejaz**). After the war, he was an adviser to **Feisal** in **Iraq.** Lawrence praises him highly in chapter 6 of *Seven Pillars of Wisdom.* See Bruce Westrate, *The Arab Bureau: British Policy in the Middle East 1916–1920.*

Corvinus Press

A press founded by **Viscount Carlow,** who met Lawrence through Lawrence's commanding officer at **R.A.F. Cattewater/ Mount Batten,** Wing Commander **Sydney Smith.** Perhaps inspired by Lawrence, Carlow began collecting and then publishing fine editions. The first item published by the press was a pamphlet commemorating Lawrence, *Lawrence of Arabia* (1936), containing speeches by **B. H. Liddell Hart** and **Sir Ronald Storrs.** Other works published by the Corvinus Press, which was named for a typeface designed in honor of King Corvinus of Hungary (1443–90), included Lawrence's *The Diary of T. E. Lawrence MCMXI* (1937) and **"An Essay on Flecker"** (1937). The press stopped operating soon after Carlow's death in 1944.

Coster, Howard (1885–1959)

Celebrity photographer who opened a studio in Essex Street, **London,** in 1926, and who in 1931 invited Lawrence to sit for a set of photographs that Lawrence himself regarded as very good likenesses. See S. E. Tabachnick and **Christopher Matheson,** *Images of Lawrence,* and **J. M. Wilson,** *T. E. Lawrence* for examples of Coster's work.

County Westmeath

The Irish county in which the family of Lawrence's father, Thomas Chapman, had lived from the second half of the eighteenth century. Thomas's 173-acre estate, **South Hill,** was located there, two miles from the village of Delvin.

Cousse, Commandant H.

Cousse succeeded **Brémond** in December 1917 as the head of the **French Military Mission** to the **Hejaz.** Lawrence mentions him favorably in chapter 28 of *Seven Pillars of Wisdom* for having supplied the Arab forces with four Schneider 65-millimeter cannons. *See also* **Artillery.**

Coward, Noël (1889–1973)

Important actor, director, and playwright. He liked Lawrence's *The Mint,* and Lawrence appreciated his *Private Lives* (1930)

and *Post-Mortem* (1931), as we see in Garnett, *Letters,* pp. 696, 702, 723.

Cox, Sir Percy Zachariah (1864–1937)

Cox served in several important administrative posts in the Persian Gulf and **India** before becoming chief political officer to the British Expeditionary Forces in **Mesopotamia** (1914–18) and high commissioner to **Iraq** (1920–24). Cox opposed Lawrence's attempt to rescue **General Townshend**'s army at **Kut-al-Amara** by bribing **Khalil Pasha,** but he was open to the ideas of Lawrence and the **Arab Bureau.** After the war, Lawrence criticized Cox in his August 22, 1920, *Sunday Times* article "Mesopotamia" for being insufficiently in favor of Arab independence, but in his role as high commissioner Cox has been praised by others for laying the foundations of the modern state of Iraq. See **Philip Graves,** *The Life of Sir Percy Cox.*

Crane, Stephen (1871–1900)

Great American writer, whose naturalistic *Maggie: A Girl of the Streets* (1893) influenced the style of Lawrence's *The Mint.* As late as 1933, Lawrence was pleased to find a copy of Crane's *Red Badge of Courage* (1895) for his **Clouds Hill** library.

Cranwell, R.A.F. Cadet Training College at

Lawrence served at Cranwell, Lincolnshire, from August 1925, when he was allowed to rejoin the **Royal Air Force,** until November 1926, when he was posted to **India,** where he arrived in early January 1927. At Cranwell, he maintained aircraft as a member of B Flight. He recorded this relatively happy period of his life in part III of *The Mint.*

Crusader Castles

See "**Influence of the Crusades on European Military Architecture—To the End of the XIIth Century, The**"

Curtis, Lionel G. (1872–1955)

Political theorist and leading member of the Round Table, a group of influential Englishmen dedicated to preserving the British Empire as a commonwealth. Lawrence was influenced by their ideas. But Curtis is probably most important to Lawrence's biography as the recipient in 1923 of a series of five very self-revealing letters from Lawrence; these are available in Brown, *Selected Letters*. Curtis's adulatory memoir of Lawrence is contained in **A. W. Lawrence**'s collection *T. E. Lawrence by His Friends.*

Curzon, George Nathaniel, Marquess Curzon of Kedleston (1859–1925)

Viceroy of **India** (1898–1905) and foreign secretary (1919–24). As chancellor of **Oxford University** in 1909, Curzon obtained letters of protection from the sultan of Turkey that enabled Lawrence to travel in **Syria.** In 1918, at a meeting of the Eastern Committee of the **War Cabinet** chaired by Curzon, Lawrence proposed that **Feisal** should rule **Syria, Zeid** upper **Mesopotamia,** and **Abdullah** lower Mesopotamia and stated further that Feisal would prefer American Zionists as advisers. These ideas were not accepted, and in 1920, he attacked Curzon in the course of a series of newspaper articles opposing British control of Mesopotamia. After Feisal was expelled from Syria in 1920, he was offered the throne of Iraq with Curzon's approval. See **Jeremy Wilson,** *Lawrence of Arabia,* pp. 576–77. Lawrence's claim that he had caused Curzon to burst into tears during the 1918 meeting was disputed by **Richard Aldington.**

Cust, Henry John Cockayne (1861–1917)

Author of the poem "Non Nobis," which Lawrence read in his copy of *The Oxford Book of English Verse* on November 22, 1917, two days after his torture by the Turks at **Deraa.** It reads in part, "Not unto us, O Lord: / To us thou givest the scorn, the scourge, the scar."

Custot, Pierre (1880–1919)

French author of *Sturly,* which **Jonathan Cape** commissioned Lawrence to translate in 1923. Lawrence was dissatisfied with his own work and abandoned it. Cape published a translation by **Richard Aldington** in 1924.

D

Dahoum (1896–1918)

Lawrence's Arab servant, whom he first met during the dig at **Carchemish,** brought home with him to Oxford for a visit in June 1913, took with him on his **Wilderness of Zin** travels, and employed as a spy behind Turkish lines during the **Arab Revolt.** According to the testimony of **Tom Beaumont,** Dahoum died of typhoid around September 1918, leaving Lawrence deeply saddened. His proper name, Salim Achmed, has led to his identification as the "S. A." of *Seven Pillars of Wisdom*'s dedicatory poem. **C. Leonard Woolley** implied that Lawrence's relationship with Dahoum was homosexual, but this has been denied by **J. M. Wilson** and others. *See also* **Sexuality.**

Dale, Colin

A pseudonym, based on the Colindale underground station in **London,** used by Lawrence when writing reviews (in the August and September 1927 and February 1928 *Spectator*) of works by **D. H. Lawrence, Hakluyt, H. G. Wells, H. M. Tomlinson, W. H. Hudson,** William Gerhardi, Arthur Machen, **Walter Savage Landor,** and others. Three of the reviews were included in *Men in Print;* all of them are reprinted in *Lawrence of Arabia, Strange Man of Letters,* ed. Harold Orlans.

Damascus, Fall of

Lawrence saw Damascus, **Syria,** as a great city whose capture from the Turks was a primary goal of the **Arab Revolt.** He admitted that his account of its capture on September 30–October 1, 1918, in chapters 119 and 120 of *Seven Pillars of Wisdom* was problematic; and indeed **General Chauvel** and writers **Richard Aldington** and **Elie Kedourie** have disputed it, claiming that the Australians, rather than the Arabs as Lawrence says, were the first to enter the city, or that the Arabs were allowed to enter first only as a courtesy. After the Arab forces came in, Lawrence played a role in deposing the Algerian brothers **Mohammed Said** and **Abd el Kader el Jesairi,** who had assumed control of the government, and then he helped establish order. See **John Mack,** *A Prince of Our Disorder* and **J. M. Wilson,** *Lawrence of Arabia,* for full discussions of this issue. The **Battle of Megiddo,** which saw **General Allenby** destroy the Turkish armies in **Palestine** with overwhelming force, beginning on September 19, 1918, led to a disorganized Turkish retreat under the pursuit of British cavalry. Some 40,000 Turkish and German troops remained along the roads leading to Damascus, but they were scattered and disorganized. On September 29, the Australian cavalry broke through around 2,000 Turkish troops guarding the southern approach to Damascus. On Sep-

Lawrence's Arab servant Dahoum standing in the reservoir at the ancient Byzantine town of Raheiba in January 1914, during the Wilderness of Zin survey. Photo by T. E. Lawrence. Courtesy of the Palestine Exploration Fund.

tember 30, the remnants of the Turkish Fourth Army were destroyed about 10 miles south of Damascus by the Arabs and the British cavalry, as Lawrence explains in chapter 116, 117, and 118 of *Seven Pillars of Wisdom.* In Damascus itself, 11,000 Turkish troops were captured, and only 4,000 Turkish troops remained to guard **Aleppo,** the final Turkish point of defense in **Syria.** See Pope and Wheal, *The Dictionary of the First World War,* and **A. P. Wavell,** *The Palestine Campaigns.*

Damascus Protocol

A document drawn up by colleagues of **Feisal** in the **Al Fatat** and **Al Ahd** societies in 1915. It set forth Arab independence as a precondition for Arab cooperation with England against Turkey and served as the basis for **Sharif Hussein**'s position in the **McMahon-Hussein Correspondence.** See **George Antonius,** *The Arab Awakening,* for details concerning this document.

Daud (died 1918)

True name Ali. One of a pair of Lawrence's Arab servants from the **Ageyl** mercenaries, Daud died in March 1918 of a sickness, leaving his partner **Farraj** (true name Othman) in despair, as related in chapter 92 of *Seven Pillars of Wisdom.* In *Seven Pillars of Wisdom,* Lawrence treats Daud's and Farraj's homosexuality sympathetically, leading several commentators, among them **Richard Aldington,** to infer Lawrence's own sexual proclivities from that, but this remains a disputed point. *See also* **Sexuality.**

The Turkish hospital in Damascus, in front of which Turkish prisoners are being led away after the British conquest of the city. Courtesy of the Australian War Memorial.

Dawnay, Lt. Col. Alan G. C. (1888–1938)

Charged in 1918 with being the liaison between **Allenby**'s forces and the **Arab Revolt,** Dawnay proved very useful in obtaining support for both the regular and the irregular Arab forces and is described very positively in chapter 92 of *Seven Pillars of Wisdom.* He also organized a raid on Tell Shahm station of the **Hejaz Railway,** the military professionalism and precision of which Lawrence regarded with bemused respect, as related in chapter 94 of *Seven Pillars of Wisdom.*

Dawnay, Brig. Gen. Guy (1878–1952)

Brother of **Alan Dawnay** and the member of **Allenby**'s staff responsible, according to Lawrence, for conceiving the attack on **Beersheba** as a means of conquering **Gaza,** 30 miles to the west, as related in chapter 69 of *Seven Pillars of Wisdom.* He also planned the attack on **Jerusalem. Wavell,** however, credits **Sir Philip Chetwode** with the plan to attack Beersheba. Dawnay was one of those who, in December 1923, conceived of the idea of a subscriber's edition of *Seven Pillars of Wisdom.* A pencil sketch of Dawnay by **Henry Lamb** is included in that and some subsequent editions. See **A. P. Wavell,** *The Palestine Campaigns.*

Dawson, Geoffrey (1874–1944)

Editor of *The Times* (1912–19; 1923–41) who proposed Lawrence for election as a fellow at **All Souls College, Oxford.** Lawrence was accepted and spent some of 1920 intermittently at the college, playing pranks and meeting **Robert Graves** there.

Day-Lewis, Cecil (1904–72)

British poet laureate (1967–72) and detective writer under the pseudonym Nicholas Blake. By praising Day-Lewis's *Beechen Vigil* (1925) to **Lady Astor** and other influential friends, Lawrence was largely responsible for the poet's early recognition, as Day-Lewis tells us in his autobiography *The Buried Day* (1960). Lawrence remained supportive despite his criticism of Day-Lewis's subsequent Marxist poetry and prose. In the 1936 mystery *Thou Shell of Death,* Day-Lewis portrayed Lawrence as the dashing Fergus O'Brien who like Lawrence has a tendency to gild the lily. Day-Lewis also wrote an insightful 1938 *Spectator* review of **David Garnett**'s edition of Lawrence's letters and a preface to **J. M. Wilson**'s edition of Lawrence's poetry anthology *Minorities* (1971).

De la Mare, Walter (1873–1956)

Poet and fantasist. Lawrence was reading him by 1923 and had many of his books in his **Clouds Hill** library.

De Setvans, Sir Roger (died 1306)

As a teenager, Lawrence rubbed a brass, located at Chartham, Kent, of this knight. Lawrence's hobby of **brass rubbing** continued into his university years.

Deedes, Brig. Gen. Sir Wyndham Henry (1883–1956)

Expert on Turkey and member of military intelligence, **London;** Gallipoli intelligence; and from 1916, **Cairo** intelligence. He worked with Lawrence on the attempt to bribe **Khalil Pasha** and save the British position at **Kut-al-Amara.** Lawrence thought highly of him, and he is mentioned positively in chapter 113 of *Seven Pillars of Wisdom*. He was later chief secretary to the administration in **Palestine.**

"Demolitions under Fire"

An article by Lawrence appearing in *The Royal Engineers' Journal* 29:1 (January 1919): 6–10 and reprinted in *Evolution of a Revolt,* edited by **Stanley** and Rodelle **Weintraub,** and in *The Essential T. E. Lawrence,* edited by **David Garnett.** In it, Lawrence explains in precise detail his methods of destroying the **Hejaz Railway** during the **Arab Revolt.** He discusses, for instance, the length of fuse and amount of blasting gelatine and guncotton necessary to destroy rails and bridges.

Deraa, Syria

Town in southwestern **Syria** that served as a vital Turkish rail junction and therefore a prime British military objective. It was taken in September 1918 by the Arab forces, leaving columns of departing Turkish soldiers open to the attacks of Lawrence's men, as related in chapters 96 and 97 of *Seven Pillars of Wisdom*. At Deraa, a branch line to **Palestine,** serving the Turkish Seventh and Eighth Armies, ran off of the main **Damascus**-to-**Medina** line of the **Hejaz Railway.** It is in this town that the **Deraa incident** occurred, during which Lawrence on a reconnaissance mission was arrested by Turkish troops and tortured.

Deraa Incident

A controversial incident related in chapter 80 of *Seven Pillars of Wisdom,* according to which Lawrence was arrested on November 20, 1917, while on a reconnaissance mission in **Deraa,** propositioned by the bey in charge, and then tortured and sexually abused by the bey's soldiers before he escaped. Lawrence's account of this incident in *Seven Pillars of Wisdom* contains several ambiguities and is contradicted or modified by other documents he wrote and by what is known about the bey, leading commentators to interpret it variously. According to **Desmond Stewart,** the incident never occurred at Deraa, but may have happened elsewhere, and points to Lawrence's masochistic and homosexual nature. Dramatist **Terence Rattigan** in his *Ross* (1960) suggests that the bey had Lawrence assaulted and deliberately let him go with his spirit broken. **Knightley** and **Simpson** researched the man who was the bey at Deraa at the time of the incident. They found that **Hajim Bey,** whom Lawrence identifies as Nahi Bey in chapter 80 of *Seven Pillars of Wisdom,* died in Izmir, Turkey, in 1965 and was known to be an aggressive heterosexual with no hint of homosexuality in his character; also, his diaries contained no mention of Lawrence, although Hajim's son remembered his father referring to Lawrence as an opponent who wanted to conquer Deraa. Even those defending Lawrence's version of events in *Seven Pillars of Wisdom,* such as **J. M. Wilson,** find it difficult to explain why he claimed in that book that the bey did not recognize him while asserting in a letter of 1919 to **Maj. W. F. Stirling,** chief political officer at general headquarters **Cairo,** that the bey did know his identity because he had been betrayed by **Abd el Kader el Jesairi.** In a letter of 1924 to **Mrs. G. B. Shaw,** Lawrence stated that he allowed himself to be raped by the bey's soldiers when he could no longer stand the pain of their beating. In the 1922 manuscript of *Seven Pillars of Wisdom,* Lawrence hints that the beating at Deraa resulted in a post-war flagellation compulsion, but he gives no details about it. Because of these many conflicting versions and views, Kaja Silverman has taken the approach that what actually happened or did not happen to Lawrence at Deraa is less important than his fantasizing about it. The central position that this incident occupies in the structure of *Seven Pillars of Wisdom* and the letters to Stirling and Mrs. Shaw seem to show that something did indeed happen to Lawrence at Deraa, but exactly what transpired will remain open to question and interpretation until more definitive evidence appears, if it ever does. *See also* **Sexuality.**

Derbyshire, SS

The crowded and foul-smelling troopship upon which Lawrence sailed to his **Royal Air Force** post in **India** in December 1926.

Deve Hüyük

At an ancient cemetery here, Lawrence recognized graves of the later Parthian period (250 B.C.E.–250 C.E.) and with **C. L. Woolley** helped retrieve valuable objects that were being looted by local peasants. P.R.S. Moorey describes these objects in his monograph *Cemeteries of the First Millenium B.C. at Deve Hüyük, near Carchemish, Salvaged by T. E. Lawrence and C. L. Woolley in 1913.*

Diary of T. E. Lawrence, MCMXI, The

Also entitled *Diary of a Journey across the Euphrates,* this is the record of Lawrence's month-long journey on foot through **Syria** during 1911, when he was on vacation from the dig at **Carchemish.** It was first published by the **Corvinus Press** in 1937 in 203 copies, of which only 150 were for sale, and has since gone through several different editions. In it, Lawrence recorded notes on Crusader castles that he wished to add to his B.A. thesis on that subject in order to publish it one day as a book. According to **Philip O'Brien,** the original Corvinus Press edition is one of the rarest Lawrence books.

Dinard, France

Town in Brittany, **France,** on the Gulf of St. Malo. At the time that Lawrence's family lived in Dinard, from 1891 to 1894, it was a small resort town. The family lived in the Chalet du Vallon and employed an English governess. T. E. and his brother Montagu Robert also studied at the Ecole St.-Marie. During his later bicycle trips in France, he visited the **Chaignon**s, who had befriended his family during their stay in Dinard. The town's medieval aspect probably influenced Lawrence's interest in castles and **archaeology.**

Dinning, Capt. Hector William (born 1887)

Author of *Nile to Aleppo: With the Light-Horse in the Middle East* (1920), which includes a chapter on Dinning's work as a pilot with Lawrence toward the end of the war.

Dixon, Alec L. (born 1900)

Author and soldier. Dixon met Lawrence in 1923 when Dixon was a corporal in the Tank Corps at **Bovington Camp.** His memoir in **A. W. Lawrence**'s collection *T. E. Lawrence by His Friends* testifies to Lawrence's love of his **Brough** motorcycle, his readiness to discuss art, literature, and music with service colleagues at **Clouds Hill,** and his unhappiness in the Tank Corps. He has also included these memories in his *Tinned Soldier: A Personal Record 1919–1926* (1941).

Dobson, Frank (1886–1963)

Painter and sculptor. A member of the Artists Rifles during **World War I,** president of the London Group of artists (1923–27), and later a leading sculptor. Dobson met Lawrence in 1921 and did the pencil sketch of **Pierce Joyce** that was included in the 1926 subscriber's edition of *Seven Pillars of Wisdom.* In a letter of 1922 (Garnett, *Letters,* p. 385), Lawrence called Dobson the finest sculptor of his generation in England. V. M. Thompson, *"Not a Suitable Hobby for an Airman"—T. E. Lawrence as Publisher,* contains a concise biography.

Dodd, Francis (1874–1935)

Artist who sketched **Dahoum** when he visited Lawrence in Oxford in June 1913. Lawrence was present during the sketching sessions. **J. M. Wilson**'s exhibition catalog *T. E. Lawrence* has a reproduction of this picture (p. 39). From 1916 to 1918 Dodd, a leading portrait painter, served as an official war artist on the western front.

Doran, George H. (1869–1956)

The American publisher of a few special copyright copies of *Seven Pillars of Wisdom* in 1926 and of **Revolt in the Desert.** In 1927, soon after the publication of *Revolt,* his firm merged with that of **Frank Doubleday.**

Dostoyevsky, Fyodor Mikhaylovich (1821–81)

Widely regarded as one of the greatest writers of all time. For Lawrence, Dostoyevsky's *The Brothers Karamazov* was a model whose intense spirituality and epic quality he tried to emulate in *Seven Pillars of Wisdom.* The other books he placed in this highest category of greatness were **Herman Melville**'s *Moby Dick* and **Friedrich Nietzsche**'s *Thus Spake Zarathustra,* as he wrote to **Edward Garnett** on August

26, 1922 (Garnett, *Letters,* p. 360). He felt that Dostoyevsky even exceeded **Tolstoy** in greatness, although in a letter of September 29, 1924 (Garnett, *Letters,* p. 467), he includes Tolstoy, as well as Whitman, Rabelais, and Cervantes, in his list of top writers. In 1928, he compared Dostoyevsky's *House of the Dead* and his own *The Mint,* indicating possible influence.

Doubleday, Frank Nelson (1862–1934)

American publisher who first met Lawrence in 1918. When in 1927 Doubleday's firm merged with that of **George Doran,** it acquired Lawrence's *Revolt in the Desert.* The company was then the largest publisher in the English-speaking world. Lawrence visited with the Doubledays several times during their visits to England (where Doubleday owned Heinemann). The Doubleday firm began publishing the American edition of *Seven Pillars of Wisdom* upon Lawrence's death in 1935 and remains the owner of the American copyright.

Doughty, Charles Montagu (1843–1926)

Explorer, travel writer, and poet, to whom Lawrence turned for advice about the Middle East before taking his first trip there in 1909. For much of his life, Lawrence regarded Doughty's *Travels in Arabia Deserta* (1888), based upon his solo travels in Arabia from 1876–1878, as a great masterpiece. He was instrumental in getting it republished by **Jonathan Cape** and Philip Lee Warner in 1921 with his own introduction, and its influence on *Seven Pillars of Wisdom* is apparent, particularly with regard to the speech and heroic portrayal of the Arab characters. But later in his life, when he became familiar with the tastes of

soldiers and airmen in the ranks and was himself serving as a simple airman, Lawrence criticized Doughty's work for a lack of structure, precious style, and Victorian feelings of superiority toward the Arabs. For further information, see D. G. Hogarth, *The Life of C. M. Doughty;* S. E. Tabachnick, *T. E. Lawrence, Charles Doughty,* and (editor) *Explorations in Doughty's "Arabia Deserta";* and Andrew Taylor, *God's Fugitive: The Life of C. M. Doughty.*

Dowson, Ernest (1867–1900)

Decadent poet and, with Lionel Johnson and **W. B. Yeats,** a member of the Rhymer's Club. His poetry deeply impressed Lawrence, for in chapter 53 of *Seven Pillars of Wisdom,* Lawrence recounts that as he lay expecting to die after having fallen off his camel (which he had accidentally shot in the head with his pistol) during the charge on **Aba el Lissan,** two lines of Dowson's "Impenitentia Ultima" came into his head.

Dowson, Sir Ernest (1876–1950)

Colonial civil servant, director of the Survey of Egypt, and postwar adviser to the **Palestine, Transjordan,** and **Iraq** governments. In his memoir in **A. W. Lawrence**'s collection *T. E. Lawrence by His Friends,* Dowson testifies to Lawrence's work in 1914–16 in **Cairo** as a liaison between the Military Intelligence Service, the **Arab Bureau,** the Survey of Egypt, and the Egyptian Government Press.

Doynel de Saint-Quentin, Lt.

French military liaison staff officer in **Cairo** who in 1917 wrote a memo praising

Lawrence as the outstanding British personality in the Middle East, as is pointed out in **Maurice Larés,** *T. E. Lawrence, la France et les Français* (p. 158).

Druse

An Arabic-speaking ethnic group living in **Lebanon, Syria,** and Israel. The Druse religion, which is secret, is not considered part of **Islam** by more orthodox believers, although it derived from a branch of Shiite Islam beginning in the eleventh century. Druse history has been marked by bloody tensions with the **Maronites** and Muslims, and in chapter 121 of *Seven Pillars of Wisdom* Lawrence accused the Druse of failing to aid in the capture of Damascus, but then looting the residents. See Shimoni and Levine, *Political Dictionary of the Middle East in the Twentieth Century.*

Dunn, George W. M. (born 1908)

Dunn, an aircraftman, met Lawrence in 1929 in the **Royal Air Force.** His piece in **A. W. Lawrence**'s collection *T. E. Lawrence by His Friends* testifies to Lawrence's love of conversation about art and many other subjects, including British fascism, which Lawrence detested. He also points to Lawrence's perfectionism and unhappiness with himself during this period. Lawrence was instrumental in getting Dunn's *Poems: Group One* (1934) published by **Jonathan Cape.**

Duval, Elizabeth W.

Librarian at Oklahoma State University and compiler of *T. E. Lawrence: A Bibliography* (1938), the fullest and most reliable listing of works by Lawrence up to the time of its publication.

E

East Cowes, Isle of Wight

Lawrence spent some time at an experimental station here in 1933, watching over the construction of **Royal Air Force** boats and equipment. During this same period, he also worked at the **Marine Aircraft Experimental Establishment at Felixstowe** and at Manchester and **Hythe** as well.

Eastern Mediterranean Special Intelligence Bureau

A branch of British intelligence, operating out of the British consulates in the eastern Mediterranean. The organization's headquarters were transferred from **Greece** to **Egypt** in December 1915. "A" Branch gathered information about the Turkish Empire, while "B" Branch monitored and tried to foil German submarine activity, Turkish attempts to break the British naval blockade, and Turkish counterintelligence operations. In early 1917, EMSIB head Rhys Samson was replaced by Philip Vickery. A Greek branch remained under the command of Compton Mackenzie, a prominent writer. EMSIB representatives sometimes encroached on Lawrence's own running of agents, especially as the **Arab Revolt** moved toward Damascus. **Alec Kirkbride**'s *An Awakening* (1971) and Lewen B. Weldon's *"Hard Lying"* (1925) discuss some of the activities of this secret agency on the basis of first-hand knowledge, while Yigal Sheffy's comprehensive *British Military Intelligence in the Palestine Campaign, 1914–1918* is based on archival sources.

Ede, Harold Stanley (born 1895)

Tate Gallery assistant keeper and author of *Savage Messiah* (1931), a life of the sculptor Gaudier-Brzeska. Lawrence liked the book and arranged to have it reviewed. Some of his correspondence with Ede was published by the **Golden Cockerel Press** under the title *Shaw-Ede: T. E. Lawrence's Letters to H. S. Ede 1927–1935* (1942).

Eden, Matthew

Author of a thriller, *The Murder of Lawrence of Arabia* (1979), claiming that Lawrence was killed by British intelligence.

Edmonds, Charles

Pseudonym of **Carrington, Charles Edmond.**

Egypt

Lawrence first visited Egypt in 1912, when he worked with archaeologist **Flinders Petrie.** At that time, he formed a negative impression of the country, which had been controlled by Britain since 1882, although it legally remained part of the Ottoman Empire until December 18, 1914, when Britain declared it a protectorate. **Lord Kitchener** was British consul general from 1911 until 1914, when he became British minister of war. Hussein Rushdi Pasha, a British appointee, was prime minister throughout the war years, while Hussein Kamel was Sultan until he was succeeded in this post by his brother Ahmad Fuad in 1917. Lawrence served in **Cairo** from 1914 to 1916 and returned there occasionally during the **Arab Revolt** to consult his superiors. Although the British did not use Egyptian troops overseas, 120,000 Egyptian volunteers served in support positions in **Palestine** and the western front. The major danger to the British forces in Egypt came from the **Senussi** revolt in Libya and rebellious forces in the **Sudan,** as well as from failed Turkish attempts on the **Suez Canal** in 1915 and 1916. Tension between the British government, represented by High Commissioner **Sir Reginald Wingate** (who had succeeded **Sir Henry McMahon** in this post in December 1916), and Egyptian nationalists under the Wafd Party led by Said Zaghlul Pasha erupted in riots in 1918 and especially in March 1919, with the imprisonment of Zaghlul. **Edmund Allenby** replaced Wingate and calmed matters by allowing Zaghlul, head of the nationalist party, to be released from prison and to present his case at the **Peace Conference** in **Paris.** On February 28, 1922, the British granted independence to Egypt, but only after Zaghlul, who had refused to accept Britain's terms, had been exiled. In fact, however, Britain continued to rule Egypt until 1936, at which time its forces withdrew from all areas except the Suez Canal Zone, which had always been Britain's preoccupation, because it controlled access to **India.** In a letter of 1925 to **Robert Graves,** who was considering a job in Egypt for which Lawrence had recommended him, Lawrence noted the gulf between British bureaucrats and the Egyptian peasantry, but now found Egypt's climate, topography, artifacts, and people positive. He especially recommended the Nile Delta swamps, Wilfrid Jennings Bramley's structures near Alexandria, and the architecture of the Divine Mosque in Cairo. For further information, see the articles on Egypt in Shimoni and Levine, *Political Dictionary of the Middle East in the Twentieth Century* and in Pope and Wheal, *The Dictionary of the First World War.*

Egyptian Expeditionary Force

A united command formed in March 1916 under **Sir Archibald Murray.** This replaced the Mediterranean Expeditionary Force, which had been evacuated to **Egypt** from **Gallipoli.** At the beginning of 1917, the E.E.F. numbered 156,000 British, Australian, New Zealand, Indian, West Indian, French, and Italian soldiers. **Gen. Edmund Allenby** assumed control of this force on June 27, 1917, and with it succeeded in ending the war in **Palestine** and **Syria** by October 1918. In August 1917, the E.E.F. was comprised of the Desert Mounted Corps (formerly the Desert Column) under **Maj. Gen. H. G. Chauvel,** the XX Corps, under **Lt. Gen. Sir Philip Chetwode,** and the XXI Corps, under Lt. Gen. Sir Edward Bulfin. Chauvel and Chetwode as well as **Maj. Gen. Sir E. W. C. Chaytor** and **Maj. Gen. Sir G. de S. Barrow** figure prominently and not always favorably in *Seven Pillars of Wisdom,* especially toward the end, during the **fall of Damascus.** The **Imperial Camel Corps Brigade** was also part of the E.E.F. See **A. P. Wavell,** *The Palestine Campaigns,* Philip Haythornthwaite, *The World War One Source Book,* Pope and Wheal, *The Dictionary of the First World War,* and Bryan Perrett, *Megiddo 1918.*

El Ula

Town about 100 miles east of **Wejh,** near which Hamid el Rifada, an ally of **Feisal,** captured a Turkish supply caravan of 70 camels around December 1916, as reported in chapter 17 of *Seven Pillars of Wisdom.* The **Hejaz Railway** passed through this town.

Elgar, Sir Edward (1857–1934)

Distinguished British composer. Lawrence's record collection at **Clouds Hill** contained 10 pieces by Elgar. In a letter of December 22, 1933, to Elgar, Lawrence singled out the violin concerto, Symphony No. 2, and Symphony No. 3 for special praise (Garnett, *Letters,* p. 785). **G. B.** and **Charlotte Shaw** had introduced him to Elgar in 1932.

Eliot, Thomas Stearns (1888–1965)

With **W. B. Yeats,** a preeminent poet of the early twentieth century. Lawrence read Eliot's *Poems 1909–1925* in December 1925 and recognized their futurity, to which he compared the neomedievalism of *Seven Pillars of Wisdom* unfavorably (Garnett, *Letters,* p. 488). He liked Eliot's essay on Dante, but he also criticized Eliot for taking an overly intellectual approach toward literary criticism and literature itself (Garnett, *Letters,* p. 756). It seems that although Lawrence desired to accommodate himself to literary Modernism as represented by Eliot, Yeats, and **James Joyce,** he could not quite do so and remained loyal to the aestheticism of the 1890s. For a comparison of Eliot's *The Waste Land* and *Seven Pillars of Wisdom,* see "The Waste Land in *Seven Pillars of Wisdom,*" in *The T. E. Lawrence Puzzle,* edited by Tabachnick.

Empty Quarter

See **Rub al Khali**

Enver Pasha (1881–1922)

With **Jemal Pasha** and **Talat Pasha,** one of the three rulers of Turkey during **World War I.** In January 1914, Enver replaced Izzet Pasha as minister of war and chief of the general staff. In this capacity, he was largely responsible for Turkey's alliance with Germany and for the repression of minorities within the empire. A poor strategist, he commanded the Second and Third Armies' failed campaign on the Caucasus front in 1914 and again ineffectually wasted resources there in 1917. In chapter 5 of *Seven Pillars of Wisdom,* Lawrence relates how **Feisal** had Enver and Jemal at his mercy during a military review in **Medina** before the **Arab Revolt** broke out but let them live. Enver is mentioned at several other points in *Seven Pillars of Wisdom,* usually disreputably, and in chapter 115, Lawrence relates a horrifying tale of Enver's sadistic methods. Enver went into exile with the rest of the Turkish leadership and was killed while fighting against Soviet rule in Turkish central Asia. See **Liman von Sanders,** *Five Years in Turkey;* Shimoni and Levine, *Political Dictionary of the Middle East in the Twentieth Century;* and Philip Haythornthwaite, *The World War One Source Book.*

Erzurum, Turkey

A Turkish fortress town captured by Russian Gen. Nicholas Yudenich (under the nominal direction of the Grand Duke Nicholas) on February 16, 1916. In chapter 6 of *Seven Pillars of Wisdom,* Lawrence alludes to having had a role in the fall of Erzurum, and to **B. H. Liddell Hart** he said that he had put the Russian grand duke in touch with disaffected Arab officers in the Turkish fortress, thus hastening its fall. This has been doubted by **Richard Aldington,** and **John Mack** feels that Lawrence overstated his role in these events, but **J. M. Wilson** has shown that Lawrence was in fact dealing with secret information about the Caucasus front while working in **Cairo Military Intelligence.** A possible reason that Lawrence could not be specific about this and other intelligence issues in *Seven Pillars of Wisdom* is that the people involved might still be living in Turkey or the surrounding areas when *Seven Pillars of Wisdom* was published and subject to reprisal for their wartime roles. See *T. E. Lawrence to His Biographers Robert Graves & Liddell Hart;* Richard Aldington, *Lawrence of Arabia: A Biographical Enquiry;* John Mack, *A Prince of Our Disorder;* and J. M. Wilson, *Lawrence of Arabia.*

Es Salt, Jordan

See **Salt**

"Essay on Flecker, An"

An impressionistic memoir of Lawrence's stay in **Beirut** in August 1911 with the poet **James Elroy Flecker,** a friend of Lawrence's who died in 1915. Lawrence wrote the short, unfinished piece in late 1924 or early 1925, but it was not published until the **Corvinus Press** and Doubleday, Doran editions of 1937 appeared, and then it was published again in 1940, in somewhat different form, by the **Golden Cockerel Press,** as part of *Men in Print,* a collection of Lawrence's literary criticism. It is also available in *Lawrence of Arabia, Strange Man of Letters,* edited by Harold Orlans.

"Evolution of a Revolt, The"

The title of an article that Lawrence published in the *Army Quarterly* 1:1 (October 1920): 55–69, to help editor **Guy Dawnay,** with whom Lawrence had worked in Arabia, get the journal started. It is also available in ***Oriental Assembly*** and in *Evolution of a Revolt,* edited by **Stanley** and Rodelle **Weintraub.** In this article, Lawrence sets forth in essential form the strategic ideas that appear in chapter 33 of *Seven Pillars of Wisdom:* surprise hit-and-run raids over a wide area using a minimum of manpower and propaganda to turn the civilian population against the enemy, all with a view to weakening his morale. The essential idea is to win the war psychologically rather than by means of force. **Liddell Hart** used it as the basis of the article on irregular warfare in the 14th edition of the *Encyclopaedia Britannica* that appeared above Lawrence's initials, as he relates in *T. E. Lawrence to His Biographers Robert Graves & Liddell Hart.*

F

Fairley, Barker (1887–1986)

University of Toronto English professor and author of *Charles M. Doughty: A Critical Study* (1927), which Lawrence criticized for maintaining that **Doughty**'s *Arabia Deserta* was consciously structured when Lawrence felt that it was meandering and haphazard (Garnett, *Letters,* pp. 526–27).

Fakhri Pasha (Omar Fahkri ud-Din Pasha)

This general, commanding the approximately 10,000–12,000 men of the Turkish Twelfth Army Corps, managed to hold **Medina** against the Arab forces during the entire war, refusing out of Muslim conviction to retreat northward up the **Hejaz Railway** even when ordered to do so by **Jemal Pasha** in March 1917. Fakhri was known for his part in the massacre of **Armenians** before being sent to Medina and for the massacre of Beni Ali tribesmen after being sent there, as recorded in chapter 13 of *Seven Pillars of Wisdom.* Lawrence thought him an unintelligent commander, but the fact is that the Arab forces never captured Medina, and the Turks there surrendered long after the war's end, in January 1919, only after Fakhri was removed by a coup. See **Konrad Morsey,** "T. E. Lawrence, Strategist," in *The T. E. Lawrence Puzzle,* edited by Tabachnick; **A. P. Wavell,** *The Palestine Campaigns;* and Pope and Wheal, *The Dictionary of the First World War.*

Faraifra Station

Hejaz Railway station located about 55 miles north of **Maan,** taken on May 24, 1918, by **Sharif Nasir** and **Capt. Hornby.**

Fareedah el Akle (1882–1976)

Christian and Arab nationalist language teacher at the **American Mission** School at Jebail, **Lebanon,** whom Lawrence first met in 1909 and with whom Lawrence studied Arabic for three months in 1911. He continued to correspond with her as late as 1927, and she has published a memoir in **A. W. Lawrence**'s collection *T. E. Lawrence by His Friends. See* **John Mack,** *A Prince of Our Disorder.*

Faris

With **Halim,** one of Lawrence's two bodyguards during the scouting trip of November 1917 that resulted in his capture and torture by the Turks during the **Deraa incident,** as related in chapter 80 of *Seven Pillars of Wisdom.* **Sheikh Tallal** was a third companion during that journey.

Farnborough, Oxford University Officers' Training Corps Camp at

From June 20 to July 2, 1910, Lawrence attended this summer camp, which took place on Farnborough Common and included various exercises, including a mock battle against Cambridge University's Officers' Training Corps.

Farnborough, R.A.F. School of Photography at

Still using the last name Ross, Lawrence was transferred to Farnborough from **Uxbridge** on November 8, 1922, and remained there until he was expelled from the **Royal Air Force** at the end of January 1923 after a newspaper disclosed his identity. During this period, he made friends with **A. E. "Jock" Chambers** and **R.A.M. Guy** and received his first birching at the hands of **John Bruce.** Chambers's memoir in **A. W. Lawrence**'s collection *T. E. Lawrence by His Friends* shows that Lawrence was accepted by his fellow servicemen. He did not like drill but was a success in the course training him to be an aerial photographer, especially in working with negatives; he had learned photography from his father while still a boy. He was also working on an abridgment of *Seven Pillars of Wisdom* with **Edward Garnett** that was never published and on the notes that resulted in *The Mint,* but he found that Uxbridge offered more interesting material than Farnborough.

Farraj

True name Othman. One of a pair of homosexual lovers who were Lawrence's servants. After his lover **Daud** died of an illness in March 1918, Farraj was desolate. So when near **Faraifra** on April 11, 1918,

Studio shot of the Emir Feisal. Photographer: Lafayette Ltd. Courtesy of the Australian War Memorial.

Lawrence had to shoot the wounded Farraj to spare him possible torture by the Turks, Farraj died willingly as related in chapter 93 of *Seven Pillars of Wisdom. See also* **Sexuality.**

Feisal ibn Hussein, Emir (1885–1933)

The third son of **Sharif Hussein ibn Ali** of **Mecca,** Feisal played a leading role in the military and political aspects of the **Arab Revolt,** both during the war and after it. Feisal made contacts with disaffected Arab groups in Damascus before the revolt, led the (failed) attack on **Medina** that began the revolt, united the **Beduin** tribes sufficiently to make them into a useful fighting force, assumed power in Damascus after its capture, and represented the

The Emir Feisal, who recently had been evicted from Damascus by French General Gouraud, inspects an honor guard in Palestine with British High Commissioner Sir Herbert Samuel in August 1920. Courtesy of the Palestine Exploration Fund.

Arab nationalist position at the 1919 **Peace Conference** in **Paris.** Lawrence's portrait of him, for instance in chapter 103 of *Seven Pillars of Wisdom,* is complex, revealing weakness as well as nobility, subtlety, and wit. At the Paris conference, with Lawrence's mediation, Feisal signed a treaty with **Dr. Chaim Weizmann,** who represented **Zionism,** but he was less successful in his attempt to assert Arab independence and thwart French designs on **Syria.** On July 28, 1920, Feisal was expelled from Damascus after two years of rule there by a French army under **General Gouraud;** but as a result of the **Cairo Conference** of 1921, in which Lawrence participated, the British installed him on the throne of **Iraq,** which he ruled until his death on September 7, 1933. He was assisted in Iraq by **Gertrude Bell.** See **George Antonius,** *The Arab Awakening;* Eliezer Tauber, *The Arab Movements in World War I;* R. Bidwell, ed., *Arabian Personalities of the Early Twentieth Century;*

and Shimoni and Levine, *Political Dictionary of the Middle East in the Twentieth Century.*

Felixstowe, R.A.F. Marine Aircraft Experimental Establishment at

Lawrence at first wanted to leave the **Royal Air Force** on April 6, 1933, but he changed his mind when he was offered the more interesting work, boatbuilding, that he wanted. He was stationed at Felixstowe, on the Suffolk coast, from April 28, 1933, until he was sent two weeks later to Manchester and then to another station at **East Cowes, Isle of Wight.** At Felixstowe he oversaw the construction of R.A.F. boats at a marine contractor's shipyard. Upon his retirement, he donated the *Biscuit,* his small speedboat capable of a speed of 40 miles per hour, to the officers at Felixstowe. **Fl. Lt. W.E.G. Beaufort-Greenwood,** whom Lawrence served as an assistant, and **Sgt. W. Bradbury,** a colleague, have left memoirs of this period (a happy one for Lawrence) in **A. W. Lawrence**'s collection *T. E. Lawrence by His Friends.*

ffoulkes, Charles J. (1868–1947)

Curator of the Armouries of the Tower of London (1913–35) and first curator and secretary, **Imperial War Museum** (1917–33). While lecturing on medieval arms and armor at **Oxford University** in 1909–10, ffoulkes would accompany Lawrence on **brass rubbing** expeditions. When ffoulkes was at the Imperial War Museum, Lawrence donated gifts, including a wreath from the tomb of Saladin, uniforms from the **Hejaz** forces, and a collection of photographs from the Arab campaign. He has left a memoir of Lawrence in **A. W. Lawrence**'s collection *T. E. Lawrence by His Friends.*

Films

Lawrence's career was bound up with film both as practitioner and subject. During the war, he saw and used aerial and ground photographs of important enemy sites and took many excellent photographs himself. After the war, he was sent to the **Royal Air Force**'s school of **photography** at **Farnborough.** He was also a subject of films and photographs: **Lowell Thomas,** with the aid of **Harry Chase**'s skilled photography, produced a famous slide show about him starting in 1919; in 1934, **Alexander Korda** wanted to film *Revolt in the Desert;* and since his death he has been the subject of several television documentaries and the full-length David Lean/**Robert Bolt** feature film *Lawrence of Arabia* (1962). Lawrence dissuaded Korda from going ahead with the film and wrote **Robert Graves** in 1935 that he detested the

idea of having a film made of him (Garnett, *Letters,* p. 851). See S. E. Tabachnick and Christopher Matheson, *Images of Lawrence,* for a review of television documentaries through 1987 and L. Robert Morris and Lawrence Raskin, *Lawrence of Arabia,* for a very complete discussion of the making of the film. The television documentary films are as follows: *T. E. Lawrence: 1888–1935,* written and narrated by David Lytton and produced by **Malcolm Brown** (1962); *Lawrence of England,* written and narrated by Alan Lomax (1979); BBC newsnight segment, written and narrated by John Witherow of the *Times* (May 13, 1985); *The Master Illusionist,* directed by Jeff Burton and Michael Caulfield and produced by Mal Read in Australia (1983); *The Shadow of Failure,* directed by Jeff Goodman, produced by Ken Seymour, and narrated by David Rogers and Richard Worthy (1985); *Lawrence and Arabia,* produced by Julia Cave and Malcolm Brown (1986); *A Dangerous Man: Lawrence after Arabia,* directed by Christopher Menaul, with Ralph Fiennes as Lawrence (1990); and *Lawrence of Arabia: The Battle for the Arab World,* directed by James Hawes and produced by Cassius Harris for Lion Films (2003).

Flaubert, Gustave (1821–80)

Lawrence wrote **Edward Garnett** in 1922 that Flaubert's *Salammbô* (1862) was stylistically brilliant, and **Jonathan Cape** suggested in 1924 that he translate it, but after his failure to translate **Pierre Custot**'s *Sturly,* Lawrence felt unequal to the job. He wrote **Charlotte Shaw** in 1928 that Flaubert was one of his favorite French writers.

Flecker, (Herman) James Elroy (1884–1915)

Poet, playwright, and British consular official. Lawrence met Flecker and his wife

Helle in August 1911 when Flecker had just become vice-consul at **Beirut.** He visited them several times in their summer home in **Lebanon** during his **Carchemish** period and worked with Flecker in smuggling some rifles from a British ship in Beirut harbor to the British consulate in **Aleppo** in 1913. Lawrence's **"Essay on Flecker"** is a brief, unfinished memoir. He especially liked the poet's *Golden Journey to Samarcand* (1913) and wrote Helle in 1923 that he had enjoyed seeing his play *Hassan* (1913) performed in **London.** Lawrence was disturbed by Flecker's early death from tuberculosis, and in a letter of 1928 to **David Garnett** (*Letters,* p. 612), he expresses dismay at the decline in Flecker's poetic reputation.

Foch, Marshal Ferdinand (1851–1929)

Author of *Principes de la Guerre* (1903), commandant of the French Ecole de Guerre, and from April 14, 1918, Allied supreme commander for the western front. An advocate of aggressive military tactics that often brought victory toward the end of the war, if at the great expense of human life, Foch was in many ways the most important Allied general of **World War I.** He also led the Armistice negotiations that imposed harsh terms upon the Germans and was the leading military adviser to **Clemenceau** during the 1919 **Peace Conference** in **Paris.** In chapter 33 of *Seven Pillars of Wisdom,* Lawrence is harshly critical of Foch's doctrines, preferring a strategy of swift thrusts, low casualty rates, and threat, to massed confrontations with the enemy. Lawrence told **Liddell Hart** that he met Foch in 1919 and also claimed that Foch had plagiarized part of his *Principes* from a German writer. See *T. E. Lawrence to His Biographers Robert Graves & Liddell Hart* and Philip Haythornthwaite, *The World War One Source Book.*

Fontana, R. A.

Lawrence met Fontana and his wife Winifred in the spring of 1911 when Fontana was the British consul at **Aleppo, Syria.** They visited him at **Carchemish** in the spring of 1912, and in 1913 he helped smuggle rifles to Aleppo to protect the consulate from a feared attack on the city by the **Kurds.** Mrs. Fontana's memoir appears in **A. W. Lawrence**'s collection *T. E. Lawrence by His Friends,* and she is also quoted in Garnett's *Letters.*

Fontevraud, Abbey of

Founded in 1101 near Saumur, **France,** this is the site of the Plantagenet family's tombs, including that of **Richard I** (Coeur de Lion). Lawrence visited the Abbey on a bicycle trip in 1907 and was very impressed with the monument of Richard there. In an *Arab Bulletin* dispatch of November 26, 1916, he compares **Feisal**'s appearance to this monument.

Foreign Office

The British government agency responsible, with the cabinet, the War Office, and the **India Office,** for Middle Eastern policy until the creation, partly because of Lawrence's urging, of the **Middle East Department** in the **Colonial Office** in 1921. Until the creation of the Middle East Department, the Foreign Office was responsible for **Egypt,** the **Sudan, Palestine,** and the **Hejaz** area, while the India Office controlled policy for **Mesopotamia,** central and southern Arabia, and Aden, and the Colonial Office covered Cyprus and Somaliland. Lawrence and the Foreign Office were often at loggerheads during the immediate postwar period, when he was working for greater Arab independence in **Syria** under **Feisal,** and the Foreign Office wanted to accommodate

French desires for a Syrian mandate. The Foreign Office and the India Office also competed with one another during this period, with the Foreign Office supporting **Sharif Hussein** of **Mecca** and the India Office supporting the **Wahabi** chieftain **Ibn Saud,** who in 1924 drove Hussein into exile. See David Fromkin, *A Peace to End All Peace;* Karsh and Karsh, *Empires of the Sand;* **E. Kedourie,** *In the Anglo-Arab Labyrinth;* R. Baker, *King Husain and the Kingdom of Hejaz;* and Briton Busch, *Britain, India, and the Arabs 1914–1921.*

Forster, Edward Morgan (1879–1970)

Preeminent British novelist and critic. Forster first met Lawrence in 1921 but their friendship developed slowly. In 1924, Forster wrote Lawrence that *Seven Pillars of Wisdom,* which he criticized sympathetically in detail in its 1922 "Oxford text" version (**A. W. Lawrence,** *Letters to T. E. Lawrence,* pp. 58–62), helped him finish his own greatest novel, *A Passage to India* (1924). In his turn, Lawrence stated that he saw in that novel, about the British in India, a reflection of his own political and cultural problems in Arabia (Garnett, *Letters,* pp. 461–62). He also offered Forster his views on Forster's other fiction, including his work with homosexual themes, and Forster visited him at **Clouds Hill** more than a dozen times. Lawrence intended to write an article about Forster, but he never finished it. He wrote **Robert Graves** in 1933 that he liked **Frederick Manning, Ernest Altounyan,** and Forster most among his friends since **D. G. Hogarth** died. Forster's *The Eternal Monument and Other Stories* (1928) is dedicated to Lawrence. Forster wrote insightfully about Lawrence in his *Abinger Harvest* (1936), *Two Cheers for Democracy* (1951), and in **A. W. Lawrence**'s collection *T. E. Lawrence by His Friends,* among other places.

France

The nature of Lawrence's attitude toward France and the French has been much disputed. **Aldington** and others have held that he was completely anti-French, while **Maurice Larés,** the author of *T. E. Lawrence, la France et les Français* (1980), has pointed out that Lawrence opposed French policy in the Middle East but that he enjoyed his trips to France, translated French literature, and had French friends. Some French detachments (under **Col. Edouard Brémond, Capt. Pisani,** and **Major Cousse**) assisted the **Arab Revolt,** but French policymakers wanted to control **Syria** rather than to grant it a degree of independence after the war. Following that policy, the French deposed **Feisal** in 1920 and kept control of Syria until 1946. Thus, the Arab Revolt succeeded militarily but failed politically because of French policy, and Lawrence remained highly conscious of that fact. Despite or because of Lawrence's ambiguity with regard to France, many French writers, including **Léon Boussard, André Malraux, Jean Béraud-Villars,** Manes Sperber, Vincent-Mansour Monteil, and Renée and André Guillaume, have written extensively and not unfavorably about him.

French Language

Lawrence's spoken knowledge of the language was adequate, and his reading knowledge was good enough for translation. He lived in **France** as a child and visited it as a teenager. During the war, he worked with French contingents in the **Hejaz,** and after the war he took part in the 1919 **Peace Conference** in **Paris,** occasionally speaking French there. Witnesses agree that his spoken French was bookish and that his English accent was strong, but he could carry on a conversation in the language. In 1923, he translated **Adrien le Corbeau**'s *Le Gigantesque* as *The Forest Giant,* and he considered translating **J. C. Mardrus**'s French translation of *The Arabian Nights* and **Pierre Custot**'s *Sturly.* **Maurice Larés,** who has done the most exhaustive study of this issue in his *T. E. Lawrence, la France et les Français,* concludes that Lawrence's understanding of the nuances of written French was excellent.

French Military Mission (Mission Militaire Française)

A deputation arriving in **Jidda** in September 1916 under **Col. Edouard Brémond** to assist **Sharif Hussein** in his uprising against the Turks and to establish a French political position. Lawrence claimed that the mission was suggested by British Military Intelligence chief **Clayton** to allay French suspicions of British intentions in the Middle East. By October 1916, the French force included eight machine gun sections, six artillery pieces, and six mountain guns, plus an engineer company and support. Brémond wanted Allied troops landed at **Rabegh** and used throughout the campaign, making the sharif dependent on them in order to forestall Arab independence in **Syria** and **Mesopotamia** after the war. Lawrence disputed this plan, wanting to rely on Arab forces with European advisers, as he explains in chapter 21 of *Seven Pillars of Wisdom.* Brémond

puts the French point of view in his *Le Hedjaz dans le Guerre Mondial* (1931), which argues against Lawrence's interpretation of events at several points while acknowledging his talents. With the departure of Brémond at the end of 1917, **Major Cousse** succeeded him and the tension between the British and French eased somewhat but never entirely. Captain Depui served with the **Emir Abdullah** during the siege of **Medina,** and French officers helped at the sharifian training center at **Mecca.** Lawrence praises the work of **Captain Pisani**'s gun crews at several points in *Seven Pillars of Wisdom.* **Larés,** in his *T. E. Lawrence, la France et les Français* (1980) corrects some of *Seven Pillars of Wisdom*'s statements about Brémond and the French role.

Freud, Sigmund (1856–1939)

Founder of psychoanalysis. In a conversation with **Liddell Hart** in 1934, Lawrence noted the influence of Freud's ideas, and in a letter of 1923 to **Lionel Curtis,** when Lawrence was in the early throes of his flagellation compulsion and had witnessed the talk about sexuality in the Tank Corps barracks at **Bovington,** he seconded Freud's emphasis on the sexual drive as essential to understanding human beings (Garnett, *Letters,* p. 414). *See also* **Sexuality.**

G

Gadara

Site near Um Keis, **Syria,** mentioned in Josephus's *Antiquities of the Jews,* in Mark 5:1, and in Luke 8:26, 37. This was a Hellenic city that flourished in the early centuries B.C.E., producing the poets Philodemus and **Meleager** and the satirist **Menippus,** all of whose work appears in the *Greek Anthology.* In chapter 70 of *Seven Pillars of Wisdom,* Lawrence very favorably mentions the Gadarene school of literature, and particularly the works of Meleager, and in *T. E. Lawrence to His Biographers,* **Robert Graves** recounts that Lawrence wanted to do a translation of the *Anthology.* See Avraham Negev, editor, *The Archaeological Encyclopedia of the Holy Land,* for more information on Gadara.

Galilee

In a long letter of August 2, 1909, to his mother, Lawrence described his travels in **Lebanon** and in what is now northern Israel (*Home Letters,* pp. 90–99). He was enthusiastic about the view from Safed and of the Sea of Galilee from Capernaum, but he compared the present unfavorably with the Roman past and concluded that Jewish settlement was positive because it might restore the country to past glory. In chapter 63 of *Seven Pillars of Wisdom,* he echoes some of these views, referring to what he saw as the cultivated if somewhat corrupt civilization of the Galilee in the time of Jesus, which allowed new thought to flourish.

Gallipoli Campaign

Disastrous British military campaign that lasted from February 1915 to January 1916. **Winston Churchill,** first lord of the Admiralty, boldly planned to break through the Dardanelles with a naval fleet and then to assault the city of Constantinople. But the fleet failed to get through owing to Turkish minefields and other obstacles, and it was decided instead to land British and ANZAC troops on the Gallipoli Peninsula. Here, inept British leadership and strong Turkish resistance under **Gen. Otto Liman von Sanders** and **Mustafa Kemal** produced enormous British and Australian losses until all three Allied beachheads were successfully evacuated on December 7, 1915. In chapter 7 of *Seven Pillars of Wisdom,* Lawrence mentions some of the negative effects of the British failures at Gallipoli and **Kut-al-Amara** on British negotiations with the Arabs. In the wake of the Gallipoli defeat, the British, including Lawrence, considered a landing at **Alexandretta** as a counterthrust against the Turks, but this idea was defeated primarily by the French, who did not want British troops in **Syria** because it might compromise their ability to control the country after the war. See Von Sanders, *Five Years* *in Turkey;* A. Moorehead, *Gallipoli;* and P. Haythornthwaite, *The World War One Source Book.*

Garland, Maj. Herbert G. (died 1921)

Bimbashi or major in the Egyptian army and inventor of the Garland grenade. As an adviser to **Feisal**'s forces, Garland instructed them in machine gunnery and demolition work and took part in demolitions himself. Lawrence praises him highly in chapter 17 of *Seven Pillars of Wisdom,* but **J. M. Wilson** notes that Lawrence was more critical of Garland privately, and also that Lawrence mistakenly writes in chapter 17 that Garland died during the war. Garland was the final director of the **Arab Bureau** and the final editor of the *Arab Bulletin,* the Arab Bureau's secret intelligence newsletter. See *T. E. Lawrence: The Selected Letters,* edited by **M. Brown,** for more information on Garland and Lawrence's view of him.

Garnett, David (1892–1981)

Novelist, publisher, and editor. The son of noted critic **Edward Garnett** and translator Constance Garnett, David was involved with bookselling, the Nonesuch Press, and *The New Statesman,* where he was literary editor from 1932 to 1934. He is perhaps best known for the fictional fantasy *Lady into Fox* (1922), which Lawrence at first criticized and then praised highly. From 1927, they corresponded often and discussed each other's works. David Garnett also is known for his edition (the first) of *The Letters of T. E. Lawrence* (1938) and for *The Essential T. E. Lawrence* (1951). When working on his edition of the letters, he was not allowed access to important correspondence and documents. Despite these obstacles and a scanty index, Garnett's edition of the correspondence has been essential for all students of Lawrence since its publication.

Garnett, Edward (1868–1937)

Literary editor, father of **David Garnett,** and son of **Richard Garnett.** Lawrence met Edward Garnett at **Jonathan Cape**'s office in 1921 and found mutual ground in their admiration for **Charles Doughty**'s *Arabia Deserta,* which Garnett had abridged in 1908. Garnett became one of the first readers of the 1922 "Oxford text" of *Seven Pillars of Wisdom,* and with Lawrence's consent worked on an abridgement of that, which was never published and is now in the **Houghton Library, Harvard.** He was also an early and enthusiastic reader of Lawrence's *The Mint* and a friend.

Garnett, Richard (1835–1906)

Supervisor of the Reading Room, then keeper of printed books at the British Museum (now the **British Library**), man of letters, and father of **Edward Garnett.** Although Richard Garnett wrote poetry and biography, he remains known for beginning the printed catalog at the museum and for his collection of stories, *The Twilight of the Gods and Other Tales* (1924). Lawrence's introduction to this work, written at Edward Garnett's request, is a paean to his own love of the British Museum as well as to the eccentricity of the book itself. Lawrence's introduction is available in Orlans, *Lawrence of Arabia, Strange Man of Letters.*

Gasim

An outlaw from **Maan** who was one of the men under Lawrence's command during the march to **Akaba** in May 1917. When he went missing in the Biseita desert, Lawrence rescued him as recounted in chapter 44 of *Seven Pillars of Wisdom.*

Gaza, Battles of

The town of Gaza is on the Mediterranean coast about 30 miles west of **Beersheba** and had a population of 20,000–30,000 in 1917. It was held by some 18,000 Turkish troops, including small German air, machine gun, and artillery units under the command of German **Col. Freiherr Kress von Kressenstein,** who reported to **Jemal Pasha.** Opposing Kressenstein's men were three British infantry and four cavalry divisions, totaling approximately 36,000 men, under General Dobell, who reported to British Commander-in-Chief **Sir Archibald Murray.** The first battle of Gaza took place on March 25–26, 1917. Dobell's forces attacked under cover of a dense fog and succeeded in holding an important ridge outside of Gaza City by the evening of March 25. The Turks were demoralized and might have surrendered had the British pressed the attack. However, the battle resulted in a British failure when von Kressenstein ordered a successful counter-attack against the ridge the next day. The British withdrew, and their casualties numbered 4,000 against 2,400 Turkish casualties. Murray presented the result to London as a victory and so was allowed to try again. He did so on April 17–19, this time using eight Mark I heavy tanks and some 4,000 gas shells, but Kressenstein's careful defensive system, manned by 18,000 soldiers, defeated British attempts to breach it, and a lack of water forced the British to withdraw. This resulted in the replacement of Dobell by **General Chetwode** and of Murray by **General Allenby.** They succeeded in taking the town on November 6, following a successful attack by 40,000 troops, including cavalry, on October 31 on **Beersheba,** 30 miles to the east, which had been left relatively unprotected owing to a brilliant deception organized by Allenby's intelligence chief **Col. Richard Meinertzhagen.** The Turks were led to believe that the British would attack at Gaza rather than at Beersheba and shifted their strength accordingly. Also, during the attack on Beersheba, Allenby feinted eastward with a raid on Hebron led by **Col. Stewart Newcombe,** leading the Turks to believe that an attack on **Jerusalem** might be imminent. The Turks withdrew from Gaza in order to move toward Jerusalem's defense and the British occupied Gaza on November 6. The Turks were pursued to Huj and then to Jerusalem, and suffered many desertions, with the result that only 15,000 Turkish troops were available to defend a new line south of Jerusalem. In chapter 56 of *Seven Pillars of Wisdom,* Lawrence is highly critical of Murray, even claiming that he lacked the will to win in Gaza; and in chapter 69, he details Allenby's brilliant planning for Beersheba and Gaza, stressing the roles of **Guy Dawnay** and Meinertzhagen. A cemetery in modern Gaza City holds 3,000 **World War I** Commonwealth soldiers' graves. See Pope and Wheal, *The Dictionary of the First World War,* and **A. P. Wavell,** *The Palestine Campaigns.*

Geographical Section of the General Staff, War Office

Until the middle of October 1914, Lawrence and **C. Leonard Woolley** were occupied with finishing writing their *Wilderness of Zin* report on Sinai and Negev antiquities. But toward the end of October, Lawrence started work as a civilian in the Geographical Section in London, whose commander was **Col. Walter Hedley,** who had also been involved with the Zin survey. During this period, he worked on **Stewart Newcombe's** maps of the Sinai desert and also on maps of **Palestine** and **Syria,** which he knew from his 1909 Crusader castle study trip and his **Carchemish** period. He became a temporary 2nd lieutenant–interpreter. According to the testimony of **Sir Ernest Dowson,** the su-

Gen. Edmund Allenby inspects a captured German Albatros aircraft in Palestine in 1918. Courtesy of the Australian War Memorial.

pervisor of his later wartime mapwork in Egypt, Lawrence excelled at Arabic transliteration and local geography but sometimes found it difficult to accept established opinion (*T. E. Lawrence by His Friends,* edited by **A. W. Lawrence**). During this period in London, he read the proofs of the *Wilderness of Zin* survey and wrote a *Military Report on the Sinai Peninsula* before being transferred to **Cairo** in December 1914.

George V, King of England (1865–1936)

Second son of King Edward VII and king of the United Kingdom during and after **World War I.** On October 30, 1918, Lawrence refused to accept a Companion of the Bath for his capture of **Akaba** and a Distinguished Service Order from King George during a private investiture ceremony because he was upset with the way England had acceded to French control over **Syria.** In December of that year, Law-

rence accompanied **Feisal** during an audience with the king. Lawrence later gave the king a copy of the 1926 subscriber's edition of *Seven Pillars of Wisdom.* The king did not hold Lawrence's refusal of honors against him, and upon his death sent a condolence to his family.

Georges-Picot, Charles François (1870–1951)

French diplomat and, with **Mark Sykes,** the author of the **Sykes-Picot Agreement** of 1916 calling for postwar French control of **Syria** and British control of **Mesopotamia** and parts of **Palestine.** Picot had been the French consul general in **Beirut** before November 1914 and came from a well-established French colonial family.

Germans

German assistance to the Turks began long before **World War I** under **Sultan Abdul-Hamid II,** who agreed to the building of the **Berlin–Baghdad Railway** by the Germans. Of the triumvirate that replaced him, however, only **Enver Pasha** was entirely pro-German, and **Jemal Pasha** was actually for the French until he changed his mind at the outbreak of the war. Already in December 1913, however, a German mission under **Gen. Otto Liman von Sanders** began to modernize the Turkish army. Once Germany and Turkey had signed an alliance, the Germans supplied officers, ships, airplanes, artillery, and munitions to the Turkish forces. By 1917, some 800 German officers played key roles in the Turkish command structure: in the **Palestine** theater, **Col. Freiherr Kress von Kressenstein** attacked the **Suez Canal** and dealt the British two defeats at **Gaza,** and **Gen. Erich von Falkenhayn,** earlier chief of staff of the German army, led the **Yilderim** force from July 1917 until he was replaced by Von Sanders in February 1918 after a series of defeats by **General Allenby.** In *Seven Pillars of Wisdom,* Lawrence writes with respect for the German forces that he confronted, especially during the retreat of the Turkish Fourth Army; in chapter 117 he notes their excellent discipline even under attack. Von Sanders' *Five Years in Turkey* (1920; English 1927) gives an account of the eastern war from the German perspective.

Ghassan, Kingdom of

A state (circa fifth–seventh century C.E.) stretching at its height from near **Petra** to Palmyra (today Tadmor, **Syria**). It was originally formed by the Beni Ghassan, a tribe from Yemen who adopted Christianity. Around the time of Justinian the kingdom served as a buffer state for the Byzantine Empire. During the reigns of its greatest kings, including al-Harith ibn-Jabalah (circa 529–69), the splendor of the Ghassanid court was recounted by well-known bards, including Hassan ibn Thabit

of **Medina** who became Muhammed's own poet laureate. Lawrence refers to the glories of Harith and the other Ghassanid kings in chapter 105 of *Seven Pillars of Wisdom,* as he visits the site of their palaces in and around **Azrak.** The kingdom came to end as a result of Arab incursions in the middle of the seventh century C.E. See P. Hitti, *A History of Syria.*

Ghazi ibn Feisal (1912–39)

Son of **Feisal ibn Hussein** and king of Iraq from 1933 to 1939. Ghazi acceded to the throne upon his father's death but died in a car crash only six years later. Despite a brief education at Harrow, he was anti-British and an Arab nationalist but had no influence on the officers who really ran the country after 1936. See Shimoni and Levine, *Political Dictionary of the Middle East,* for a Hussein family tree.

Gill, Colin (1882–1940)

An official war artist and later faculty member at the Royal College of Art, Gill contributed the chalk drawing of **Gen. William H. Bartholemew** that appears in the 1926 subscriber's edition of *Seven Pillars of Wisdom.* See V. M. Thompson, *"Not a Suitable Hobby for an Airman"—T. E. Lawrence as Publisher.*

Gillman, Gen. Webb

Sent by the War Office in **London** in 1916 to investigate the situation in **Mesopotamia,** including the **Kut-al-Amara** siege of the British by the Turks, General Gillman left Mesopotamia in May on the same troopship that carried Lawrence, who was also writing a report on the same problems. Lawrence told **Liddell Hart** that Gillman read Lawrence's report before working on his own. See *T. E. Lawrence to His Biographers Robert Graves & Liddell Hart.*

Gilman, Capt. L. H.

Commander of an armored car unit who worked with Lawrence. He helped build a road through **Wadi Itm** in 1917, for which he is praised in chapter 82 of *Seven Pillars of Wisdom,* and later defended Lawrence against **Aldington**'s allegations, as related in **John Mack**'s *A Prince of Our Disorder.*

Glubb Pasha, Lt. Gen. Sir John Bagot (1897–1986)

British army officer who served in **Iraq** during **World War I,** then in the Iraqi civil service (1926–30), and finally as commander-in-chief of the Transjordian Arab Legion (1938–56). In his *Britain and the Arabs* (1959), he stresses the importance of the **Arab Revolt** to **Allenby**'s campaign.

Golden Cockerel Press

Perhaps the preeminent small press in England from its founding in 1920 by Harold Taylor until its demise in 1960. The press is especially known for its wood engravings by artists such as **Blair Hughes-Stanton** and **Paul Nash,** among others whose work was also included in the 1926 subscriber's edition of Lawrence's *Seven Pillars of Wisdom.* The press posthumously published four of Lawrence's own works, including *Crusader Castles* (1936), *Secret Despatches from Arabia* (1939), *Men in Print* (1940), and *Shaw–Ede, T. E. Lawrence's Letters to H.S. Ede 1927–1935* (1942).

Gorringe, Gen. Sir George (1868–1945)

Commander of a British force sent in April 1916 to relieve **General Townshend,** whose men were surrounded by the Turks at **Kut-al-Amara** in **Mesopotamia.** When this attempt and an attempt to break the Turkish river blockade failed, Lawrence and **Aubrey Herbert** were allowed to try (unsuccessfully) to bribe the Turkish commander, **Khalil Pasha.** After his unsuccessful attempt to rescue Townshend, Gorringe commanded the 47th Territorial Division for the rest of the war. See R. Millar, *Kut: The Death of an Army.*

Goslett, Maj. Raymond

Supply officer at **Wejh** and then **Akaba.** Lawrence praises him in chapter 57 of *Seven Pillars of Wisdom.* After the war he went into business and supplied the bathtub for Lawrence's **Clouds Hill** cottage in 1933.

Gouraud, Gen. Henri Joseph (1867–1946)

As commander of the French Fourth Army, Gouraud played a major role in stopping Ludendorff's Marne offensive in July 1918 by blocking the advance of the German First and Third Armies. From late 1919, he was the commander-in-chief of French forces in **Syria** and based in the coastal region; then, on July 14, 1920, he gave an ultimatum to **Feisal** to accept the French mandate over the whole territory. Feisal accepted the French terms, and the French army moved to occupy **Damascus,** but 2,000 Arabs, acting against Feisal's instructions, tried to stop them at the Meissaloun Pass. On July 24, the one-armed Gouraud's army easily went through, and Feisal was forced to leave the country on July 28. Gouraud became high commissioner in Syria and remained in that capacity until 1923. See **G. Antonius,** *The Arab Awakening;* P. Hitti, *History of Syria;* and **M. Larés,** *T. E. Lawrence, la France et les Français.*

Goytisolo, Juan (born 1931)

Noted Spanish writer of fiction, including *Juan the Landless* (English version 1977), in which Juan daydreams that he is Lawrence.

Gramophone Records

According to Warwick James in **A. W. Lawrence**'s collection *T. E. Lawrence by His Friends,* Lawrence was a dedicated record collector. His Ginn gramophone was the best available, and he took excellent care of it. He kept his records, including the liner notes, meticulously and weeded unsuitable ones. He disliked jazz and was not partial to any kind of vocal music, but had wide-ranging tastes in orchestral and chamber music and was a focussed and considerate listener when in the company of others, including **Royal Air Force** and Tank Corps colleagues. James includes a complete list of the records in **Clouds Hill** at the time of Lawrence's death.

Granville-Barker, Harley (1877–1946)

Actor, playwright, and Shakespeare scholar. As director at the Court Theatre from 1904 to 1907 he helped establish **George Bernard Shaw** as a famous playwright. Lawrence, who probably met him through Shaw, in 1924 gave Granville-Barker the 1922 Oxford text of *Seven Pillars of Wisdom* to read. He himself enjoyed Granville-Barker's play *The Secret Life* (1923).

Graves, Philip Perceval (1876–1953)

Half-brother of **Robert Graves,** London *Times* correspondent in the Middle East before **World War I,** and from January 1915 a member of the **Cairo Military Intelligence Department.** An expert on Turkey, he was responsible for the 1916 edition of the secret *Handbook of the Turkish Army,* to which Lawrence also contributed information. During this period, he probably introduced Lawrence to his brother Robert's poetry, which Lawrence said he had first read in **Egypt** in 1917. He wrote several books about the Middle East, including a biography of **Sir Percy Cox.**

Graves, Robert (1895–1985)

Major twentieth-century historical novelist and poet and author of a classic **World War I** memoir, *Goodbye to All That* (1929). In his essay in **A. W. Lawrence**'s collection *T. E. Lawrence by His Friends* and in *T. E. Lawrence to His Biographers,* Graves explains that he met Lawrence at **All Souls College, Oxford,** in 1920 and then details his long association with Lawrence, including his writing of the biography *Lawrence and the Arabs* (1927) with Lawrence's help (which he made Graves deny). In these works, Graves offers insight into Lawrence's character and informed impressions of Lawrence's literary efforts. Lawrence respected Graves's poetry and offered criticism of it, but he rarely submitted his own work for Graves's comments; Graves did, however, help Lawrence rewrite the *Seven Pillars of Wisdom* dedicatory poem "To S. A." Lawrence lent Graves money early on in the relationship but may have resented Graves's later financial and literary success, as explained in S. E. Tabachnick, "T. E. Lawrence and Robert Graves: A Friendship?" *T. E. Notes* 9:1 (1998): 1–8. See also Harold Orlans, "The Friendship of Lawrence and Graves," *Journal of the T. E. Lawrence Society* (Spring 1995): 50–60.

Great Britain

Lawrence loved the literature, history, culture, and people of Great Britain and served them well; except for his wartime and postwar military and diplomatic service, he never lived anywhere else, nor wanted to. But he had serious reservations about **World War I** and post–World War I British policy in the Middle East, and his appearance at the 1919 **Peace Conference** in **Paris** as **Feisal**'s adviser led to doubts about his British loyalty on the part of some policymakers and writer **Richard Aldington.** In the famous introductory chapter to *Seven Pillars of Wisdom,* he makes it clear that he opposed the peace agreements, which he regarded as having betrayed Feisal to French interests and the native population of **Mesopotamia** to British interests. While in the **Colonial Office** under **Winston Churchill,** he was able to help Britain fulfill its promises to the Arabs in his view by influencing the **Cairo Conference** participants to give Feisal the throne of **Iraq** and to confirm **Abdullah** as ruler of **Transjordan.** In his postwar letters, he evolves the view that the British Empire should move toward a commonwealth of independent states. His postwar service in the **Royal Air Force** as an airman allowed him an outlet for his patriotism; and his value to Great Britain has been testified to in tributes by Churchill and others.

Greece

In December 1910 Lawrence wrote his parents about his brief stop in **Athens** on his way to **Carchemish** in **Syria** (Garnett, *Letters,* pp. 87–90). He did not like the unhygienic condition of the port at Piraeus, but he delightedly saw the Greeks in terms of characters in **Aristophanes**'s plays, enjoyed the Temple of Athena in the Parthenon, and questioned whether his romanticism had distorted his view of Athens. He returned to Athens briefly during the war, but only in 1919 did he manage to tour a bit, seeing the Aegean islands.

Greek Language and Literature

E. F. Hall testifies in **A. W. Lawrence**'s collection *T. E. Lawrence by His Friends* that Lawrence had a copy of the *Odyssey* with him almost always when he was at **Oxford University.** According to Lawrence's letters, by 1912 he was able to read **Meleager** and other poets in the *Greek Anthology* with a dictionary. He read **Aristophanes**'s *Peace* during the Arab campaign and later accomplished one of the finest prose translations of **Homer**'s *Odyssey* (1932), although he complained to **Harley Granville-Barker** in 1932 that his Greek had deteriorated. At that time, he wrote that he could read parts of the works he liked (in addition to those mentioned here, Xenophon's *Anabasis* and the plays of Aeschylus) without a dictionary but could not read unfamiliar works without help. He wrote **C. Day-Lewis** that there was much more worthwhile Greek than Latin literature (Garnett, *Letters,* p. 839). His library at **Clouds Hill** had more than 30 books in the Loeb classical series.

Grey, Sir Edward (1862–1933)

As British foreign secretary (1905–16), Grey proposed reform rather than dismemberment of the Ottoman Empire, and his general policy was one of caution. However, he supported the forced cession of the Sinai Peninsula from **Turkey** to British **Egypt** in 1906, and in 1914 he subsidized

Abdul Aziz el Masri, the founder of the **Al Ahd Society,** dedicated to the overthrow of Turkish rule. Lawrence's opinion of late 1916 that no British troops should be sent to the **Hejaz** pleased Grey, and in June 1916 Grey had advocated taking **Akaba,** an idea that Lawrence eventually carried out with Arab forces. **D. G. Hogarth** was a former schoolmate of Grey's, making it relatively easy for ideas to pass from the **Arab Bureau** to Grey himself. Grey was replaced by Lord Balfour in **Lloyd George**'s government in December 1916. See Pope and Wheal, *The Dictionary of the First World War.*

Grosvenor, Charles (born 1952)

A Hollywood artist, animator, producer, and director by profession, Charles Grosvenor has pursued an interest in Lawrence portraits and sculptures, thus filling a gap in the study of Lawrence. Beautifully designed and produced as well as carefully researched, his *An Iconography: The Portraits of T. E. Lawrence* (which is the second edition of his original study) is a pioneering work on this subject. Grosvenor's article on the design of the 1926 subscriber's edition of *Seven Pillars of Wisdom* in *The T. E. Lawrence Puzzle* (ed. Tabachnick) is perhaps the most acute analysis of that edition's aesthetic triumphs and problems written to date. Grosvenor also has a deep interest in the Alamo and the historic battle that took place there.

Guerrilla Warfare

Lawrence's contribution to this subject has been praised by **Liddell Hart,** who used Lawrence's writings on it as the basis for an article in the *Encyclopaedia Britannica* (14th edition), and by many other authorities, including British **Gen. A. P. Wavell,** British military writer Douglas Orgill, and

German military historian **Konrad Morsey.** Lawrence's influence has been felt around the world, including in the U.S. Army War College and the forces of **Mao Tse-Tung.** Chapter 33 of *Seven Pillars of Wisdom* and his 1920 article **"The Evolution of a Revolt"** provide the best summary of Lawrence's strategic principles, perhaps influenced by some retrospective thinking. In these pieces, Lawrence sees excellent intelligence, hit-and-run raids, and propaganda as the keys to guerrilla warfare; for him, the most successful war would be one in which the enemy was defeated without any fighting at all. **Aldington,** however, doubted that Lawrence read all of the strategists that he claimed to have read in chapter 33, and indeed in *T. E. Lawrence to His Biographers, Robert Graves & Liddell Hart* (p. 2:96) Lawrence seems to indicate that his Oxford tutor, **Reginald Lane Poole,** rather than Lawrence himself, had read these writers. See Konrad Morsey, "T. E. Lawrence, Strategist" in *The T. E. Lawrence Puzzle,* edited by Tabachnick; D. Orgill, *Lawrence;* and G. Gawrych, "T. E. Lawrence and the Art of War in the Twenty-First Century," in *The Waking Dream of T. E. Lawrence,* edited by Stang.

Guilfoyle, Wing Commander W.J.Y. (died 1946)

Lawrence's commanding officer at **Farnborough,** who doubted if Lawrence's value as an airman could compensate for the publicity trouble his presence was causing once it became known.

Guweira

Howeitat trading center, about 25 miles northeast of **Akaba,** in the midst of a beautiful sandy plain. The Turkish garrison here was captured by **Beduin** under **Sheikh ibn Jad,** which helped Lawrence in his attack on Akaba in June 1917 from the north. Guweira then became a base, including an airfield and armored car facility, for the Arab and British forces. It was at Guweira on August 5, 1917, after the capture of Akaba, that Lawrence confronted **Auda abu Tayi** and **Nasir** about their possible double-dealing with the Turks, as related in chapter 57 of *Seven Pillars of Wisdom.*

Guy, R.A.M.

A friend of Lawrence's in the **Royal Air Force** at **Farnborough.** Guy was very handsome and known by the nicknames of "Poppet" or "Rabbit." This has led **Jeffrey Meyers** to speculate on the possibility of a homosexual relationship between Guy and Lawrence, but this has been vigorously denied by **J. M. Wilson.**

H

Hai Tribes

A group of Shiite tribes, fiercely jealous of their independence, about whom Lawrence wrote in his 1916 report on **Mesopotamia** that they would resist any occupying force, including the British. See **J. M. Wilson,** *Lawrence of Arabia,* Appendix III, for the text of Lawrence's report.

Haifa

City in **Palestine** (now Israel), which Lawrence visited during his 1909 summer walking tour of Crusader castles. In Lawrence's time, the city offered an anchorage but no port facilities; it was also the terminus of one branch of the **Hejaz Railway.** In 1915, **Lloyd George** considered the Haifa anchorage a good reason for attaining British control of Palestine, in addition to Palestine's usefulness as a buffer against attacks on the **Suez Canal.** In February 1911 Lawrence again visited the city on his way to the dig in **Carchemish.** Haifa was also the home city of Charles Boutagy, a spy whom Lawrence ran during his years in **Cairo Military Intelligence,** as reported in **Knightley** and **Simpson,** *The Secret Lives of Lawrence of Arabia.* During **World War I,** the city was captured by British forces on September 23, 1918.

Hajim Bey (died 1965)

Chief of police at Izmir (1914–17) and governor of the Hauran region of Ottoman **Syria** from March 1917. In a letter of 1919 to Chief Political Officer **W. F. Stirling** in **Cairo** general headquarters, Lawrence wrote that Hajim was the bey at **Deraa** who assaulted him and had him tortured. In the 1922 Oxford text of *Seven Pillars of Wisdom* he is less definite, saying the bey might have been Hajim, and in the published version for some reason he changed the bey's name to Nahi. **Knightley** and **Simpson,** who have investigated Hajim Bey's character, find that he had a reputation not as a homosexual but as an active heterosexual. **John Mack** found that he had a reputation for brutality, but neither he nor any other biographer has been able to definitively confirm (or deny) Lawrence's account. In the absence of any solid evidence, the issue of whether or not Lawrence was assaulted by Hajim Bey at Deraa rests on Lawrence's testimony alone. After the war, Hajim became the governor of Bursa and was subject to an inquiry for a military failure against the Greek army. A photo of Hajim Bey is available in J. N. Lockman, *Scattered Tracks on the Lawrence Trail* (p. 53).

Hakluyt, Richard (1552–1616)

Geographer, translator, and influential Elizabethan travel writer. Under the pseudonym **Colin Dale,** Lawrence reviewed Hakluyt's three-volume *Principal Navigations, Voyages, Traffiques and Discoveries of the English Nation* (1589) in the *Spectator* (September 10, 1927), at the request of its literary editor, **Francis Yeats-Brown.** In "Hakluyt—First Naval Propagandist," Lawrence finds that Hakluyt wanted to make a point rather than to write artistically, with the result that his work is boring.

Halim

With **Faris,** one of Lawrence's two bodyguards during the scouting trip of November 1917 that resulted in his capture and torture by the Turks at **Deraa,** as related in chapter 80 of *Seven Pillars of Wisdom.* Sheikh Tallal was a third companion on that trip.

Hall, Canon E. F. (born 1888)

Lawrence's friend at **City of Oxford High School** and **Jesus College, Oxford.** His memoir in **A. W. Lawrence**'s collection *T. E. Lawrence by His Friends* contains some of the most famous anecdotes about Lawrence's youthful escapades, including his firing a pistol with blanks into the Turl (a street in Oxford) from Hall's rooms and his taking an exploratory canoe trip through a sewer in Oxford with Hall as a companion.

Hall, M. Radclyffe (1866–1943)

Popular novelist. In letters of 1928 to **Charlotte Shaw** and **E. M. Forster,** Lawrence defended her right, which was under attack by the British government, to write about lesbian themes in her novel *The Well of Loneliness* (1928). However, he found the novel itself boring.

Hallsmith, Janet

See **Laurie, Janet**

Hama, Syria

Town and province of northern **Syria,** mentioned in Lawrence's 1915 intelligence report to his chief, **Gilbert Clayton.** The report, "Syria. The Raw Material," appeared in the *Arab Bulletin* (March 12, 1917). Lawrence includes Hama (with Damascus, **Homs, and Aleppo**) among the four oldest cities of Syria and emphasizes its productivity and its local character. He repeats these remarks in chapter 59 of *Seven Pillars of Wisdom.*

Hamd, Wadi

A dry riverbed about a mile wide beginning on the **Red Sea** coast about 50 miles below **Wejh** and extending to **Medina,** about 300 miles to the southeast. **Feisal**'s army crossed this wadi in January 1917 on the way to its belated arrival at Wejh, as described in chapter 26 of *Seven Pillars of Wisdom.* The British navy and its landing parties, including Arab forces under **Major Vickery,** had already driven the Turks out of the town.

Hamed the Moor

As related in chapter 31 of *Seven Pillars of Wisdom,* on March 12, 1917, Hamed, a Moroccan member of Lawrence's force, killed an **Ageyl** mercenary. To prevent a blood feud, Lawrence had to carry out Hamed's execution himself, and this incident continued to haunt him, as in the bad dream he recounts in chapter 32.

Hamoudi ibn Sheikh Ibrahim el Awassi, Sheikh (circa 1880–circa 1950)

Born at **Jerablus, Syria,** the site of the **Carchemish** excavation in which Lawrence participated, Hamoudi was the *hoja,* or foreman, at the dig from 1911 to 1914. Lawrence hosted him and **Dahoum** in Oxford in July 1913, reciprocating for the many acts of kindness that Hamoudi had shown him in Syria. In an interview with **E.H.R. Altounyan** included in **A. W. Lawrence**'s *T. E. Lawrence by His Friends,* Hamoudi presented a heroic view of Lawrence, even as a young man before the war. From 1922 to 1934, he worked for **C. Leonard Woolley** at Ur and then at Souedia, Syria.

Hamra

Arabian village of about 100 dwellings in Lawrence's time, about 70 miles southwest of **Medina.** Lawrence met **Feisal** at his camp here for the first time in October 1916 during his mission to the **Hejaz,** as reported in chapter 12 of *Seven Pillars of Wisdom.*

Handbook of the Turkish Army 1916

A detailed guide to the Turkish army, covering topics such as conditions of service, administration, organization, and all branches of service. There are detailed chapters, too, on manufacturing establishments and defenses and sections on military law, rates of pay and decorations, and even a glossary of military terms. The estimate of 480,000 men under arms in October 1914 seems accurate; a recent estimate of the Turkish army at its peak during the war counts 650,000 men. Although no author appears in the book, according to **Liddell Hart,** it was compiled by **Philip Graves** and Lawrence, who both interrogated Turkish prisoners to glean information for the book. Lawrence was responsible for the printing of some of the several editions of the book. In 1996 it was reprinted by the **Imperial War Museum** and the Battery Press in Nashville, Tennessee.

Hankey, Maurice P. A., 1st Baron (1877–1963)

Assistant secretary to the Committee for Imperial Defence and then secretary of the War Cabinet. Lawrence told **Liddell Hart** that he admired Hankey, who held some of the most powerful positions in the British government during **World War I,** for being able to be interesting without giving away secrets. Hankey authored several books, including *The Supreme Command 1914–18* (1961).

Hanley, James (1901–85)

Irish-born seaman and brutally naturalistic author of *Drift* (1930), *Men in Darkness* (1931), and *An End and a Beginning* (1958), among other works. Lawrence liked his work, particularly *Boy* (1931), which he read in a draft. He offered C. J. Greenwood, an editor at Boriswood, which published the novel, his advice when the book was charged with indecency. He also gave his permission for a quotation from a letter of his to Hanley to be used on the jacket of *Boy.*

Harb Tribe

Beduins of the **Nejd** region of Arabia.

Hardinge, Charles, 1st Baron Hardinge of Penshurst (1858–1944)

As viceroy of **India** (1910–16), Hardinge in 1915 vigorously opposed the attempts of the British authorities in **Cairo** to support Arab nationalism in Arabia. In 1918, Hardinge agreed that Lawrence should be permitted to attend the 1919 **Peace Conference** in **Paris** as an adviser to the British, but he was then dismayed because Lawrence did not subordinate himself to British policy and officials there and instead represented **Feisal**'s claim to **Syria.**

Hardinge, HMS

A former Royal India Mail steamship that was armed and used as a transport in the British **Red Sea** fleet. Lawrence traveled from **Egypt** to **Akaba** on the *Hardinge* to persuade **Auda** not to go over to the Turks, as related in chapter 57 of *Seven Pillars of Wisdom.*

Hardy, Florence Emily (1879–1937)

Writer **Thomas Hardy**'s second wife. **Robert Graves** gave Lawrence an introduction to the Hardys, and during 1923 he became a regular visitor at Max Gate, their home. He wrote several letters to Mrs. Hardy, and in 1925 she asked if Lawrence was interested in editing her husband's diary. In 1923 Lawrence arranged to have **Augustus John** paint Hardy's portrait, delighting Florence, and in a moving letter of January 15, 1928 (Garnett, *Letters,* p. 564), he consoled her concerning Hardy's death.

Hardy, Thomas (1840–1928)

Great British novelist and poet of rural England. Lawrence held Hardy in the highest esteem, visited him frequently in the 1920s after having received a letter of introduction from **Robert Graves,** and had many of Hardy's books in his **Clouds Hill** library, including *Tess of the D'Urbervilles*

(1891), *Jude the Obscure* (1896), and his poems. He especially liked Hardy's *Dynasts* (1908), a poetic drama of the Napoleonic wars. It was therefore a great honor for Lawrence when he was able to report in a letter to **D. G. Hogarth** that Hardy had praised *Seven Pillars of Wisdom* highly (Garnett, *Letters,* p. 429).

Harry Ransom Humanities Research Center

This rare books library, part of the University of Texas at Austin, is a prime repository of published and unpublished Lawrence material, including hundreds of letters, a 1926 subscriber's edition of *Seven Pillars of Wisdom* (only approximately 200 were printed), and a rare first American copyright edition of *The Mint.* A listing of the library's Lawrence holdings is accessible through its online catalog and that of the University of Texas library.

Hashemites

Name of the dynasty of the sharifs of **Mecca,** who ruled the city and the surrounding area from the tenth century. This name indicates the Banu Hashem, the family of the Qureish tribe from which the Prophet Muhammad himself descended. As Lawrence explains in chapter 5 of *Seven Pillars of Wisdom,* the title sharif signifies descent from Mohammed himself through his daughter Fatima and her oldest son Hassan. In the twentieth century, prominent members of the family included **Sharif Hussein ibn Ali** and his sons **Ali, Abdullah, Feisal,** and **Zeid,** who began and led the **Arab Revolt.** See Shimoni and Levine, *Political Dictionary of the Middle East in the Twentieth Century,* for a family tree (p. 153).

Hauran

A large lava plateau, about 60 miles square, in central and southern **Syria.** While lacking in trees and water, it is good pasture and wheat land and includes many Roman and Byzantine ruins. As a Turkish district, it extended far beyond the plateau region. The nearest oasis was **Azrak,** one of Lawrence's favorite places. As the **Arab Revolt** moved north, Lawrence added three peasants from this area—Rahail, Assaf, and Hemeid—to his force so he could learn about it from them. The **Yarmuk Valley Bridges,** by way of which the **Hejaz Railway** ascended to the Hauran region, were prime targets for Lawrence, as was the city of **Deraa,** an important railway junction in the Hauran itself.

Hedley, Col. Sir Walter Coote (1865–1937)

Member of the council of the Royal Geographical Society, the committee of the **Palestine Exploration Fund,** and head, **Geographical Section, General Staff.** He was a friend of **D. G. Hogarth** and Lawrence's supervisor during his three months in **London** before Lawrence was sent to the Middle East at the end of 1914 upon Hedley's recommendation.

Hejaz

Red Sea coastal and inland area, including **Mecca** and **Medina,** of Arabia; its name means "borderland." The **Arab Revolt** extended its influence northward through all the cities along the 600-mile Hejaz coast, including **Jidda, Rabegh, Yenbo,** and **Wejh.**

Hejaz Railway

A 900-mile railway, planned by Izzat Pasha el Abd with the consent of Turkish **Sultan Abdul-Hamid II,** financed in large part by donations from the Muslim world, and constructed by German engineers under Meissner Pasha from 1901 to 1908. It extended from Damascus to **Medina** with 21 strongly built stations and watering stops inbetween. From Damascus northward, it joined the **Berlin–Baghdad Railway** line just above **Aleppo.** As **Antonius** points out in *The Arab Awakening,* a journey from Damascus to Medina that took 40 days by caravan or 10–15 days with the aid of ships now took five days. The line was not extended to **Mecca,** 250 miles farther south, because the local Arabs wanted to collect road pilgrimage tolls; the Arabs also opposed it because it enhanced Turkish control of the **Hejaz.** The railroad was inaugurated on September 1, 1908, and in the same year, **Hussein** was appointed sharif of Mecca. During the war, the Turks guarded the railway with station garrisons totaling perhaps 5,000 men, but between stations the tracks offered an easy target for Lawrence's demolitions, which are described in colorful detail in many chapters of *Seven Pillars of Wisdom.* In chapter 33, he states that his strategy was to keep the railroad barely operational, as a drain on Turkish resources. As Matthew Hughes points out in *Allenby and British Strategy in the Middle East, 1917–1919,* in fact the Turks were able to keep the line operating throughout the war despite these attacks (p. 78). See W. Ochsenwald, *The Hijaz Railroad.*

Hemingway, Ernest (1898–1961)

Very important American novelist whose books Lawrence had in his **Clouds Hill** library and who (according to scholar Joel Hodson in his *Lawrence of Arabia and American Culture*) was influenced by Lawrence and *Seven Pillars of Wisdom* in constructing his hero, Robert Jordan, of *For Whom the Bell Tolls* (1940).

Herbert, Aubrey N.H.M. (1880–1923)

Son of Egyptologist Lord Carnarvon, member of parliament, and expert on the Ottomans who served with Lawrence in the **Cairo Military Intelligence Department** from 1915. Herbert was sent with Lawrence on their failed mission of April 1916 to bribe **Khalil Pasha,** whose army surrounded **General Townshend**'s expeditionary force at **Kut-al-Amara.** Herbert is the author of the classic travel book *Ben Kendim* (1924), about which Lawrence offered some suggestions, as well as *Mons, Kut and Anzac* (1919), a book Lawrence recommended to **Robert Graves.**

Hermes, Gertrude (1901–83)

Wood engraver and sculptor, wife of **Blair Hughes-Stanton.** Hermes supplied the woodcut *High Explosive* for the 1926 subscriber's edition of *Seven Pillars of Wisdom.* See **J. M. Wilson,** *T. E. Lawrence* (p. 170), for a reproduction of this engraving.

Hesa, Wadi

Dry riverbed running east to west about five miles north of **Tafileh,** in west-central Jordan. After Lawrence's defeat of **Fakhri Pasha** at Tafileh on January 25, 1918, the Arabs pursued the Turks through Wadi Hesa, as related in chapter 86 of *Seven Pillars of Wisdom,* but the exact facts of this battle remain unclear, for Lawrence admitted in that chapter that his official report was not accurate.

Hesa Station

A station on the **Hejaz Railway,** about 50 miles above **Maan,** in what is now Jordan.

On May 23, 1918, this station was taken by an Arab force under **Sharif Nasir,** with the demolition assistance of **Capt. H. S. Hornby** and **Maj. F. G. Peake,** as described in chapter 96 of *Seven Pillars of Wisdom.*

Hira

Capital of the Lakhmid kingdom, a buffer state (circa third–seventh century C.E.) in **Syria** guarding the border of the Persian Empire during the fifth–sixth centuries C.E. The pro-Persian Lakhmid kings were rivals of the pro-Byzantium kings of **Ghassan,** who in 580 C.E. burned Hira. In 602, the Lakhmid kingdom was destroyed by a Persian king, who in so doing opened his own borders to Arab incursions from the desert. Lawrence mentions Hira positively in chapter 75 of *Seven Pillars of Wisdom.*

Hirtzel, Sir Arthur (1870–1937)

Secretary of the Political Department of the **India Office,** who, like most of his colleagues, opposed the **Arab Bureau**'s pro-**Hashemite** policy in both **Syria** and **Mesopotamia.** He therefore also opposed Lawrence's appointment as adviser at the 1919 **Peace Conference** in **Paris** and looked askance at his role in the **Royal Air Force** in **India** in the late 1920s.

Hittites and Neo-Hittites

The Hittites ruled much of the Middle East from the fourteenth century B.C.E. to the mid-twelfth century B.C.E., when their empire fell. From 1000 B.C.E. to 800 B.C.E., they were replaced by the Neo-Hittites, a group of many peoples. The Hittites are mentioned in the Bible at several points;

Uriah, the husband of Bathsheba, was a Hittite, and Solomon sold the Hittites chariots. The viceregal city of the Hittites, and then the capital of the Neo-Hittites, was **Carchemish,** near **Jerablus, Syria.** During his work at Carchemish from 1910 to 1914, Lawrence catalogued and photographed discoveries, made some discoveries himself, and helped solve mechanical problems. This dig set the course for all future British study of the Hittites. Along with **Hogarth, Woolley,** and P.L.O. Guy, Lawrence is listed as one of the authors of the report *Carchemish: Report on the Excavations at Djerabis on Behalf of the British Museum* (1914, 1921, 1952). In a letter of 1912 to **Mrs. André Rieder,** Lawrence places Hittite sculpture above Egyptian and most Greek sculpture of comparable periods, and he was clearly impressed with the Carchemish finds. See O. R. Gurney, *The Hittites,* and J. Garstang, *The Hittite Empire.*

Left to right: Lawrence, his mentor Comdr. D. G. Hogarth, and Col. Alan Dawnay. Photograph at Cairo Headquarters, 1918, by Harry Chase. Courtesy of Corbis.

Hoare, Sir Samuel (Samuel John Gurney Hoare, 1st Viscount Templewood) (1880–1959)

British statesman, variously secretary of state for **India,** foreign secretary, home secretary, and special ambassador to Spain. As secretary of state for air (1922–24, 1924–29, 1940) Hoare in January 1923 approved the discharge of Lawrence, who was serving in the **Royal Air Force** under the name of Ross, when his presence attracted publicity and Lawrence's officers complained. During a dinner with Lawrence on January 27, Hoare turned down Lawrence's appeal for reinstatement. He was overruled in 1925 owing to the intervention of **John Buchan,** who influenced **Prime Minister Stanley Baldwin,** and Lawrence was permitted to rejoin. Hoare was the author of *A Flying Trip to the Middle East* (1925) and other books.

Hogarth, Comdr. Dr. David George (1862–1927)

Keeper of the **Ashmolean Museum** (1908–27), supervisor of the **Carchemish** dig (1911–14), deputy director of the **Arab Bureau** (from 1916), and friend and mentor to Lawrence from their first meeting at the Ashmolean in January 1909. Hogarth is credited with having turned Lawrence's attention toward the Middle East and of having sponsored him throughout his career. **Knightley** and **Simpson** have claimed that Hogarth worked for intelligence before the war and that the Carchemish dig was only a cover for organized spying activities, but these claims have not been substantiated by later research. Lawrence related to Hogarth as a father figure, often turning to him for advice and guidance. He respected Hogarth's work, which (in addition to joint authorship of a report on the excavation at Carchemish and several other books) includes the historical volume *The Penetration of Arabia* (1904), the wartime intelligence compilation *Handbook to Arabia* (1916–17), the travel book *A Wandering Scholar in the Levant* (1925), and *The Life of Charles M. Doughty* (1928). Lawrence has left an admiring view of Hogarth's Arab Bureau activities in chapter 6 of *Seven Pillars of Wisdom.* Hogarth encouraged Lawrence to rewrite *Seven Pillars of Wisdom* after the first manuscript was lost, and he helped Lawrence plan for the 1926 subscriber's edition of the book. A. H. Sayce has written a brief biography, *David George Hogarth, 1862–1927. See also* **Seven Pillars of Wisdom, Texts of.**

Holdich, Col. Thomas

Chief of the British Intelligence Department at Ismailia, **Egypt,** which was in rivalry with **Cairo Military Intelligence** under **Gilbert Clayton.** Lawrence told **Liddell Hart** that Holdich was good at operations but not intelligence. Holdich won the rivalry, and in September 1916 Clayton was deprived of some of his military intelligence role and continued to direct the **Arab Bureau.** By deliberately irritating Holdich and his staff, Lawrence got himself transferred from their control to the Arab Bureau and continued to work with Clayton, whom he respected, as related in chapter 7 of *Seven Pillars of Wisdom.* See *T. E. Lawrence to His Biographers Robert Graves & Liddell Hart* (p. 2:92) and Y. Sheffy, *British Military Intelligence in the Palestine Campaign, 1914–1918.*

Homer

Ancient Greek author of *The Iliad* and *The Odyssey.* Lawrence greatly respected Homer as the poet of *The Iliad,* but he found *The Odyssey* a much weaker work stylistically and in terms of characterization,

and in his preface to his *Odyssey* translation Lawrence wonders if the same man could have written both works. He sees the Homer of *The Odyssey* as a middle-aged bookworm lacking authentic knowledge of battles and seafaring. See M. Cohen's and Stephanie Nelson's essays in Charles Stang, editor, *The Waking Dream of T. E. Lawrence,* and James A. Notopoulos, "The Tragic and the Epic in T. E. Lawrence," *Yale Review* 54:3 (spring 1965): 331–45.

Homosexuality

See **Sexuality**

Homs, Syria

City in west-central **Syria,** once called Emesa, that was renamed when the Arabs conquered it in 636 C.E. This was one of the four important ancient cities of Syria (Damascus, **Hama,** and **Aleppo** were the others), according to Lawrence in chapter 59 of *Seven Pillars of Wisdom* and in his 1915 intelligence report, "Syria. The Raw Material," that was published in the *Arab Bulletin* (March 12, 1917). He further states that Homs produced cotton and wool and was a rival of Hama, but like it, was provincial rather than cosmopolitan in culture.

Hornby, Charles Harry St. John (1867–1946)

Director of the bindery W. H. Smith and from 1894 owner-operator of the Ashendene Press, the beauty of whose publications Lawrence greatly admired. In 1924 he asked Hornby for a critique of the proposed typography of *Seven Pillars of Wisdom.*

Hornby, Capt. H. S.

A British military adviser to the Arabs and specialist in demolitions who worked with

Col. Stewart Newcombe. In chapter 41 of *Seven Pillars of Wisdom,* Lawrence states that the Arabs believed that Hornby bit the **Hejaz Railway** rails when he was unable to blow them up. He took part in the demolitions of **Hesa** and **Faraifra** stations, among other actions.

Horses

Lawrence preferred **camels** to horses, but during the **Arab Revolt** he sometimes rode a blood mare, as he states in chapter 46 of *Seven Pillars of Wisdom.* Moreover, like **Feisal** and **Nuri el Said,** Lawrence became an honorary member of the Arab Horse Society in 1919 and remained one until 1930. It is rumored that the Beduin gave Lawrence a mare as a present; in such cases, the animal is left with the tribe, and the owner also owns any offspring. Thus Lawrence may have owned a horse (or horses) without ever possessing it.

Houghton Library, Harvard University

Harvard's rare books library and one of the most important repositories of Lawrence materials. The collection, partially based on the private collection of Bayard Kilgore, Jr., includes three 1926 subscriber's editions (out of approximately 200 that Lawrence had printed) of *Seven Pillars of Wisdom* and two 1922 Oxford texts of *Seven Pillars of Wisdom* (out of only eight printed). A listing of the items in the collection may be viewed by accessing Hollis, the Harvard University Library's online catalog. *See also* **Seven Pillars of Wisdom, Texts of.**

House, Col. Edward Mandell (1858–1938)

President Wilson's emissary to the **Peace Conference** in **Paris.** On March 29, 1919,

House met with **Feisal,** who approved the idea of the **King-Crane Commission,** which would visit **Syria** in June and July in an attempt to determine the wishes of the native population about self-government. Lawrence acted as interpreter during the March meeting, and a transcript of the conversation can be found in **David Garnett'**s edition of the *Letters* (p. 275).

Howard, George Wren (1893–1968)

Partner of **Jonathan Cape,** responsible for the production and publicity of Lawrence's *Revolt in the Desert.*

Howard, Leslie (1893–1943)

Actor. In 1934, Lawrence wittily proposed that, since Leslie Howard was so unlike him, Howard should play him in **Alexander Korda'**s projected film, which was never made.

Howe, Irving (1920–93)

American literary critic, man of letters, and author of an influential 1962 *Hudson Review* article, "T. E. Lawrence: The Problem of Heroism" (15:3, pp. 333–64), that portrayed Lawrence as "a prince of our disorder." This phrase was adopted by **John Mack** for the title of his biography.

Howeitat Tribe

An important **Beduin** tribe of what is now southern Jordan, extending from around **Akaba** to the surroundings of **Maan. Auda abu Tayi** was the sheikh of the Maan area branch of the tribe. The Howeitat played a major part in the capture of Akaba, as related in chapter 53 of *Seven Pillars of Wisdom.*

Hudd, Walter (1897–1963)

British actor who played the Lawrence figure, Pvt. Napoleon Trotsky Meek, in **George Bernard Shaw**'s *Too True to Be Good* when the play opened in 1932. Lawrence later wrote **Robin Buxton** that Hudd had been superb in the role. As **Stanley Weintraub** notes in *Private Shaw and Public Shaw,* Lawrence personally congratulated Hudd on his performance, and Hudd was impressed by Lawrence's relaxed manner.

Hudson, William Henry (1841–1922)

British novelist, naturalist, and travel writer. Born in Argentina of American parents, Hudson immigrated to England in 1869. Lawrence was a great admirer of Hudson's style, and Hudson influenced Lawrence's romantic nature writing in *Seven Pillars of Wisdom.* Lawrence's **Clouds Hill** library had many of Hudson's works, particularly those he loved, such as *Idle Days in Patagonia* (1893), *The Purple Land* (1895), and *Green Mansions* (1904). See S. E. Tabachnick, *T. E. Lawrence* (pp. 22–26) for Hudson's influence on Lawrence's writing.

Hughes-Stanton, Blair (1902–81)

Painter and woodcutter, husband of sculptor **Gertrude Hermes.** Hughes-Stanton contributed 11 metaphysically oriented woodcuts to the 1926 subscriber's edition of *Seven Pillars of Wisdom,* some of which depict Lawrence as the puppet of a higher power. See **J. M. Wilson,** *T. E. Lawrence* (pp. 172–74), for reproductions of these woodcuts, and **Charles Grosvenor,** "The Subscribers' *Seven Pillars of Wisdom*" in *The T. E. Lawrence Puzzle,* edited by Tabachnick, for a discussion of their import.

Humber, HMS

British light river or coastal defense warship commanded by Captain Snagge and stationed at **Akaba** in August 1917 as a guardship and to bolster Arab morale. In chapter 60 of *Seven Pillars of Wisdom,* Lawrence relates how this ship, luxuriously appointed originally for use in Brazil, served him as a much-needed resthouse. **J. M. Wilson**'s *T. E. Lawrence* has Lawrence's photo of this ship (p. 90).

Huntington Library

This elegant rare books library, on the former estate of railroad magnate Henry E. Huntington, houses many items from the **Edwards Metcalf** collection of Lawrence materials. It includes several 1926 subscriber's editions (only approximately 200 were printed) of *Seven Pillars of Wisdom.* A listing of the items in the collection is available by means of the Huntington Library online catalog. *See also* **Seven Pillars of Wisdom, Texts of.**

Hussein ibn Ali el Aun, Sharif (circa 1854–1931)

Claimed descendant of Mohammed's daughter, guardian of **Mecca** and **Medina,** and instigator of the **Arab Revolt.** Hussein, with his sons **Ali, Abdullah, Feisal,** and **Zeid,** was kept in custody in Constantinople by **Sultan Abdul-Hamid II** for 18 years, until the advent in 1908 of the **Young Turks,** who allowed him to return to the **Hejaz** and assume the title of sharif of Mecca. When **World War I** began in 1914, he refused the Turks' request to declare a holy war, or jihad, and instead entertained the entreaty of the Syrian secret societies **Al Fatat** and **Al Ahd** to declare independence from the Turks. Through Abdullah he contacted **Kitchener** in **Egypt** in 1914. The famous **McMahon-Hussein**

Correspondence, about how the spoils of war would be divided between the British and the Arabs in the event of victory, was conducted from October 1915 to March 1916. At the same time, Hussein was negotiating with an Ottoman government that he continued to fear would replace or assassinate him. Britain very much wanted the sharif on its side, to nullify a possible Turkish call for jihad. When he received word from **Sir Henry McMahon,** the British high commissioner in Egypt (1914–16), that British support would be forthcoming, Hussein on June 5, 1916, declared the Arabs' independence from the Turks, and on June 10 his forces ousted the Turks from Mecca. Lawrence describes this history in chapter 5 of *Seven Pillars of Wisdom.* In October 1916, Hussein proclaimed himself king of Hejaz but let his sons command his armies. During the war Hussein was difficult to deal with but was even more so when the war was over. Lawrence as a member of the **Colonial Office** tried for two months in 1921 to get Hussein to accept the British position in **Palestine** and **Iraq** but without success, although Hussein was receiving a British subsidy and was also offered British protection against his rival **Ibn Saud.** In March 1924, he proclaimed himself caliph, but by October Ibn Saud had captured Mecca, forcing Hussein (and his son Ali, who had succeeded him) into exile in Cyprus and **Transjordan,** where he died. See **George Antonius,** *The Arab Awakening,* and Randall Baker, *King Husain and the Kingdom of Hejaz,* for more information.

Hussein ibn Mubeirig, Sheikh

Chief of the **Beduin Masruh Harb** tribe, which lived near the **Hejaz** port of **Rabegh.** A rival of **Sharif Hussein,** he became pro-Turkish, threatening the sharif's supplies and forces through late 1916.

Hythe

Site near Southampton of the **British Power Boat Company** shipyard, where Lawrence was posted off and on from 1931 to 1935 during the last phase of his **Royal Air Force** career. Here in early 1931 Lawrence met **Hubert Scott-Paine,** the company's founder, and learned how to handle and maintain the fast new 37½-foot seaplane tender that Scott-Paine had developed. He also developed a manual for the care of this fast rescue boat.

I

Ibn Bani

Swordsmith of the **Ibn Rashid** dynasty in Hail, northern Arabia. In chapter 46 of *Seven Pillars of Wisdom,* Lawrence says that he was the most highly reputed member of his profession in Lawrence's time.

Ibn Bani, Sheikh

Leader of the **Serahin** tribe who gathered with other leaders of the Arab forces in September 1918 at **Azrak** in preparation for the final push northward toward Damascus, as related in chapter 107 of *Seven Pillars of Wisdom.*

Ibn Dakhil, Sheikh

An **Ageyl** sheikh, Ibn Dakhil went from supporting the Turks to joining the **Arab Revolt.** He and his men took part in January 1917 in the march on **Wejh,** which is colorfully described in chapter 24 of *Seven Pillars of Wisdom.* When the Arab forces arrived at Wejh itself, the Ageyl rebelled against the severity of Ibn Dakhil and he resigned his position.

Ibn Dgeithir, Sheikh

Sheikh of the **Ageyl Beduin** who took part in the march on **Akaba** in May–July 1917. In chapter 39 of *Seven Pillars of Wisdom,*

Lawrence describes him as detached and self-sufficient.

Ibn Jad, Sheikh

Sheikh who captured the Turkish garrison at **Guweira** after deciding that the sharifian forces were stronger than the Turks'; at Lawrence's urging, he then (as recounted in chapter 54 of *Seven Pillars of Wisdom*) captured the Turkish post at Kathira with no resistance because the Turks were afraid of a lunar eclipse, which Lawrence had correctly foreseen from his diary, and were superstitiously trying to end it by making noise, thus neglecting their military duties.

Ibn Rashid, House of

Dynasty of the Shammar tribe of northern **Nejd,** based in Hail. In *Travels in Arabia Deserta,* **Doughty** discusses Mohammed ibn Rashid, a powerful ruler during the late nineteenth century who began to understand the usefulness of oil, and his rivalry with the **Ibn Saud** dynasty based in Riyadh. In 1890–91, Ibn Rashid forced the Saudis into exile, but early in the twentieth century Abdul Aziz ibn Saud recaptured Riyadh. The Rashids remained loyal to the Turks, while Ibn Saud was a British ally. In 1921, he succeeded in forcing the Ibn Rashids to surrender all power and influence. See Shimoni and Levine, *Political*

Dictionary of the Middle East in the Twentieth Century.

Ibn Saud, House of

Wahabi, or purist Sunni Muslim rulers of southern **Nejd,** based in Riyadh. Their rivals were the house of **Ibn Rashid** in Hail in the nineteenth and early twentieth centuries and **Sharif Hussein** in the **post–World War I** period. Their leading representative was Abdul Aziz ibn Saud (1880–1953), otherwise known simply as Ibn Saud, who conquered the pro-Turkish Ibn Rashids in 1921 and the pro-British Husseins in 1924–25. He was sent into exile by the Turks when a child but was restored by a revolt of **Beduins** in 1902. He expanded his kingdom in 1913 when he conquered a gulf province, el Hasa. He looked on Sharif Hussein of **Mecca** as a heretic and was against both British and Turkish rule in Arabia, but he allied himself with the British from 1916 as a tactical move and accepted British assistance to defeat the pro-Turkish confederacy of Shammar tribes. In 1926, he proclaimed himself king of **Hejaz,** Nejd, and its dependencies, and in 1927 the British, who had prevented him from expanding into **Iraq** and **Transjordan,** recognized his independence. He also conquered the Asir region, south of the Hejaz, in the 1920s and in the 1950s became immensely wealthy owing to development of oil reserves by the Aramco company. His family, based on his 40-odd sons, continues to rule Saudi Arabia, which was largely his creation. In 1919, when Lawrence was on his way to **Cairo,** his plane crashed in **Rome,** preventing him from aiding Sharif Hussein's forces against the incursions of Ibn Saud. To **Robert Graves** much later, however, Lawrence indicated that he personally approved of Ibn Saud's rule. During the war, Lawrence and the **Arab Bureau** preferred Sharif Hussein to Ibn Saud because the sharif's religious influence was much broader than Ibn Saud's. As **Hogarth** later commented, this was an expedient war-time policy and the Arab Bureau was not looking beyond the war in making it. See Gary Troeller, "Ibn Saud and Sharif Hussein: A Comparison in Importance in the Early Years of the First World War," *History Journal* 14 (September 1971): 627–33; H. St. John Philby, *Sa'udi Arabia* and *Arabia of the Wahhabis;* D. Howarth, *The Desert King: Ibn Saud and His Arabia;* Pope and Wheal, *The Dictionary of the First World War.*

Ibn Wardan, Palace of

A ruined palace 35 miles northwest of **Hama, Syria,** built by Byzantine Emperor Justinian, which Lawrence visited with **Dahoum** in the summer of 1912. It appears in chapter 3 of *Seven Pillars of Wisdom* as the place where Dahoum taught Lawrence that the best smell in the world was not the supposed perfumes embedded in the walls of the palace, but the wind of the desert. For a description of the site, see R. Burns, *Monuments of Syria* (pp. 201–2).

Idrisi, The (Sayid Mohammed ibn Ali) (1876–1923)

In the middle of the nineteenth century, Sayid Ahmed al Idris, a north African, became a Sufi religious and political leader in the Asir region (between **Yemen** and the **Hejaz**) of Arabia after settling there in 1830. He claimed descent from the fourth caliph, Ali ibn Abi Talib, and was influenced by the **Wahabi,** or purist strain of Sunni **Islam.** His great-grandson Sayid Mohammed set up a state in the Asir that lasted from 1906 to 1934, when **Ibn Saud** annexed it to Saudi Arabia. In 1912–13, **Feisal** took part in warfare against the Id-

A unit of the Imperial Camel Corps above Ain Sir, Transjordan, in early 1918. Photo by Capt. Arthur Rhodes. Courtesy of the Palestine Exploration Fund.

risi state. In 1915, Lawrence felt that Sayid Mohammed would be a powerful ally (Garnett, *Letters,* p. 196) because he was attacking the pro-Turkish Imam Yahya of **Yemen,** but since he was a rival of **Sharif Hussein** the British decided not to risk alienating the sharif by cultivating Sayid Mohammed, much to Lawrence's disappointment. In 1918, however, Lawrence predicted in a report to the British Cabinet (reprinted in Garnett's *Letters,* pp. 265–69) that the Idrisi would fall because of his attempt to incorporate African fetishism into Islam. See Anne K. Bang, *The Idrisi State in Asir, 1906–1934,* and D. Nicolle and R. Hook, *Lawrence and the Arab Revolts.*

Imperial Camel Corps Brigade

In January 1916, **Gen. Archibald Murray,** commander-in-chief of the Egyptian army, formed some camel companies, and on December 19 these companies became the basis of the ICC Brigade under the command of Brig. Gen. C. L. Smith. It included 18 companies composed of Australian, British, and New Zealand troops, with some Indian army gunners. Troops were trained for about six weeks at a riding school near **Cairo,** and they used excellent Sudanese camels. Usually, the ICC was employed as mounted infantry rather than as a swift, attacking cavalry force. *Seven Pillars of Wisdom*'s chapter 99 records Lawrence's shock when seeing, in July 1918, the British and Australian ICC soldiers side by side with the Arabs for the first time; chapter 101 tells of the ICC Brigade's successful attack (without Lawrence present) on **Mudowwara** station in early August 1918; and chapter 104 reveals that, under **Robin Buxton**'s skilled leadership, the ICC had become adept at irregular warfare within a month of their arrival at **Akaba.** When the ICC was disbanded in 1918, Lawrence received 2,000 camels from **Allenby** for use against **Deraa,** as recounted in chapter 95 of *Seven Pillars of Wisdom.* See H. S. Gullett's *Aus-*

tralian Imperial Force in Sinai and Palestine, 1914–18, and **A. P. Wavell,** *The Palestine Campaigns.*

Imperial War Museum, London

Museum of Britain's military history that includes paintings of the **Palestine** campaign by James McBey, Richard and **Sydney Carline,** and others, the materials used by **Knightley** and **Simpson** and others when writing their Lawrence biographies, and photos and other documentary material relating to Lawrence.

Imperialism, Lawrence's Attitude toward

Lawrence has been attacked by **Knightley** and **Simpson** and Edward Said, among others, for ardent imperialism and by **Aldington** for being too pro-Arab. The Arabs themselves saw him as a military hero during the **Arab Revolt** but later attacked him for imperialism (see **Antonius,** *The Arab Awakening,* pp. 323–24; **Mack,** *A Prince of Our Disorder,* pp. 194–95). During the war his thinking contained both imperial and anti-imperial elements, and it evolved after the war into a clearly anti-imperial position. Lawrence's letter of March 22, 1915, to **Hogarth** (Garnett, *Letters,* pp. 195–96) tells us that by this time he had already formulated the idea of having **Sharif Hussein**'s forces take **Syria** with British help and forcing the French, whom he saw as unfit to rule the country, out of the picture. As he participated in the **Arab Revolt,** he remained loyal to this idea, even when he learned of the **Sykes-Picot Agreement,** which included British agreement to postwar French control of Syria, as he explains in chapter 48 of *Seven Pillars of Wisdom.* Clearly he wished the British to win, as **Suleiman Mousa** has claimed, but during the war, he wrote in

his diary that he could not stand asking the Arabs to fight unless their hope of independence would be honored. He felt that the British would give more to the Arabs than would the French, and he wanted to serve both British and Arab goals. Lawrence's basic idea of Arab semi-independence in alliance with the British or under a British mandate was progressive for his period. He remained true to it after the war when at the **Cairo Conference** of 1921 he recommended **Feisal**'s becoming king of **Iraq** under British guidance, with an eye toward eventual independence. Feisal's accession to the throne of Iraq in 1921 calmed the situation of open revolt that had broken out in June 1920 against **Sir Arnold T. Wilson**'s harsh colonial rule. At that time, Lawrence showed determined opposition to purely British control of the country in his letters to and articles in the **London** *Times* (Garnett, *Letters,* pp. 306–8, 311–17) as well as in the introductory chapter of *Seven Pillars of Wisdom,* where he openly stated that oil and empire were no longer worth dying for. His postwar letter to **D. G. Pearman** makes it clear that he envisioned the British empire becoming a voluntary commonwealth (Garnett, *Letters,* p. 578). It is important to view Lawrence in the context of his period and not to judge him with hindsight.

India

Lawrence left for India in December 1926 on board the troop ship **SS** *Derbyshire.* From January 7, 1927, to May 26, 1928, he served in the Engine Repair Section at the **Royal Air Force** depot at Drigh Road, **Karachi.** During this time *Revolt in the Desert* was published in England and America, he finished *The Mint,* and **Robert Graves** published his Lawrence biography. He was then transferred to **Miranshah,** near the **Afghanistan** border, where he served as a clerk. Here he worked on his *Odyssey* translation in tranquillity.

However, in September 1928 newspapers began false accounts of his alleged spying activities in Afghanistan, and on January 12 he was sent to England on board the **SS Rajputana.** Both Karachi and Miranshah are in what is now Pakistan. **A. W. Lawrence**'s *T. E. Lawrence by His Friends* contains three memoirs by servicemen who knew him during this period. He displayed little interest in India and did not leave either camp.

India, Government of

The British government agency responsible for controlling India and adjacent territories. During the **World War I** period, **Charles, Baron Hardinge of Penshurst,** was viceroy until April 1916, when he was succeeded by Frederic, Baron Chelmsford. Lord Hardinge in 1915 strongly opposed British sponsorship of Arab nationalism because the government of India wanted to annex **Mesopotamia** and because it was suppressing nationalism in India itself, but the **India Office** in London accepted the British pledges of Arab independence in the **McMahon-Hussein Correspondence.** During the war and after, the Indian government supported **Ibn Saud** against the **Arab Bureau**'s **Sharif Hussein** of **Mecca,** thus increasing the rivalry between these agencies. Lawrence opposed the Indian government's postwar treatment of Mesopotamia as a colony rather than as an independent state in the making. The government of India was responsible for the British campaign in **Mesopotamia,** which included the surrender of a division under **General Townshend** to the Turks. Lawrence, who was sent in 1916 to rescue Townshend's force by means of bribery, wrote a scathing report about Mesopotamian operations, earning himself the permanent hostility of the government of India and the Indian army. Sir Frederick Maude, the British commander in Meso-

potamia from August 1916, defeated the Turks in the Second Battle of **Kut-al-Amara** (February 22–23, 1917), conquered **Baghdad** on March 11, and succeeded in conquering Ramadi (September 22–23, 1917) before dying of cholera. See B. Cooper Busch, *Britain, India and the Arabs.*

India Office

The British government agency in London responsible for Indian affairs. In 1915, the secretary of state for **India,** Austen Chamberlain, was not completely opposed to **Sharif Hussein**'s demand for postwar independence but wanted to limit it. He reluctantly supported the **McMahon-Hussein Correspondence** pledges to Hussein, which put him at odds with **Charles Hardinge,** viceroy of the **government of India,** who strenuously opposed them as a threat to Indian interests. At the end of chapter 14 of *Seven Pillars of Wisdom,* Lawrence shows that he understood the Indian government's position when he candidly explains that the British could not have risked arousing Arab nationalism if they thought that it would present a threat to their own strategic interests. See B. Cooper Busch, *Britain, India and the Arabs.*

Indian Army Expeditionary Force

A detachment of 5,000 Indian army troops (Force "D") under General Barrett that disembarked in the Shatt al Arab in November 1914, took Basra on November 23, and was subsequently enlarged, taking (under its new commander from April 1915, Gen. Sir John Nixon) all of southern **Mesopotamia** by July 1915. The force had originally been sent to secure an oil pipeline but the scope of the mission steadily increased. The report of the Mesopotamian Commission held that Nixon's overconfidence led him to send **General Towns-**

hend northward with 15,000 men toward **Baghdad** without adequate transport and provisions. Defeated at Ctesiphon by a superior Turkish force, Townshend fell back on **Kut-al-Amara** and was forced to surrender in April 1916 after a long siege. With **Aubrey Herbert,** Lawrence was sent to ransom Townshend's force. The attempt failed, and Lawrence wrote a scathing report (reproduced in **J. M. Wilson,** *Lawrence of Arabia,* pp. 949–59) about Mesopotamian operations that earned him the permanent hostility of the **government of India.** Under Gen. Stanley Maude, its commander from August 1916 (when Sir Percy Lake, who had relieved Nixon, left), the IEF recovered from this defeat and went on to conquer Baghdad on March 11, 1917. See A. J. Barker, *The Neglected War;* R. Millar, *Kut: The Death of an Army;* C. Townshend, *My Campaign in Mesopotamia;* R. Braddon, *The Siege;* and F. J. Moberly, *The Campaign in Mesopotamia 1914–1918.*

"Influence of the Crusades on European Military Architecture—To the End of the XIIth Century, The"

The title of Lawrence's **Jesus College, Oxford,** B.A. honors thesis, researched during a 1,100-mile walking trip through parts of what are now **Lebanon, Syria,** and Israel from July 8 to September 19, 1909, and written during the 1909–10 academic year. In this controversial work, which covers 36 Crusader castles, Lawrence claimed that they were influenced almost exclusively by European models, with the exception of the newer fortresses of the Templars, which he thought were influenced by some Eastern castles. This contradicted the prevailing opinion at the time, held by such authorities as **Oman** and **Rey,** which was that all of the Crusaders had been strongly influenced by Eastern castle designs. It is now generally

agreed that all Crusader orders were influenced by both Eastern and Western castle architecture and that they often created their own unique designs. Even if Lawrence's work now appears extreme in claiming almost exclusively Western influence, the issue is not definitely resolved, and Lawrence's thesis continues to be respected by such authorities as R. C. Smail, in his *Crusading Warfare* (1956), and Denys Pringle in his introduction to the 1988 Clarendon Press edition of *Crusader Castles,* under which title Lawrence's thesis has been published three times. It earned Lawrence a first, the highest possible grade.

Intelligence

Lawrence was one of the last important generalist intelligence agents in the nineteenth century tradition, equally good at reconnaissance, collection, counterintelligence, covert operations, and assessment. Before the war, during the **Carchemish** period, he took part with **Woolley** in the *Wilderness of Zin* survey, an ostensibly archaeological project that disguised **Stewart Newcombe**'s military spying on Turkish defenses in the **Negev desert.** During that survey, Lawrence for the first time explored the city of **Akaba,** which would later become his most important conquest of the war. In early 1914, Newcombe sent Woolley and Lawrence down the track of the **Berlin–Baghdad Railway,** and they secured the plans for it from a disgruntled Italian engineer. During his **Cairo** period in military intelligence, from 1914 to 1916, Lawrence made situation maps of actual and potential Middle Eastern fronts, helped **Philip Graves** compile the *Handbook of the Turkish Army 1916,* and ran agents, such as Charles Boutagy. In 1916, he and **Aubrey Herbert** were sent to ransom **General Townshend**'s force at **Kut-al-Amara, Mesopotamia,** and to assess the possibility of an Arab uprising against the Turks there. When he transferred to the **Arab Bureau** in late 1916, he helped edit the secret *Arab Bulletin* and contributed analyses to it. After he went into the field with **Feisal**'s forces, he himself became an operative and in June 1917 embarked on a dangerous solo trip behind Turkish lines. During this trip he met with **Ali Riza Pasha Rikabi,** the governor of Damascus under the Turks, who was furtively working for the Arab forces. It was during a reconnaissance trip into **Deraa** that he was caught and tortured by the Turks. Lawrence himself says in chapter 69 of *Seven Pillars of Wisdom* that because the Arab population was sympathetic to the Arab rather than Turkish forces, the **Arab Revolt**'s intelligence was excellent. See G. Gera, "T. E. Lawrence: Intelligence Officer," in Tabachnick, editor, *The T. E. Lawrence Puzzle,* and Y. Sheffy, *British Military Intelligence in the Palestine Campaign, 1914–18.*

Iraq

Previously known as **Mesopotamia,** or as the three Ottoman provinces (or *vilayets*) of **Baghdad, Mosul,** and Basra. After the **Young Turk** revolution of 1908, there were nationalistic stirrings centered upon **Sayid Taleb el Nakib,** but Britain invaded one week after **World War I** was declared and steadily expanded its control from Basra to Mosul by the time of the armistice. In June 1920 an insurrection broke out, and Britain was given a League of Nations mandate at **San Remo** in the same year. Lawrence strongly criticized the British administration of Mesopotamia in letters to newspapers and in the introductory chapter in *Seven Pillars of Wisdom.* **Feisal,** having been expelled from **Syria** by the French, was appointed king by the British in August 1921 and ruled with the assistance of British advisers. Iraq became independent on October 3, 1932, and Feisal died in September 1933, at which time his son **Ghazi** succeeded him. A series of dictators, coups, and instability followed. See A. T. Wilson, *Loyalties: Mesopotamia;* Shimoni and Levine, *Political Dictionary of the Middle East in the Twentieth Century.*

Ireland

Lawrence's father, originally named Chapman, was the lord of a manor in Ireland. But Lawrence never received the benefits of this estate, which remained in the hands of Thomas Chapman's first wife and daughters. Although Lawrence never visited Ireland and wrote that family, politics, and finances kept him in England, **Robert Graves** claimed that Lawrence had many Anglo-Irish qualities in his personality. In 1933, Lawrence wrote to **Edward Garnett** that Irish writers, compared to English ones, did not seem to grow, but in 1932 he humbly accepted his appointment to the **Irish Academy of Letters** in a letter to **W. B. Yeats** (Garnett, *Letters,* pp. 743–44, 775).

Iris III Flying Boat

On February 4, 1931, while at **R.A.F. Mount Batten,** Lawrence witnessed the crash of an Iris III seaplane. He was one of the first to arrive at the site in a rescue boat, and six men were saved. Lawrence appeared before a court of inquiry and an inquest.

Irish Academy of Letters

An organization of Irish writers formed in 1932 and continuing to this day. **G. B. Shaw** immediately nominated Lawrence for membership in the organization, and right after the organization's first meeting in September the great poet **W. B. Yeats** invited Lawrence to join, which he did.

Isham, Ralph H. (1890–1955)

American businessman and collector of James Boswell papers. Isham, who had served as an officer with the British army in **France,** first met Lawrence in 1919 in **London** and enjoyed literary and musical discussions with him thereafter. **Winston Churchill** asked Isham to find out if Lawrence would accept a **Colonial Office** position, which he did. In 1927, Isham asked Lawrence if he would translate the *Odyssey* for printer **Bruce Rogers.** He left an insightful and affectionate but not uncritical memoir in **A. W. Lawrence**'s collection *T. E. Lawrence by His Friends.*

Isherwood, Christopher (Christopher William Bradshaw-Isherwood) (1904–1986)

Novelist and coauthor, with **W. H. Auden,** of *The Ascent of F.6,* whose central character, Ransom, is based on Lawrence.

Islam

Lawrence's attitude toward Islam appears in chapter 63 of *Seven Pillars of Wisdom,* where he writes that he felt that, compared to Christianity, Islam was abstract and static, until he met a prophetlike old man in the Wadi Rumm who spoke of God's love. This emphasis on a dynamic principle of love led Lawrence to see Islam in a more positive light. However, Lawrence himself was a secularist and pleased that **Feisal** was amenable to work with non-Muslims and did not unduly emphasize Islamic religiosity during the **Arab Revolt.**

Ismailia, Egypt

City on the **Suez Canal,** north of the Great Bitter Lake. This was the location of headquarters of the Intelligence Department of the **Egyptian Expeditionary Force** under **Colonel Holdich** from 1916 on. In chapter 7 of *Seven Pillars of Wisdom,* Lawrence explains how he deliberately irritated the staff in Ismailia in order to get himself transferred to the **Arab Bureau.** It was at the Ismailia train station in July 1917 that Lawrence, still in Arab dress after a camel trip across Sinai, fortuitously was able to announce the news of his capture of **Akaba** to **Admiral Wemyss,** who sent the *Dufferin* there with supplies for the Arab forces.

Itm, Wadi

Dry river bed running northeast above **Akaba,** through which Lawrence's forces passed on their way to the capture of that city from the north. In 1917 the British forces built a road through Wadi Itm from Akaba to **Guweira,** a distance of about 25 miles.

J

Jaafar Pasha el Askari, Maj. Gen. (1880–1936)

Formerly a Mesopotamian officer in the Ottoman forces, he was captured while fighting against the British during the **Senussi** rebellion, as explained in chapter 28 of *Seven Pillars of Wisdom.* He then joined the **Arab Revolt** and became **Feisal**'s chief of staff and commander of the Arab regular forces, who were advised by **Lt. Col. Joyce** and based at **Akaba** from August 1917. He and his forces, including many former Turkish prisoners of war who had also joined the revolt, took part in the battle of **Tafileh** in January 1918. He also led the attack on **Maan** in April 1918 and the siege on that Turkish base until September 1918. After the war, he was prime minister of **Iraq** under Feisal but was assassinated in 1936. He contributed an essay to **A. W. Lawrence**'s collection *T. E. Lawrence by His Friends.* See William Facey, editor, *A Soldier's Story: From Ottoman Rule to Independent Iraq—The Memoirs of Jaafar Pasha al-Askari.*

Jacobsen, Jens Peter (1847–85)

Danish poet and fiction writer, perhaps known best for his *Gurresange,* because they form the text of Arnold Schönberg's *Gurrelieder,* and for his novel *Niels Lyhnne* (1880), considered an atheist tract. Law-rence had this novel as well as Jacobsen's *Marie Grubbe* (1876), both in English translation, in his **Clouds Hill** library.

James, Henry (1843–1916)

American-born essayist and fiction writer. Lawrence had only a copy of James's *A Little Tour in Italy* (1900) in his **Clouds Hill** library, but Lawrence's reference to his will as a wild beast in chapter 103 of *Seven Pillars of Wisdom* may show his familiarity with James's story "The Beast in the Jungle." James, however, was not apparently one of Lawrence's favorite writers because his letters are devoid of references to James's work.

James, William (1842–1910)

Henry James's brother and an important American philosopher known for his *Varieties of Religious Experience* (1902). William James developed the philosophy of **neutral monism,** which was later taken up by **Bertrand Russell.** Traces of this philosophy appear at the end of chapter 83 of *Seven Pillars of Wisdom,* where Lawrence indicates that thoughts and things are both made of the same material, atoms. There is no indication that Lawrence read William James, but he may have learned of neutral monism through his friend **Vyvyan Richards,** a philosophy major at Oxford, or through a reading of Russell.

Jane, Lionel Cecil (1879–1932)

Lawrence's private tutor in history during his last year at the **City of Oxford High School for Boys** and during his three years at **Oxford University.** In a letter of 1927 to **Robert Graves,** Jane stressed Lawrence's effortless originality of thought; Lawrence also respected Jane and recommended him to his brother Will.

Jarvis, Claude Scudamore (born 1879)

British military governor of the Sinai peninsula in the post–**World War I** period. He praises Lawrence highly in his *Three Deserts* (1936) as an outstanding guerrilla strategist.

Jauf

Oasis in northern Arabia about 200 miles east of the **Hejaz Railway,** where **Nuri Shaalan,** sheikh of the **Rualla tribe,** was centered.

Jebail, American Mission School at

See **American Mission**

Jefer

An oasis east of **Maan.** In June 1917 the Turks tried to destroy the well there, but Lawrence's men, on their way to capture **Akaba,** were able to restore it, as shown in chapter 52 of *Seven Pillars of Wisdom.* The way to the oasis was over the hard mud plain surrounding Jefer. In August and September 1918 Lawrence crossed the plain in an armored car, raising a dust cloud, as described in *Seven Pillars of Wisdom*'s chapters 105 and 107.

Jemadar Hassan Shah (died 1918)

An Indian Muslim officer commanding a unit of Indian volunteers participating in the **Arab Revolt.** Lawrence mentions Hassan Shah favorably at several points in *Seven Pillars of Wisdom,* notably in chapter 76, when he accompanied Lawrence on his **Yarmuk Valley Bridges** attack, and in chapter 79, when he was assigned to clean out the mosque and post machine guns at **Azrak.** Hassan Shah's death by shooting and torture at the hands of the Turks at the village of **Tafas** precipitated the killing of 200 Turkish prisoners by the Arabs, who were already incensed by the Turks' slaying of villagers, as related in chapter 117. The extent to which Lawrence was responsible for allowing this massacre to take place remains controversial, as does the issue of whether or not he himself participated in it.

Jemal Kuchuk, Gen. Mehmet

Commander of the Turkish Fourth Army at the time of **General Allenby**'s 1918 "Megiddo" offensive. He was called Jemal "the lesser" to distinguish him from **Jemal Pasha,** to whom he was not related. In his *Five Years in Turkey,* **Liman von Sanders,** the German commander-in-chief of the Turkish armies in **Palestine** and **Syria** from February 1918 on, praises Jemal Kuchuk as a wise, just, and reliable general. See also **A. P. Wavell,** *The Palestine Campaigns,* and Bryan Perrett, *Megiddo 1918.*

Jemal Pasha, Ahmed (1872–1922)

Turkish minister of marine from 1913 and—with **Enver Pasha** and **Talat Pasha**—one of the three rulers of the country during **World War I.** After his overtures to the Entente were rejected, he favored

Jemal Pasha, a member of the ruling Turkish triumvirate and commander of the Turkish armies on the Palestine front until December 1917. Courtesy of Corbis.

friendship with Germany. During the war, he was governor of **Palestine** and **Syria** until **Gen. Edmund Allenby**'s capture of **Jerusalem** in December 1917, when he returned to Constantinople until the fall of the Turkish government in October 1918. With **Col. Kress von Kressenstein,** he was responsible for the daring but failed Turkish attack on the **Suez Canal** in 1915. Lawrence mentions him at many points in *Seven Pillars of Wisdom* as a ruthless leader whose life was spared by **Feisal** even when he had the chance and reason to take it, as explained in chapter 5. **Wavell** describes him as a poor commander but an able administrator. Jemal was assassinated after the war by **Armenians** while working as a military adviser in **Afghanistan.** He was the author of *Memories of a Turkish Statesman—1913–1919.* Jemal Pasha was

sometimes called "the greater" to differentiate him from **Jemal Kuchuk** "the lesser." See **George Antonius,** *The Arab Awakening;* Pope and Wheal, *The Dictionary of the First World War;* and A. P. Wavell, *The Palestine Campaigns,* for further information.

Jemil el Midfai (1890–1958)

Commander of the Arab army's artillery, he accompanied **Feisal, Nuri el-Said,** and **Capt. Pisani** when they joined Lawrence at **Azrak** in September 1918 in preparation for an attack on **Deraa,** as related in chapter 107 of *Seven Pillars of Wisdom.* El Midfai served in the Ottoman army until he deserted in 1916 to join the Arab forces. He was appointed chief of public security by Lawrence when the Arabs first took Damascus and was an aide to Feisal during his two-year rule in **Syria.** He later became prime minister of **Iraq** five times.

Jerablus, Syria

Town in northern **Syria,** and the site of the **Hittite** viceregal capital of **Carchemish,** which Lawrence excavated from 1911 to 1914 under the direction of **D. G. Hogarth** and **C. Leonard Woolley.**

Jerdun

Station on the **Hejaz Railway** about 10 miles north of **Maan,** taken for a third and final time by the Arab regular forces in May 1918, as related in chapter 95 of *Seven Pillars of Wisdom.*

Jericho

Town about 10 miles northwest of the Dead Sea, captured in February 1918 by **Gen. Sir Philip Chetwode,** commanding XX Corps. In July 1918 **General Allenby** erected a dummy camp near there as a deception; his final offensive would come in the coastal sector of **Palestine,** far to the west, as Lawrence explains in chapter 98 of *Seven Pillars of Wisdom.*

Jersey

British island in the English Channel. Lawrence's parents stayed here briefly in 1890, when he was two years old, after they had left **Kirkcudbright,** Scotland, and the Isle of Man. They used Jersey as a base while they looked for a place to live in **France,** which they found in 1891, at **Dinard.** In early 1893, Lawrence's family returned to Jersey so Lawrence's mother could give birth to **Frank Helier Lawrence** on English soil; from there they moved, in 1894, to **Langley Lodge,** near the New Forest, in England.

Jerusalem

In chapter 59 of *Seven Pillars of Wisdom,* Lawrence criticizes the atmosphere of Jerusalem, but in chapter 81 he says that his presence at the December 11, 1917, Jaffa gate ceremony celebrating **Allenby**'s capture of the city (December 9, 1917) was the high point of the war for him, undoubtedly for historical reasons. He appears in newsreel footage of this event now in the **Imperial War Museum, London.** To his parents he wrote on December 14, 1917, that during the ceremony there were airplanes overhead accompanied by antiaircraft fire (Brown, *Selected Letters,* p. 131). In 1921, as a member of the **Colonial Office,** he returned to Jerusalem to work with **Abdullah,** who had taken control of **Transjordan.**

Jerusalem, Battle for

After the Turks were defeated at **Beersheba** and withdrew from **Gaza** on November 6, 1917, they put up resistance at Huj, north of Gaza, but **Allenby**'s forces took that supply base with a cavalry charge on November 8. The Turks lost 10,000 prisoners and 100 guns in the Gaza and Huj actions, but the bulk of their army escaped. However, after Huj, they became so disorganized that they lost most of their troops to desertions with the result that only 15,000 troops of the Turkish Seventh Army under Fehvzi Pasha took up a line of defense southwest of Jerusalem on November 10. Allenby was very aware of the difficulties of attacking Jerusalem, which is situated in very hilly country and at the time had few good roads, all of which made it easy for a few defenders to hold back a large force of attackers. On November 21, the British succeeded in capturing Nebi Samwil, which overlooked the Turks' Jerusalem defenses, and held it despite three fierce Turkish counterattacks. After consolidation of British positions around Jerusalem in the face of many Turkish counterattacks, the British resumed their attack on the city on December 8, hampered by a heavy rainfall the night before. Already on the evening of the 8th, the Turks, demoralized by their inability to shake the British defenses and by the loss of many troops in counterattacks, retreated from the city, and the mayor of Jerusalem gave the keys of the city to General Shea in the afternoon of December 9. Allenby had outmaneuvered his opponent, **Marshal Erich von Falkenhayn,** completely and had all but destroyed his plan for a **Yildirim** shock force. Falkenhayn, however, did not give up easily, and on the night of December 26, the Seventh Army, now up to 20,000 troops, attacked just north of Jerusalem but was pushed back. Total British casualties since the Beersheba attack were 18,000, while the Turks lost 25,000 troops. The British presented the capture of Jerusalem as a Christmas present to their nation, and it offset negative results in Russia, Caporetto, and Cambrai around the same time. The Turks were demoralized by the loss of this holy city in addition to their previous loss of **Mecca** and **Baghdad,** but they held **Medina** to the end of the war. See **A. P. Wavell,** *The Palestine Campaigns,* and Pope and Wheal, *The Dictionary of the First World War.*

Jesty, Simon

Pen name of W. W. Vickery, for the manuscript of whose novel **River Niger** Lawrence wrote an ambiguous reader's report in 1934 at the request of Boriswood editor C. J. Greenwood. Lawrence's letter to Greenwood was used as a preface when the novel was published in 1935.

Jesus

Although Lawrence was far less religious than his mother or his brother **M. R. Lawrence,** in his early letters home he sometimes refers to Jesus as "Our Lord," and in chapter 63 of *Seven Pillars of Wisdom* he mentions Christ, if only as the inhabitant of a sophisticated, corrupt, and Hellenized Galilee. He also compares his ordeal of leadership of the Arab movement to a crucifixion in chapter 100, and in *Seven Pillars of Wisdom* as a whole there are several references to Jesus' sayings.

Jesus College, Oxford

Oxford University college at which Lawrence studied from 1907 to 1910. He was admitted at the age of 19 with a Meyricke Exhibition in Modern History, a modest scholarship. During this period, under the influence of **D. G. Hogarth** at the **Ashmolean Museum** he melded his interest in medievalism with an interest in the Middle East, producing in 1909–10 an outstanding honors thesis, **"The Influence of the Crusades on European Military Architecture—To the End of the XIIth Century."** Although he did not live in the college but behind his family's home in a cottage built especially for him, he made many friends,

including the American philosophy student **Vyvyan Richards,** whose *Portrait of T. E. Lawrence* (1936) offers the best picture of his attitudes, personality, reading tastes, and adventures during this period.

Jews

Lawrence's attitudes toward the Jews were positive, if expressed with the global generalizing tendency that Lawrence, like most Europeans of his period, applied to all groups. In chapter 2 of *Seven Pillars of Wisdom,* he sees the continued existence of the Jews as miraculous; in chapters 3 and 59, he writes positively of **Zionism;** and in chapter 101, he writes sarcastically that the **Balfour Declaration** only promised something ambiguous to the Jews. At the same time, he attributes the extremes of lust and self-denial to the Jews as to the Arabs (chapter 3), at first felt that Judaism and Islam were too abstract to allow love between God and man (chapter 63), and found that the Orthodox Jews of **Jerusalem** were the most uncongenial of the groups in **Palestine** (chapter 58). His letters confirm his positive attitude toward Zionism: in 1909 he writes that he wants the Jews to farm Palestine, and in a letter of 1922 he defends **Chaim Weizmann** against the aspersions of the Anglican archbishop of Jerusalem. In 1919 he was instrumental in bringing together Weizmann and **Feisal** at the **Peace Conference** in **Paris,** where they signed a treaty, the first ever between Jewish and Arab nationalists, and both Weizmann and Feisal regarded him as a friend. See Weizmann's memoir in **A. W. Lawrence's** *T. E. Lawrence by His Friends.* **George Antonius** includes the text of the Feisal-Weizmann agreement in *The Arab Awakening.* A Jewish Legion of the British army, founded by Zionist politicians Vladimir Jabotinsky and Joseph Trumpeldor, fought in Palestine, but Lawrence apparently had no contact with this unit. See Roman Freulich, *Soldiers in Judea.*

Jezirah

A region of northern **Mesopotamia** with a large **Kurdish** population. In 1918, Lawrence recommended to the Eastern Committee of the **War Cabinet,** chaired by **Lord Curzon,** that Jezirah be kept separate, at least administratively, from the rest of Mesopotamia until the Kurds and other nomadic peoples could be convinced to join a local Arab government.

Jidda

Arabian Red Sea port, about 30 miles west of **Mecca. Col. C. E. Wilson** was sent there in August 1916 by **Sir Reginald Wingate,** sirdar (or commander-in-chief) of the Egyptian army and governor-general of the **Sudan,** to serve as liaison with the Arab forces. When Lawrence first visited Jidda on October 16, 1916, to assess the situation of the **Arab Revolt** as reported in chapters 8 and 9 of *Seven Pillars of Wisdom,* it seemed a strange city—boiling hot, unhygienic, and sinister. In time he became more used to Arabia. He visited Jidda again in July 1921 in an unsuccessful attempt to convince **Sharif Hussein** to accept the British position in the Middle East in exchange for British protection from **Ibn Saud,** who eventually succeeded in overthrowing Hussein's rule.

Jihad

On November 14, 1914, Sultan Mehemed V of Turkey (brother of the deposed **Sultan Abdul-Hamid II**) proclaimed a jihad or holy war against the Russians and British, while exempting the Germans, who were allied with the Turks. **Sharif Hussein of Mecca,** still nominally allied with the Turks but considering an alliance with the

British, did not support the jihad. The British, who feared a Muslim uprising in **India,** were pleased with **Hussein**'s failure to support jihad, and his value as a bulwark against the call to jihad was a leading reason for their decision to support him when he decided to revolt against the Turks on June 27, 1916. See Gary Troeller, "Ibn Saud and Sherif Husein: A Comparison in Importance in the Early Years of the First World War," *Historical Journal* 14 (Sept. 1971): 627–33.

Jinman, Fl. Lt.

An engineering officer with whom Lawrence worked on tests of the **200 Class Seaplane Tender** during the last two years of his **Royal Air Force** service.

John, Augustus (1878–1961)

Painter and etcher, recipient of the Order of Merit (1942), and friend of Lawrence. John first painted Lawrence in 1919 during the **Peace Conference** in **Paris** and contributed an oil of **Feisal,** a charcoal drawing of **D. G. Hogarth,** and a pencil sketch of Lawrence to the 1926 subscriber's edition of *Seven Pillars of Wisdom.* **Charles Grosvenor**'s *An Iconography: The Portraits of T. E. Lawrence* (1988) describes 16 Lawrence portraits by John, some of which are in the National Portrait Gallery, London. Lawrence considered John the best British painter of the period, but John's powers notably declined in the late 1920s. See also **J. M. Wilson,** *T. E. Lawrence,* for a group of John portraits relating to Lawrence.

Jones, Ira T. (born 1896)

Royal Air Force squadron leader who served in France during **World War I,** in **Iraq** from 1923–26, and with Lawrence in 1929 as part of the British **Schneider Tro-**

phy team. In his memoir in **A. W. Lawrence**'s *T. E. Lawrence by His Friends,* he recalls excellent advice that Lawrence gave him about writing a biography, as well as Lawrence's modest demeanor during his **Royal Air Force** service.

Jordan, Kingdom of

See **Transjordan**

Jordan Valley

The deep valley extending along the banks of the Jordan River from the Sea of Galilee to south of the Dead Sea, including the lowest point on earth. While the river itself is usually no more than 70 or 80 feet across, the mountains on either side and the great heat of the valley in the summer make this a difficult campaign site. In January 1918, 70 **Beersheba**-area **Beduin** under Abdulla el Feir raided the Turkish naval base at Kerak on the Dead Sea shore and scuttled the boats there, as related in chapter 87 of *Seven Pillars of Wisdom.* The Jordan Valley was also the scene of **Allenby**'s failed raid on **Salt** and **Amman** in April 1918, as told in chapter 93 of *Seven Pillars of Wisdom* and in **Wavell**'s *The Palestine Campaigns.* The valley also was the site of Allenby's deception of the Turks in the summer of that year, when by stationing some forces there he made them believe that he would attack again in the Jordan Valley (chapter 98), rather than farther to the west in **Palestine,** which he did in the fall.

Joyce, James (1882–1941)

Widely regarded as the greatest twentieth-century author. Lawrence read *Ulysses* (1922) in 1927 and saw Joyce as an avant-garde genius who made Lawrence's own *Seven Pillars of Wisdom* look dated; but he also had reservations about the difficulty of Joyce's writing (Garnett, *Letters,* pp. 488, 522–24).

Joyce, Lt. Col. Pierce Charles (1878–1965)

Commander of all British soldiers in **Feisal**'s area, including Lawrence, with overall responsibility for the success of the **Arab Revolt.** When he first met Lawrence in Port Sudan in 1916, Joyce was irritated by Lawrence's scruffy uniform, but during the Arab campaign he came to appreciate Lawrence's bravery, endurance, and love of speed. Unpublished transcripts of 1939 and 1941 BBC talks given by Joyce can be found in **John Mack,** *A Prince of Our Disorder* (pp. 201–2). Lawrence writes of Joyce at many points in *Seven Pillars of Wisdom,* always with respect.

Juheina Tribe

A **Beduin** tribe occupying the area of the **Hejaz** between **Jidda** and **Wejh.** They proved unreliable allies, at one point leaving a battle to drink coffee, as Lawrence mentioned to **Robert Graves** in his *T. E. Lawrence to His Biographers Robert Graves & Liddell Hart.*

Junner, Elizabeth (born 1833)

Lawrence's grandmother on his mother Sarah's side. Elizabeth died of alcoholism and never married Sarah's father, thought to be a ship's carpenter named John Lawrence, 10 years her senior; Elizabeth worked as a servant in John Lawrence's father Thomas's house in Sunderland, County Durham. Elizabeth's parents were John and Jane Junner, born circa 1807 and 1813, respectively. See **J. M. Wilson,** *Lawrence of Arabia,* for more details.

Junner, Sarah

See **Lawrence, Sarah Junner**

Junor, Lieutenant

A Royal Flying Corps pilot of the "X" Flight in the Arabian theater. In chapter 109 of *Seven Pillars of Wisdom,* Lawrence relates how Junor, in September 1918, single-handedly used his outdated B.E. 12 to distract Turkish planes from attacking Lawrence and his men on the ground. Then, when he tried to land with enemy planes on his tail, his plane blew over in the wind and was destroyed by an enemy bomb after he had fortunately gotten away from it. Junor then requested a car and blew up some rails under enemy fire.

Jurf el Derwish

A plain extending from **Tafileh** and **Shobek** in the west to around **Bair** in the east. Jurf is also the name of a **Hejaz Railway** station located in the middle of the plain. A strong station, protected by a mountain gun as well as two machine guns, it was captured in January 1918 by Arab forces under **Sharif Nasir,** as described in chapter 84 of *Seven Pillars of Wisdom.*

K

Kadesh Barnea

An oasis in the northern Sinai desert at the crossroads between the Way of Shur and the road to Arad and Hebron that was the site of a lengthy sojourn of the Children of Israel during the Exodus, as stated in Deuteronomy 1:46. During their archaeological **Wilderness of Zin** survey (for the **Palestine Exploration Fund**) of early 1914 that was used as a cover for then-Capt. **Stewart Newcombe**'s military spying work, Lawrence and **C. Leonard Woolley** established Ain el Qudeirat rather than the nearby Ain Kadeis (previously thought to be the site) as the correct location of the biblical Kadesh Barnea, and their results were confirmed by Israeli archaeologist Rudolf Cohen in 1978–79. Lawrence and Woolley stated their reasoning in their *The Wilderness of Zin,* which remained the most important book on the area's archaeology until Professor Nelson Glueck's *Rivers in the Desert* (1959), which also confirmed many of their findings about the **Nabataean**/Byzantine cities in the Negev desert. See R. Cohen, "Did I Excavate Kadesh Barnea?" *Biblical Archaeology Review,* 7:3 (May/June 1981): 20–33, and S. E. Tabachnick, "Lawrence of Arabia as Archaeologist," *Biblical Archaeology Review,* 23:5 (Sept./Oct. 1997): 40–47, 70–71.

Karachi, R.A.F. Depot at

Lawrence served as a clerk in the Engine Repair Section of this depot in Drigh Road near Karachi, in what was then **India** and is now Pakistan, from January 1927 to May 1928, when he was transferred, at his request, to a **Royal Air Force** base at **Miranshah.** During his Karachi period he watched from afar the publication of his *Revolt in the Desert,* thought of writing a biography of **Roger Casement,** finished *The Mint,* and began translating *The Odyssey.*

Kedourie, Elie (1926–92)

Middle East historian, author of *In the Anglo-Arab Labyrinth: The McMahon-Husayn Correspondence and Its Interpretations 1914–1939* (1976), and a Lawrence skeptic. In his *The Chatham House Version and Other Middle-Eastern Studies* (1970), Kedourie charges that in *Seven Pillars of Wisdom* Lawrence deliberately concealed the fact that it was the Australians rather than the Arabs who entered Damascus first, and in his critical review of **John Mack**'s biography ("The Real T. E. Lawrence," *Commentary* 64:1 [July 1977]: 49–56), Kedourie charges that Lawrence wrongly used politics to solve his personal problems and that he romanticized terrorism.

Kelmscott Press

A famous private press set up by **William Morris** in 1891. In 1916, Lawrence wrote **Vyvyan Richards** (Garnett, *Letters*, p. 201) that he felt aesthetically uplifted by the Kelmscott edition of Coleridge, and his own desire to make the 1926 edition of *Seven Pillars of Wisdom* a "book beautiful" was undoubtedly owing to Morris's inspiration.

Kemal Pasha, Mustapha (1881–1938)

Turkish military hero and founder of the modern, Westernized Turkish state. Kemal played a major role in the British defeat at **Gallipoli,** commanded the Turkish Seventh Army in **Palestine,** and defeated the Greek army's attempt to capture Smyrna in 1919. He went on to become the first president of the Turkish Republic in 1924 and took the name Ataturk or "Father of the People" in 1934. Lawrence claimed that he actually spoke to Kemal in September 1918, when as the commander of the retreating Turkish Seventh Army, Kemal might have been captured briefly by the Arabs north of **Deraa,** but there is no evidence confirming this (See **J. M. Wilson,** *Lawrence of Arabia,* pp. 557–58). Lawrence also claimed to **Liddell Hart** that he had once shot at and barely missed Kemal, but this too has not been confirmed (*T. E. Lawrence to His Biographers*, p. 1:108). **Feisal** was in correspondence with Kemal (as well as with **Jemal Pasha**) about a possible separate peace with Turkey, even in the last year of the war, according to chapter 101 of *Seven Pillars of Wisdom* and Lawrence's statement to Liddell Hart. Lawrence also told Liddell Hart that he viewed Kemal as a great Turkish patriot. See H. C. Armstrong, *The Grey Wolf: The Life of Kemal Ataturk.*

Kennington, Eric H. (1880–1960)

British painter and sculptor, official war artist in **World War I** and World War II. Kennington served as art editor of the 1926 subscriber's edition of *Seven Pillars of Wisdom* and himself contributed 48 woodcuts, drawings, and painted portraits to the edition—more than any other artist. In 1921, he exhibited at the Leicester Galleries the work that he had done on a trip to Arabia; *Catalogue of an Exhibition of Paintings, Pastels, Drawings, and Woodcuts,* with an introduction by Lawrence, is a very rare collectors' item. Kennington also did the effigy of Lawrence lying down, which is found in St. Martin's Church, Wareham, Dorset, as well as the headstone for Lawrence's grave at **Moreton** and the bronze in St. Paul's Cathedral. See V. M. Thompson, *"Not a Suitable Hobby for an Airman"—T. E. Lawrence as Publisher* (1986). **J. M. Wilson'**s *T. E. Lawrence* contains numerous reproductions of Kennington's work relating to Lawrence.

Kenyon, Sir Frederic G. (1863–1952)

Major archaeologist and from 1909 director of the British Museum, which sponsored **D. G. Hogarth'**s dig at **Carchemish,** in which Lawrence took part from 1911 to 1914. Kenyon wrote an introduction to the 1936 edition of **The Wilderness of Zin,** in which he particularly praises Lawrence and **Woolley'**s demonstration that the climate of the **Negev Desert** had not changed over thousands of years.

Khalfati

In chapter 80 of *Seven Pillars of Wisdom,* where Lawrence describes the **Deraa** torture of November 21, 1917, he mentions

Lawrence's effigy by Eric Kennington, at St. Martin's Church, Wareham, Dorset, dating from 1939. Courtesy of Corbis.

that five years before (or 1912, when he would have been working on the **Carchemish** dig), he had been subjected to a similar but less mortifying ordeal at Khalfati, which is in northern **Syria.** Lawrence claimed that he was beaten by **Kurdish** robbers during his walking tour of Syria, but that was in 1909, so the Khalfati incident remains mysterious.

Khalil Pasha (1864–1923)

Turkish commander who besieged and captured British **Major General Townshend**'s force of 14,000 troops at **Kut-al-Amara, Mesopotamia,** in March 1916. Lawrence and **Aubrey Herbert** were sent to try to ransom Townshend by means of

a bribe (suggested by Townshend himself as a way of making sure that his men would be taken care of in captivity) of one and then two million pounds sterling, but Khalil refused after consultations with his nephew **Enver Pasha,** the Turkish minister of war. Lawrence's report of May 1916 (reprinted in **J. M. Wilson,** *Lawrence of Arabia*) states that Khalil was alert, forceful, and impatient, but in his *Five Years in Turkey,* German **Gen. Liman von Sanders** criticizes Khalil for not following up the success at Kut. Khalil was involved in campaigns against the **Kurds** before the war and in a massacre of **Armenians** in the Melazgherd area; upon capturing Kut, he hanged nine people. See also R. Millar, *Kut: The Death of an Army,* and C.V.F. Townshend, *My Campaign in Mesopotamia.*

Khartoum

Main city of the **Sudan.** In the company of **Admiral Wemyss,** Lawrence was in Khartoum in November 1916 to show the governor-general, **Reginald Wingate,** his report on the promise of the **Arab Revolt.** While Lawrence was at Khartoum, word came that Wingate would replace **Sir Henry McMahon** as high commissioner of **Egypt.** During his two or three days at Khartoum, Lawrence read **Malory**'s *Morte d'Arthur,* according to his account in chapter 16 of *Seven Pillars of Wisdom.*

Killua Castle

An ancestral home of a branch of Lawrence's father's family, the Chapmans, now in ruins, located at Killua in **County Westmeath.** In medieval times, this house belonged to the Knights Hospitalers. During his life in **Ireland,** Lawrence's father Thomas lived in **South Hill,** a large house near Delvin. In 1914 he received the title but not actually the property of the Killua estate. See **J. M. Wilson,** *Lawrence of Arabia,* for more information.

King-Crane Commission

Composed of Dr. H. C. King and C. R. Crane, an advocate of self-determination, this was an American mission sent to **Palestine** and **Syria** in June and July 1919 at the urging of **President Woodrow Wilson** to ascertain the attitude of the people of Syria toward a possible French mandate over them. This was supposed to be an inter-Allied commission, but only the Americans participated, while the British ignored it and the French were hostile. **Feisal** made his anti-French sentiments clear, and on August 28 the commission presented a report stating that only the Catholic population was in favor of French rule and that the rest of the population preferred independence or American or British rule. But the Americans did not want such a role, the British deferred to the French, and the report remained unpublished and ignored. Garnett reprints the memorandum of a conversation about the commission between Feisal and **Col. Edward House,** Wilson's envoy, during which Lawrence acted as interpreter (*Letters,* p. 275). See H. C. Howard, *The King-Crane Commission.*

Kinglake, Alexander (1809–91)

British travel writer and historian and author of *Eothen* ("Toward the Dawn," 1844), which Lawrence considered a stylistic marvel. See S. E. Tabachnick, *T. E. Lawrence* (pp. 20–22), for a discussion of Kinglake's influence on Lawrence.

Kipling, Rudyard (1865–1936)

British poet, fiction writer, and journalist. Writing to **Frank Doubleday** from **Miranshah, India,** in 1928, Lawrence stated that he especially liked "The Light that Failed" and "The City of Dreadful Night" and thought Kipling a superb stylist but felt that Kipling's portrayal of India was superficial (Orlans, *Lawrence of Arabia, Strange Man of Letters,* p. 195). Lawrence wrote **Robert Graves** in 1927 that he liked the school of realism as opposed to modernism that Kipling represented, but he also stated that Kipling could be "mean," perhaps referring to his anti-Semitism and other prejudices (*T. E. Lawrence to His Biographers Robert Graves & Liddell Hart,* pp. 1:134, 1:144). He visited Kipling in Doubleday's company and also flew over his house in a Gypsy Moth aircraft.

Kirkbride, Sir Alec Sneath (1897–1978)

Kirkbride, an Arabic-speaking British lieutenant, first met Lawrence in February 1918 at **Tafileh,** to which he had been sent to collect intelligence about the conditions on the Arab front, as Lawrence reports in chapter 90 of *Seven Pillars of Wisdom.* He is portrayed in subsequent chapters, particularly during the occupation of Damascus, as ruthless and summary in judgment. In his own account of these events, *A Crackle of Thorns* (1956) and *An Awakening: The Arab Campaign 1917–18* (1971), Kirkbride largely affirms the accuracy of Lawrence's view of Kirkbride himself and of events. From 1947 to 1951 he was a British resident in **Transjordan.**

Kirkcudbright

The town in southwest Scotland, on the river Dee, to which Lawrence's parents moved from **Tremadoc, Wales,** in September 1889, when Lawrence was 13 months old. His brother **William George Lawrence** was born in Kirkcudbright. The family stayed in Kirkcudbright until 1891, when they moved to the Isle of Man, then to **Jersey,** and finally to **Dinard, France.**

Kiswe

Town, about 10 miles southwest of Damascus. There, on September 9, 1918, an Arab force under **Sharif Nasir** and **Nuri Shaalan** headed off a column of 2,000 Turks, a remnant of the once-powerful Fourth Army, who were then destroyed by a force of Arabs and British yeomanry, as described in chapter 118 of *Seven Pillars of Wisdom.* Lawrence also discussed this battle in an *Arab Bulletin* piece on "The Destruction of the Fourth Army" (Garnett, *Letters,* pp. 247–57).

Kitan, Wadi

A dry riverbed of west-central Arabia, about 10 miles northeast of Um Lejj. In chapter 81 of *Seven Pillars of Wisdom,* Lawrence describes the wadi's beauty but also his forced execution of **Hamed the Moor** there on March 12, 1917.

Kitchener, Field Marshal Lord Horatio Herbert, 1st Earl Kitchener (1850–1916)

British soldier and statesman. A member of the Royal Engineers, Kitchener served in **Palestine,** Cyprus, and the **Sudan,** where at Omdurman in 1898 he defeated the Mahdi, thus reasserting British prestige after Gordon's loss 10 years earlier. He was commander-in-chief of British forces at the end of the Boer War and then held the same post in **India.** He then became British agent and consul-general in **Egypt** from 1911 to August 1914 and secretary of state for war in **London** from August 3, 1914. His career was damaged by his desultory support of the **Gallipoli** campaign. He died on June 5, 1916, when the ship he was on struck a mine and sank. Kitchener worked on a military survey of Palestine in 1874, and while ruling Egypt he authorized **Newcombe,** Lawrence, and **Woolley** to do the **Wilderness of Zin** survey of 1914. In the synopsis of *Seven Pillars of Wisdom*'s first chapter and in chapter 6, Lawrence credits Kitchener as the driving force behind the British alliance with **Sharif Hussein** and says that Kitchener advocated an aggressive military policy toward Turkey, including a proposed landing at **Alexandretta** that never took place and an Arab uprising in **Mesopotamia** to relieve pressure on the British force surrounded by the Turks at **Kut-al-Amara.** Lawrence claimed to **Liddell Hart** that he had met Kitchener in Egypt in 1913 and in London in 1914, but this has not been confirmed. In *T. E. Lawrence to His Biographers Robert Graves & Liddell Hart,* Lawrence calls Kitchener limited, dogmatic, and uncharismatic, but sometimes far-seeing, a view that has been confirmed by several historians. See Pope and Wheal, *The Dictionary of the First World War,* and W. Jerrold, *Earl Kitchener of Khartoum: The Story of His Life.*

Knightley, Phillip (born 1929)

Prolific Australian-born journalist, London *Times* correspondent resident in England, and author (with **Colin Simpson**) of *The Secret Lives of Lawrence of Arabia* (1969). Based on a series of articles first appearing in the *Times,* this biography revealed details of Lawrence's flagellation disorder, which until then had been only hinted at by **A. W. Lawrence** in his memoir in *T. E. Lawrence by His Friends.* The book also shed new light on the **Deraa incident** and accused Lawrence of imperialism. Knightley also wrote an article on the attempt to prevent **Aldington** from publishing his work and has remained involved in the Lawrence field. See "Aldington's Enquiry concerning T. E. Lawrence," *Texas Quarterly* 16 (Winter 1973): 98–105.

Knowles, Pat (1906–81)

Eldest son of Sgt. Arthur Knowles of the Tank Corps, who originally owned the **Clouds Hill** property that Lawrence bought, and from 1933 a neighbor of Lawrence's at Clouds Hill. He often chatted with Lawrence and made some improvements to the cottage for him. Knowles heard Lawrence's motorcycle approach on May 13, the day of Lawrence's fatal accident, and he served as a pallbearer at Lawrence's funeral. With Joyce Knowles and Bob Hunt, Knowles is the author of *Clouds Hill, Dorset "An handful with quietness"* (1994),

which includes his piece "T. E. Lawrence as I Knew Him." This work also includes a memoir about Pat Knowles himself, and Knowles appears in the 1962 BBC documentary by **Malcolm Brown,** *T. E. Lawrence 1888–1935.*

Korda, Sir Alexander (1893–1956)

British filmmaker who proposed in 1934 to do a film of Lawrence's *Revolt in the Desert.* Lawrence wrote **Mrs. G. B. Shaw** in January 1935 that he had persuaded Korda to postpone the film until Lawrence died or approved of the notion.

Kunfida

City on the southwestern coast of Arabia controlled by **The Idrisi.** In 1915, Lawrence thought he and **Newcombe** would go there to enlist The Idrisi's aid in the war against Turkey. But because **Sharif Hussein** was in dispute with The Idrisi and the British preferred to work with Hussein, the plan was abandoned and Lawrence never went.

Kuntilla

British airstrip about 50 miles northwest of **Akaba,** to which British planes returned in August 1917 after raiding **Maan,** at Lawrence's request, and **Aba el Lissan,** upon the initiative of the energetic pilot Stent, as indicated in chapter 60 of *Seven Pillars of Wisdom.*

Kurds

An ancient nation, largely Sunni Muslim and speaking Kurdish, living in adjacent parts of **Turkey,** Iran, **Mesopotamia,** and **Syria.** In 1909, Lawrence was attacked by Kurds during his Crusader castles walking tour, according to **H. Pirie-Gordon** in

A. W. Lawrence's *T. E. Lawrence by His Friends.* In 1913, Lawrence smuggled rifles from **Beirut** to the British consulate at **Aleppo** to guard against possible raids by Kurds who sensed Turkish weakness in the aftermath of the Balkan war of 1912. At **Carchemish,** he tried to keep the friendship of the Kurdish workers, and this seems to have been reciprocated (Garnett, *Letters,* pp. 158–59). In a report to the British Cabinet written after on November 4, 1918, he states that Kurdish independence will be more difficult to satisfy than Armenian independence (Garnett, *Letters,* p. 269). In 1920, the Kurds gained a pledge of autonomy in the **Treaty of Sèvres** between the Allies and the Turks, but this was rescinded in the **Treaty of Lausanne** of 1923, owing to Turkish opposition. The Kurds' situation remains volatile to this day, which often finds the Kurds fighting for autonomy with Turkey, Iran, **Iraq,** and Syria.

Kut-al-Amara

Town on the Tigris River in **Mesopotamia.** After a siege beginning in December 1915, the 6th Indian Division of 14,000 troops under British **Major General Townshend** was forced to surrender to Turkish Gen. **Khalil Pasha** here on April 29, 1916. Lawrence and **Aubrey Herbert** were sent to try to rescue the British with a bribe of one and then two million pounds sterling and to see if a rebellion of Arabs in the Turkish army could be fomented as a way of relieving pressure on the British garrison. Lawrence's mission as well as an attempt in early April by General Sir Stanley Maude, the commander-in-chief in Mesopotamia, to relieve the garrison failed, and Lawrence wrote a report criticizing the Indian army. Lawrence mentions the British defeat at Kut in chapters 5, 6, and 7 of *Seven Pillars of Wisdom.* Seventy percent of Townshend's force died on the way to captivity in Turkey, but he survived the war as a prisoner in Constantinople. Outside of the British defeat at **Gallipoli** in 1916, the fall of Kut was the major success of the Turks against the British in **World War I.** But Kut was retaken by Maude in February 1917, and he went on to capture **Baghdad** in March. See R. Millar, *Kut: Death of an Army;* F. J. Moberly, *The Campaign in Mesopotamia 1914–1918;* and C.V.F. Townshend, *My Campaign in Mesopotamia.*

L

Laforgue, Jules (1860–1887)

Innovative French poet and prose writer, known especially for his influence on **T. S. Eliot.** In 1922, when he was working on *Seven Pillars of Wisdom,* Lawrence wrote **Edward Garnett** (Garnett, *Letters,* p. 359) that he considered Laforgue's *Moralités legendaires,* a prose retelling of six old tales, a stylistic wonder on the order of some of his other favorite examples of style at this time—**Flaubert**'s *Salammbô* (1862), **Kinglake**'s *Eothen* (1844), and **Hudson**'s *Idle Days in Patagonia* (1893).

Lamartine, Alphonse Marie Louis Prat de (1790–1869)

French poet, travel writer, and diplomat. After a trip to the Levant in 1832–33, he wrote *Un Voyage en Orient* (1835). Lawrence esteemed him, like **Kinglake,** because Lawrence shared, at least early on, his romantic sentiments about the Middle East.

Lamb, Henry (1883–1960)

Portrait and landscape painter. Lamb served in **France,** Macedonia, and **Palestine** during **World War I** and was an official war artist during World War II. A student of **Augustus John,** he contributed *Irish Troops in the Judaean Hills Surprised by a Turkish Bombardment* and a pencil portrait of

Guy Dawnay to the 1926 subscriber's edition of *Seven Pillars of Wisdom.* In 1927, Lawrence wrote **Robert Graves** that he was especially impressed by a portrait of Lytton Strachey, the historian, by Lamb. See **J. M. Wilson,** *T. E. Lawrence* (p. 139), for a reproduction of this picture.

Lamotte, Sublieutenant

French artillery officer and **Colonel Brémond**'s representative with **Feisal**'s forces. He took a photo of Lawrence, **Sharif Nasir,** and **Auda abu Tayi** and their men as they began the **Akaba** expedition on May 9, 1917, as recounted in chapter 39 of *Seven Pillars of Wisdom,* but did not go on the march himself. He seems to have accompanied the Arab forces through most of 1918, as mentioned in Brémond's book *Le Hedjaz dans la Guerre Mondial* (1931).

Landor, Walter Savage (1775–1864)

Poet and stylist, noted especially for his *Poems from the Arabic and Persian* (1800) and *Imaginary Conversations* (1824–28), consisting of 150 prose pieces. Lawrence's review, probably written in March 1928, of T. Earle Welby's 1927 edition of Landor's complete works appeared in Lawrence's ***Men in Print*** and is available in Orlans's *Lawrence of Arabia* (1993). Lawrence writes that Landor's style is beautiful, but that ultimately Landor's work is too assured, smooth, and superficial.

Lane, Edward William (1801–76)

Author of *An Account of the Manners and Customs of the Modern Egyptians* (1836) and translator of *The Arabian Nights* (1838–41). Lawrence disliked the English translations by **Sir Richard Burton,** John Payne, and Edward Lane, preferring the French version of **Mardrus,** as he wrote in 1923 to **Jonathan Cape,** who had suggested that Lawrence himself do a translation of Mardrus. See Cape's memoir in **A. W. Lawrence's** *T. E. Lawrence by His Friends* for details.

Langley Lodge, New Forest

In 1894 the Lawrence family moved from **Dinard, France,** to the Isle of Wight, and then to Langley Lodge, an isolated house in Hampshire, about an hour southwest of Southampton. They remained here, enjoying their proximity to the sea, until 1896, when they moved to Oxford so the boys could receive a better education. Here Lawrence met **Janet Laurie,** who would later claim that he had proposed to her.

Languages, Knowledge of

See **Arabic, French,** and **Greek**

Larés, Maurice Jean-Marie (born 1926)

French author of *T. E. Lawrence, la France, et les Français* (1980), which is a shorter version of his two-volume doctoral thesis. Larés has also translated numerous works by and relating to Lawrence, including the manuscript of an unfinished Lawrence biography by **André Malraux.** His most recent work is *T. E. Lawrence avant*

L'Arabie 1888–1914 (T. E. Lawrence before Arabia 1888–1914).

Laurie, Janet

Lawrence met the Laurie family when he and his parents lived at **Langley Lodge** from 1894 to 1896. She went to boarding school in Oxford and was a frequent guest at the Polstead Road home of the Lawrences in Oxford. She later claimed that in 1910 Lawrence had suddenly proposed marriage to her and that she had laughed at him, but her account has not been fully accepted. In 1920, as **J. M. Wilson** points out in his *Lawrence of Arabia,* Lawrence generously gave her 3,000 pounds that his deceased brother **William Lawrence** had inherited from his father and that Will, who had been in love with her, had wanted her to have.

Lausanne, Treaty of

The treaty that resulted from a conference held in Lausanne, Switzerland, in 1923. It removed the humiliating terms imposed on Turkey by the **Treaty of Sèvres** in 1920, which Turkey had been forced to sign after being on the losing side in **World War I.** As a result of the Treaty of Lausanne, the Dardanelle Straits were demilitarized but Turkey retained sovereignty over all of Anatolia. The treaty also removed the Capitulations, or special privileges for foreigners in Turkey, and prevented the rise of an Armenian state or a Kurdistan, thus making Turkey the only country that was able to negotiate its own terms despite having been defeated in World War I. See David Fromkin, *A Peace to End All Peace.*

Lawrence, Arnold Walter (1900–91)

Lawrence's youngest brother, professor of classical archaeology at Cambridge University (1930–51), director of the National Museum, Ghana (1951–57), and Lawrence's literary executor. A. W. was a firm guardian of Lawrence's reputation, especially when countering **Richard Aldington**'s and **Suleiman Mousa**'s claims of Lawrence's untruthfulness and when disagreeing with some aspects of the 1962 David Lean film *Lawrence of Arabia.* In the postscript in his edited collection, *T. E. Lawrence by His Friends* (1937), he hinted at Lawrence's flagellation syndrome but did not openly state it. This collection, consisting of memoirs by people from all walks of life, is an invaluable addition to the Lawrence literature, as is A. W.'s edition *Letters to T. E. Lawrence* (1962).

Lawrence, David Herbert (1885–1930)

Important British fiction writer and poet. Lawrence greatly admired D. H. Lawrence, who in *Lady Chatterley's Lover* (1926–27) refers to Lawrence denigratingly as "Col. C. E. Florence." Lawrence did not hold it against him, because in his letter of 1930 to **Henry Williamson,** he shows an appreciation of D. H. Lawrence's novel and does not mention the slight to himself (Garnett, *Letters,* p. 687). Under the pseudonym **Colin Dale,** Lawrence reviewed D. H. Lawrence's novels, particularly *The Plumed Serpent* (1926), which he thought unsuccessful, in the *Spectator* 6 (August 1927): 223. This was reprinted in Lawrence's *Men in Print* and is available in Orlans, *Lawrence of Arabia, Strange Man of Letters.*

Lawrence, Frank Helier (1893–1915)

Frank Helier was born at (and named for) St. Helier, **Jersey,** to which the Lawrence family had traveled from **Dinard, France,** where they were living, in order to ensure that he would never be subject to the French army draft, Jersey being an English island. Frank was the fourth of the five Lawrence brothers, after Montagu Robert, T. E., and William George. Nicknamed Chimp, he was the only one to enjoy organized sports and was **Sarah Lawrence**'s favorite. His death in France on May 9, 1915, was devastating to her, especially since it was followed in the fall of 1915 by Will Lawrence's death in war. Lawrence took it stoically (Garnett, *Letters,* p. 199), but in chapter 117 of *Seven Pillars of Wisdom,* Lawrence refers to the death of his brothers, revealing that it was very much on his mind.

Lawrence, Montagu Robert (1885–1971)

Eldest of the five Lawrence brothers and the most dutiful. He served as a doctor in **France** during **World War I.** He then became a medical missionary, accompanying his mother **Sarah** to China in the early 1920s, much to Lawrence's disapproval. He edited the essential *Home Letters of T. E. Lawrence and His Brothers.*

Lawrence, Sarah Junner (1861–1959)

Lawrence's mother, born in Sunderland, County Durham, in the north of England. She was illegitimate, the daughter of **Elizabeth Junner** and (probably) John Lawrence, the son of a man in whose household Elizabeth was a servant. Sarah repeated this history when she became a governess in the house of Lord and Lady Thomas Chapman. She became pregnant, and Thomas set her up in an apartment in Dublin and eventually left his wife to move with Sarah to Wales, where the couple took the name Lawrence. Because Lady Chapman never granted her husband a divorce, Thomas and Sarah were never able to marry. As a result, Sarah became very religious, bringing up the five Lawrence brothers strictly and doing missionary work in China in the 1920s. See **J. M. Wilson,** *Lawrence of Arabia.*

Lawrence, Thomas Edward (1888–1935)

The subject of this encyclopedia, Lawrence was the second of five sons born to **Thomas Lawrence** (formerly Chapman) and **Sarah Junner Lawrence,** a couple that was never able to marry. Lawrence was born in **Tremadoc, Wales,** on August 16, 1888, lived in **Dinard, France,** as a child, and grew up in a house on Polstead Street, Oxford. He attended the **City of Oxford High School for Boys** then **Oxford University** (1907–10). After that came an apprenticeship under **D. G. Hogarth** and **C. Leonard Woolley** at a dig at the **Hittite** viceregal capital **Carchemish,** near **Jerablus, Syria** (1911–14). In early 1914, he also participated in the **Wilderness of Zin** survey, a study of the **Nabataean** and Byzantine sites in the northern Sinai desert, that covered a spying expedition by then-Capt. **Stewart Newcombe** of the Royal Engineers. When **World War I** began, Lawrence was in **London,** working on the proofs of *The Wilderness of Zin,* the **Palestine Exploration Fund** report about the archaeological results of the survey. After a brief stint making maps in the **Geographical Section, General Headquarters** in London, he was sent to **Cairo Military Intelligence.** During this period, he participated in an attempt to ransom **General Townshend**'s force that was surrounded by the Turks in **Mesopotamia.** In late 1916 he transferred to the **Arab Bureau** and then became involved in the **Arab Revolt.** Living and fighting like a **Beduin,** he developed a guerrilla strategy that would be emulated later in the century. He paid a personal price for the eventual victory of the British and Arab forces

when he was captured by the Turks at **Deraa** and abused. After the war, Lawrence worked at the **Peace Conference** in **Paris** to establish the **Emir Feisal**'s rule in **Syria** (as he had during the revolt); this failed when the French evicted Feisal in 1920, but in the meantime Lawrence had become one of the century's first electronic celebrities owing to the slide shows of American journalist **Lowell Thomas.** He joined the **Royal Air Force** as a simple airman in 1922 under the name **John Hume Ross,** was discharged when the media discovered this, and joined the Tank Corps in 1923 as **T. E. Shaw.** He served unhappily in the Tanks until 1925, when he was allowed to rejoin the R.A.F. Starting in 1922 and continuing at intervals until the end of his life, he suffered from a flagellation compulsion, but he was also very productive during this period. He produced the 1926 subscriber's edition of *Seven Pillars of Wisdom,* book reviews, a translation of **Pierre Custot**'s *Sturly* from the French, and, partially while he served with the R.A.F. in **India,** a translation of **Homer**'s *Odyssey.* After returning to England and serving at **R.A.F. Cattewater** (later **Mount Batten),** he became a superb marine mechanic, learning to help design, test, and overhaul fast boats, particularly the **200 Class Seaplane Tender.** His cottage, **Clouds Hill,** which he had acquired while in the Tank Corps and which held a rich collection of his books and records, became a place of refuge to which he finally retired in February 1935, only to die on May 19 as the result of a motorcycle accident. He is buried in the cemetery of St. Nicholas' Church, **Moreton.** Lawrence owes much of his fame to the interesting life he led during the Arab Revolt, to Lowell Thomas's publicity in the 1920s, to **Richard Aldington**'s debunking of the "Lawrence image" in the 1950s, and to David Lean's 1962 film *Lawrence of Arabia.* But Lawrence's reputation persists and grows because he was a brilliant polymath, who left his imprint on the fields of archaeology, intelligence work, strategy, diplomacy, literature, fine printing, and mechanics; because his life and career touched on many of the most important themes of the twentieth century, including wartime heroism, colonialism, and personal identity; and because he was a spiritual figure whose personal struggles and contradictions have inspired an almost religious devotion in many people. More than 50 biographies and numerous academic studies testify to his permanent interest to the general public and to scholars in many fields. *See* the introduction in this volume for a more detailed account. The best biographies are **John Mack,** *A Prince of Our Disorder,* and **J. M. Wilson,** *Lawrence of Arabia.*

Lawrence, Sir Thomas Robert Tighe Chapman (1846–1919)

Lawrence's father's family, the Chapmans, were related to Sir Walter Raleigh, through whose influence they received **Killua Castle** in **County Westmeath, Ireland.** Thomas Robert, however, became the lord of **South Hill,** a manor house near Delvin, also in County Westmeath. After attending Eton, he seemed destined for an unexceptional life as a settled, wealthy member of the Anglo-Irish gentry, especially when in 1873 he married Edith Sarah Hamilton. The couple had four daughters—Louisa, Rose Isabel, Florence Lina, and Mabel Cecele. But **Lady Edith Chapman** was religiously rigid and puritanical, and the unhappy Thomas ran off with a young governess, whom he had gotten pregnant, and took the name of Lawrence. They could never marry, but they lived together as man and wife and had five sons, of whom T. E. Lawrence was the second. The family lived in **Tremadoc, Wales** (where Lawrence was born), **Kirkcudbright,**

Scotland, and **Dinard, France,** among other places before settling down with their five sons in Polstead Road, Oxford. Lawrence's father taught the boys bicycling, **photography,** and sailing, but Lawrence saw him as someone who, owing to love, had been transformed from a free-wheeling aristocrat into a more cramped bourgeois role. In *Heart-Beguiling Araby,* Kathryn Tidrick speculates that Lawrence may have sought a princely role among the Arabs in an attempt to experience something of his own lost aristocratic position. Thomas Robert died in the influenza epidemic that swept the world after **World War I.** See **John Mack,** *A Prince of Our Disorder,* and **J. M. Wilson,** *Lawrence of Arabia.*

Lawrence, William George (1889–1915)

The third of the Lawrence brothers, born on December 10 in **Kirkcudbright,** Scotland. Lawrence felt closer to "Beadle" than to his other brothers. Will visited him at **Carchemish** in 1913 and wrote a poem to him. Will was a teacher in **India** when **World War I** began and returned to England to enlist. He was a Royal Flying Corps observer and had been in **France** less than a week when he was killed. Lawrence felt not only depressed, but guilty because he was still working in an office in **Cairo** rather than in a combat role. Later in life Lawrence gave **Janet Laurie** Will's share of his father's inheritance because Will had liked her greatly and had wanted him to do so.

"Lawrence Bureau"

A loosely organized group of Lawrence admirers headed by **B. H. Liddell Hart** and, to a lesser extent, **A. W. Lawrence,** that attempted to prevent the publication

Anthony Quinn as Auda abu Tayi whispers in the ear of Peter O'Toole, playing Lawrence, in this still from the 1962 film *Lawrence of Arabia,* written by Robert Bolt and directed by David Lean. Courtesy of Corbis.

of **Richard Aldington**'s *Lawrence of Arabia: A Biographical Enquiry* (1954 French edition; 1955 English). This was Aldington's term for the group, which also included **Eric Kennington** and **Robert Graves,** among others. These men may have felt that they were protecting Lawrence's reputation against scurrilous attack, but their attempt to interfere with Aldington's book, both before and after its publication, was controversial. See Fred Crawford, *Richard Aldington and Lawrence of Arabia: A Cautionary Tale,* for a history of this famous literary controversy that takes Aldington's side. See also **P. Knightley,** "Aldington's Enquiry concerning T. E. Lawrence," *Texas Quarterly* 16 (winter 1973): 98–105.

Lawrence of Arabia

This well-known film of 1962, produced by Sam Spiegel, directed by David Lean, and written by Michael Wilson and then **Robert Bolt,** featured the fine acting of **Peter O'Toole** as Lawrence, Alec Guinness as **Feisal,** Anthony Quinn as **Auda abu Tayi,** Omar Sharif as **Sharif Ali,** Claud Rains as **D. G. Hogarth** (called "Dryden" in the film), and Jack Hawkins as **General Allenby.** It inaccurately depicts Lawrence deliberately burning his finger with a match and confessing that he enjoyed killing and shows him being beaten rather than raped at **Deraa,** but it is nonetheless a very credible attempt to render the complexities of his political and personal dilemmas during the **Arab Revolt.** It has become a classic because of its excellent script, exceptional acting, and epic cinematography by Freddie Young. It regularly appears on lists of the best film epics, and many Lawrence enthusiasts date their interest from their first viewing of the film. See L. Robert Morris and Lawrence Raskin's *Lawrence of Arabia: The Thirtieth Anniversary Pictorial History;* and Steven Caton, *Lawrence of Arabia: A Film's Anthropology.*

Lawrence of Arabia Fact File, The

A Web site maintained by **Jeremy Wilson** containing valuable information about all aspects of Lawrence's life and work. Its Web address is http://www.lawrenceof arabia.info.

Lawrence of Arabia Memorial Medal

A silver medallion designed by **Eric Kennington** and struck in 1935 by the Royal Mint for the Royal Central Asian Society. The list of recipients includes **J. B. Glubb, Peake Pasha,** Orde Wingate, and **Wilfred Thesiger.** See **C. Grosvenor,** *An Iconography: The Portraits of T. E. Lawrence.*

Leachman, Lt. Col. Gerard Evelyn (1880–1920)

Officer of the Royal Sussex Regiment stationed in **India,** who became a political and intelligence operative among the Arabs of **Mesopotamia** during **World War I.** After the war, there was a period of unrest when the tribes rose against the British. Leachman died when Sheikh Dhari of the Zoba tribe had him shot; the British retaliated by burning Zoba villages. Lawrence met Leachman during the **Kut-al-Amara**

ransom attempt and in April 1917 in **Wejh.** As he wrote to **Alec Dixon** (Garnett, *Letters,* pp. 489–91), Lawrence felt that Leachman was brave, but a bully, and unsuited to work with people of other cultures. **Gertrude Bell** had a similar opinion of him. See **N.N.E. Bray,** *A Paladin of Arabia,* and H.V.F. Winstone, *Leachman: "OC Desert,"* for further details concerning Leachman's character and work.

"Leaves in the Wind"

A manuscript consisting of a few pages and kept in the **British Library,** apparently written by Lawrence as a projected sequel to *The Mint.* Garnett's *Letters* (pp. 502–3) reproduces a section detailing the unsanitary conditions during Lawrence's trip to **India** aboard the troopship SS *Derbyshire.*

Lebanon

Ottoman territory on the eastern Mediterranean coast until 1918, then a French mandate, and an independent country from 1946. Under the Ottomans, Lebanon was part of three large districts: **Beirut,** Damascus, and Mt. Lebanon, a Christian area ruled by a governor with some Great Power supervision. When **World War I** broke out, the Ottomans abrogated this special Mt. Lebanon arrangement, and in 1915–16 they hanged some Lebanese notables on suspicion of Arab nationalism. In 1918, at the end of the **Palestine** campaign, the British occupied the area and placed it under an Allied (largely French) administration. However, on October 3, 1918, before the entry into Beirut of Allied soldiers, **Shukri el Ayoubi** raised **Feisal's** flag there. The French (who were promised Lebanon and **Syria** in the **Sykes-Picot Agreement**) protested, and **Allenby** ordered the flag removed, causing a disturbance among the Arabs in Damascus.

Lawrence maintained (Garnett, *Letters,* pp. 670–72) that **Ali Riza Pasha** and other Damascene notables sent Shukri there right after the conquest of Damascus without Feisal's or Lawrence's consent; but as early as 1915 Feisal's father **Sharif Hussein** of **Mecca** in the **McMahon-Hussein Correspondence** had claimed Lebanon for the Arabs. The result of the flag-raising incident was the **Anglo-French Declaration** on November 7, which proclaimed the Allies' respect for the consent of the governed; it calmed the immediate tension, but on August 31, 1920, the French created Greater Lebanon, even before they received a mandate from the League of Nations. This was accepted by the Maronite Christian community, but less so by the Muslims of Lebanon and Syria. The French ruled the country, establishing its first constitution in 1926, until 1945–46 when they evacuated their troops. See **G. Antonius,** *The Arab Awakening;* Shimoni and Levine, *Political Dictionary of the Middle East in the Twentieth Century;* and M. E. Yapp, *The Making of the Modern Near East 1792–1923.*

Le Corbeau, Adrien (1886–1932)

French author of *Le Gigantesque,* the life story of a giant Sequoia tree, which Lawrence translated as *The Forest Giant* (1924). Lawrence felt that he had improved on the French version, because le Corbeau's style was in his opinion deficient. See **M. Larés,** *T. E. Lawrence, la France et les Français.*

Leeds, E. T. (1877–1955)

Assistant keeper at the **Ashmolean Museum** in **Oxford** from 1908 and friend of Lawrence from then on. In Leeds's memoir in **A. W. Lawrence**'s collection *T. E. Lawrence by His Friends,* he stresses Law-

rence's archaeological enthusiasm, which lasted until his death. See **J. M. Wilson,** editor, *T. E. Lawrence: Letters to E. T. Leeds* (1988).

Letters

Lawrence was a voluminous and brilliant correspondent, and his letters are an important facet of his literary production as well as an essential source about his life. Despite the valiant efforts of researchers to locate all of Lawrence's letters, the task never perhaps will be complete. **J. M. Wilson** has been working on a more complete edition than now exists and has published several full volumes of correspondence, including that with **G. B.** and **Charlotte Shaw** and a **Henry Williamson** volume. The letters can also be found in several other volumes: **J. Mack,** *A Prince of Our Disorder* (1976), contains Lawrence's letters relating to his flagellation; **B. Rogers,** *Letters from T. E. Shaw to Bruce Rogers* (1933); *More Letters from T. E. Shaw to Bruce Rogers* (1936); **D. Garnett,** *The Letters of T. E. Lawrence* (1938); **Clare Sydney Smith,** *The Golden Reign* (1940); **H. S. Ede,** *Shaw-Ede: T. E. Lawrence's Letters to H. S. Ede* (1942); **M. R. Lawrence,** *The Home Letters of T. E. Lawrence and His Brothers* (1954); **R. Graves** and **Liddell Hart,** *T. E. Lawrence to His Biographers* (1963); H. Montgomery Hyde, *Solitary in the Ranks* (1977); **M. Brown,** *T. E. Lawrence: The Selected Letters* (1988); **J. M. Wilson,** *T. E. Lawrence: Letters to E. T. Leeds* (1988); H. Orlans, *Lawrence of Arabia: Strange Man of Letters* (1993). See **Jeffrey Meyers,** "T. E. Lawrence in His Letters" in his collection *T. E. Lawrence: Soldier, Writer, Legend.*

Lewis, C. Day

See **Day-Lewis, Cecil**

Lewis, Percy Wyndham (1884–1957)

British novelist, painter, leader of the Vorticist movement, and, briefly, supporter of Adolf Hitler. Lawrence commissioned Lewis to do some illustrations for the 1926 subscriber's edition of *Seven Pillars of Wisdom,* but Lewis failed to produce, seriously disappointing Lawrence, who had given him a 50-pound advance. Lawrence wrote **Robert Graves** in 1927 that he could not understand Lewis's philosophy, and he was highly critical of Lewis's short-story collection *The Wild Body* (1927). For his part, Lewis felt that Lawrence had wasted his talents in the **Royal Air Force.** See **Jeffrey Meyers,** *The Enemy: A Biography of Wyndham Lewis.*

Liddell Hart, Capt. Basil Henry (1895–1970)

Influential military writer, author of numerous books on strategy and history, and journalist. Liddell Hart's *"T. E. Lawrence": In Arabia and After* (1934) claimed for Lawrence a position as one of the great military figures because of his use of the indirect attack. He followed this biography with *T. E. Lawrence to His Biographers Robert Graves & Liddell Hart* (1963; Graves's and Liddell Hart's portions of this book were originally published separately in 1938). Although Liddell Hart realized that Lawrence had told Graves and himself conflicting stories about his ride of June 1917 behind Turkish lines and other matters, he remained one of Lawrence's strongest advocates, becoming the unofficial leader of the **"Lawrence Bureau"** that sought to protect Lawrence's reputation against **Aldington**'s attack of 1954–55 and even to prevent the publication of Aldington's book. In addition to his work on Lawrence, Liddell Hart was the military correspondent for the *Daily Telegraph,* the *Times,* and the *Encyclopaedia Britannica.*

In the latter role, he wrote the article on guerrilla warfare in the 14th edition of the *Britannica* on the basis of Lawrence's writings, after Lawrence turned down the task of writing the article himself. The Liddell Hart Centre for Military Archives is at King's College, **London.** See Alex Danchev, *Alchemist of War: The Life of Basil Liddell Hart,* and Fred Crawford, *Richard Aldington and Lawrence of Arabia: A Cautionary Tale.*

Lloyd, Sir George Ambrose, 1st Baron Lloyd (1879–1941)

Honorary attaché in Constantinople, 1905; head of the British trade mission to **Mesopotamia,** 1907; Unionist member of parliament for South Staffordshire; member of **Cairo Military Intelligence Department** from 1914; in charge of Sinai Intelligence, 1917–18; secretary to the British delegation at the **Peace Conference** in 1918; governor of Bombay; and high commissioner of **Egypt** (to 1929). Lloyd was a specialist in economic matters who was a member of the known banking family. In chapter 6 of *Seven Pillars of Wisdom,* Lawrence praises Lloyd as a guide to the future of trade and politics in the Middle East, and in chapters 70 and 73 he praises his character. Lloyd accompanied Lawrence part of the way on the **Yarmuk Valley Bridges** expedition, and he wrote a report about Lawrence's plans. In 1934, Lawrence wrote a lengthy letter to Lloyd, commenting on his *Egypt since Cromer* (1933) in detail (Garnett, *Letters,* pp. 819–24).

Lloyd George, David, 1st Earl (1863–1945)

Liberal Party politician and prime minister of England, 1916–22. In his view of self-determination for small nations, Lloyd George held a stance between **Clemen-**

ceau's overt imperialism and **President Woodrow Wilson**'s pro-independence position. On November 30, 1918, Lloyd George and Clemenceau signed an agreement that modified the **Sykes-Picot Agreement** by placing an enlarged **Palestine** under British (rather than international) control and the **Mosul** area of **Mesopotamia** in the British sphere of influence, while giving France control over **Lebanon** and the coastal areas of **Syria,** as well as some share of the Mosul area's oil revenues. **Feisal** was to receive Damascus, **Homs, Aleppo,** and **Hama.** Lawrence encouraged **Feisal,** who protested any French occupation, to accept this deal as the best that he was likely to get. Lawrence told **Liddell Hart** in 1933 that he admired Lloyd George more than the other leading politicians at the **Peace Conference,** and he was pleased to visit him in retirement in Liddell Hart's company; but because of Lloyd George's acquiescence to Clemenceau's designs on Syria, he may figure as one of the unspecified "old men" of whom Lawrence complains in the introductory chapter of *Seven Pillars of Wisdom.* See D. McCormick, *The Masks of Merlin: A Critical Biography of Lloyd George;* and B. Gilbert, *David Lloyd George: A Political Life.*

London

Lawrence lived in London for a relatively sustained amount of time only when, in late 1919–early 1920, he retreated from his lodgings at **All Souls College, Oxford,** to a loft in Barton Street, Westminster, owned by **Sir Herbert Baker,** to work on *Seven Pillars of Wisdom,* and when in 1921 he worked with **Winston Churchill** in the **Colonial Office,** but he was absent from England much of that time. He also lived in London until August 1922, when he enlisted in the **Royal Air Force** under the name **John Hume Ross.** Although Lawrence seems to have preferred living outside of London, it is clear from his letters that he enjoyed wandering the streets there, and in 1927 he contemplated working in the City as a night watchman after retiring from the R.A.F.

Lucas, Frank Laurence (1894–1967)

King's College, Cambridge, literary critic whom Lawrence met through **E. M. Forster** in 1925 and with whom he corresponded thereafter. Lucas, an influential traditionalist critic, greatly admired *Seven Pillars of Wisdom.*

Lynden-Bell, Maj. Gen. Sir Arthur L. (1867–1943)

A captain in the Boer War and subsequently a division commander. Chief of staff to **Gen. Sir Archibald Murray** in **Egypt.** Lawrence characterized Lynden-Bell, in chapter 7 of *Seven Pillars of Wisdom,* as a stodgy traditional soldier, but in chapters 16 and 28, he praises him for his support of the **Arab Revolt.** Lynden-Bell, known by the nickname Belinda, was removed by **General Allenby** when he took command in the summer of 1917 and was replaced with Allenby's chief of staff, **Maj. Gen. Louis Bols.**

M

Maan

City about 60 miles northeast of **Akaba** (in what is now Jordan), the site of a **Hejaz Railway** station, and the command headquarters of Behjet Pasha. According to chapter 60 of *Seven Pillars of Wisdom,* in August 1917 it was held by 6,000 Turkish infantry soldiers and a regiment of cavalry and was a major supply dump. It was heavily entrenched and had its own airfield and planes. At that time, Lawrence began a series of air raids, railroad attacks, and armored-car skirmishes, some of which were successful, but a direct attack on Maan under **Jaafar Pasha el Askari** and **Nuri el Said** in April 1918 met with failure. The Arabs besieged but were never able to capture Maan in a battle. However, in September 1918 the Turkish force there retreated and their commander Ali Bey Wahaby surrendered his 4,500 troops on September 28 to Australian **General Chaytor**'s force. See **A. P. Wavell,** *The Palestine Campaigns,* and William Facey, editor, *A Soldier's Story.*

Mack, John E. (born 1929)

Harvard professor of psychiatry and author of *A Prince of Our Disorder: The Life of T. E. Lawrence* (1976). This book is notable for its insights into the connection between the public and the private in Lawrence's life and for its accurate historical presentation. Because it is very pro-Lawrence, it has been criticized by **Elie Kedourie** and others skeptical of Lawrence's role. In the years after writing this book, Mack became embroiled in controversy over his seeming acceptance of alien abduction theories.

Mafrak

Town in what is now Jordan, about 25 miles south of **Deraa,** with a **Hejaz Railway** station. It was destroyed in September 1918 by a British Handley-Page bomber that dropped several 100-pound bombs, setting it on fire. Soon after, the Arab forces were able to capture a number of prisoners and arms from the Turkish forces attempting to escape from the station, as described in chapter 115 of *Seven Pillars of Wisdom.*

Maggs Bros.

Leading **London** dealer of Lawrence books. The firm is located in Berkeley Square, and its Web site is http://www.maggs.com.

Mahmas

A camel driver who had a knife fight with Awad, another of the 28 men who lived with Lawrence in two cramped rooms at **Tafileh** in January 1918, as described in chapter 87 of *Seven Pillars of Wisdom.* Awad bore his punishment of whipping bravely; but Mahmas cried and then left because he felt humiliated by his failure of nerve. Lawrence comments that this incident reminded him of his own perceived failure during his beating in the **Deraa incident.**

Mahmud

One of Lawrence's bodyguards. As described in chapter 71 of *Seven Pillars of Wisdom,* he was from the Yarmuk area, 19 years old, and easily angered.

Malory, Sir Thomas (died 1471)

British author of *Morte d'Arthur* (originally entitled *The Book of King Arthur and His Noble Knights of the Round Table*). **Vyvyan Richards** testifies that Malory was one of Lawrence's favorite authors during his years at **Oxford University,** along with **William Morris, Charles Doughty,** and **Aristophanes.** In chapters 16 and 87 of *Seven Pillars of Wisdom,* Lawrence writes that he was reading Malory to relieve the stress of the campaign, and elsewhere he compares **Auda abu Tayi**'s ageless quality to that of Malory's work. In a letter of April 7, 1927, to **D. G. Hogarth,** he stated that his reading during the Arab campaign consisted of Malory, Aristophanes, and *The Oxford Book of English Verse* (Garnett, *Letters,* p. 512).

Malraux, André (1901–76)

French man of action and novelist who some writers have compared to Lawrence. Malraux himself was fascinated by Lawrence and based Vincent Berger, the hero of his *Walnut Trees of Altenburg* (English edition, 1952) on him. In the 1940s, he also wrote an unfinished Lawrence biography that has been edited by **Maurice Larés.**

Manning, Frederic (1882–1935)

Author of the war novel *Her Privates We* (1930) and a book about the Somme, among other works. Lawrence liked Manning's writing from the time he was an undergraduate, but he became friends with Manning only in 1930 and wrote in that year to **Robert Graves** that he felt closest to Manning, **Altounyan,** and **Forster** since **Hogarth**'s death (Garnett, *Letters,* p. 760). Manning's essay "Apologia Dei" in his *Scenes and Portraits* (1930) is dedicated "To **T. E. Shaw,**" Lawrence's adopted name. When Manning died, Lawrence wrote a moving letter to Manning's publisher Peter Davies (Garnett, *Letters,* p. 859). See Jonathan Marwil, *Frederic Manning: An Unfinished Life.*

Mao Tse-Tung (1893–1976)

Leader of the Great March (1934–35) of the Chinese Communist army and founder of the People's Republic of China (1949). Writers on guerrilla warfare have claimed that Mao was influenced by Lawrence, and that Lawrence's **"Twenty-Seven Articles"** exceed the usefulness of Mao's "Eight Points" as a text for practitioners of guerrilla warfare. It has been rumored that Mao had a Chinese edition of *Seven Pillars of Wisdom.* See **K. Morsey,** "T. E. Lawrence: Strategist," and **P. O'Brien,** "Collecting T. E. Lawrence Materials" in *The T. E. Lawrence Puzzle,* edited by Tabachnick.

Mapmaking

Lawrence began work on maps before the war, when he and **Woolley** assisted **Newcombe** during the **Wilderness of Zin** survey and made archaeological maps. When the war began, Lawrence's first position was in the **Geographical Section** of the War Office in **London,** where he worked on maps of Sinai. He worked again on maps as part of his assignment as a general staff intelligence officer in **Cairo,** where he was transferred in December 1914. As a liaison between Military Intelligence and the Survey of **Egypt,** Lawrence worked on maps of Sinai, the Dardanelles, and **Syria** and played a role in the early development of aerial photography. **Ernest Dowson,** director-general of the Survey of Egypt from 1909, testifies in **A. W. Lawrence**'s *T. E. Lawrence by His Friends* that Lawrence's work was outstanding. His most extraordinary talent, according to Dowson, who worked with him during as well as before the war, was a photographic memory that enabled him to remember topographic features of any ground that he covered. It has been claimed by David Kimche (*Jerusalem Post,* December 22, 1984) that in 1915 Lawrence made a map of the **Akaba** region, based on his own trip there in 1914 as part of the Zin survey, that moved the boundary of British Egypt farther north than it actually should have been, and that this map figured much later in the negotiations between Egypt and Israel over the Taba area in the early 1980s.

Mardrus, Dr. Joseph Charles (1868–1949)

Egyptian-born scholar and translator who lived in **France** from an early age. In 1923, **Jonathan Cape** suggested that Lawrence translate Mardrus's French version of *The Arabian Nights* into English. Lawrence was enthusiastic because he felt that Mardrus's translation was the best in any language with which he was familiar, but the French publisher already had assigned the rights to translation in English, and Edward Powys Mathers did it instead of Lawrence. See Cape's memoir in **A. W.**

Lawrence's collection *T. E. Lawrence by His Friends.*

Maronites

A group of Eastern Christians, in communion with the Catholic Church, whose center is in **Lebanon.** In 1860–61, massacres of Maronites by Druses caused the creation by the European powers of the autonomous area of Mt. Lebanon, which had a Maronite majority. During **World War I,** the Maronites worked with French intelligence, and the French viewed themselves as the Maronites' protector. After 1920, the Maronites, while a minority, became the largest group in the French-created and French-controlled Greater Lebanon. Until recently, the president and commander-in-chief of Lebanon's army were always Maronites by law, and the Maronite party was the Phalanges, which also functioned as a military group. In chapter 59 of *Seven Pillars of Wisdom,* Lawrence mentions influential Christian merchants of **Beirut,** but he seems to have had few dealings with them or with other Maronites, although according to **Knightley** and **Simpson,** during his **Cairo intelligence** period he supervised Charles Boutagy, a Lebanese Christian spy. See Shimoni and Levine, *Political Dictionary of the Middle East in the Twentieth Century.*

Marsh, Edward (1872–1953)

Private secretary to **Winston Churchill** in the 1920s, translator of La Fontaine's *Fables,* and literary executor of war poet Rupert Brooke. Lawrence first met Marsh in 1918. Marsh approached Lawrence in 1921 to see if he would join the **Colonial Office** to advise Churchill on Arab affairs. Because Marsh was the editor of *Georgian Poetry* and a patron of the arts, he was able to introduce Lawrence to **Siegfried Sassoon** and **Thomas Hardy.** Lawrence liked Marsh as a person (Garnett, *Letters,* pp. 601–2) but did not fully respect his intellect (p. 752).

Marshall, Ken (died circa 1950)

London bookseller. Marshall mistook Lawrence for a furnace repairman when Lawrence first came into his bookshop, but they soon became friends because of their literary interests. In 1935, Lawrence wrote Marshall, who was then affiliated with Boriswood Publishers, about the prosecution of **James Hanley**'s novel *Boy* (published by Boriswood) for indecency (Garnett, *Letters,* pp. 847–48). Lawrence lent Marshall his cottage, **Clouds Hill,** when he was out of work. Marshall suffered divorce and a breakdown after World War II.

Marshall, Maj. W. E.

Scottish doctor who was assigned to the Arab forces. Lawrence roomed with him when at the **Akaba** base, as he relates in chapter 83 of *Seven Pillars of Wisdom.* Marshall accompanied the Arab forces when they moved toward **Syria** and is consistently described by Lawrence as being reliable and good-natured even when faced with difficult circumstances.

Matheson, Christopher (born 1949)

A Londoner resident in California, Matheson has amassed one of the finest private photo collections of Lawrence. In addition to photos, his collection includes television documentaries about Lawrence, and he has been a consultant to the BBC and, most recently, assisted JAK films with a forthcoming documentary on Lawrence. He supplied the photos and captions for *Images of Lawrence,* the centenary volume

published by **Jonathan Cape** in 1988, with text by Stephen Tabachnick.

Maxwell, Gen. Sir John Grenfell (1859–1929)

General officer in command of **Egypt,** followed in early 1916 by **Sir Archibald Murray.** On December 18, 1914, he formally severed Egypt's ties to Turkey and declared the country a British protectorate. Although Lawrence mentions him only once in *Seven Pillars of Wisdom,* Lawrence viewed Maxwell favorably, perhaps because from 1914 he supported the idea of an Arab revolt against the Turks, to be initiated by an Allied landing at **Alexandretta, Syria.** Since Maxwell had supported the idea of an Alexandretta landing before Lawrence did, Lawrence was mistaken in his claim to **Liddell Hart** (in *T. E. Lawrence to His Biographers, Robert Graves & Liddell Hart,* p. 17) that he had initiated the Alexandretta scheme. See **John Mack,** *A Prince of Our Disorder,* and **J. M. Wilson,** *Lawrence of Arabia,* for more details.

McDonnell, Denis W. (born 1952)

A leading American bookseller of Lawrence materials and, with Mary McDonnell and Janet Riesman, a founding editor of the newsletter *T. E. Notes,* which began publication in 1990. The Web site of his firm, which is located in Honesdale, Pennsylvania, is http://www.denismcd.com.

McMahon, Sir Arthur Henry (1862–1949)

Minister for foreign affairs, government of **India,** 1911–14; high commissioner of **Egypt,** 1915–16, following **Kitchener;** and author of the British side of the **Mc-**

Mahon-Hussein Correspondence, which set forth the terms under which the British and Arabs would fight against the Turks. In chapter 6 of *Seven Pillars of Wisdom,* Lawrence praises McMahon for his support of the Arab movement and claims in chapter 48 that McMahon was unaware of the **Sykes-Picot Agreement,** which to some degree contradicted the McMahon-Hussein Correspondence, while he was negotiating with the Arabs. In a letter of 1918 to *Times* editor **Geoffrey Dawson,** Lawrence indicates that McMahon was dismissed in December 1916 from the High Commission because the **Arab Revolt** seemed to be a failure in its early days (Brown, *Selected Letters,* pp. 161–62). Lawrence told **Liddell Hart** that after the war he had met McMahon in a train and had chatted amiably with him, while **H. G. Wells** was in the same carriage and introduced himself to them.

McMahon-Hussein Correspondence

A correspondence consisting of 10 letters, initiated on July 14, 1915, by **Sharif Hussein** of **Mecca** and ending on March 30, 1916. In his letters, Hussein asked Britain, represented by **Sir Henry McMahon,** the high commissioner in **Egypt,** to accept the independence of the Arab countries and the reestablishment of an Arab caliphate. In exchange for this, Hussein would ally himself with the British against the Turks. McMahon accepted these principles, but in his responses he excluded from Arab control areas of **Syria** west of Damascus, **Homs, Aleppo,** and **Hama,** as well as Basra (now in **Iraq**) and two port cities, Mersin and **Alexandretta** (now in **Turkey**). Hussein did not accept these conditions and broke off the correspondence. After the war, the exclusion of the western Syrian areas became the focus of a dispute, with the Arabs claiming that **Palestine** was not part of the excluded area, and the Brit-

ish (including McMahon himself) contending that it was. Various British, Zionist, and Arab nationalist historians, including **Antonius,** have rendered opinions on this issue, according to their political outlooks. In any case, the **Sykes-Picot Agreement,** which McMahon may not have known about while he was negotiating with Hussein, clearly awards Palestine and **Mesopotamia** to the British; **Lebanon** and most of Syria to the French; Trebizond, Erzerum, Lake Van, and Bitlis to the Russians; and only Arabia to the Arabs, thus nullifying McMahon's pledges and rendering the argument over his correspondence moot. In the event, the League of Nations mandate system did not allow any formal direct possession of areas by the British and French, awarding them only indirect control as mandatory powers. The British and French did, however, remain in de facto control of Palestine and Syria respectively until they were forced to leave in the late 1940s. The British left Mesopotamia (now called Iraq) in 1932. See G. Antonius, *The Arab Awakening,* and **E. Kedourie,** *In the Anglo-Arab Labyrinth: The McMahon-Husayn Correspondence and Its Interpretations 1914–1939.*

Mecca

Muslim holy city in Arabia, about 50 miles east of **Jidda,** containing the Kaaba and the shrine of Abraham. Under Ottoman rule, the city was administered for the caliph or sultan by a sharifian family, but Turkish troops were garrisoned there. **Sharif Hussein**'s forces revolted against the 1,400 Turkish troops in the city on June 10, 1916, forcing their surrender on July 4 after the arrival of Egyptian army artillery supplied by **Sir Reginald Wingate.**

Medici Society

Scholarly society that agreed to Lawrence's request to republish **Doughty**'s

Arabia Deserta (1888), in concert with Philip Lee Warner and **Jonathan Cape,** who had just set up his own imprint. The book was published in 1921 with Lawrence's introduction, which was insisted upon by the publishers to help the book's sales. Lawrence's introduction asserts the uniqueness of *Arabia Deserta* and its uniquely high place in Anglo-Arabian and indeed all travel writing.

Medina

Muslim holy city in **Arabia,** about 100 miles east of the port of **Yenbo,** containing the tomb of the prophet Mohammed. The city was Mohammed's base, providing him with the resources for a victory over the Meccans in 630 C.E. and serving as his home after that. During the **Arab Revolt, Sharif Hussein**'s forces besieged the city, held by **Fakhri Pasha** and some 10,000–12,000 Turkish troops with artillery and machine guns, but were never able to conquer it. **Enver Pasha** instructed Fakhri to evacuate the city, but he ignored the order and surrendered undefeated only in January 1919, after his starving troops mutinied and **World War I** had already ended. There is some debate over whether Lawrence decided not to try to conquer Medina in order to draw Turkish troops to the **Hejaz** by harassing the city, as Lawrence claims in chapter 33 of *Seven Pillars of Wisdom,* or if this apparently ingenious strategy was merely an acquiescence to the fact that the Arabs were unable to take the city. See **K. Morsey,** "T. E. Lawrence: Strategist," in *The T. E. Lawrence Puzzle,* edited by Tabachnick, and Pope and Wheal, *The Dictionary of the First World War.*

Mediterranean Expeditionary Force

Also called Medforce, this was a British army assembled in spring 1915 for the pur-

pose of landing in the **Gallipoli** peninsula. Part of Lawrence's job as an intelligence officer in **Cairo** involved serving this force. After Medforce's evacuation from Gallipoli to **Egypt** in January 1916, it was placed under **Gen. Sir Archibald Murray,** and in March 1916 it was melded into the British army in Egypt.

Megiddo, Battle of

Also known as the Battle of Armageddon because Megiddo (now in Israel) is the site of Armageddon, or the final battle of all, according to the Bible. The Battle of Megiddo was the most important battle of **World War I** in **Palestine,** and for all important purposes the final major battle of the eastern war. After elaborate preparations (including the building of a false camp with 3,000 surplus tents and many noncombatant troops who were told to raise dust) to mislead the Turks into thinking that his major offensive would come in **Transjordan,** on September 19, 1918, Allenby attacked along a 60-mile line north of **Jerusalem.** With 57,000 troops, 12,000 additional cavalry troops, and 540 guns, plus 30,000 troops in reserve, he completely overwhelmed the Turkish forces, which numbered no more than 29,000 troops, 3,000 cavalry, and 400 guns. His air power, including 105 SE-5s, Bristol fighters, and Airco DH9 bombers, completely overwhelmed the five remaining aircraft of the German Air Service in Palestine. The British forces completely overran the Turkish trenches along the line and by late afternoon of the first day had captured the Turkish Eighth Army headquarters, some 15 miles behind the line. British **General Chetwode** attacked north of Jerusalem and forced the Turkish Seventh Army back until it was melded into the disorganized and reeling Eighth Army. Meanwhile, the Turkish Fourth Army's base at **Deraa** was surrounded by Lawrence's Arab forces, and the British moved to seal all escape routes for the collapsing Turkish armies. By the evening of September 24, thousands of Turkish troops had been captured. German **Gen. Liman von Sanders,** whose headquarters in Nazareth had been captured on the 20th, attempted to hold a line south of the Sea of Galilee with a few hundred troops who were quickly overwhelmed. By September 26, the remnants of the Turkish armies in Palestine were in full retreat toward Damascus, pursued by Allenby's cavalry. The Turks never recovered from this attack, and by October 1 Damascus itself was in British and Arab hands. *See* **Damascus, Fall of.** For more information, see Pope and Wheal, *The Dictionary of the First World War;* **A. P. Wavell,** *The Palestine Campaigns;* Cyril Falls, *Armageddon 1918;* and Bryan Perrett, *Megiddo 1918.*

Meinertzhagen, Col. Richard (1878–1967)

British intelligence chief during the East African campaign against German guerrilla **Gen. Paul von Lettow-Vorbeck.** An eager combatant, Meinertzhagen at one point narrowly missed von Lettow-Vorbeck with a bullet. He later became **Allenby**'s head of intelligence during the **Palestine** campaign. In chapter 69 of *Seven Pillars of Wisdom,* Lawrence credits "Meiner" (who was British, but whose name was of Danish origin) with a brilliant implementation of **Guy Dawnay**'s plan to conquer **Gaza** by means of a surprise attack first on **Beersheba.** In addition to other shrewd maneuvers, Meinertzhagen rode near the Turkish lines with a false and blood-stained set of plans and deliberately dropped it when the Turks chased and shot at him. The story is also told in Simon Wincer's film *The Light Horsemen* (1988). Meinertzhagen might have told Lawrence of von Lettow-Vorbeck's tactics, thus inspiring Lawrence's own, but this is speculative. In his *Middle East Diary, 1917–1956,* Meinertzhagen alleges homosexuality on Lawrence's part, but several biographers have questioned the accuracy of this and other recollections because some of Meinertzhagen's entries seem to be retrospective rather than contemporary. For his part, Meinertzhagen disagreed with Lawrence's portrayal of him in *Seven Pillars of Wisdom* as a brutal warrior. See P. Capstick, *Warrior: The Legend of Colonel Richard Meinertzhagen;* M. Cocker, *Richard Meinertzhagen: Soldier, Scientist, Spy;* J. Lord, *Duty, Honor, Empire: The Life and Times of Col. Richard Meinertzhagen;* and J. Lockman [Jon Loken], *Meinertzhagen's Diary Ruse.*

Meissaloun, Battle of

A battle that took place on July 24, 1920, at the Meissaloun Pass between 2,000 of **Feisal**'s followers (acting against his orders) and French forces that were marching on Damascus under **Gen. Henri Gouraud.** The Arabs, including Feisal's Minister of War Yusuf el-Azmeh, were decimated, and the French went on to occupy the city on July 25. They evicted Feisal, who left the country on July 28. This marked the end of the **Arab Revolt,** and it occurred during the time that Lawrence was writing *Seven Pillars of Wisdom,* undercutting the triumphant military story in that work. See **G. Antonius,** *The Arab Awakening,* and **J. M. Wilson,** *Lawrence of Arabia.*

Meleager (c. 100 B.C.E.)

Greek poet of ancient **Gadara,** or modern Um Keis, **Syria,** whose poetry survives in the *Greek Anthology,* which he originally compiled. In chapter 70 of *Seven Pillars of Wisdom,* Lawrence refers to Meleager's work as the high point of Syrian literature.

Melville, Herman (1819–91)

Widely regarded as the greatest American novelist. Lawrence considered Melville's *Moby Dick,* along with **Dostoyevsky**'s *The Brothers Karamazov* and **Nietzsche**'s *Thus Spake Zarathustra,* as one of the three books he was competing with when writing *Seven Pillars of Wisdom* (Garnett, *Letters,* p. 360). He also read Melville's *Redburn* and *White Jacket,* which might have served as a model for Lawrence's ***The Mint,*** and he greatly admired Melville's Civil War poetry. In 1923 he declined **Jonathan Cape**'s invitation to write introductions to *Typee, Omoo,* and *Moby Dick,* but only because he did not want to write under the name Lawrence.

Men in Print, Essays in Literary Criticism

Published in 1940 by the **Golden Cockerel Press,** with an introduction by **A. W. Lawrence,** this collection includes Lawrence's "A Note on **James Elroy Flecker**," "A Review of Novels of **D. H. Lawrence**," "A Review of Short Stories of **H. G. Wells**," "A Criticism of **Henry Williamson**'s *Tarka the Otter*," and "The Works of **Walter Savage Landor**." All of these items, and other reviews and literary letters written by Lawrence, are available in Orlans's *Lawrence of Arabia, Strange Man of Letters.*

Menippus (3rd century B.C.E.)

Like **Meleager,** a Greek poet of ancient **Gadara** or modern Um Keis, **Syria,** and mentioned with him by Lawrence in chapter 70 of *Seven Pillars of Wisdom.* Menippus satirized society in a mixture of prose and poetry, but only imitations of his work survive.

Merton, Wilfred (1889–1957)

Outstanding printer and book collector. Partner, with **Sir Emery Walker,** in the production of the beautiful 1932 **Bruce Rogers** edition of Lawrence's *Odyssey* translation.

Mesopotamia

The Tigris-Euphrates Valley, site of the ancient Sumerian and Babylonian civilizations, and an important theater of Turkish-British contention during **World War I,** especially because of the importance of oil fields necessary for the British navy. After the **Young Turk** revolution of 1908, a group of Mesopotamian Sunni officers in the Ottoman army, and the Shiite **Sayid Taleb,** began plotting Arab independence from Turkey, which controlled the area. As soon as World War I began, a British army from **India** invaded, and by July 1915 all of southern Mesopotamia was under British control. In April 1916, **Maj. Gen. Charles Townshend,** after an ill-prepared and over-extended advance along the Tigris toward Baghdad, was forced to surrender his 10,000 men to the Turks at **Kut-al-Amara.** But by March 11, 1917, Baghdad was conquered by a force under General Sir Stanley Maude, and by November 1, 1918, the British controlled all of the territory up to and including **Mosul.** General Maude died of cholera in November 1917, but General Marshall took over, and the 50,000 Turkish troops in this theater were unable to stop the 250,000 troops that the British were able to deploy against them. This campaign cost 98,000 British casualties (one-third of which were deaths) and even higher Turkish losses. After the war, Arab hopes of independence were dashed, and in June 1920 a large-scale insurrection broke out against the British, until in 1921 **Feisal,** who had been expelled from **Syria** in 1920 by the French, took over as king under a British League of Nations mandate. He was assisted by British advisers, including **Gertrude Bell.** On October 3, 1932, the state of **Iraq,** covering most of the territory of Mesopotamia, was admitted to the league as a fully independent state. See Pope and Wheal, *The Dictionary of the First World War,* and F. J. Moberly, *The Campaign in Mesopotamia 1914–1918.*

Metcalf, Edwards (died 2001)

A businessman, Edwards Metcalf began collecting Lawrenciana in the 1930s and developed an outstanding collection, including several 1926 editions of *Seven Pillars of Wisdom,* first editions of most of Lawrence's works, and numerous letters. His collection was housed at the **Huntington Library,** in San Marino, California, where Metcalf lived, and formed the basis for **Philip O'Brien**'s award-winning Lawrence bibliography. A true arts patron, Metcalf funded the first-ever conference on Lawrence, at Pepperdine University in 1988, as well as a second conference at the Huntington Library. He also had a collection of **Sir Richard Francis Burton**'s work, which is housed at the Huntington, and he sponsored a Burton conference there. In addition to his Lawrence and Burton collections, Metcalf was also a collector of works about papermaking. At the time of his death, the ultimate fate of his collections was not clear.

Meyers, Jeffrey (born 1939)

American-born scholar and prolific author of literary biographies. Meyers, a Berkeley Ph.D. in English, wrote the first analytic book on Lawrence as a writer, *The Wounded Spirit* (1973; bibliography revised 1989), and edited a collection, *T. E. Lawrence: Soldier, Writer, Legend* (1989),

on him. He also had numerous book chapters and articles on Lawrence to his credit.

Mezerib

Hejaz Railway station, on the branch line to **Palestine,** about 10 miles west of **Deraa.** Lawrence relates the capture on September 16, 1918, of this station, with its 40 Turkish survivors and its abundant supplies, as well as the looting by the local peasants that accompanied it, in chapter 110 of *Seven Pillars of Wisdom.*

Middle East Department

A new department of the **Colonial Office** proposed by Lawrence, **D. G. Hogarth, Lionel Curtis,** and Arnold Toynbee in 1920 to administer Arab affairs in place of the **Foreign Office** and the **India Office.** When **Winston Churchill** took over the Colonial Office in January 1921, he invited Lawrence to join its new Middle East Department, so their agitation had succeeded.

Mifleh el Gomaan

Lawrence's Arab guide during the failed **Yarmuk Valley Bridges** expedition. Lawrence testifies to Mifleh's good work in chapters 76 and 78 of *Seven Pillars of Wisdom.*

Milli-Kurds

Nomadic Kurdish tribe who planned in 1912, when Turkey was occupied with the Balkan Wars, to sack **Aleppo** because their crops had failed. Because they planned to go through **Jerablus** where Lawrence and **Woolley** were digging, the pair did their best to keep on good terms with the **Kurds,** who seemed eager to loot from Europeans as well. Lawrence helped smuggle arms from **Beirut** into the British consulate at Aleppo to protect it from the possible Kurdish attack, as recorded in Garnett, *Letters,* pp. 150–51 and 158. Knowledge of the Kurds was undoubtedly one of the elements that Lawrence had in mind when he wrote at the beginning of chapter 6 of *Seven Pillars of Wisdom* that he had learned something of the political forces in the Middle East during the prewar period.

Minifir

Site on the **Hejaz Railway** about 50 miles south of **Deraa** and 50 miles west of **Azrak** where Lawrence and Zaal destroyed some curved rails in June 1917 (as recounted in chapter 50 of *Seven Pillars of Wisdom*) and where on November 10 of the same year Lawrence was spotted by a Turkish train when his mine failed to explode (*Seven Pillars of Wisdom,* chapter 77). On November 11, Lawrence was wounded there when he succeeded in blowing up a train.

Minorities

Lawrence's personal anthology of poetry, assembled from 1919 to 1927. The 112 poems range from the well-known, such as Keats's "La Belle Dame Sans Merci" and Coleridge's "Kubla Khan," to the less famous, such as Charles Sorley's "Song of the Ungirt Runners" and Humbert Wolfe's "The Harlot, I." Lawrence stated that his intention in making the anthology was to gather works that he personally liked, with a special (but clearly not exclusive) emphasis on lesser known poems by important poets and good poems by minor poets. He displays a preference for late nineteenth-century and Edwardian romantics, but there are much earlier works as well. **William Morris** has 10 entries, more than anyone else, while **D. G. Rossetti** and James Thomson are tied for second, with six po-

ems each. Lawrence also gives space to **World War I** and postwar poems, including work by **D. H. Lawrence** and John Crowe Ransom. Poets whom he knew personally, such as **James Elroy Flecker** (four poems), **Siegfried Sassoon** (four poems), **Thomas Hardy** (five poems), and **Robert Graves** (one poem), are substantially but not overwhelmingly represented. The manuscript, which was not intended for publication according to Lawrence and was given to **Charlotte Shaw** in 1927, was edited by **J. M. Wilson** and published in 1971.

Mint, The

A continuation of the autobiographical project that Lawrence began in *Seven Pillars of Wisdom,* this time about his service in the **Royal Air Force** after the war. The book is based on notes he made concerning the **Uxbridge R.A.F. Depot** from August through December 1922 and then at **Cadet Training College, Cranwell,** in 1925. These notes were reworked while Lawrence served in **India** from 1927, and the work was completed by early 1928. Lawrence hoped that *The Mint* would serve as a tribute to this relatively new branch of the service, and it does contain much information about what life was like in the R.A.F. during the early 1920s. But it focuses almost exclusively on Lawrence himself, detailing his difficulties in adjusting as a simple airman (or private) to "the mint" of the Royal Air Force. Lawrence, a colonel at the end of **World War I,** never reveals the reasons that led him to join the R.A.F. at such a substantial reduction in rank and comfort, and so the book has an air of mystery about it from the very beginning. It opens with his hesitation over walking into the recruiting office and continues with the difficulty of fitting in with his service companions and with his weary disgust with his onerous physical duties during basic training as well as with the attitudes of some of his officers. However, the book concludes with a feeling of great personal satisfaction and almost mystical oneness with his unit. Written in a clipped, realistic style replete with dialogue containing obscenities, and therefore strongly reminiscent of the documentary photography techniques that Lawrence was learning in the R.A.F. during his service, *The Mint* contrasts strongly with the high romanticism of *Seven Pillars of Wisdom* and was considered innovative and daring when it was first written. Lawrence was dismissed from the R.A.F. in 1923 because of the publicity surrounding him and was allowed to rejoin it only in 1925, after a bitter period of service in the Tank Corps. He feared that publication of this candid book would result in another dismissal and therefore showed the typescript to **Air Marshal Trenchard** in 1928 after he had finished writing. When Trenchard proved uneasy about its publication Lawrence agreed to delay it until 1950. In 1936, one year after his death, 50 copies of the book were published to protect copyright in the United States, but the work was not widely published in either England or America until 1955, when it appeared in both an unexpurgated and an expurgated edition. *The Mint* has attracted some prominent admirers, such as **George Bernard Shaw, Edward Garnett,** and V. S. Pritchett, but most critics have found it less exciting and aesthetically pleasing than *Seven Pillars of Wisdom.* Moreover, the fact that Lawrence does not refer to his flagellation syndrome, which was causing him great misery and soul-searching during the time of the action of *The Mint,* leads some critics to deny Lawrence's final claim of happiness in the book and to charge him with dishonesty. Others reply that while it is true that he concealed this important personal problem, on the whole during the latter part of his R.A.F. service Lawrence was in fact happier than he had ever been (except perhaps at **Carchemish** before the war) and

that he seems while in the R.A.F. to have often achieved precisely the feeling of wholeness and satisfaction that he claims for himself. For a statement of the skeptical attitude toward *The Mint* as art and as autobiography, see **J. Meyers,** "T. E. Lawrence: The Mechanical Monk," in Tabachnick, editor, *The T. E. Lawrence Puzzle,* and **T. J. O'Donnell,** *The Confessions of T. E. Lawrence.* For a more positive view of the book, see Tabachnick, *T. E. Lawrence.* Whether its biographical contents are seen in a positive or negative light, *The Mint* is a worthy artistic experiment and (with his letters) is essential reading for an understanding of Lawrence's attitudes and self-perception during the 1920s.

Miranshah, India, R.A.F. Outpost at

Lawrence was posted to this distant outpost in northwest **India,** very close to the Afghan border, following his request of April 1928 to **Sir Geoffrey Salmond,** the head of the **Royal Air Force** in **India.** Small, with only 25 R.A.F. personnel, including three officers, and 700 Indian troops, the post offered quiet, especially because Lawrence found the commanding officer, I. E. Brodie, the best officer he had yet served under in the R.A.F. Lawrence not only did clerical work, but also translated some of the *Odyssey* here. He was abruptly recalled to England on January 8, 1929, after false rumors that he was involved in espionage in **Afghanistan** began to circulate in the press throughout the world.

Mirzuk el Tikheimi

A notable assistant of **Feisal,** responsible for hosting his guests and handling other important duties. Of the **Juheina** clan, he was good at recounting anecdotes about Feisal's family and others. He is described in chapter 19 of *Seven Pillars of Wisdom.*

Mohammed Ali el Bedawi

Emir of the **Juheina,** who met **Feisal** during the march on **Wejh** in January 1917, as described in chapter 24 of *Seven Pillars of Wisdom.* He was later responsible for a delay of two months when, after a failed attempt to conquer **Mudowwara** station in early 1918, he kept the **Beni Atiyeh** at an oasis (chapter 88).

Mohammed el Dheilan

Cousin of **Auda abu Tayi** and second in command of the **Abu Tayi,** he tutored Lawrence in the spoken Arabic of **Medina** and in the desert accent, as recounted in chapter 40 of *Seven Pillars of Wisdom.* He is described in chapter 45 as tall, powerful, and thoughtful, with a cynical sense of humor. He accompanied Lawrence on the march to **Akaba** that resulted in its capture, but after that he and Auda engaged in treacherous correspondence with the Turks, as related in chapter 57. However, like Auda, he accompanied Lawrence to Damascus, even taking part in the fracas at the town hall after its capture, as told in chapter 119.

Mohammed el Kahdi (circa 1899)

A strong and quiet son of Dakhil-Allah of the **Juheina,** Mohammed was 18 years old in March 1917 when he guided Lawrence to the **Emir Abdullah**'s camp at **Wadi Ais** and then on to **Feisal** at **Wejh,** as described in chapter 34 of *Seven Pillars of Wisdom.*

Mohammed Hassan

A Yemenite from **Taif** whom the **Emir Abdullah**'s men would torment for amusement, as recounted in chapter 36 of *Seven Pillars of Wisdom.* There it is recorded that Abdullah shot a coffee pot off of Mohammed's head three times in a row and then gave him three months' pay as a reward for his suffering.

Mohammed Said, Emir

Brother of **Abd el Kader** who may have betrayed Lawrence to the Turks at **Deraa** by describing him, according to Lawrence's report of June 28, 1919, to the chief political officer at general headquarters, Cairo, **W. F. Stirling.** In that report, Lawrence says that these Algerian brothers were anti-Christian religious fanatics, but **Knightley** and **Simpson** in their *Secret Lives of Lawrence of Arabia* claim that they simply favored the French against the British and the Turks. Their loyalties seem fluctuating and inconsistent, and they probably remained loyal only to themselves. In chapter 101 of *Seven Pillars of Wisdom,* Lawrence states that **Jemal Pasha** sent Mohammed Said to **Feisal** in August 1918 as an emissary; Feisal promised to come over to the Turks only if Turkey would abandon **Amman** and the surrounding province, which he knew the Turks would not do. Mohammed Said and his brother seemed to support the sharifian cause in October 1918 when their assistants helped **Shukri Pasha el Ayoubi,** Feisal's representative, raise the sharifian flag over the **Damascus** town hall, but as recounted in chapter 120 of *Seven Pillars of Wisdom,* Lawrence had to turn the brothers out of the hall soon after, when they tried to take over the government. Abd el Kader was shot on November 7 by an Arab police contingent. Mohammed Said later backed French rule in Damascus.

Montaigne, Michel de (1533–92)

French essayist. Lawrence states in a letter of February 16, 1928 (Orlans, *Lawrence of Arabia, Strange Man of Letters,* p. 254), to **David Garnett** that he prefers **Montes-**

Lawrence's grave at Moreton cemetery, Dorset, where he was buried on May 21, 1935, after being fatally injured in a motorcycle crash on May 13. Courtesy of Corbis.

quieu to Montaigne because Montesquieu is more masculine, a cryptic comment that he fails to explain. In 1908, he had respectfully visited Montaigne's chateau, later noting that the writer had inscribed his favorite sayings on the wooden beams there (Garnett, *Letters,* p. 86). Lawrence's **Clouds Hill** library contained a three-volume set of Montaigne's essays in English translation.

Montesquieu, Charles-Louis de Secondat (1689–1755)

French philosopher and satirist. In 1928, Lawrence stated that he preferred Montesquieu's essays to **Montaigne**'s (Orlans, *Lawrence of Arabia,* p. 254), and his **Clouds Hill** library contained a two-volume set of Montesquieu's works in the original French.

More, Capt. J. C.

British Secret Service officer in Basra. In Lawrence's report on **Mesopotamia** of May 1916, he mentions More favorably as the only Intelligence Staff member who spoke Arabic and praises him for his knowledge of Persian and of **Syria** and the Arabs as well. More was responsible for placing pro-British agents in much of Syria and Mesopotamia. See **J. M. Wilson,** *Lawrence of Arabia* (Appendix III).

Moreton, Dorset

The site of St. Nicholas' Church, in the cemetery near which Lawrence was buried, following his own request, in the afternoon of Tuesday, May 21, 1935, after his fatal motorcycle accident on May 13.

The funeral of T. E. Lawrence on May 21, 1935, at Moreton cemetery. Photo by Philip Somerville. Courtesy of the Huntington Library.

There were many mourners, and the service was brief. Lawrence's headstone in the small cemetery reads "To the dear memory of / T. E. LAWRENCE / Fellow of All Souls College / Oxford / Born 16 August 1888 / Died 19 May 1935 / The hour is coming & now is / When the dead shall hear / The voice of the / SON OF GOD / And they that hear / Shall live." A footstone at the grave reads "DOMINUS ILLUMINATIO MEA," a Latin translation of Psalm 27:1, which in English is "The Lord is my light." This is also the motto of **Oxford University.**

Morley, Frank V. (1899–1980)

Chairman of the publishing firm of Faber and Faber, to whom Lawrence made comments about **T. S. Eliot**'s criticism and

D. H. Lawrence's letters in the 1930s (Orlans, *Lawrence of Arabia, Strange Man of Letters,* pp. 153, 154, 198–99). Morley reviewed the 1935 edition of *Seven Pillars of Wisdom* in the magazine *Now and Then* (Summer 1935).

Morning Post

The newspaper in which Lawrence published (on July 20, 1922) his letter of resignation from the **Colonial Office.** Lawrence, however, disapproved of its simple-minded patriotism, writing to **Stewart Newcombe** in 1920 that the paper's editorial policies struck him as insane and in 1923 to **Sydney Cockerell** that he would respect **Charles Doughty** more if he did not read the paper (Garnett, *Letters,* pp. 321, 438).

Morris, William (1834–96)

Creator of neomedieval poetry, prose fantasies, and handmade furniture and books. Morris remained Lawrence's favorite author and artistic inspiration throughout his life. **Vyvyan Richards,** Lawrence's fellow student, emphasizes in his *Portrait of T. E. Lawrence* the importance of the Morris cult in vogue while he and Lawrence were at Oxford. In 1927 Lawrence himself wrote **Robert Graves,** then working on a biography of Lawrence, that Morris was his favorite writer (*T. E. Lawrence to His Biographers, Robert Graves & Liddell Hart,* p. 1:56), and in a letter of 1928 to **David Garnett,** Lawrence praised Morris very highly (Garnett, *Letters,* p. 612). He mentions or alludes to the Morris prose fantasies *The Wood beyond the World* (1894) and *The Well at the World's End* (1896) in letters from 1910 onward. In a letter of 1927 to **Charlotte Shaw** he ranked Morris's neo-Icelandic *Story of Sigurd the Volsung* (1876) with Milton's *Paradise Lost* and also praised his short poems (Orlans, *Lawrence of Arabia, Strange Man of Letters,* pp. 256–57). Given this lifelong admiration, it is no surprise that Morris's influence on *Seven Pillars of Wisdom*'s writing and design is very pronounced. It appears in such areas as Lawrence's medievalizing of the Arab characters, such as **Auda abu Tayi,** in his art prose style, and in his careful design and printing of the 1926 subscriber's edition as a "book beautiful" modeled on Morris's Kelmscott editions, of which Lawrence had several in his **Clouds Hill** library. Morris's socialist politics did not, however, influence Lawrence in any way.

Morrison, Walter (1836–1921)

Palestine Exploration Fund board member and wealthy benefactor of **D. G. Hogarth**'s dig at **Carchemish.** In *The T. E. Lawrence Puzzle* (ed. Tabachnick), Gideon Gera speculates that Morrison had intelli-

gence connections, but this has been disputed by **J. M. Wilson.** See Wilson's *T. E. Lawrence* (p. 42) for a brief biography of Morrison.

Morsey, Konrad

German military historian and T. E. Lawrence scholar. Morsey received his Ph.D. in 1975 at the Westfalischen Wilhelms-Universität in Münster. His dissertation became the important book *T. E. Lawrence und der arabische Aufstand 1916–18* (1976), which, on the basis of archival evidence, argues for the importance of Lawrence's strategic theories.

Mosley, Sir Oswald (1896–1980)

Controversial British politician who founded the British Union of Fascists after he visited Mussolini's Italy. The party, of which he was head, supported Adolf Hitler and caused violence in the largely Jewish East End of **London.** Suppressed during World War II, he went on in 1948 to found the racist Union Movement. **Basil Liddell Hart** records that on June 25, 1934, Lawrence told him that the fascists had been soliciting his support but that he had turned them down, and he explicitly named Mosley as a fascist (*T. E. Lawrence to His Biographers Robert Graves & Liddell Hart,* p. 2:223). In his autobiography, Mosley himself denied ever having met or written to Lawrence, and **J. M. Wilson** has cited convincing evidence that Lawrence completely rejected Mosley's movement (*Lawrence of Arabia,* pp. 917–18).

Mosul

A city and district in what is now northern **Iraq,** opposite the site of ancient Nineveh, about 60 miles south of the Turkish border, Mosul played a prominent role in the oil politics of Lawrence's period. On December 1, 1918, British Prime Minister **Lloyd George** and French President **Clemenceau** agreed that **France** would receive control over all of **Syria,** in exchange for which Britain would take control of the oil-rich Mosul district of **Mesopotamia,** which had been placed in the French zone by the **Sykes-Picot Agreement,** as well as receive a mandate over **Palestine,** which had been slated for international control. In return for the concession of Mosul to Britain, France would receive some oil rights in Mosul, and British agreement to France's control of **Lebanon** as well as Syria, among other concessions. At the **San Remo Conference** of April 1920, the Lloyd George–Clemenceau interpretation of the Sykes-Picot Agreement was finalized, with France receiving de facto rule over Lebanon and Syria and Britain getting mandates over Iraq (including Mosul), Palestine, and **Transjordan.** Turkey protested that Mosul had not been under British control when the Turko-British **Mudros Armistice** had been signed on October 30, 1918, but in 1926 the League of Nations decided to award the district to **Iraq,** still under a British mandate. For 25 years Turkey was given in compensation a 10 percent share in Iraq's oil profits. Lawrence refers scathingly to the British jockeying for control of oil in Iraq, including Mosul, in the introductory chapter of *Seven Pillars of Wisdom.* See also Shimoni and Levine, *Political Dictionary of the Middle East in the Twentieth Century.*

Motlog el Awar, Sheikh

The owner of el Jedha, the best female camel in northern Arabia, Sheikh Motlog also liked traveling on a Ford truck until he fell out, complaining good-naturedly that he had not yet learned how to ride this vehicle. In February 1918 he and his men were entrusted by **Feisal** and Lawrence with the transportation of a large shipment of gold (worth 24,000 pounds sterling)

from **Guweira** to the **Emir Zeid** at **Tafileh.** Lawrence learned upon his own later arrival at Tafileh that Zeid had spent all of it. This caused the collapse of Lawrence's plans for a spring campaign and almost resulted in his quitting the movement altogether, but **Allenby** sent him back to the Arab forces. This story is recounted in chapters 88–91 of *Seven Pillars of Wisdom.*

Motorcycles

The first motorcycle that Lawrence used in Arabia was a Triumph. After the war, he owned a series of **Brough** motorcycles, seven in all, and he died before he rode an eighth one that he had ordered. The first of these, a Mark I bought in 1922, he named Boanerges after the New Testament's Mark 3:17, in which Jesus calls James and John "the sons of thunder," referring to their loud voices. He also called this machine "Boa" for short, or George I after its builder, **George Brough;** it was damaged on March 31, 1923, during a trip from **London** to Lawrence's base at **Bovington.** Subsequent machines were George II (a 1922 SS100), III, IV (1925), V (damaged on a wet street and sold for 100 pounds just before he left for **India** in late 1926), VI, and VII. Chapter 16 of *The Mint* is devoted entirely to Lawrence's delight in Boanerges's performance on the road, including a race with a Bristol fighter aircraft at more than 90 miles per hour; and he states there that he prefers a good motorcycle to any riding animal because of the way in which it seems a part of his body and because it never grows tired. **Malcolm Brown**'s *Selected Letters* includes numerous references to Lawrence's motorcycles, while **J. M. Wilson**'s *T. E. Lawrence* contains several photos of Lawrence on motorcycles as well as photos of his last motorcycle, George VII, a **Brough Superior** SS100, registration number GW2275, showing its condition after the crash on which Lawrence met his death, and in its restored condition (pp. 230–31).

This motorcycle was on sale for over three million dollars in 1997. For more information, see Mike Leatherdale, "Lawrence and His Brough Motorcycles," *Journal of the T. E. Lawrence Society* (Winter 1991–92): 63–96.

Mount Batten, R.A.F. Station (previously Cattewater)

The **Royal Air Force** flying-boat station on Plymouth Sound at which Lawrence served as a machine and workshop section clerk from March 10, 1929 (one month after his return from **India**), to April 7, 1933. In late 1929, the station changed its name from Cattewater to Mount Batten, partially as a result of Lawrence's urging. Much of this period was Lawrence's happiest in the R.A.F. He liked **Wing Comdr. Sydney Smith** (whose wife **Clare Sydney Smith** wrote a memoir, *The Golden Reign,* 1940), and the station was small (about 100 men). Lawrence assisted Smith in setting up the international **Schneider Trophy** seaplane race that took place in September 1929, helped rescue survivors of the crash of an R.A.F. Iris III seaplane that he witnessed on February 4, 1931, and tested the **R.A.F. 200 class boats.** He also enjoyed the small Biscayne Baby boat, named *Biscuit,* that he owned jointly with Sydney Smith. The period is important from a literary point of view because during it Lawrence finished his translation of **Homer's** *Odyssey* and saw it through its publication in 1932 by famed book printers and publishers **Bruce Rogers, Wilfred Merton,** and **Sir Emery Walker.** He also received an invitation from **W. B. Yeats** to join the new Irish Academy of Letters, which he accepted.

Mousa, Suleiman (born 1920)

Jordanian author of *T. E. Lawrence: An Arab View* (Arabic edition 1962; English edition 1966), which, based on sources in Arabic, charges Lawrence with underestimating the importance of the Arab contribution to the events recounted in *Seven Pillars of Wisdom.* Mousa, a government employee and journalist, also authored many articles about Lawrence.

Mudowwara

A water station on the **Hejaz Railway,** about 50 miles east of **Akaba** and 80 miles south of **Maan.** In September 1917, this was the planned target of one of Lawrence's raids, but as he tells us in chapter 64 of *Seven Pillars of Wisdom,* the station's garrison of 200 seemed too strong for his party of 116 and its stone buildings too sturdy for his explosives, so he passed on it. However, Lawrence managed to blow up a train near the station on September 19, as he tells us in the next chapter. Not until August 1918 was Mudowwara station successfully attacked by the **Imperial Camel Corps** under **Robin Buxton,** as recounted in chapter 101.

Mudros Armistice

On October 29, 1918, **Sharif Nasir's** forces reached Muslemiya, the northernmost limit of the Allied advance in **Syria.** On October 30, the Turks, represented principally by Hussein Rauf Bey, Ottoman naval minister, signed an armistice with the Entente, represented by Vice-Admiral Calthorpe, head of the British fleet in the Aegean. This took place at Mudros, a port on the island of Lemnos, and ended the Turkish role in **World War I.** The armistice enjoined upon the Turks not only an immediate end to hostilities and the demobilization of their land and sea forces, but a break with the German and Austro-Hungarian empires and the expulsion of their nationals from all Turkish territories. This surrender marked the end of the **Young Turk** government and led to the flight of its co-leaders, **Enver Pasha, Talat**

Pasha, and **Jemal Pasha.** The deliberate exclusion of the French from the talks led to lasting suspicions by them and the Turks that the British were seeking their own advantage amid the possible dismemberment of the Ottoman Empire.

Murray, Gen. Sir Archibald (1860–1945)

As chief of staff to Sir John French, commander of the British Expeditionary Force on the western front, from August 1914 to early 1915, Murray suffered a nervous breakdown; he then served as deputy chief and from September 1915 chief of the Imperial General Staff before being replaced by Sir William Robertson. He then took command in **Egypt,** becoming commander-in-chief of the British forces in the Middle East starting in March 1916. As such, he was responsible for two abortive attacks on the Turkish forces at **Gaza** on March 26 and April 17–18, 1917, and was replaced by **Allenby** in June of that year. He remained in home positions until he retired in 1922. Murray was regarded on the western front as a nervous and undistinguished commander. Lawrence strengthens this impression when he records in chapter 16 of *Seven Pillars of Wisdom* that Murray's chief of staff, **Gen. Lynden-Bell,** warned Lawrence not to make Murray nervous; he also records Murray's support for Lawrence's idea that no European troops outside of advisers were necessary in the early stages of the **Arab Revolt** to supplement the sharifian forces in Arabia. Although according to Lawrence, Murray was lukewarm about the usefulness of the **Arab Revolt** at first, he came to realize its value as a diversionary force after the capture of **Wejh,** as recorded in chapter 28. See **A. P. Wavell,** *The Palestine Campaigns;* Pope and Wheal, *The Dictionary of the First World War;* and Y. Sheffy, *British Military Intelligence in the Palestine Campaign, 1914–1918.*

Music

Lawrence took music lessons as a child but did not go on with them, and he came seriously to building a collection of recordings only after the war. His service companions testify that Lawrence disliked jazz but loved classical music, and he was especially pleased when he could escape to his **Clouds Hill** cottage to listen to recordings from his large and carefully chosen collection. He had a room upstairs dedicated to music listening, and in February 1924 he bought a Columbia gramophone; this was followed by one made by Ginn. According to **R. G. Sims,** he liked gramophones with long and straight horns and dusted his records with graphite before playing them. He insisted that anyone playing his records had to wash his hands first. In **A. W. Lawrence**'s collection *T. E. Lawrence by His Friends,* W. Warwick James described Lawrence's tastes, as did **Alec Dixon** and Sims in that volume. Beethoven was Lawrence's favorite composer, but he also liked Bach, Brahms, and Mozart as well as Schubert, Schumann, Wagner, and Wolf. Among contemporary composers, Delius, Elgar, Hindemith, Milhaud, Prokofiev, and Ravel are included among the complete list of Lawrence's records found at the time of his death that James has appended to his article. Lawrence's choice of performers is exemplary, including pianist Artur Schnabel on the "Emperor Concerto" of Beethoven; Alfred Cortot, piano, and Jacques Thibaud, violin, on Beethoven's "Kreutzer" sonata; and Yehudi Menuhin on Bruch's Violin Concerto No. 1. Lawrence was clearly a sophisticated music lover without however playing an instrument himself.

Mustapha Kemal

See **Kemal Pasha, Mustapha**

N

Nabataeans

A people (flourished circa 400 B.C.E. to 106 C.E., when they were conquered by the Romans) of the Sinai, **Negev,** and Transjordanian deserts, famous for their towns, dams, and extensive agriculture methods. In *The Wilderness of Zin,* which he wrote with **C. Leonard Woolley,** Lawrence made some contribution to the understanding of this important people, although the book focuses largely on the Byzantine layer of archaeological evidence, which succeeded the Nabataean and Roman layers. Lawrence and Woolley did not have the knowledge, which was developed later, to date the potsherds on the surface or the time to probe beneath the surface, with the consequence that they were unable to devote full attention to the Nabataean layer. However, their plan of the Nabataean/Byzantine city of Shivta is one of the best to date according to recent authorities, such as Arthur Segal of Haifa University. Woolley is probably responsible for drawing up this plan, because he visited the city while Lawrence headed south toward **Akaba** on the **Red Sea,** but because Lawrence and Woolley consulted about every aspect of their book, Lawrence may well have had a hand in this plan. Even more impressively, Lawrence and Woolley determined that the climate of the desert had not changed at least since Byzantine (and by implication Nabataean) times, and later authorities such as Nelson Glueck, in his *Rivers in the Desert,* have supported them in this idea. See Avraham Negev, editor, *The Archaeological Encyclopedia of the Holy Land;* P. Hammond, *The Nabataeans;* S. E. Tabachnick, "Lawrence of Arabia as Archaeologist," *Biblical Archaeology Review* 23:5 (Sept./Oct. 1997): 40–47, 70–71.

Nablus

Important town about 50 miles southeast of **Haifa,** headquarters of the Turkish Seventh Army, occupied on September 21, 1918, by French Colonial and British forces during **Allenby**'s great final offensive that effectively ended Turkish resistance in **Palestine.** This success, which also included the captures of Haifa, Afula, Beisan, and Semakh, is reported by Lawrence in chapter 114 of *Seven Pillars of Wisdom.* See **A. P. Wavell,** *The Palestine Campaigns.*

Nafi Bey

Egyptian major and commander of the Egyptian Army troops sent by **Sir Reginald Wingate** to help with the **Arab Revolt.** In chapter 13 of *Seven Pillars of Wisdom,* Lawrence says that Nafi was not enamored of his task because he preferred the relative ease and security of **Egypt.**

Nakhl Mubarak

Oasis populated by Bnei Ibrahim **Beduin** of the **Juheina** tribe, consisting of a village, date palms, and gardens, and located about 20 miles northeast of **Yenbo;** used as a camp by **Feisal** in late 1916 and early 1917. Here on December 9, 1916, the Arab forces, already forced out of **Bir Said,** were again forced to retreat toward Yenbo by Turkish troops under Ghalib Bey, as related in chapter 20 of *Seven Pillars of Wisdom.* The Turks were deterred from attacking Yenbo by the floodlights of the British ships *Dufferin* and *M.31* in Yenbo harbor, which raked the shore. Turkish commander **Fahkri Pasha,** the defender of **Medina** throughout the war, accompanied Ghalib Bey. Two British airplanes bombed his forces in Nakhl Mubarak and forced him to retreat to Medina in January 1917. For a time he threatened **Rabegh,** which was not well defended, but sickness in his ranks and tribal raids caused him to forego that objective. See **J. M. Wilson**'s *T. E. Lawrence,* p. 80, for a photo of the Nakhl Mubarak camp.

Namier, Sir Lewis B. (1888–1960)

Originally an immigrant to England from Poland, Namier became influential while serving as a professor of modern history at Manchester University from 1931 to 1953. He was one of the foremost historians of eighteenth-, nineteenth-, and twentieth-century British politics and political secretary of the Jewish Agency for **Palestine** from 1929 to 1931. In his memoir in **A. W. Lawrence**'s *T. E. Lawrence by His Friends,* Namier mentions that he met Lawrence at **Oxford** in 1920 and again at intervals until 1930. He testifies to Lawrence's positive attitude toward **Zionism,** which he hoped would reinvigorate all of Palestine.

Nash, Paul (1889–1946)

British painter, engraver, and theater artist who served in the Artists' Rifles during **World War I,** becoming an official war artist in 1917. He served in the same capacity in World War II. According to Valerie Thompson's *"Not a Suitable Hobby for an Airman"—T. E. Lawrence as Publisher,* Lawrence first met Nash after the war and bought Nash's first sea painting for the **Colonial Office** (pp. 97–98). In 1922 Lawrence asked him to do drawings from his photographs for use in the 1926 subscriber's edition of *Seven Pillars of Wisdom.* After going through 200 photos that Lawrence brought him, Nash executed five works for the book: *A Garden, Dhat el Haj,* and *The Prophet's Tomb* are interspersed with the text, and *Waterfall* and *Mountains* follow the text. In his essay in *The T. E. Lawrence Puzzle* (edited by Tabachnick), **Charles Grosvenor** discusses Nash's work for *Seven Pillars of Wisdom,* and an annotated proof plate for *Mountains* appears in **J. M. Wilson**'s *T. E. Lawrence* (p. 175).

Nasir, Sharif of Medina

In chapter 26 of *Seven Pillars of Wisdom,* Lawrence describes Sharif Nasir in a heroic light as the man who fired the first and last shots of the **Arab Revolt.** Lawrence first met him when he came into **Feisal**'s camp on January 21, 1917, and in *Seven Pillars of Wisdom* he mentions Nasir's presence on October 1, 1918, in the Damascus town hall after the city had been captured by the Allied forces. He was one of Feisal's leading guerrilla commanders, especially influential in controlling the **Beduin** during the march on **Akaba.**

Naval Intelligence, British

The British Navy had the responsibility for landing agents along the coasts of **Pales-**

tine, **Syria,** and Asia Minor. As early as December 1915, **Stewart Newcombe** sent a British lieutenant, soon captured by the Turks, on a spying mission along the northern Sinai coast, where he attempted to recruit agents among the **Beduin.** The navy also provided the means of contact between British Intelligence in **Cairo** and the NILI spy ring, a pro-British network run by Zionists **Aaron Aaronsohn** and his sister **Sarah.** The navy's methods of dropping off, picking up, and signaling agents can be found in L. B. Weldon's memoir, *"Hard Lying,"* and in Yigal Sheffy's *British Military Intelligence in the Palestine Campaign 1914–1918. See also* **Eastern Mediterranean Special Intelligence Bureau.**

Naval Intelligence Division, Geographical Section

Created in 1915 to write geographical handbooks. **D. G. Hogarth** was one of several academic specialists recruited for this division by the head of **Naval Intelligence,** Sir Reginald Hall, and he produced the secret *Handbook to Arabia* for this agency.

Nawaf Shaalan

Eldest son of **Nuri Shaalan,** emir of the **Rualla Beduin.** When **Feisal** was at **Wejh,** still early in the **Arab Revolt,** Nawaf sent him a mare as a pledge of allegiance, as recorded in chapter 30 of *Seven Pillars of Wisdom.* Later, the Turks attempted to take him hostage and to force him to lead a column in search of **Feisal**'s rebels, but his relative Trad went instead.

Nefud Desert

Also called the Great Nefud, a series of sand dunes separating the northern Shammar area of Arabia from the Syrian desert.

In chapter 63 of *Seven Pillars of Wisdom,* Lawrence relates how he wanted to enter it during the march on **Akaba,** if only to pay tribute to the previous explorers— **W. G. Palgrave,** the **Blunts,** and **Gertrude Bell,** as well as George Augustus Wallin and **Capt. Shakespear**—who had crossed it, but he was prevented from this unnecessary excursion by **Auda abu Tayi.**

Negev Desert

The desert in what is now Israel starting in **Beersheba** and continuing south to the Egyptian border. It is a northern extension of the Sinai Desert. Lawrence visited this desert when he and **C. Leonard Woolley** collaborated on *The Wilderness of Zin,* which remained the best work on the **Nabataean** and Byzantine ruins in the Negev until the publication of Nelson Glueck's *Rivers in the Desert* half a century later. Lawrence and Woolley were the first to notice what is now called Negev pottery. The Negev and Sinai deserts were crossed by a Turkish force of 20,000 men under **Jemal Pasha** and his German chief of staff **Col. Kress von Kressenstein,** who unsuccessfully attacked the **Suez Canal** in February 1915 and again in 1916 after a march of some 150 miles. These deserts also were crossed by **Gen. Edmund Allenby**'s forces when they successfully attacked Beersheba in October 1917, but by that time the British had laid a railroad line and water pipe from the Suez Canal zone to El Arish, making the crossing much easier.

Nejd

Plateau region on the border of the **Hejaz,** in the center of Arabia, ruled during Lawrence's time and after by **Ibn Saud,** the **Wahabi** leader. Ibn Saud eventually defeated **Sharif Hussein** of the Hejaz, and **Ibn Rashid** of the Shammar area of northern Arabia, uniting the three regions and creating the kingdom of Saudi Arabia. Lawrence had relatively little contact with the areas of Arabia outside the Hejaz.

Nekhl

A crossroads in the mid-Sinai, which Lawrence passed on his way to announce his capture of **Akaba** to British headquarters in **Cairo** in July 1917, as told in chapter 55 of *Seven Pillars of Wisdom.* As explained in MacMunn and Falls, *Military Operations, Egypt and Palestine,* the Turks held Nekhl with a unit of 100 cavalry as late as early February 1917, but on February 18, a British column forced them to fall back and captured a field gun and 11 Turkish prisoners.

Nesib el Bekri

A prominent Damascus landowner and member of the secret nationalist society **Al Fatat.** According to **George Antonius,** it was at his urging that his younger brother Fauzi brought **Sharif Hussein** the message that the society would like him to lead a revolt against the Turks. Nasib was among the three or four notables who accompanied **Feisal** on his return to the **Hejaz** in May 1916 on the orders of **Jemal Pasha,** who thought that they would secure sharifian loyalty to the Turks; instead they helped Feisal initiate the **Arab Revolt** against the Turks, and Nesib was subsequently exiled from Damascus. He took part in the march on **Akaba** and later represented Feisal to the Syrian villagers. In chapter 39 of *Seven Pillars of Wisdom,* Lawrence praises his political savvy, intelligence, and love of adventure, but Lawrence also criticized him in chapter 48 for urging a premature assault on Damascus, which Lawrence refused to undertake. Toward the end of the campaign, Nesib helped organize Syrian **Druse** support for the sharifian forces. In **Suleiman Mousa**'s

T. E. Lawrence: An Arab View, el Bekri's retrospective statements are used as evidence to deny that Lawrence secretly rode to Damascus in June 1917 during the march on Akaba, but **J. M. Wilson** and others have shown that this daring trip certainly did take place.

Neutral Monism

A philosophical doctrine, first espoused by **William James** in 1912 and then adopted by **Bertrand Russell** in 1921, that may have influenced Lawrence while he was writing *Seven Pillars of Wisdom.* The doctrine holds that both mental and material things are made out of the same "neutral" stuff. Lawrence seems to adopt this position when in chapter 83 he states that the mental and the physical or material are really one thing and constructed from one basic material. Lawrence may have heard about this doctrine from **Vyvyan Richards,** a friend at **Oxford University** who was a philosophy major. See the introduction to S. E. Tabachnick, editor, *The T. E. Lawrence Puzzle,* for a full discussion of Lawrence's position on the mind-body problem.

Newcombe, Col. Stewart Francis (1878–1956)

A notable soldier and participant in Lawrence's career, who served in the Boer War, then in the Egyptian Army, and who during **World War I** had numerous roles. As a captain in the Royal Engineers in November 1913, Newcombe requested and was entrusted with the survey of the Sinai Desert that in January 1914 included Lawrence and **C. L. Woolley** and resulted in the publication of *The Wilderness of Zin,* which is dedicated to Newcombe. **Kitchener** had mapped the northern Sinai area in 1884, but as he admitted and Newcombe noticed, it had been an inaccurate job. Newcombe cataloged wells, topography, and Turkish fortifications, while as a cover Lawrence and Woolley wrote up the archaeological sites of interest. Newcombe's essay in **A. W. Lawrence's** *T. E. Lawrence by His Friends* recounts this mission. When the six-week Sinai survey was over and Lawrence and Woolley had returned to **Carchemish,** Newcombe visited them there in May 1914 and directed them to gather information about the **Berlin–Baghdad Railway,** which the Germans were building through the Amanus Mountains, near the Carchemish site. As recounted in Woolley's *As I Seem to Remember,* the pair had great success in this mission, getting the plans for the railway from an Italian engineer. When Lawrence worked in intelligence in **Cairo** with Woolley, **Aubrey Herbert,** and **George Lloyd** in 1914–16, Newcombe was his immediate boss and reported to **Gilbert Clayton.** Newcombe was sent to the **Hejaz** in January 1917 at the head of the **British Military Mission,** consisting of **Majors Vickery** and **Cox** and medical **Major Marshall** to assist the **Arab Revolt,** and became Lawrence's immediate if only nominal commander. Lawrence mentions Newcombe favorably at several points in *Seven Pillars of Wisdom,* praising his energy and dedication. In June 1917, Newcombe deliberately lost papers containing a false plan of attack, thus deceiving the Turks and causing them to keep a unit in Tadmor, **Syria,** for no reason until the end of the war, as related in chapter 49 of *Seven Pillars of Wisdom.* In July 1917, as recounted in **Liddell Hart's** *"T. E. Lawrence": In Arabia and After,* Newcombe's great exertions caused him to be shipped back to recover his strength in **Egypt,** where he convinced **Gen. Edmund Allenby** that he could be useful during Allenby's planned attack on **Beersheba** in October 1917 by cutting the Beersheba-Hebron road with **Beduin** help. During that engagement, Newcombe's unit sus-

tained heavy losses, and he was forced to surrender to the Turks. He spent the rest of the war in Constantinople, living in the elegant Pera Palace Hotel with **General Townshend** of the **Kut-al-Amara** debacle, among others. He tried to escape three times. After the war, Newcombe was a friend and correspondent of Lawrence's and served as one of six pallbearers at his funeral. See **J. M. Wilson,** *T. E. Lawrence,* for a portrait of Newcombe by **William Roberts** (p. 83).

Nicholson, Sir William (1872–1949)

Artist. Creator of a pen-and-wash portrait of **Gilbert Clayton,** British intelligence chief in **Cairo,** that Lawrence included in the 1926 subscriber's edition of *Seven Pillars of Wisdom.* Knighted in 1936, he was known for his posters and portraits, as described in V. M. Thompson's *"Not a Suitable Hobby for an Airman."* Lawrence considered him a very fine artist, as he wrote to Clayton on August 15, 1922 (Brown, *Selected Letters,* p. 198). See **J. M. Wilson,** *T. E. Lawrence* (p. 86), for Nicholson's portrait of Clayton.

Nicolson, Sir Arthur, 1st Baron Carnock (1849–1928)

Permanent undersecretary for foreign affairs, 1910–1916. His committee was responsible for negotiations with the French over the future of the Arab territories, dealing with the **McMahon-Hussein Correspondence** and the **Sykes-Picot Agreement,** which he supported, as related by **Jeremy Wilson** in his *Lawrence of Arabia* (p. 247).

Nietzsche, Friedrich Wilhelm (1844–1900)

Influential philosopher. In a letter of August 26, 1922, to **Edward Garnett** (D.

Garnett, *Letters,* p. 360), Lawrence calls Nietzsche's *Thus Spake Zarathustra,* along with **Dostoyevsky**'s *The Brothers Karamazov* and **Melville**'s *Moby Dick,* one of the three great books with which he was competing when writing *Seven Pillars of Wisdom.* **Jeffrey Meyers,** in his *Wounded Spirit,* claims that Lawrence accepted Nietzsche's view that pain leads to self-knowledge, and that will transforms knowledge into achievement. In an essay in *The T. E. Lawrence Puzzle,* edited by Tabachnick, **Thomas O'Donnell** has shown that Lawrence fluctuates between extremes of assertion of the will and self-denial and found it difficult to find a balance between the two. Indeed, in *Seven Pillars of Wisdom,* Lawrence often seems to seek peace from a willful romantic striving for an impossible-to-attain absolute. In the group activity portrayed in Part 3 of *The Mint* he appears at last to have found that peace, at least upon occasion. He seems, therefore (perhaps like many other intellectuals), to have eventually outgrown a youthful fascination with Nietzsche and to have found a more quiet, mundane reconciliation of will and world.

Nuri el Said, Gen. (1888–1958)

Important participant in the **Arab Revolt** and later prime minister of **Iraq** multiple times. In *The Arab Awakening,* **George Antonius** writes that he was a member of the secret nationalist society of Arab officers in the Turkish army, **Al Ahd.** He was briefly deported to India by the British, but joined the sharifian forces in 1916. He became chief of staff to **Jaafar Pasha el Askari,** his brother-in-law, who was the commander of **Feisal**'s regular (as opposed to his guerrilla) army. At the **Hejaz Railway** station in Jurf, Nuri fired the Turks' own cannon into the station, forcing the surrender of 200 soldiers, as reported in

chapter 84 of *Seven Pillars of Wisdom,* and, ceremonially attired, he accepted the surrender of the Turkish station at **Mezerib,** as told in chapter 110. He was appointed commander of Feisal's troops in Damascus by Lawrence and helped him hold the city against **Abd el Kader el Jesairi,** as written in chapters 120 and 121. In 1921, he became the first chief of staff of the Iraqi army under King Feisal, then minister of defense twice, and in 1930 prime minister for the first of 14 times. A proponent of good relations with Britain and an anti-Communist, Nuri was assassinated during the coup of 1958 in Baghdad that put an end to Hashemite rule in Iraq. See Shimoni and Levine, *Political Dictionary of the Middle East in the Twentieth Century.*

Nuri Shaalan

Powerful sheikh of the **Rualla Beduin** tribal confederation, centered on **Jauf,** in the southern Syrian desert. Nuri had ruled his tribes for 30 years and was approximately 70 years old when Lawrence met him, as described in chapter 30 of *Seven Pillars of Wisdom.* He offered shelter to **Feisal** and his entourage at the beginning of the **Arab Revolt,** as related in chapter 5 of *Seven Pillars of Wisdom,* and his tribes played an increasingly active role in it when the revolt reached **Syria.** Like other Beduin leaders and tribes, he was paid for his services by the British (*Seven Pillars of Wisdom,* chapter 45), but as revealed in chapter 48 of *Seven Pillars of Wisdom,* where he questions Lawrence about conflicting British pledges to the Arabs, he was suspicious of the British role. Lawrence's answer was to believe the latest communication from the British, which undoubtedly did not inspire Nuri's confidence. Although primarily loyal to Feisal, he played both the Turkish and British/Arab sides (as Lawrence relates in chapter 30 of *Seven Pillars of Wisdom*) until it was clear in 1918 that the British and Arabs would win the war, at which time he openly declared his support for Feisal. He was forced on occasion to support the Turks, as when he had to allow his nephew Trad who was held semi-hostage to guide a Turkish force in search of the Arab forces. Trad deliberately took them on a difficult route lacking water supplies, as retold in chapter 52 of *Seven Pillars of Wisdom*. Nuri was present at the town hall in Damascus when Lawrence asserted sharifian control of the government.

Nutting, Anthony (1920–99)

British Conservative politician and author, who resigned a position as deputy foreign secretary in Prime Minister Anthony Eden's government as a protest against British participation in the 1956 **Suez** crisis, when **France,** Britain, and Israel invaded **Egypt.** In addition to having written books about that crisis, Egyptian President Nasser, and the **Balfour Declaration,** Nutting was the author of *Lawrence of Arabia: The Man and the Motive* (1961), in which he asserted that Lawrence discovered his own masochism during the **Deraa incident,** that he had encouraged the slaughter of Turkish prisoners by the Arabs at **Tafas,** and that he had a suicidal intent during many engagements. He also saw no indication of homosexuality in Lawrence's life outside of the **Carchemish** period and thought that "S. A." was an imaginary conception rather than a real person. Nutting served as an advisor to the makers of the 1962 David Lean film *Lawrence of Arabia.*

O

O'Brien, Philip M. (born 1940)

Director of the Wardman Library at Whittier College, Pasadena, California, Dr. O'Brien was the compiler of the standard *T. E. Lawrence: A Bibliography* (1988), which won the Besterman Award for the best bibliography published in Great Britain during that year. The work was based on the great **Edwards Metcalf** collection of Lawrenciana at the **Huntington Library,** as well as on O'Brien's own considerable personal collection and research. A supplement, nearly double in size, was published in 2000. He also published, in *Explorations in Doughty's "Arabia Deserta,"* edited by Stephen Tabachnick, a descriptive bibliography of the editions of **Charles Doughty**'s *Travels in Arabia Deserta* as well as bibliographies of Rebecca West's and children's books. In *The T. E. Lawrence Puzzle,* edited by Tabachnick, Dr. O'Brien detailed some of his experiences while collecting Lawrence materials.

Ocampo, Victoria (1890–1979)

Argentinian critic and translator. Ocampo's brief *338171 T. E. Lawrence of Arabia* (Buenos Aires: Sur, 1942), which uses Lawrence's serial number in the **Royal Air Force** in 1930, was written in two months.

Ocampo focuses on Lawrence's self-denial as the key to his character.

O'Donnell, Thomas J. (born 1938)

English professor. Dr. O'Donnell's "The Dichotomy of Self in T. E. Lawrence's *Seven Pillars of Wisdom*" (University of Illinois, 1970) was the first Ph.D. dissertation in any field to focus on Lawrence. It was published in 1979 in revised form as *The Confessions of T. E. Lawrence: The Romantic Hero's Presentation of Self* (Ohio University Press). In this provocative and polished work, O'Donnell posits a Lawrence character divided between masochistic and sadistic impulses and who belongs to the nineteenth-century literary tradition of the divided self.

Odyssey, The

Lawrence's English translation of **Homer**'s poem of Odysseus's wanderings is his only literary work (other than letters) published under the name **T. E. Shaw.** It is considered one of the finest prose renditions ever achieved and has been praised by **Sir Maurice Bowra,** among others. Lawrence's introduction, however, is notable for its attack on Homer as a man and as a writer. He found Homer's writing in this poem overly decorative and his heroes less than ideal, and he even doubted that

The Bruce Rogers edition of Lawrence's *Odyssey* translation is considered one of the most beautifully produced twentieth-century books. Courtesy of the Huntington Library.

Homer wrote both this work and *The Iliad,* which he considered far superior. **Ralph Isham** proposed the project to Lawrence in 1928, while he was serving in **India,** and Lawrence completed it in October 1931, when he was working on **Royal Air Force** boats in England. It was published in 1932 in an edition of 530 copies produced by **Emery Walker, Wilfred Merton,** and **Bruce Rogers. Philip O'Brien** considers this one of the most beautifully produced twentieth-century books. The most thorough work on the quality and significance of Lawrence's translation is Maren Ormseth Cohn's 561-page 1995 University of Chicago Ph.D. dissertation, "T. E. Lawrence and Odysseus." See also her and Stephanie Nelson's articles in Charles Stang, editor, *The Waking Dream of T. E. Lawrence,* and James A. Notopoulos, "The Tragic and the Epic in T. E. Lawrence," *Yale Review* 54:3 (spring 1965): 331–45.

Oman, C.W.C. (1860–1946)

Oman was the author of *The Art of War,* considered an authoritative work on me-

dieval architecture at Oxford during Lawrence's studies there. In his B.A. thesis, entitled "The Influence of the Crusades on European Military Architecture—To the End of the XIIth Century," Lawrence contradicted this work's idea that Western military architects learned exclusively from the East, positing instead that they brought their knowledge with them. It now appears that both Lawrence and Oman were right and that the Crusaders both brought some architectural ideas with them and learned from Eastern architects.

Orage, A. R. (1875–1934)

Editor of *The New Age* (in association with **G. B. Shaw**) from 1907 to 1922 and of *The New English Weekly* from 1931 to 1934, he was interested in social and literary reform. In a letter of August 17, 1922, to Shaw, Lawrence says that he likes Orage's criticism (Brown, *Selected Letters,* p. 201). Writing on December 7, 1934, to **Ezra Pound,** he laments Orage's death but not his interest in Guild Socialism and Social Credit schemes (Orlans, *Lawrence of Arabia, Strange Man of Letters,* p. 287).

Oriental Assembly

This collection of Lawrence's writings, edited by **A. W. Lawrence** and published by Williams & Norgate in 1939, includes *Diary of a Journey across the Euphrates,* **"The Changing East," "The Evolution of a Revolt,"** the previously suppressed introductory chapter of *Seven Pillars of Wisdom,* "On Eric Kennington's Arab Portraits," and 129 of Lawrence's war photographs. The diary was republished as ***The Diary of T. E. Lawrence, MCMXI,*** and the piece on **Kennington** was the preface to the Leicester Gallery catalog of the portraits in the 1926 edition of *Seven Pillars of Wisdom.* The introductory chapter is now available in Penguin editions of *Seven*

Pillars of Wisdom, and "The Evolution of a Revolt" was republished in the collection of Lawrence's writing of that name edited by **Stanley** and Rodelle **Weintraub.**

Orontes

A river in Turkey and **Syria** flowing from Antioch through **Hama** and **Homs** and eventually to the Sea of Galilee in present-day Israel. The valley of the Orontes is mentioned twice in chapter 58 of *Seven Pillars of Wisdom* as the dwelling-place of **Armenian** and **Circassian** populations.

Orpen, Sir William (1878–1931)

Oil and watercolor portraitist and official war artist. Orpen painted one portrait of Lawrence in early 1919 at the **Peace Conference** in **Paris** on the basis of two 90-minute sittings. As **Charles Grosvenor** points out in his *An Iconography: The Portraits of T. E. Lawrence,* this was not one of Lawrence's favorite paintings of himself. But it was one of Lawrence's mother's favorite paintings of him, and the actor **Peter O'Toole** has stated that he felt that it was the truest and perhaps cruelest of all of the Lawrence portraits. Of Irish origins himself, like Lawrence and O'Toole, Orpen was able to capture some of the weaknesses of the Irish landed gentry in Lawrence's face, according to O'Toole.

Othman

See **Farraj**

O'Toole, Peter Seamus (born 1932)

British actor. Although he has acted in numerous plays and films, O'Toole remains most famous for his role as Lawrence in the David Lean epic *Lawrence of Arabia.*

He bears a strong resemblance to Lawrence and has claimed that he is, indeed, a distant cousin. His justly praised performance, grounded in **Robert Bolt**'s excellent script, captures Lawrence's many contradictions, especially those between self-assertiveness and self-denial, and seems to be based on deep insight into Lawrence's character. *Lawrence of Arabia: The 30th Anniversary Pictorial History* by Morris and Raskin contains many details concerning the making of this film, including O'Toole's performance.

Oxford, City of

Lawrence lived in Oxford with his family from 1896 at the age of eight until he graduated from **Oxford University** in 1910. He also spent some time as a fellow at **All Souls College,** Oxford, from September 1919 through the fall of 1920. Lawrence's family lived at 2, Polstead Road, a modest home, and Lawrence had a small bungalow to himself in the garden. The family went to church at St. Aldate's, an Evangelical congregation. Lawrence attended the **City of Oxford High School for Boys.** Lawrence and his friend **C.F.C. Beeson** went to Oxford Archaeological Society meetings and roamed around the city and its environs looking for Roman and medieval artifacts, especially armor, weapons, and coins. He took advantage of the **Ashmolean Museum** and became known while still a schoolboy to archaeologists **C. Leonard Woolley,** with whom he would work before and during **World War I.** During his years at Oxford University, his most famous exploit was to canoe through Trill Mill Stream, which runs through tunnels under the city streets. He brought his Arab friends from the **Carchemish** archaeological dig, **Dahoum** ("S. A.") and **Hamoudi,** the dig foreman, home during the summer of 1913 and delighted in showing them Oxford. For the early period of Lawrence's life, see particularly Paul J. Marriott, *Oxford's Legendary Son—The Young Lawrence of Arabia, 1888–1910* (1977), as well as the essays in *T. E. Lawrence by His Friends,* edited by **A. W. Lawrence.** After the war, which saw the deaths of two of his brothers, then the influenza epidemic that killed his father, and finally his own involvement in the **Royal Air Force,** he seemed to feel less attracted to Oxford. Except for his year at All Souls he seems to have visited only infrequently, and then largely to visit **D. G. Hogarth** and the surviving members of his own family.

Oxford Book of English Verse, The

In a letter of 1927 to **D. G. Hogarth,** Lawrence wrote that his reading during the Arab campaign consisted of **Aristophanes, Malory,** and *The Oxford Book of English Verse.* The **Houghton Library** at Harvard has the 1915 edition of this work that Lawrence purchased in **Cairo** in 1916 and kept with him throughout the campaign. The poems that he read during the revolt include Arthur Shaughnessy's "Ode," John Davidson's "Song," William Watson's "The Great Misgiving," Henry Cust's "Non Nobis," Kipling's "Dedication," and Clough's "Say Not the Struggle Nought Availeth." See the notes in **J. M. Wilson**'s edition of Lawrence's own poetry anthology, *Minorities,* for the connections between these poems and events taking place in the course of the revolt when Lawrence read each of them.

Oxford *Times*

Because he was short of money, Lawrence had an early draft of *Seven Pillars of Wisdom* (now held at the **Bodleian Library** and known as the Bodleian manuscript) printed up on the linotype press of the Oxford *Times* newspaper from January 20, 1922, to June 24, 1922. This printed version of the Bodleian manuscript has since become known as the Oxford text. Of eight copies so printed, five bound copies were circulated among friends and a sixth one, now at the **Houghton Library,** Harvard, was given to **Edward Garnett** for use in a possible abridgement. **J. M. Wilson** edited and published the Bodleian manuscript/Oxford text in two volumes under his Castle Hill imprint in 1999. It is considerably longer than the 1926 subscriber's edition of *Seven Pillars of Wisdom* and includes important statements and events omitted from the 1926 version, which was eventually published widely in 1935. Although authorities have been divided about whether or not the Oxford version was better than the 1926 version of *Seven Pillars of Wisdom,* Lawrence was never in any doubt that the 1926 version was better written and more cogent. *See* **Seven Pillars of Wisdom, Texts of,** for more details.

Oxford University

Lawrence, who attended **Jesus College, Oxford,** from 1907 to 1910 and then was at the University again in 1919–1920 as a fellow at **All Souls College,** was intimately associated with this venerable institution of learning and can rightly be considered one of its most famous and important graduates. Lawrence was tutored by **Dr. Lane Poole** and was sent to **Prof. Ernest Barker** in 1909–10 for work in medieval history, as Barker informs us in his essay in **A. W. Lawrence**'s *T. E. Lawrence by His Friends.* **L. C. Jane** coached him in his studies. Barker mentions that he was impressed by Lawrence's honors thesis, entitled **"The Influence of the Crusades on European Military Architecture—To the End of the XIIth Century,"** which was published in 1936 under the title *Crusader Castles.* In this work, based on an 1,100-mile solo walking tour to 37 Crusader castles in the Middle East during the summer of 1909, Lawrence argues for the influence of Western military architecture on Eastern castle designs. Poole was so impressed that he threw a party in Lawrence's honor, and it is no wonder that he graduated with a first, the highest possible mark. During these years, Lawrence also made the acquaintance of **D. G. Hogarth,** keeper of the **Ashmolean Museum,** with whom he worked at a dig at **Carchemish, Syria,** after he graduated, and then in the **Arab Bureau** in **Cairo** during **World War I.** After the war, Lawrence received a small scholarship for residence at **All Souls College** and met poet **Robert Graves** during this period. According to

Graves, who became his second biographer, he carried out several pranks at this time, including ringing the Tell Shahm **Hejaz Railway** station bell out of his room window and flying the sharifian flag from a roof pinnacle. But the war had ended his desire to become a permanent fixture at Oxford, and he eventually left to work in the **Colonial Office** and then in the **Royal Air Force** and Tank Corps. For an excellent description of Lawrence as an undergraduate, see **Vyvyan Richards**'s *Portrait of T. E. Lawrence.* For Lawrence at All Souls, see Graves's *Lawrence and the Arabian Adventure.*

P

Palestine

In the period from 1516 to 1917–18, Palestine was under Turkish control and was divided into three areas: the north was assigned to the *vilayet* or province of **Beirut,** the south to the special district of **Jerusalem,** and the east, or **Transjordan,** to the *vilayet* of Damascus. Thus, when Lawrence visited the area during his Crusader castles walking tour, it was under Turkish control and largely desolate. In a lengthy descriptive letter of August 2, 1909, to his mother, filled with biblical references, he stated that the land benefited greatly from recent Jewish farming and supported the continuation of this effort (Garnett, *Letters,* pp. 63–75). In early 1914, he and **C. L. Woolley,** under the auspices of the British army and the **Palestine Exploration Fund** (as cover) took part in a survey of the **Wilderness of Zin,** which constitutes the northern Sinai and southern **Negev** regions. While Lawrence and Woolley surveyed the biblical, **Nabataean,** and Byzantine remains in the area, **Stewart Newcombe** of the Royal Engineers was mapping Turkish defenses in the area. In 1917–18, Palestine was conquered by **Gen. Edmund Allenby,** who made good use of the survey materials for military purposes. *Seven Pillars of Wisdom* records some details of that campaign, especially the clever ruse by means of which Allenby was able to conquer **Beersheba** by surprise and then **Gaza** and the historic conquest of **Jerusalem,** which Lawrence felt was the high point of the war for him, given his knowledge of its biblical associations. *Seven Pillars of Wisdom* also records Allenby's use of a second ruse for his final offensive, when he built a false camp indicating that an attack would come toward **Amman** when in fact he eventually attacked along the plain of Palestine, much farther to the west. After the war, Lawrence was instrumental in the separation of Transjordan from the rest of Palestine as a participant in the **Cairo Conference** of 1921, which essentially recognized the conquest of that area by **Feisal**'s brother, **Abdullah.** Lawrence supported both Arab and Jewish aspirations in Palestine and was the main force behind the signing (during the **Peace Conference** in **Paris** in 1919) of the Feisal-**Weizmann** agreement, which pledged both sides to future cooperation. In *Seven Pillars of Wisdom*'s chapter 101, Lawrence criticizes the British government for making ambiguous promises to both Arabs and Jews. See **A. P. Wavell,** *The Palestine Campaigns;* **Antonius,** *The Arab Awakening;* and A. Klieman, *Foundations of British Policy in the Arab World.*

Palestine Exploration Fund

Formed in 1865 under the initiative of George Grove, secretary of the Crystal

Palace Company, with the support of Queen Victoria and leading figures from the world of British art, science, religion, and politics, the fund's purpose was to investigate the biblical culture of **Palestine.** In the course of the succeeding decades, the fund organized several important surveys of Palestine, including the **Wilderness of Zin** exploration in which Lawrence participated, as well as a previous survey conducted by **Horatio Kitchener,** later a field marshal. It is now understood that these ostensibly archaeological surveys were actually the cover for spying on the Turkish deployments in southern Palestine. Nonetheless, the cover survey conducted by Lawrence and **C. L. Woolley** resulted in their important coauthored work of biblical and later archaeology, *The Wilderness of Zin.* See Neil Silberman, *Digging for God and Country,* for an interesting exploration of the many roles of the P.E.F.

Palgrave, William Gifford (1826–88)

Author of *Narrative of a Year's Journey through Central and Eastern Arabia* (1862–63), which recounts the adventures experienced by this British explorer and possible spy. On May 22, 1933, Lawrence wrote Brig. Gen. Sir Percy Sykes, then writing his *History of Exploration,* that Palgrave was a superb explorer and wonderful writer, and Palgrave is mentioned with respect in chapter 43 of *Seven Pillars of Wisdom.* Palgrave's work, however, has been challenged by **H. St. John Philby,** who accuses him of inventing incidents. Palgrave also wrote *A Vision of Life* (1891), a long autobiographical poem discussing among other matters his religious quest, which took him from Judaism to Protestantism and finally to Catholicism. See Mea Allan, *Palgrave of Arabia: The Life of William Gifford Palgrave, 1826–88.*

Palmyra

Town in **Syria,** about 130 miles northeast of Damascus, where an Arab kingdom flourished in the third century C.E. Lawrence visited Palmyra surreptitiously in June 1917 during his secret northern ride behind Turkish lines. A **Wuld Ali** sheikh friendly to the sharifians gave him an escort of 35 men here, and he also visited the Kawakiba sheikh, but other people whom he wished to contact at Palmyra did not show up. See **Antonius,** *The Arab Awakening,* and "T. E. Lawrence: Intelligence Officer" by Gideon Gera in Tabachnick, editor, *The T. E. Lawrence Puzzle.*

Pan-Arabism

A political ideology, largely associated with the **Hussein** family, including the sharif of **Mecca** and his sons **Feisal** and **Abdullah,** that asserted the unity of Arab territories and peoples, especially in the Fertile Crescent. The idea persisted even after World War II with Abdullah's urging but was opposed by other Arab rulers and has not been achieved even in the early twenty-first century. At the end of chapter 14 of *Seven Pillars of Wisdom,* Lawrence admits openly that only because of Arab weakness and the need to defeat the Turks was it possible for the British to think of stirring up their nationalistic ardor, lest it prove too difficult to control.

Pan-Islam

A political and religious ideology, begun by the Turkish **Sultan Abdul-Hamid II** in the late nineteenth century, claiming that the Muslim world is one unified entity. Abdul-Hamid was deposed by the **Young Turks** in 1908 and replaced by Mohammed V in 1909. He tried to use this doctrine in 1914 to unite the Muslim world against Britain and the Allies, but Britain wisely had taken the countermeasure of allying itself with **Hussein,** the sharif of Mecca, and his family. Turkey could not claim that it represented all Muslims against the European powers, because it was allied with Germany, just as the sharif was allied with Britain. Moreover, the Arabs were alienated from the Turks after centuries of having been ruled by them. In **India,** the sultan's *fatwa,* or religious pronouncement, calling for war against the Allies, failed to stir up the Muslims against Britain, and in the Ottoman Empire it also fell on deaf ears. Lawrence discusses this issue in chapter 5 of *Seven Pillars of Wisdom.* Attempts to revive the caliphate, or Turkish religious authority, which was dissolved in 1924, were unsuccessful. Despite the appeal of the Pan-Islamic ideology to ordinary Muslims, no universal organization then or now arose to implement it, and indeed Lawrence felt that the Arabs were too fractious to achieve unification.

Pan-Turanism (or Pan-Turkism)

A nationalistic movement asserting unity among all Turkish-speaking groups within and outside of the Ottoman Empire. "Turan" is the Turkish name for the Turks' pre-Turkey territory in Asia, and Yeni-Turan the name of the movement in Turkish. Beginning at the end of the nineteenth century and gaining force in 1908 with the ascension of the **Young Turks** movement, it persisted into **World War I,** when **Enver Pasha** hoped to cause an uprising of the Turkish peoples in **Russia.** In chapter 4 of *Seven Pillars of Wisdom,* Lawrence describes how the Young Turks at first talked of cooperation among Ottoman Empire nationalities but were then upset by the nationalistic fervor this unleashed and eventually retreated into a Pan-Turkish ideology that involved the suppression of other nationalities, including the Arabs.

Enver, for instance, tried to limit the use of the Arabic language. This ideology underwent periods of weaker or stronger support since it was conceived, and it still survives in expressions of Turkish support for compatriots in areas outside of Turkey, such as Cyprus and Europe.

Paris

Lawrence liked French culture, especially French medieval architecture, and it is fitting that he began his most important literary work when he was at the 1919 **Peace Conference** in **Paris.** According to his own notes, he began to write the first draft of *Seven Pillars of Wisdom* on January 10 and completed it on July 25, even working on it while he took a round-trip airplane ride to **Cairo,** which lasted from mid-May to August, having been delayed by an air crash in which he was injured. **J. M. Wilson** however says that he had finished only seven of the work's 11 books at that time. On January 30, 1919, Lawrence complained to his mother that he had not yet been able to visit a bookstore because of his busy conference schedule. See M. Larés, *T. E. Lawrence, la France et les Français,* for a full discussion of Lawrence's interaction with French culture.

Parker, Col. Alfred C. (1874–1935)

Member of the **Cairo Military Intelligence Department.** Governor of Sinai from 1906 to 1912, in which capacity he surveyed Sinai with special attention to possible routes of attack on the **Suez Canal** that might be used by the Turks in the event of war. In late 1916 he began setting up an intelligence system in the **Hejaz.** In chapter 6 of *Seven Pillars of Wisdom,* Lawrence includes Parker along with **Newcombe, Herbert, Graves,** and **Hogarth** among those devoted to the sharifian cause. In chapter 10 he mentions that Parker was **Sharif Ali ibn Hussein**'s liaison with the British. Parker as a professional soldier had little respect for irregular warfare and the military abilities of the Arabs and first suggested that armored cars could function well in the desert.

Peace Conference, Paris

Sometimes also called the Versailles Conference because of the signing of the Versailles Treaty on June 28, 1919. This important meeting for the purpose of settling borders and war claims took place between January 18, 1919, and January 20, 1920. Lawrence played a highly visible role at this conference, wearing an Arab headdress and serving as an adviser to **Feisal.** Lawrence also acted as Feisal's translator and as the financial manager of Feisal's grant from the **Foreign Office.** These roles clashed with his position as technical adviser to the British government from January 1919 on, and several British officials complained about that conflict of interest. In the event, the actual Middle East claims were resolved by the mandate system only at the **San Remo Conference** that was held in April 1920. At the Paris conference, Feisal, with Lawrence's help, made the case for Arab independence in the former Ottoman territories, appearing in front of the Supreme Council on February 6, 1919. Acting as interpreter, Lawrence first spoke in English but then switched to French at the request of the French and Italian delegations. Lawrence hoped that **President Woodrow Wilson** would secure Arab independence, but after the conference he felt that Arab hopes had not been fulfilled because the French insisted on a major role in **Syria** regardless of Feisal's claims, and he expressed his feeling of disgust in the introductory chapter of *Seven Pillars of Wisdom.* But as **Elie Kedourie** maintained, it is not clear that the sharifians, who were based in Arabia, had any greater claim to Syria than did the French. Regardless of the outcome of this claim, Lawrence had one clear accomplishment at the conference when he persuaded Feisal and **Chaim Weizmann,** head of the Zionist organization, to sign a treaty of cooperation; this was to be the first and last such agreement until the Begin-Sadat accord of 1979. See E. Kedourie, "The Real T. E. Lawrence," *Commentary* 64 (July 1997): 49–56, and (October 1997): 10–18; D. Fromkin, *A Peace to End All Peace;* and **George Antonius,** *The Arab Awakening.*

Peake, Pasha Frederick G. (1886–1970)

Soldier and participant with Lawrence in the **Arab Revolt.** Peake served in **India** before coming to **Egypt.** In chapter 94 of *Seven Pillars of Wisdom* he is mentioned as **Alan Dawnay**'s camel master, and Lawrence says that Peake was not fluent in Arabic. Captain Peake commanded the newly formed Egyptian Army Camel Corps at the capture of Tell Shahm station on April 19, 1918, and also took part in the demolition of **Hesa** station at the end of May 1918. Lawrence credits him with the co-invention of the tulip explosive, which he used to good effect against the **Hejaz Railway.** In 1920 he commanded the Trans-Jordanian Arab Legion, which he led until 1939. See C. S. Jarvis, *Arab Command: The Biography of Lieutenant-Colonel F. C. Peake Pasha.* Peake authored *A History and Tribes of Jordan* (1958).

Pearman, Capt. Douglas George

Participant in the **Arab Revolt** with Lawrence. Pearman was the author of *The Imperial Camel Corps with Colonel Lawrence* (London: Newton, 1928), which is a series of lectures illustrated with slides. Lawrence wrote him a letter in 1928 stating that he saw no future for British colonialism but a bright future for a British Commonwealth (Garnett, *Letters*, p. 578).

Petra

The "rose-red city half as old as time" discovered by J. L. Burckhardt in 1812. A city carved into a cliffside in what is now southwestern Jordan and containing some 750 monuments, Petra was founded by the **Nabataeans** approximately in the sixth century B.C.E. and was occupied by the Romans around 100 C.E. and then by the Byzantines. It continued in some form under the Byzantines and the Crusaders until the thirteenth century C.E. Lawrence was no less attracted to this fabled site than were many other desert travelers and praises it in chapter 118 of *Seven Pillars of Wisdom*. He first saw it during the **Wilderness of Zin** survey, and in February 1914 he wrote a friend that it surpassed all that had been written about it.

Petrie, Sir William Matthew Flinders (1853–1942)

Important British archaeologist who excavated Egyptian and Palestinian sites. In January 1912 Lawrence worked under Petrie at Kafr Ammr, **Egypt,** for several weeks to learn new methods that he could apply at **Carchemish.** He found Petrie eccentric but very knowledgeable, and Petrie liked him enough to invite him to work with him again.

Philby, H. St. John Bridger (1885–1960)

British official, adviser to the Saudi throne, and travel writer. Philby was the father of the British spy for the Russians, Kim Philby. Philby served with the British army

in **Iraq** during **World War I** as chief of its political administrative office, then in 1920 he became an adviser in the Iraqi Ministry of the Interior, in which position he opposed **Feisal**'s ascension to the throne. Philby also served as British resident in **Transjordan** from 1921 to 1924 after Lawrence vacated that post and praised Lawrence for his work there. After working as a businessman in Saudi Arabia for some years, he converted to **Islam** in 1930 and became an adviser to **Ibn Saud.** He crossed the **Rub al Khali,** the forbidding Empty Quarter, of Arabia in 1932, following **Bertram Thomas**'s feat by a different route. He was expelled from Arabia in 1954 following Ibn Saud's death. He wrote many books about his experiences, including *Arabia of the Wahhabis* (1928), which confirms details of **Doughty**'s trip in Arabia as reported in his *Travels in Arabia Deserta,* and the autobiography *Arabian Days* (1948), in which he praises Lawrence for wanting Arab independence but blames him for favoring Feisal over Ibn Saud. Lawrence, for his part, regarded Philby as a superb traveler but a mediocre writer. See Elizabeth Monroe's *Philby of Arabia* for more information.

Photography

Lawrence learned photography from his father, who was an enthusiastic amateur. During his tour of French castles in the summer of 1907, he took many photos, some of which appear in *Crusader Castles.* In a letter of May 23, 1911 (Garnett, *Letters,* pp. 106–7), he tells his mother that the telephoto lens for his camera is better than the human eye at a range of two miles. During **World War I,** Lawrence interested himself in aerial photography, and when he was in the **Royal Air Force** he was sent to photography school at **Farnborough.** See Yigal Sheffy, *British Military Intelligence in the Palestine Campaign, 1914–1918,* for a discussion of the state of aerial photography at that time, with examples. Many of Lawrence's wartime photos can be seen in *Oriental Assembly,* edited by **A. W. Lawrence.**

Picot, François Georges

See **Georges-Picot, Charles François**

Pike, Roy Manning

With Henry J. Hodgson, printer of the 1926 subscriber's edition of *Seven Pillars of Wisdom.* An American, he was a student at the London School of Printing. The two addresses at which the work was printed were 44 Westbourne Terrace North, London W2, and 25 Charles Street, London W11. Lawrence was quite pleased with Pike's work on the edition. Hodgson wrote a memoir of the job, which took three years: *Henry Hodgson Printer. Work for T. E. Lawrence & at Gregynog* (London: Fleece Press, 1989). *See also* **Seven Pillars of Wisdom,** Texts of and **Printing.**

Pirie-Gordon, Lt. Col. H.

Archaeologist, expert on the military architecture of the Crusades, and member of the **Arab Bureau** and of the Political Mission in **Palestine.** Pirie-Gordon recounts in his entry in **A. W. Lawrence**'s *T. E. Lawrence by His Friends* that he briefed Lawrence on the castles in Palestine and **Syria** before Lawrence set out for them in the summer of 1909. Lawrence returned the map Pirie-Gordon loaned him for the trip, apologizing for bloodstains on it. He worked with Lawrence in **Cairo** during the war and once helped him arrive at intelligence chief **Gilbert Clayton**'s location in **Egypt** after a policeman had questioned Lawrence, who refused to speak English and was clad only in Arab robes. Pirie-Gordon edited *A Brief Record of the Advance of the Egyptian Expeditionary Force under the Command of General Sir Edmund H. H. Allenby, July 1917 to October 1918.*

Pisani, Captain

Commander of a French contingent of troops at **Akaba** from August 1917 and later with Lawrence throughout the remainder of the **Arab Revolt,** often supplying artillery cover with his two 65-millimeter mountain guns and two 80-millimeter cannons. In chapter 68 of *Seven Pillars of Wisdom,* Lawrence notes that Pisani was fond of honors, but he also makes it clear that Pisani was an excellent soldier. Larés's *T. E. Lawrence, la France et les Français* offers an account of his activities.

"Playground Cricket"

A semi-humorous essay Lawrence published in the *Oxford High School Magazine* for July 1904 discussing how the game was played at the school, including variants. It is signed "Lawrence ii," indicating that he was the second-born of his five brothers.

"Playground Football"

An essay Lawrence (under the pseudonym "Goalpost") published in the *Oxford High School Magazine* for March 1904 giving a joking view of how football was played at the school and explaining the school's variants on the standard rules.

Plymouth

See **Mount Batten, R.A.F. Station**

"Politics of Mecca, The"

A memorandum written by Lawrence in January 1916 in which, as a member of **Gilbert Clayton**'s intelligence unit in

Cairo, he argues that **Sharif Hussein** would suit British purposes because he was a noted Arab leader who also lacked the wherewithal to unite the Arabs in one strong state. See **P. Knightley** and **C. Simpson,** *The Secret Lives of Lawrence of Arabia,* pp. 58–59.

Poole, Reginald Lane (1857–1939)

Lawrence's tutor at **Oxford University.** In 1910, he gave a dinner party to celebrate the success of Lawrence's honors thesis about Crusader architecture. A known medievalist, he was the author of *Illustrations of the History of Medieval Thought and Learning* (1920) and many other works on that period. **Aldington** has charged that Lawrence learned of the strategists he mentions prominently in chapter 33 of *Seven Pillars of Wisdom* not by reading them, but from Lane Poole, who participated in an Oxford Kriegspiel, or war games club.

Port Said

Port city on the extreme north end of the **Suez Canal.** It was the first city Lawrence saw when he sailed to the Middle East to study Crusader castles, but according to a letter of July 2, 1909, to his mother (**M. R. Lawrence,** editor, *The Home Letters of T. E. Lawrence and His Brothers,* pp. 84–85), he found it an ugly and relatively uninteresting place. **Basil Liddell Hart**'s biography says that Lawrence helped coal ships there briefly, and **J. M. Wilson** in his *Lawrence of Arabia* thinks this must have been for a few days on his return journey from the castle study in the summer of 1909. Lawrence also stopped off at this city on his way to **India** in 1927 and on his way back in 1929, when the police tried unsuccessfully to arrest him, thinking him a spy, as Wilson reports.

Pottery

During their survey of Zin in early 1914 that is recorded in *The Wilderness of Zin,* Lawrence and **C. Leonard Woolley** were the first to identify the crude earthenware pottery now called Negev pottery. However, as modern Israeli archaeologist Rudolph Cohen also notes in his article about Kadesh Barnea, they lacked the technical means to date this (or any other pottery), a process that would not be discovered until much later. See R. Cohen, "Did I Excavate Kadesh Barnea?" *Biblical Archaeology Review* (May/June 1981): 21–33.

Pound, Ezra (1885–1972)

American poet living in London with whom Lawrence corresponded. Lawrence felt that Pound, later notorious for his anti-Semitic views and support of Mussolini during World War II when he was resident in Italy, was histrionic and always unjustifiably angry about something or other. Pound, author of the complex *Cantos,* was associated with the modernist Imagist school, but Lawrence, with his **pre-Raphaelite** predilections, preferred Pound's neo-medieval "The Ballad of the Goodly Fere" to all of his other poems.

Pre-Raphaelites

The group of Victorian writers and artists influenced by **Dante Gabriel Rossetti** and committed to a neomedieval style in literature and art. Lawrence had a strong preference for their work, which included **Ruskin**'s praise of the Gothic in architecture and **William Morris**'s creation of handmade furniture and home decorations. In planning for the publication of *Seven Pillars of Wisdom,* Lawrence followed Morris's precepts about fine **printing,** also a pre-Raphaelite concern. While appreciative of the modern, such as **James Joyce**'s *Ulysses,* Lawrence never fully made the transition from the Victorian to the modern taste in the arts and remained loyal all his life to the same works that he had enjoyed as a teen.

Printing

Inspired particularly by **William Morris**'s beautifully printed *Kelmscott Chaucer,* Lawrence discussed with Oxford friend **Vyvyan Richards** the possibility of setting up a press for the purpose of art printing. While this ambition was never realized, Lawrence pulled out all the stops when designing the 1926 subscriber's edition of *Seven Pillars of Wisdom,* as related in V. M. Thompson's *"Not a Suitable Hobby for an Airman"—T. E. Lawrence as Publisher.* **Manning Pike** was retained for the print job, while **Sangorski and Sutcliff** did the binding. Some of the best artists of the period, including **Augustus John, William Rothenstein,** and **Eric Kennington** were retained for the portraits and woodcuts used to illustrate the edition. But as **Charles Grosvenor** has noted in his essay in *The T. E. Lawrence Puzzle* (edited by Tabachnick), the edition, seen in terms of design, was not entirely a success because the various styles of the illustrations were sometimes jarring rather than harmonious.

Prost, Sgt. Claude

An Arabic and Turkish speaker, the French Sergeant Prost had been the tutor of the **Emir Abdullah, Feisal**'s brother. In chapter 36 of *Seven Pillars of Wisdom,* Lawrence describes how Prost innocently delivered a letter to Abdullah from **Colonel Brémond,** commander of the French mission to the **Arab Revolt,** backbiting the British.

Public Record Office

Repository of British government documents in **London.** In 1968, many documents relating to Lawrence's military and political role from this archive were made available for the first time, prompting **Knightley** and **Simpson** to write *The Secret Lives of Lawrence of Arabia.* By 1975 almost all of the documents had been released, allowing **John Mack** and **J. M. Wilson** to write more accurate biographies than had previously been possible.

Pugh, Sgt. A.

A service companion of Lawrence in "B" Flight at **Cranwell R.A.F.** base from 1925, who testified to Lawrence's ignoring the pain of a broken arm in order to help a man involved in an auto accident.

Punctuation

Lawrence and **George Bernard Shaw** disagreed about punctuation during Shaw's editing of *Seven Pillars of Wisdom* in manuscript. In a letter of October 7, 1924 (in *T. E. Lawrence: Correspondence with Bernard and Charlotte Shaw 1922–26,* edited by **Jeremy** and Nicole **Wilson**), Shaw explains his own use of colons and semicolons and criticizes Lawrence's use of same. In his introductory note to *Seven Pillars of Wisdom,* Lawrence jokingly thanks Shaw for all of the semicolons in his book.

R

Rabegh

Port on the **Red Sea** coast of Arabia, about 60 miles north of **Jidda.** In chapter 8 of *Seven Pillars of Wisdom,* Lawrence states that in October 1916, four months after the **Arab Revolt** began, **Abdullah ibn Hussein** wanted a British brigade to be sent to Rabegh to hold it against the Turks. Lawrence instead proposed that the British send only advisers and materiel, a position accepted by the British high command in **Cairo** because they were loathe to divert troops from **Palestine** and possibly from Europe. Lawrence himself was then sent back to advise the revolt.

R.A.F. 200 Class Boats

In much of 1931 and 1932 Lawrence was assigned to the shipyard at **Hythe,** near Southampton, run by **Hubert Scott-Paine.** There and also at **R.A.F. Mount Batten** he helped test a new 37½-foot speedboat for which he wrote the maintenance manual, entitled **"200 Class Seaplane Tender— Provisional Issue of Notes."** *See also* **Boats.**

Railways

See **Berlin–Baghdad Railway; Hejaz Railway**

Rajputana, SS

The boat on which, from January 12 to February 2, 1929, Lawrence returned from his posting in **Karachi** to a **Royal Air Force** base near Plymouth. The ship was scheduled to dock in Gravesend, but Lawrence disembarked before that, in Plymouth, because the Air Ministry wanted to avoid the publicity of false spying rumors surrounding Lawrence's service in **India.** Lawrence was, however, photographed when climbing down a ladder into a speedboat, and all of the attempted secrecy regarding his disembarkment led to more publicity rather than less.

Ras Baalbek

City, about 50 miles north of Damascus, in what is now **Lebanon.** The Roman city of Heliopolis stood here, including three temples and an altar, and an oracle was consulted there by the Emperor Trajan. In Lawrence's time, it was the site of an Ottoman training depot. During his famous ride behind enemy lines in June 1917, Lawrence blew up a small bridge on the **Aleppo-**Damascus Railway near here in order to impress the local tribes, as he explained in a report to **Gilbert Clayton** (Garnett, *Letters,* p. 225).

Rashid, House of

Traditional rulers of northern Arabia, descended from the Shammar tribe, and based in Hail. **Charles Doughty** recounts his discussion with Mohammed ibn Rashid in *Travels in Arabia Deserta.* In Lawrence's time, the Rashids remained loyal to the Ottomans, but in 1921, **Ibn Saud** defeated the Rashids and after a victory over the **Hussein** family in 1924, he consolidated all of what became Saudi Arabia. Unlike the Saudis, the Rashids were not **Wahabi** Muslims.

Rattigan, Sir Terence (1911–77)

Playwright. His play *Ross* (1960) proposed the theory that the bey at **Deraa** knew who Lawrence was, deliberately had him raped and forced to acknowledge his homosexuality in order to break his will, and then let him go, confident that he could not be a good leader again. This theory once seemed farfetched, but in a letter of 1919 to **W. F. Stirling** discovered by **Knightley** and **Simpson** in the late 1960s, Lawrence claimed (unlike his version of this story in *Seven Pillars of Wisdom*) that the bey did indeed recognize him and took a homosexual fancy to him. According to this letter, Lawrence resisted and the bey then had him tortured and sent to a hospital, from which he escaped. Because the bey was chagrined about the escape, he hushed up the whole matter, according to Lawrence. So Rattigan's theory, while still farfetched, seems a bit more plausible today.

Read, Sir Herbert (1893–1968)

Poet, critic, and author of numerous books on the arts. In his *Coat of Many Colours* (1945), Read includes his 1927 piece that is highly critical of *Seven Pillars of Wisdom,* calling it artificial and Lawrence not a hero on the scale of **Doughty,** but he concedes that the book does limn Lawrence's personality. Lawrence answered this critique in a letter of December 1, 1927, to **Edward Garnett,** countering that Read's idea of a hero was too narrow and claiming that he did not intend to write an epic as Read had said (Garnett, *Letters,* pp. 547–51).

Reading Railway Station

The station at which Lawrence claimed that the first manuscript of *Seven Pillars of Wisdom,* which he was carrying in a bank messenger's bag and which he left under his table when he went into a refreshment room, was stolen from him in 1919 during a trip from **London** to Oxford (Garnett, *Letters,* p. 296; *T. E. Lawrence to His Biographers Robert Graves & Liddell Hart,* p. 2:145). A slightly different version of the story appears in **J. M. Wilson**'s biography. Lawrence suggested to **Liddell Hart** that he might unconsciously have wanted to lose it. In any case, **D. G. Hogarth** and **Charles Doughty** encouraged him to rewrite it, and he did so, taking it through several more drafts. *See also **Seven Pillars of Wisdom,** Texts of.*

Red Sea

The sea extending from the port of **Akaba** in the north approximately 1,250 miles to the Bab el Mandab, or Gate of Tears, in the south, where it meets the Gulf of Aden. In Lawrence's time this sea was bordered by **Egypt,** Anglo-Egyptian **Sudan,** and Eritrea (controlled by Italy) on the western shore, and Arabia, Asir, and **Yemen** on the eastern shore. During the **Arab Revolt,** this important waterway was completely under the control of the British navy, which rendered many valuable support services to the Arab forces, as recounted in *Seven Pillars of Wisdom*. The main ships that supported the revolt were the Indian troopship **Hardinge,** the *Dufferin,* the *Fox,* and the **Suva.** Among the navy's achievements were the capture of **Wejh** in January 1917 by a landing party from the *Hardinge,* and logistical support after the capture of **Akaba** on July 6, 1917, as well as the constant transport of men and materiel. See Capt. C. Parnell**,** "Lawrence of Arabia's Debt to Seapower," *United States Naval Institute Proceedings* 105 (August 1979): 75–83.

Religion

As a reaction against his mother's intense religiosity, which was itself the result of her living with Lawrence's father in an adulterous condition, Lawrence was not overtly religious. However, as a boy in Oxford, Lawrence attended St. Aldate's Church, an Evangelical congregation, whose minister, **Canon A.W.M. Christopher,** was a leader of that movement in England. The Bible was read aloud in the Lawrence home every morning, and at the age of 16, Lawrence won a prize in an examination of religious knowledge. In *Seven Pillars of Wisdom,* Lawrence draws on many biblical allusions, including even the title, from Proverbs 9:1. He also explains, in chapter 63, that he thought that **Islam** and Judaism were too abstract to win over Europeans, but he revised this opinion when, as if in a baptism, he met an old man declaring God's love near a pool in the **Wadi Rumm.** Perhaps the most interesting religious element in Lawrence is a mystical strain that appears in *Seven Pillars of Wisdom* and *The Mint.* Lawrence is the archetypal self-conscious introvert, always in danger of mental fragmentation because he thinks about himself too much. The dangers of this tendency are glimpsed especially after the **Deraa incident** when he seemed to house several selves talking to one another

and saw madness approaching, as described in chapter 81 of *Seven Pillars of Wisdom.* This can be seen as his "Dark Night of the Soul." However, in brief moments of self-loss in battle, or in mindless rest, he is able to attain stillness. He enters the **Royal Air Force** seeking the unity with others and with himself that was denied him in Arabia when he was unable to fuse with the Arab movement or to overcome his bodily pains completely. By the end of *The Mint,* he has found wholeness loafing on the grass with his military unit, and with nature (his motorcycle rides and in the water of a swimming pool), and integration as a person. He has gone from fragmentation to a sense of oneness with men and world. **André Malraux** once wrote that Lawrence was a great religious spirit, and however secular he may have seemed or told himself he was, there are enough elements in his life and writings to indicate that Malraux was correct. Certainly, as his brother **A. W. Lawrence** said, many people's attitudes toward Lawrence have a religious basis. In his combination of the soldierly and the spiritual Lawrence may resemble Joan of Arc, especially given his early interest in medieval French culture. *See **Seven Pillars of Wisdom,** **Spiritual Journey in.***

Revolt in the Desert

This is Lawrence's own abridgement of the 1926 subscriber's edition of *Seven Pillars of Wisdom* for popular consumption, published on March 10, 1927, in England and a few weeks later in America. Lawrence's letters inform us that he needed money to pay for the sumptuous subscriber's edition of *Seven Pillars of Wisdom* and so decided to make a popular, abridged edition, which he did with two service friends in 1926 after having abandoned an earlier attempt by **Edward Garnett.** About half the length of the original, the abridgment omits the introspective passages that give depth to

Seven Pillars of Wisdom but leaves the military plot line intact. As Lawrence wrote to Edward Garnett on June 10, 1927, he considered *Revolt* a parody of the original. Be that as it may, **Philip O'Brien**'s *T. E. Lawrence: A Bibliography* informs us that it sold 90,000 copies within four months, and it made the fortunes of the relatively new firm of **Jonathan Cape,** Ltd. O'Brien counts five impressions in England alone, and the book was also being serialized in the *Daily Telegraph.* It has been translated into Czech, Danish, Hebrew, Finnish, Hungarian, and Arabic, among many other languages, and by 1962 had gone into three editions in Japanese. In February 2004 it held the amazon.co.uk sales rank of approximately 230,000 while *Seven Pillars of Wisdom* held the approximate rank of 3,600.

Rey, Emmanuel Guillaume (born 1837)

French scholar, author of *L'Architecture militarie des Croises en Syrie* (1871). In his thesis on Crusader castles, Lawrence attacks Rey for inaccuracy and for using his imagination to fill in gaps in his knowledge. Lawrence disputed Rey's view that the Crusaders were influenced by Eastern castle designs, holding to the idea that they brought their designs with them from the West. It now appears that the truth lies between the two extremes and that the Crusaders were influenced by both Western and Eastern designs.

Richard I, Coeur de Lion (1157–99)

English king, Crusader commander, and opponent of **Saladin.** Lawrence wrote his mother on August 11, 1907, that **Chateau Gaillard,** in **France,** showed Richard's design genius (**M. R. Lawrence,** *Home Letters,* p. 55). In an ***Arab Bulletin*** report,

Lawrence compares **Feisal** to the statue of Richard I at Fontevraud Abbey, France, that he had seen during his bicycle tour of the castles in the area, and his description of Feisal's appearance in chapter 12 of *Seven Pillars of Wisdom* reflects that comparison. Ideas of Richard's nobility undoubtedly fed Lawrence's vision of the Middle East and the battles in which he fought.

Richards, Vyvyan (1886–1968)

Oxford University friend of Lawrence and author of *A Portrait of T. E. Lawrence: The Lawrence of The Seven Pillars of Wisdom* (1936) and the less detailed *T. E. Lawrence* (1939). Richards is convincing about personal reminiscences, such as Lawrence's reading tastes as an undergraduate and his desire to set up a fine printing press, but less so when he speaks of the **Arab Revolt,** where he was not present.

Rich, Barbara

See **Graves, Robert,** and **Riding, Laura**

Riding, Laura (1901–91)

Born Laura Reichenthal in New York City, she had early poetic success with the Fugitive group in America and came to England in 1925. During 13 years in England and Majorca, during which she was **Robert Graves**'s girlfriend, she wrote many volumes of her own and in collaboration with him. Lawrence met her through Graves and disliked her intensely. He did however contribute a science-fiction piece on an imaginary **autogiro** for airplanes, to *No Decency Left,* a book that was published under the pseudonym Barbara Rich, a cover for Riding and Graves. She eventually went to Canada and married Walter

Jackson, a scholar at the University of Toronto.

Rieder, Mrs. André

Lawrence's teacher of French language at the **American Mission** school at Jebail, **Lebanon,** when Lawrence studied French, Arabic, and Assyrian there in early 1911. She is mentioned often and always favorably in Lawrence's letters dating from the **Carchemish** period, 1911–14, and even later.

Roberts, William (1895–1980)

Painter and official **World War I** artist. According to V. M. Thompson's *"Not a Suitable Hobby for an Airman"—T. E. Lawrence as Publisher,* Roberts was the second-largest artistic contributor to the subscriber's edition of *Seven Pillars of Wisdom,* with a total of 35 works, including 27 line drawings and many portraits in oil, pencil, or chalk. Roberts's work was Lawrence's favorite among all the *Seven Pillars of Wisdom* illustrations according to **Vyvyan Richards**'s *Portrait of T. E. Lawrence.* **Charles Grosvenor** in his essay in *The T. E. Lawrence Puzzle* (edited by Tabachnick) points out one main design flaw in the book, and it has to do with Roberts: according to Grosvenor, Lawrence's preference for the Vorticist style favored by Roberts, which is very angular and machine-oriented, does not sit well with the lush late romanticism of his prose and with other, more romantic portraits. Roberts also became an official artist in World War II. See **J. M. Wilson,** *T. E. Lawrence,* for many portraits by Roberts.

Robinson, Edward (born 1897)

Author of the youth biography *Lawrence: The Story of His Life* (1935) and the adult biography *Lawrence the Rebel* (1946). Robinson claimed to have served with Lawrence but only a T. R. Robinson appears in the rosters in *Seven Pillars of Wisdom.* His 1946 work recounts new tales about Lawrence, for instance that he ate with Turkish headquarters staff during his June 1917 ride behind enemy lines. While this seems speculative, Robinson was the first to connect Lawrence's torture at **Deraa** with a desire for revenge at **Tafas,** where the Arabs took no Turkish prisoners. The credibility of Robinson's books has been affected by **A. W. Lawrence**'s 1937 claim that he did not return papers loaned to him for his biography, and his conviction on that charge as well as on a charge of forgery in 1929.

Rodman, Selden (1909–2002)

American poet and critic. In 1937, Rodman published a long biographical poem, *Lawrence: The Last Crusade,* that turns Lawrence's own writings into verse and seeks to present his life from his own perspective. This involves some speculation, as when the poem tries to show what Lawrence was thinking as his motorcycle crashed. According to **Stanley Weintraub**'s essay in *The T. E. Lawrence Puzzle* (edited by Tabachnick), Rodman's poem is influenced by literary Futurism.

Rogers, Bruce (1870–1957)

Outstanding book designer and printer. An American, he had worked for the Cambridge University Press as well as for Random House. In 1928, under a commission from Random House, Rogers suggested that Lawrence translate **The Odyssey** so that he could set it up beautifully. Featuring handmade paper and a black morocco binding, the Rogers edition, limited to 530 copies, is considered one of the most beautiful books of modern times. See Philip O'Brien, *T. E. Lawrence: A Bibliography.*

Rolls-Royce

See **Armored Cars**

Rome

Site of the air crash on May 18, 1919, from which Lawrence escaped with a broken shoulder blade and muscle strain. He was on his way from **Paris** to **Cairo** in a Handley-Page bomber in order to retrieve some papers for use in the composition of *Seven Pillars of Wisdom* when his plane hit a tree upon landing in Rome. While in the hospital he spent his time writing the introduction to *Seven Pillars of Wisdom,* the prose of which, he claimed, had been influenced by the sound of the airplane's engines. By May 29 he was well enough to resume his trip.

Ross, John Hume

The pseudonym under which Lawrence joined the **Royal Air Force** in August 1922 and used until he was discharged in January 1923 and joined the Tank Corps under the name **T. E. Shaw.** Lawrence used the names Ross and Shaw in an attempt to avoid being recognized as Lawrence of Arabia.

Rossetti, Dante Gabriel (1828–82)

Pre-Raphaelite painter and poet. With Holman Hunt and John Millais, Rossetti shared a distaste for science and a desire to escape into the medieval period. He later worked with Algernon Swinburne and **William Morris,** who was Lawrence's favorite writer. In a letter of June 14, 1928, to **David Garnett,** Lawrence complains that Rossetti, another favorite of his, has fallen out of favor with the critics (Garnett, *Letters,* p. 612).

Rota, Bertram

London rare book dealer specializing in Lawrence materials, among others. The firm's address is 31 Long Acre (First Floor), Covent Garden, London WE2 9LT, and its Web site is http://www.bertram rota.co.uk.

Rothenstein, Sir William (1872–1945)

Painter and lithographer. An official war artist in 1917–18, famous especially for his portraits. He contributed a chalk of **Alan Dawnay** to the subscriber's edition of *Seven Pillars of Wisdom.* In a letter of May 7, 1920, to **C. M. Doughty (**Garnett, *Letters,* p. 304), Lawrence says that Rothenstein is a solid draftsman rather than a genius, which he considered **Augustus John,** for instance, to be. Rothenstein produced a red chalk portrait of Lawrence in 1920. See V. M. Thompson, *"Not a Suitable Hobby for an Airman"—T. E. Lawrence as Publisher,* and **Charles Grosvenor,** *An Iconography: The Portraits of T. E. Lawrence.*

Round Table, The

See **Curtis, Lionel G.**

Royal Air Force

Having been formed in 1918 from the Royal Flying Corps and the Royal Naval Air Service that had participated in **World War I** (Lawrence's brother **Will Lawrence,** a member of the R.F.C., had died on the western front), in Lawrence's time the R.A.F. was a relatively new service, comparable perhaps to a space agency today. Lawrence saw the air as the new element for technological progress, so the R.A.F. was his natural first choice of service and he decided to enlist in 1922 as a

Lawrence in the Royal Air Force at Miranshah, India, in 1928. Courtesy of Corbis.

simple airman under the pseudonym **John Hume Ross.** He needed the help of **Air Marshal Trenchard** to get through the physical exam, which he failed, and was finally given the serial number 352087. A/c Ross first underwent basic training at **Uxbridge** for three months. This was difficult for a former colonel, but he persevered and learned to get along with the men as an equal. On November 7 he was sent to **Farnborough** for photographic training. He was discharged in early 1923 when his identity was discovered by the press. In February 1923 he reenlisted as a private in the Tank Corps under the number 7875698 and the new name **T. E. Shaw.** He served unhappily at the Tank Corps base at **Bovington,** in what he regarded as crude mental and physical conditions, until August 1925 when he was allowed to reenlist in the R.A.F. During this whole period, through 1926, he was preoccupied with the writing and publi-

cation of the subscriber's edition of *Seven Pillars of Wisdom* as a fine book. When readmitted to the R.A.F., he served first at **Cranwell,** where he was very happy, and in June 1927 was moved to **Karachi,** then in **India,** where he served as a clerk in the Engine Repair Section of the air station. In May 1928 he was transferred to **Miranshah,** 10 miles from **Afghanistan,** where he again served as a clerk. During this period, he finished *The Mint* and worked on his translation of **Homer**'s *The Odyssey.* In January 1929, after sensational (and false) rumors about his alleged adventures in Afghanistan, he was sent to the **Cattewater** (later **Mount Batten**) naval air station near Plymouth. **Mrs. Clare Sydney Smith**'s *The Golden Reign* is a memoir of this period; as the wife of his commanding officer, she got to know him well, and he made their house a second home. In 1929 he helped **Wing Commander Smith** with the preparations for the **Schneider Trophy Race** for seaplanes. He continued working on the *Odyssey* and in 1930 helped rescue men from a crashed plane. For the rest of his service in the R.A.F., he tested boats rather than planes, at Plymouth and at **Hythe,** Southampton, and wrote a manual for 37½-foot boats of the 200 class. During his service, Lawrence suggested some useful reforms and helped develop faster boats. He also enjoyed the camaraderie of his service companions, and *The Mint* testifies at the end to a man who has found peace with himself and his comrades. However, we know now that he suffered from his flagellation problem during this time as well as earlier, and so his peace even during this excellent R.A.F. period was, perhaps, only partial.

Royal Artillery

In 1906, at the age of 17, Lawrence ran away from home and enlisted in the Royal Garrison Artillery, where he served for either six or eight months according to the testimony he gave to **Liddell Hart** (*T. E. Lawrence to His Biographers Robert Graves & Liddell Hart*). According to **J. M. Wilson**'s biography, he served in the Falmouth Garrison as a boy soldier, a position reserved for youths between the ages of 14 and 18. He was unhappy there because of the roughness of the others serving, and following his appeal his father bought him out.

Royal Navy

According to *Seven Pillars of Wisdom,* the 11 ships of the Royal Navy's **Red Sea** fleet, including two seaplane carriers, two old cruisers, three troopships, one river monitor, one patrol boat, and two armed boarding steamer monitors, played a major role in Lawrence's campaign. The British, under the command of **Rear Adm. Sir Rosslyn Wemyss** with the assistance of the senior naval officer, **Red Sea, Capt. W.H.D. Boyle,** controlled this waterway since very early in the war, and this control and the firepower of the fleet were crucial to the control and capture of the ports of **Jidda, Yenbo,** and **Wejh** as well as the supply of men, materiel, and communications. Seaplanes, including the Short 184, Short 827, Sopwith Baby, and the Sopwith Schneider, bombed Turkish positions during the defense of Yenbo. After the capture of **Akaba** by Lawrence from the landward side, Wemyss immediately sent the troopship *Dufferin* and his own flagship, the old cruiser *Euryalus,* to the city with supplies and support. See Capt. Charles Parnell, "Lawrence of Arabia's Debt to Seapower," *United States Naval Institute Proceedings* 105 (August 1979): 75–83, for a full discussion. In the **Palestine** campaign, the navy was also crucial, especially for collecting material from spies and denying the Turks the use of the coast for supply, as explained in L. B. Weldon's book *"Hard Lying."*

Rualla Tribe

A **Beduin** tribe whose territory extended through much of present-day Jordan and southern **Syria.** Their chief was **Nuri Shaalan,** who had sheltered **Feisal** when he began the **Arab Revolt** and whose tribe took part in the destruction of the Turkish Fourth Army at the end of it. In chapter 104 of *Seven Pillars of Wisdom,* Lawrence describes him as old, tired, and cynical, yet apparently committed to the revolt. During the struggle for power at the town hall in Damascus between Lawrence and **Abd el Kader el Jesairi** at the end of the revolt, Nuri committed the Rualla to the sharifians, as described in chapter 120 of *Seven Pillars of Wisdom.*

Rub al Khali

Known in English as the "Empty Quarter," the Rub al Khali is a vast desert in southern Arabia. In 1929, Lawrence proposed to **Sir Hugh Trenchard,** marshal of the **Royal Air Force,** that it be crossed by new airships then being tested. His idea was never acted on, and in 1931 **Bertram Thomas** became the first European to accomplish this feat, using camels.

Rumm, Wadi

A beautiful wadi or dry riverbed, surrounded by towering cliffs, located about 30 miles east of **Akaba,** and one of Lawrence's favorite places in the Middle East. In chapter 62 of *Seven Pillars of Wisdom,* Lawrence compares Rumm to Byzantine architecture but finds it unimaginable in its size and grandeur. According to his description, a squadron of planes could turn around in it and it dwarfed the Arab army. In chapter 118, he compares it to **Azrak,** Batra, and **Petra,** three other unusually beautiful places.

Ruskin, John (1819–1900)

Art critic and prose stylist. Ruskin, who started and supported the Gothic revival in England, was an important influence on Lawrence's own love of Gothic castles and his prose style. In a letter of 1906 he tells his mother of his enthusiasm for Ruskin's work (Garnett, *Letters,* p. 48).

Russell, Pvt. Arthur

One of Lawrence's Tank Corps companions, who enjoyed reading and classical music. He served as a pallbearer at Lawrence's funeral in 1935.

Russell, Bertrand (1872–1970)

Philosopher, mathematician, and writer. At the end of chapter 83 of *Seven Pillars of Wisdom,* a passage about body and mind offers evidence that Lawrence was influenced by the idea, first invented by **William James,** and then expressed in Russell's *Essays in Radical Empiricism* and *Analysis of Mind,* of a "neutral stuff" out of which the material of both mind and matter are built. Yet in a letter of 1932 he calls Russell foolish (Garnett, *Letters,* p. 756). See S. E. Tabachnick, "A Fragmentation Artist," in *The T. E. Lawrence Puzzle. See also* **Neutral Monism.**

Russia

Russia's long history of engagement with Turkey made it a natural ally of Britain during **World War I,** until the Bolsheviks seized power in 1917 and took Russia out of the war. Up to 1917, the Russians under the Grand Duke Nicholas and Gen. Nicholas Yudenich kept up pressure on the Turks in the Caucasus region, thus aiding the British in **Egypt** and **Palestine.** During his work in the intelligence department in **Cairo** in 1916, Lawrence helped the grand duke gain control of the Turkish city of **Erzurum** by putting him in contact with disaffected Arab officers within the city, as he told **Liddell Hart** (in *T. E. Lawrence to His Biographers Robert Graves & Liddell Hart*). **John Mack** claimed that Lawrence exaggerated his role in the capture of Erzurum, but this has been challenged by **J. M. Wilson.**

S

Safra, Wadi

Dry riverbed about 50 miles south and east of the port **Yenbo** on the coast of Arabia. The site of 13 villages occupied by former slaves, in one of which, Hamra, Lawrence first met **Feisal.** Feisal had fallen back to Hamra after having been chased out of the town of Kheif, at the head of the wadi, by the Turks. Lawrence's statement that the place was fine but distant from Damascus, the goal of the **Arab Revolt,** sent shock waves through Feisal's group of commanders, as reported in chapter 12 of *Seven Pillars of Wisdom.*

Sahyun Castle

In his B.A. thesis on **"The Influence of the Crusades on European Military Architecture—To the End of the XIIth Century"** (republished as *Crusader Castles*), Lawrence states that he regarded Sahyun (or Saone) as the finest of all the castles that he saw on his Mideast walking tour of 1909. Near Antioch, **Syria,** this castle is distinguished by a very large square keep and a moat, both beautifully carved out, and a 110-foot-high column for holding a drawbridge, as well as a magnificent position. Lawrence stayed at the site for two days to study the castle and to correct **Rey**'s inaccurate plan of it.

Saladin (1137–93)

Foe of the Crusaders. Born of Kurdish descent in **Mesopotamia** and educated in Damascus, Saladin became sultan of **Egypt** after a series of political intrigues. He decided to conquer **Palestine** and **Syria,** thus coming into protracted conflict with the Crusaders. At the battle of Hittin in 1187 near present-day Tiberias in Israel, he defeated the Christian rulers. A third Crusade was mounted in Europe as a result, with **Richard I** facing Saladin in a series of battles made mythical for their chivalric aspect. Richard succeeded only in conquering Acco, and in 1192 a treaty signed with Saladin effectively ended Christian rule in the Holy Land, except for a narrow strip along the coast. Lawrence, who discussed Saladin with **Liddell Hart,** told him that **Feisal** would regard himself as having a higher status than Saladin (*T. E. Lawrence to His Biographers Robert Graves & Liddell Hart,* p. 101).

Salmond, Air Vice Marshal Sir Geoffrey (1878–1933)

Air Chief in **India** when Lawrence was at **Karachi** in 1928. Lawrence wrote Salmond, whom he knew from the **Palestine** campaign and who is mentioned positively at several points in *Seven Pillars of Wisdom,* requesting a posting elsewhere. Salmond transferred him to **Miranshah.** In 1933 he again wrote Salmond, requesting a transfer from mundane routine at **Mount Batten.** But Geoffrey Salmond retired, and it was his brother John Salmond, his replacement, who acceded to Lawrence's request, moving him first to **Felixstowe,** an experimental boat station, and then to another station at **East Cowes** on the Isle of Wight. Lawrence claimed to **Liddell Hart** that he had told Geoffrey Salmond of his desire to join the **Royal Air Force** as early as 1919 (*T. E. Lawrence to His Biographers Robert Graves & Liddell Hart,* p. 1:77).

Salt

City in what is now Jordan, about 25 miles northwest of **Amman.** As related in **A. P. Wavell**'s *The Palestine Campaigns,* it was first occupied on March 25, 1918, by Australian cavalry under Gen. J.S.M. Shea and used as a base for covering forces during an attack on Amman. It was abandoned by the British forces on March 30–31 when the raid on Amman failed and the Turks counterattacked. On April 29 the British forces, this time under **Gen. Sir H. G. Chauvel,** again attacked Salt, capturing it the next day. However, they had to yield it to the Turks on May 3. A force of **Beni Sakhr Beduins** had promised to help the British but did not appear. While the raids on Salt were a failure, **General Allenby,** with the help of many deceptive devices, exploited that failure to convince the Turks that further raids on Amman would be forthcoming, when in fact in the fall of 1918 his forces first struck farther north and closer to the coast in the decisive final assault of the war, which took the Turks completely by surprise. In chapters 93, 95, and 101 of *Seven Pillars of Wisdom,* Lawrence discusses these events. He explains that the two failed raids did divert Turkish attention to the east bank of the Jordan River, leaving scant forces to confront the

final British offensive on the coastal plain in the fall of 1918, but the perception of British failure at Salt also emboldened **Jemal Pasha** to try to convince **Feisal** to make a separate peace with Turkey even during the last summer of the war, in 1918. Salt was finally captured and held by a force of New Zealanders on September 23, 1918, during the retreat of the Turkish Fourth Army. See Matthew Hughes, *Allenby and British Strategy in the Middle East, 1917–1919.*

Samuel, Sir Herbert, 1st Viscount (1870–1963)

English politician. Samuel was variously postmaster general, home secretary, and leader of the Liberal Party in the House of Commons and House of Lords. Lawrence worked with Samuel in his role as high commissioner for **Palestine** (1920–25), both at the **Cairo Conference** of March 1921 and then later when Lawrence was chief political officer in **Transjordan,** a role that Samuel offered Lawrence with **Winston Churchill**'s approval. Samuel opposed the separation of Transjordan from Palestine, which the conference decided upon in order to give **Abdullah,** Feisal's brother, a kingdom.

San Remo Conference

The conference held in April 1920 in Italy with the participation of **Great Britain, France,** Italy, Japan, **Greece,** and Belgium that assigned Britain the mandate for **Palestine** and **Mesopotamia** and France the mandate for **Syria** and **Lebanon.** The French also were granted oil exploitation rights in Mesopotamia. The **Treaty of Sèvres** (August 1920) between the Ottomans and the Allies confirmed these agreements, and already in July 1920 France sent an army under **General Gouraud** into Damascus, ousting **Feisal** and establishing total control of the country when the Arabs tried to resist. Turkey, however, never ratified the Treaty of Sèvres, which was superceded by the **Treaty of Lausanne** (1923). In that treaty, Turkey renounced claims to the former Ottoman Empire territories but retained sovereignty over all parts of Turkey proper. See Shimoni and Levine, *Political Dictionary of the Middle East in the Twentieth Century.*

Sangorski and Sutcliffe

Founded in 1901 by Francis Sangorski and George Sutcliffe, this bindery became famous for its elaborate work on a *Rubaiyat of Omar Khayyam,* which was lost with the *Titanic* in 1912, the same year that Sangorski died in an accident. When Lawrence used them for work on the 1926 subscriber's edition of *Seven Pillars of Wisdom,* the firm was being run by Sutcliffe and his nephew Stanley Bray. *See Seven Pillars of Wisdom,* **Texts of.**

Sassoon, Siegfried (1886–1967)

War poet, war protester, and memoir writer. Sassoon served bravely on the western front during **World War I,** but after having been sent home wounded in 1917, he became a war protester. He was however not arrested but sent to a sanatorium where he decided to serve again and was sent to **Palestine** and then to **France,** where he again was wounded. He dabbled in Labour Party politics for a time but retired to write in the country. He produced notable war poems as well as *Memoirs of a Fox Hunting Man* (1928) and *Memoirs of an Infantry Officer* (1930). There is also a further three-volume work of autobiography: *The Old Century and Seven More Years, The World of Youth,* and *Siegfried's Journey.* Lawrence, who admired Sassoon's antiwar poetry, met him through

Edward Marsh, who was **Winston Churchill**'s secretary, in 1918. He subsequently showed him the 1922 Oxford text of *Seven Pillars of Wisdom* in 1923 and maintained a correspondence with him, based on literary interests and fellow-feeling about the war. Lawrence wrote to **C. Day-Lewis** in 1934, however, that the war had damaged Sassoon's lyricism (Garnett, *Letters,* p. 825).

Savage, Raymond (born 1888)

Lawrence's literary agent from 1922 on. Savage was the manager of the Curtis Brown agency and had served with Lawrence in the war. He also wrote *Allenby of Armageddon: A Record of the Career and Campaigns of Field-Marshal Viscount Allenby* (1925).

Sayid Taleb (el Nakib)

Arab nationalist leader in Iraq. Founder of the Reform Society of Basra in 1913, a party demanding autonomy from the Ottoman Empire for the district of Basra and the use of the Arabic language there. During the summer when the war began, he had briefly assumed power in Basra, but **Talat Pasha** ordered his arrest, and he fled to Kuwait to offer his support to the British. This attempt to play off the British against the Turks failed because he was regarded mistrustfully by the British too, and in January 1915 they sent him and **Nuri el Said** into exile in Bombay. He was tried in absentia by a Turkish military court in 1916. Taleb was allowed to return to Iraq by the British in 1920, but when he tried to force them to accede to his rule, he was exiled to Ceylon for the remainder of his life. **Feisal,** who had been supported by the British, including Lawrence, and opposed by Taleb, was elected king of **Iraq** on August 23, 1921. In chapter 4 of *Seven Pillars* *of Wisdom,* Lawrence calls Taleb a corrupt revolutionary; but Taleb has had partisans, such as **H. St. John Bridger Philby.** See Karsh and Karsh, *Empires of the Sand,* and Tauber, *The Arab Movements in World War I.*

Schneider Trophy Race

A seaplane competition, named for French aviation enthusiast Jacques Schneider, and held on a fairly regular basis from 1913 to the present day. Lawrence assisted with the preparations for the 1929 race held at Plymouth between British, American, French, and Italian planes, which was won by the British plane. But he was almost expelled from the **Royal Air Force** when he was seen talking to the Italian air marshal, General Balbo. It was about some oil left on the Italians' runway that needed cleaning up, but Lawrence, as a humble airman, was under orders not to talk to exalted people.

Scott-Paine, Hubert (1890–1954)

Legendary builder of the Spitfire aircraft and fast gunboats. He was the managing director of the Supermarine Aviation Works, which was founded by Noel Pemberton-Billing in 1916. In 1919 the company's entry failed to win the **Schneider Trophy Race** for seaplanes, but in 1922 at Naples, a Supermarine Sea Lion came in first, as noted in Michael Sharpe's *Biplanes, Triplanes and Seaplanes* (p. 293). In 1923, Scott-Paine turned his attention to boats, founding the **British Power Boat Company** in **Hythe** and working to convince the British armed forces that the future lay in fast, powerful gunboats rather than in large ships. Lawrence met him when in 1931 he was assigned to Scott-Paine's factory to test new **Royal Air Force** marine craft to be used in airplane rescue efforts,

especially the 37½-foot 200 class seaplane tender. The tests moved up and down the coast between Plymouth, Hythe, and Dover, and Lawrence played a role in the development of this craft. He also wrote the maintenance manual for it, **"200 Class Seaplane Tender—Provisional Issue of Notes."** In November 1934 Lawrence was transferred to **Bridlington** pending his discharge. See A. Rance, *Fast Boats and Flying Boats: A Biography of Hubert Scott-Paine, Solent Marine and Aviation Pioneer,* and Rance's "T. E. Lawrence at the British Power Boat Company," *Journal of the T. E. Lawrence Society* 2:1 (summer 1992): 49–68.

Sculptures

Charles Grosvenor's book on the portraits of Lawrence includes several sculptures made of him, including two by Elsie March, one by Walter Marsden, one by Sidney Spedding, and one by Thomas Wright. There are also pieces by Derwent Wood and Lady Scott. The most famous however are by **Eric Kennington,** including the bronze bust made in 1926 and the five casts of that now located at the **Harry Ransom Humanities Research Center** at The University of Texas, Austin; St. Paul's Cathedral, **London,** which was unveiled at the memorial service of December 1935 for him; the **Houghton Library,** Harvard University; **Clouds Hill;** and the Tate Gallery, London. In a letter of February 15, 1927, Lawrence expresses his admiration for Kennington's achievement in this bust (Garnett, *Letters,* p. 507). In a letter to **H. S. Ede,** he briefly discusses his aesthetic ideas about sculpture (Garnett, *Letters,* pp. 590–91); and in a letter to **Edward Garnett** he ranks **Frank Dobson** as the best contemporary sculptor (*Letters,* p. 385), while in one to **Sydney Cockerell** he compares the merits of Jacob Epstein, Dobson, Kennington, and Eric Gill. Perhaps even better known is Kennington's recumbent stone effigy sculpted from a three-ton block of Portland stone and found in St. Martin's Church, Wareham. In that effigy Lawrence remains in a state similar to that of the knights and lords that he so loved to make **brass rubbings** of when he was a teenager.

Seil el Hesa, Battle of

See **Tafileh, Battle of**

Senussis

Adherents of a semi-mystical Sunni religious order, founded in 1837, and based in Jaghbub, Cyrenaica, in what is now Libya. The order established lodges along the central routes. In 1911 when the Italians invaded, making the first use of extensive aerial bombing and armored cars before **World War I,** the Senussis became a guerrilla movement resisting them. The Turks aided the order with officers and equipment and encouraged the movement, now equipped with heavy weapons and an army of approximately 25,000 men, to attack British **Egypt** in November 1915 under **Jaafar Pasha el Askari,** a Turkish officer from Baghdad. The British at first were preoccupied with **Gallipoli,** but after their retreat from there released many units, they were able to confront the Senussis at Akakir in February 1916. The British, with superior firepower including armored cars, charged the Senussi position and achieved decisive victory, capturing the wounded Jaafar in the process. (As recounted in chapter 28 of *Seven Pillars of Wisdom,* **Feisal** secured his release from captivity so he could serve against the Turks in the **Arab Revolt.** This he did with distinction, accompanying Lawrence's forces with artillery in many actions, including the isolation of **Medina,** and receiving a decoration from **General Allenby.**) But to defend their gains in the Western Desert of

Egypt, the British had to build a 210-mile railroad and a series of small forts. As David Nicolle in his *Lawrence and the Arab Revolts* points out, peace talks between the Senussis, the Italians, and the English started in July 1916 but did not end until the Italians, British, and Senussis signed a truce at Akrama in April 1917. By encouraging the Senussis, the Turks diverted no less than 35,000 British, 60,000 Italian, and even some 15,000 French soldiers from other fronts (including **Palestine**) at very little cost to themselves. With the actions of **von Lettow-Vorbeck** in German East Africa, **Wassmuss**'s guerrilla campaign in Persia, and Lawrence's own campaign among the Arabs, the Turkish support of the Senussis is one of the outstanding guerrilla actions of World War I. Even after the truce was signed and the Senussis were expelled from Egypt, they continued to harass the Italians off and on right through World War II (now with British aid), and in 1951 the order's leader gained control of all of Libya, becoming King Idris. The order was removed from power by an officers' coup in 1969.

Serahin Tribe

Beduin tribe of the area that is now northern Jordan and southern **Syria.** Some Serahin porters took part in the abortive raid on the **Yarmuk** bridges, but when firing broke out after someone accidentally dropped a rifle, the porters dumped the explosives they were carrying into a ravine and fled, as recounted in chapter 76 of *Seven Pillars of Wisdom.*

Seven Pillars of Wisdom, Characterization in

As an epic work, *Seven Pillars of Wisdom* has numerous characters. While all are based on fact, Lawrence had considerable leeway when deciding which aspects of them to convey, and so the reader receives subjective painted portraits rather than photographic likenesses. **Richard Meinertzhagen,** for instance, told Lawrence that he did not agree with how Lawrence portrayed him in the book, but Lawrence did not change his portrayal. However subjective Lawrence's portraits may be, the major characters are often complex and develop across the book, like the characters in a good novel. **Feisal** for instance, is shown at first in a heroic light as the noble leader of an oppressed people, but Lawrence later on does not refrain from presenting him as a weak leader and a political manipulator of his supporters. In the famous self-reflective chapter 103, and indeed throughout the work, Lawrence is even harsher with regard to himself as the locus of unreconciled and contradictory drives: wanting to be known and not liking himself for wanting to be known; wanting both to follow and to lead; expressing interest in sexuality and yet regarding it as unclean; and being both a man of action and a man of thought. Furthermore, he shows himself reluctantly joining the **Arab Revolt;** then becoming absorbed in it; and at the end of the revolt awakening to find himself neither British nor Arab; and finally, in his role as narrator, appearing apologetic for many of his actions, which often of necessity involved violence and killing. Other important characters are sometimes portrayed powerfully but one-dimensionally. Arab chieftains, such as **Auda abu Tayi** or **Sheikh Ali,** often appear epic, larger than life, and are notable for one or two characteristics. Most major British military and political characters, such as **Allenby, Storrs, Clayton,** and **Hogarth,** are presented as intelligent, dedicated, and highly competent but as less colorful than the important Arab characters and without many facets to their personalities. Some British characters, such as **Gen. Sir Archibald Murray** and his chief of staff **Lynden-Bell,** are presented as

basically incompetent but well-meaning, and there is not much more to their character portrayals. The French are treated largely in terms of their attitudes toward Lawrence's desire to put the Arabs in charge of Damascus. They are either political opponents, such as **Colonel Brémond** and **Georges-Picot,** or competent military technicians, such as **Cousse** and **Pisani,** who receive some praise. The Germans sometimes receive Lawrence's praise for military prowess, as in the case of the machine gunners that kept their positions during the rout of the Turkish Fourth Army, but even important figures like **Gen. Liman von Sanders** and **Gen. Erich von Falkenhayn** are barely mentioned. The Turkish officers, on the other hand, are consistently shown as cruel (**Jemal Pasha**), perverse (the bey at **Deraa**), or stupid. Only **Fakhri Pasha,** who held onto **Medina** throughout the war, receives any praise, though it is mixed with blame for his cruelty. The minor characters, whom the reader meets only in a brief scene or two, form a background for the work and often have one characteristic highlighted, as in the case of **Farraj**'s and **Daud**'s concern for one another. While Lawrence's characterizations are clearly subjective, and may or may not reflect reality precisely, the major characters are unforgettable and help make *Seven Pillars of Wisdom* the outstanding work of epic autobiography that it is. Any reader of *Seven Pillars of Wisdom* will forever after see Lawrence in terms of his own contradictory, ambiguous, and most of all artistically powerful self-presentation. The Lawrence who narrates and acts in *Seven Pillars of Wisdom* is in fact one of the most interesting and most complex characters ever portrayed in a literary work. See **J. Meyers,** *The Wounded Spirit;* **T. O'Donnell,** *The Confessions of T. E. Lawrence;* and S. E. Tabachnick, *T. E. Lawrence,* for more on characterization in the book.

Seven Pillars of Wisdom, History in

In a letter of 1927 to **Lionel Curtis** (Garnett, *Letters,* p. 559), Lawrence decried historians' slavish adherence to documents, asserting that documents are never entirely truthful; and he praised the use of the historian's instinct in understanding historical events. To **George Bernard Shaw** he wrote in 1928 that he had used his dramatic sense when writing *Seven Pillars of Wisdom* (Garnett, *Letters,* p. 603). Clearly Lawrence subscribed to a school of historiography that favored the artistic and the insightful over the baldly factual. This has led some of his critics, such as **Aldington** and **Desmond Stewart,** to charge him with outright lying. But, as **J. M. Wilson** has shown, the documents often support his account of history, where they exist. Yet while he is usually accurate and truthful in *Seven Pillars of Wisdom,* Lawrence's sense of the dramatic and colorful feeling for style, as well as his desire to conceal painful personal events and to push the sharifian cause, may sometimes put him as an historian in a gray area between strict truth and fabrication, as in his accounts of the **Deraa incident** and the **fall of Damascus.** In his *Orientations,* **Ronald Storrs** finds that Lawrence's account in *Seven Pillars of Wisdom* of their conversation on their **Red Sea** voyage to **Jidda** has been heightened for artistic effect but is a model of accurate content. Fear of betraying intelligence secrets still current when he was writing (such as the names of spies active during the war and after it), and a desire to guard his own privacy, may also have led him to appear more mysterious than he otherwise might have been in his writing. This combination of fine writing, reticence, and subjectivity may be questioned by some historians today, but they have earned Lawrence apparently permanent readership, much like that of Thucydides, who invented most of the speeches his characters give but who continues to be read and regarded as perhaps the greatest historian of all time. See S. E. Tabachnick, *T. E. Lawrence,* pp. 49–54, for a discussion of this issue. For a discussion of some points under dispute, see for instance **E. Kedourie,** "The Capture of Damascus, October, 1918," in *The Chatham House Version and Other Middle-Eastern Studies;* **J. M. Wilson,** *Lawrence of Arabia,* pp. 1105–6; **J. Mack,** *A Prince of Our Disorder;* **G. Antonius,** *The Arab Awakening;* R. Storrs, *Orientations,* p. 171; **S. Mousa,** *T. E. Lawrence: An Arab View;* and **R. Aldington,** *Lawrence of Arabia: A Biographical Enquiry.*

Seven Pillars of Wisdom, Spiritual Journey in

According to Evelyn Underhill's *Mysticism,* the mystical journey includes the stages of awakening, purification, illumination, the Dark Night of the Soul, union, and (sometimes) return to society. Lawrence, who outwardly rejected religious belief in reaction to his mother's guilty evangelism, was nonetheless familiar with many religious as well as philosophical sources and was undoubtedly influenced by them. **André Malraux** has called him a great religious spirit, and his brother **A. W. Lawrence** felt that Lawrence served a religious need for his admirers. He arouses these feelings on the part of some of his readers because, whether consciously or unconsciously done on his part, the stages of the mystical journey are written into the pages of *Seven Pillars of Wisdom* and ***The Mint.*** As he moves into his unique role in the **Arab Revolt,** the Lawrence character in *Seven Pillars of Wisdom* evinces instances of awakening (his first attraction to and repulsion from Arabia), purification (his learning the pure smell and ways of the desert), and illumination (the capture of **Jerusalem,** peace at **Azrak,** and moments of self-loss in battle are times when he glimpses another, better reality beyond self-doubt and self-division). During the **Deraa incident** he experiences the Dark Night of the Soul and falls back into fragmentation, with several selves conversing in the void, as reported in chapter 81 of *Seven Pillars of Wisdom.* He does not recover until the very end of *The Mint,* when he experiences oneness with self, society, and nature; the final swimming pool scene in that work is very possibly an example of mystical union. Given his flagellation syndrome that continued until the end of his life in 1935, and which seems to indicate the mind and the body at loggerheads, we cannot say that Lawrence achieved a permanent sense of wholeness, but we can feel certain that he experienced a deep sense of unity often as he grew older. John Updike once called Kafka the "last holy writer," but that term may apply to Lawrence equally well. See S. E. Tabachnick, introduction to *The T. E. Lawrence Puzzle.*

Seven Pillars of Wisdom, Structure of

There are two plot lines in *Seven Pillars of Wisdom:* the military plot and the personal plot, in which Lawrence discusses his personality, his attitudes toward the **Arab Revolt,** and his personal trials in managing his role as adviser to the revolt and to British and Arab leaders. The military plot is relatively straightforward: after a slow start and setbacks around **Medina,** the Arab forces, with British help, including Lawrence's, take a succession of seaports on the **Red Sea** and finally **Akaba,** Lawrence's best military achievement. Then comes the failure of Lawrence's **Yarmuk bridges** attack, **Gen. Edmund Allenby**'s capture of **Jerusalem,** Lawrence's successful leadership at the **Battle of Tafileh,** his loss of confidence when **Zeid** squandered money that Lawrence had provided for a campaign, the failure of Al-

lenby's raid on **Amman,** the success of Allenby's final offensive in **Palestine,** the pursuit and destruction of the Turkish Fourth Army, and the entrance into Damascus. This is an upward curve despite a few downticks, and it charts the success of the Arab (and the British) forces. The second plot line, showing Lawrence's introspections, is less easy to chart. It begins with Lawrence's cheeky spirit in the **Cairo Military Intelligence Department** office, his feeling of strangeness as he arrives in **Jidda,** Arabia, for the first time, his hopeful meeting with **Feisal** in **Wadi Safra,** and his first disappointing attempts at tribal warfare, and proceeds through his successful assumption of the mantle of a war leader and absorption in the Arab Revolt's goals. There follows his corrosive feeling of double-crossing the Arabs with whom he is working, his torture at **Deraa** and felt fragmentation, his self-examination of his leadership role in chapter 100, his pitiless exposure of his own motives in chapter 103, revelations of his own feelings of revenge against the Turks at **Tafas,** and finally his awakening at the end of the adventure to find that he is a stranger to British and Arabs, and even to himself. This personal plot line is of necessity much less clearly defined than the military plot line and fluctuates violently, often without adequate explanation. Lawrence's moods do not correlate directly with the military action, making them often inexplicable. Why, for instance, was Lawrence disappointed after his capture of Akaba rather than jubilant? He explains that a fulfilled desire leads to emptiness; but we must add that this is so only for a hyper-romantic person, and that most normal people enjoy their triumphs. So Lawrence's disappointment is not wholly understandable. Also, how could it be that just a few weeks after his torture at Deraa, which seems to have been soul-destroying, he seems to be perfectly well and happy when celebrating the capture of Jerusalem?

Seven Pillars of Wisdom, Style of

In a letter of February 1924 to Lawrence, **E. M. Forster** first pointed out that *Seven Pillars of Wisdom* has several styles: one for airplanes and other machines, one for regular narrative functions, one for meditations, and one for peaks of emotion or beauty, and he offered the criticism that Lawrence's meditative style was not under full control and tended to become obscure (**A. W. Lawrence,** editor, *Letters to T. E. Lawrence,* p. 60). Stephen Tabachnick has arranged Lawrence's styles in a spectrum, ranging from the most introspective to the most objective and has noted that Lawrence's most romantic styles, full of heightened adjectives and many interlocking sentence elements, are reserved for subjects having to do with the Arabs and the **Arab Revolt,** while his most objective styles, built of simple elements and relatively colorless adjectives, are used to describe the British side of the war (*T. E. Lawrence,* pp. 115–21). It is as if the perceived exoticism of the Arabs and their nationalistic struggle excited him while the British were more familiar and predictable in their goals and their personalities and therefore more mundane, even during **Allenby**'s successes in the war. When Lawrence writes about himself in the **Deraa incident** chapter, there is a strange combination of attraction and repulsion in his stylistic choices, while in the "Myself" chapter (103), his style goes muddy when he tries to differentiate between the different parts of his personality. This shows that Lawrence had difficulty understanding himself and his own motives.

Seven Pillars of Wisdom, Texts of

The story of the composition of *Seven Pillars of Wisdom* has been told by **Jeffrey Meyers, Thomas O'Donnell, J. M. Wilson,** and V. M. Thompson, in her *"Not a Suitable Hobby for an Airman"—T. E. Lawrence as Publisher* (pp. 1–59). Essentially, according to Lawrence's own record, which can be found in a note in draft three, which is now in the **Bodleian Library, Oxford,** there were several drafts: (1) The first draft was begun on January 10, 1919, in Paris, and finished on July 25, 1919. This draft was lost in **Reading Station** in November 1919. (2) The second draft was begun on December 2, 1919, at Oxford, and then put aside until January–February 1920, when 95 percent of it was written at Barton Street, where Lawrence was given a garret, in 30 days. It was finished on May 11, 1920, still at Barton Street, and then corrected and added to for a further two years. It was destroyed by Lawrence on May 10, 1922, except for one sample page that he inserted after the epilogue of draft 3. (3) The third draft, preserved in the Bodleian Library. This was begun on September 1, 1920, and finished on May 9, 1922. Parts of it were written in **Jidda** and **Amman.** It is 335,000 words long. This is called the Bodleian manuscript. (4) This is the third draft, or Bodleian manuscript, as it appeared when printed up in eight copies on the press of the Oxford *Times* from January 20, 1922, to June 24, 1922. It is referred to as the Oxford text. In 2001, one copy of this text sold for almost $1,000,000 at Christie's auction house. (5) The fourth draft is a cut version (250,000 words) of the Oxford text, printed in 1926 utilizing the finest quality materials, illustrations, and techniques. It is called the subscriber's edition because it was made available to approximately 200 private subscribers. In 2003, one copy of this edition was worth approximately $70,000–$100,000 on the rare books market. (6) The final version, identical to the subscriber's edition in all except small details, was published for the general public in 1935. (7) In addition, there was the 1927 ***Revolt in the Desert,*** an abridgment lacking the introspective chapters. The Oxford text has been published in a handsome edition by J. M. Wilson, so readers can compare it to the final version. Some critics, including **Robert Graves,** have felt that the Oxford text is superior to the final version, but Lawrence himself was never in doubt that the final edition was tighter and better phrased. **Stanley** and Rodelle **Weintraub**'s collection, *Evolution of a Revolt* (1967), makes available the articles that Lawrence, utilizing some of the same material, published in journals and magazines while he was composing *Seven Pillars of Wisdom.* See http://www.telstudies.org; J. M. Wilson, editor, *Seven Pillars of Wisdom: The Complete 1922 Text;* J. Meyers, *The Wounded Spirit;* T. O'Donnell, *The Confessions of T. E. Lawrence;* V. M. Thompson, *"Not a Suitable Hobby for an Airman"—T. E. Lawrence as Publisher;* and S. Tabachnick, *T. E. Lawrence.*

Seven Pillars of Wisdom, Title and Motto of

In the introductory matter to *Seven Pillars of Wisdom,* Lawrence informs us that his title is based on Proverbs 9:1: "Wisdom hath builded her house; she hath hewn out her seven pillars." There are other biblical allusions too: in Deuteronomy 1:13 and Exodus 18:21 leaders of the people of Israel are said to have seven qualities: wisdom, understanding, experience, ability, fear of God, trustworthiness, and incorruptibility. The Five Pillars of Faith of **Islam** also resonate in Lawrence's title. As Lawrence pointed out, the number seven implies fullness in the Semitic languages, and so *seven pillars* indicates a complete structure of knowledge (Garnett, *Letters,* p. 514). In Harvard's **Houghton Library** there is a manuscript in which Lawrence delineates the book divisions of *Seven Pillars of Wisdom* with titles indicating that he saw them as courses in the building of

a house. Traces of this scheme remain in the final edition, where the subtitle of the introduction includes the word Foundations and Book X is titled "The House is Perfected." But at the same time, *pillars* implies a ruined desert palace along the lines of Shelley's poem "Ozymandias," and while he was writing *Seven Pillars of Wisdom* Lawrence already knew that the **Arab Revolt** had ultimately failed when the French drove **Feisal** out of Damascus in 1920. So the book's subtitle, "A Triumph," can as easily be read ironically as well as triumphantly. There are also allusions to **John Ruskin**'s "Seven Lamps of Architecture" (as **Jeffrey Meyers** points out in his book) and to the seven biblical lands that must be governed morally, as Lawrence told **Liddell Hart** (see *T. E. Lawrence to His Biographers Robert Graves & Liddell Hart*). The motto that appears on the cover of some editions, about the sword indicating cleanness and death, is also allusive because *Feisal* means a downward sword stroke in Arabic. Thus there are both biblical and Arabic allusions, making *Seven Pillars of Wisdom* a very Eastern as well as a Western book. The vast number of allusions in *Seven Pillars of Wisdom* to writing as disparate as Keats's and Shelley's poetry, Shakespeare's plays, and the *Moallakat* or pagan songs of ancient Arabia, also lead to the conclusion that, as in his campaign, Lawrence as an author has been able to bridge the East and West better than almost any British writer except perhaps his mentor **Charles Doughty,** who has worked Arabic speech rhythms into his very sentences in *Travels in Arabia Deserta.*

Sèvres, Treaty of

This treaty, reluctantly signed by the Turks on August 10, 1920, embodied the results of the First Conference of **London** (February 1920) and the **San Remo Conference** of April 1920. The terms of the treaty included the loss of Turkish control over the Dardanelle Straits, the loss of the non-Turkish-speaking parts of the Empire, the loss of some parts of Anatolia, and the rise of an independent Armenia and an independent Kurdistan. Moreover, the prewar Capitulations, or special privileges for foreigners in Turkey, would be restored. When, however, a Greek army attempted to take land beyond that which the treaty allowed, the Turks under **Mustapha Kemal** resisted, also defeating some Allied forces, with the result that the **Treaty of Lausanne,** which included much more favorable terms for Turkey, replaced the Treaty of Sèvres. See David Fromkin, *A Peace to End All Peace.*

Sexuality

There has been much speculation about the nature of Lawrence's sexuality. All scholars agree that he did not much like women sexually and could relate only to mature married women, like **Clare Sydney Smith** and **Mrs. G. B. Shaw,** whom he treated as confidants and mother-figures rather than as sexual companions. There the agreement ends. One school of thought, represented by **J. M. Wilson,** holds that he was completely celibate and that he cannot be connected to homosexuality in any way. A second school, represented by Stephen Spender, says that he may have been celibate, but that he was a repressed homosexual. Another group of critics, represented by **C. Leonard Woolley,** implies or says (Daniel Wolfe) that he acted on his homosexual tendencies, most probably with **Dahoum,** or Salim Achmed, his Arab servant at **Carchemish.** To date, there has been no concrete evidence that he was a practicing homosexual, but the fifth paragraph of the first chapter of *Seven Pillars of Wisdom,* about sex between members of

the **Arab Revolt,** and his very sympathetic treatment of the **Farraj** and **Daud** story have aroused biographers' suspicions. However, the clearest evidence of his sexual nature is the testimony of **John Bruce,** first produced by **Knightley** and **Simpson** in their biography, and the letters to Bruce from an "Old Man," in fact Lawrence himself, that **Mack** published in his life of Lawrence. This evidence indicates that, beginning around the time of his service in the Tank Corps, he paid Bruce to whip him. The whippings took place anywhere from several times to once a year and continued until the year of his death. This practice has variously been attributed to his ascetic, puritanical nature that demanded punishment for his sins as a commander during the **Arab Revolt;** to his attempt to kill his sexual urges, which had always made a man who did not like to be touched uncomfortable; and finally to a perverse sexuality that could achieve orgasm only through whipping. All biographies since Knightley and Simpson's have attempted to explain this flagellation complex. At this point, it seems clear that whatever sexual satisfaction Lawrence received was experienced through these bouts of whipping, and that any other sexual activities attributed to him have been unproved. In any case, the whipping explains Lawrence's disgust with himself in some of his letters dating from the postwar period and his idea that he was unworthy of any of the fame that he was, ironically, simultaneously accruing because of the slide show that **Lowell Thomas** was presenting to tens of thousands of spectators in the early 1920s.

Shakespear, Capt. William Henry Irvine (1878–1915)

British political agent in Kuwait and explorer, who in 1913–14 traveled from the Persian Gulf through Arabia to **Akaba,**

Sinai, and Suez. After his return to Kuwait, he was sent by **Sir Percy Cox,** chief political officer of the Mesopotamian Expeditionary Force, as representative to the court of **Ibn Saud.** Shakespear easily enlisted him on the British side of **World War I** because Ibn Saud always was determined to conquer northern Arabia from **Ibn Rashid,** who had already sided with the Turks and Germans. Shakespear, however, was killed in battle against the Rashidi forces at Jarrab in January 1915. It is speculated by **H. St. John Bridger Philby** in his *Arabia* (1930) that if Shakespear had not been killed and the Saudi forces been successful on this occasion, Shakespear and Ibn Saud would have gone on to conquer all of Arabia from the Turks, thus obviating the need for Lawrence's campaigns with **Feisal.** In chapter 45 of *Seven Pillars of Wisdom,* Lawrence mentions that members of the **Ageyl** mercenaries told him of this battle and Shakespear's end. See H.V.F. Winstone, *Captain Shakespear: A Portrait.*

Shakir, Sharif (born 1888)

Emir Abdullah's cousin and the second in command of Abdullah's army, who aided Lawrence in an attack on the **Hejaz Railway,** as related in chapters 34 and 35 of *Seven Pillars of Wisdom.* He is described in chapter 36 by Lawrence as the best warrior in Abdullah's group and a fine horseman who also liked dancing and sport but as something less than a steady and serious companion.

Shaw, Mrs. Charlotte (née Charlotte Payne-Townshend; 1857–1943)

Sydney Cockerell brought Lawrence to meet Charlotte and **George Bernard Shaw** on Saturday, March 28, 1922, as she noted in a diary excerpt published in *T. E. Law-rence Correspondence with Bernard and Charlotte Shaw 1922–1926,* edited by **Jeremy** and Nicole **Wilson.** From that time on, Charlotte became an enthusiastic supporter of Lawrence and even a mother figure toward him. It was to her that he confessed, in a famous letter of March 26, 1924, now in the **British Library,** that he had allowed himself to be raped at **Deraa** when he could not stand the pain of his torture by the Turks. And in a letter of September 28, 1925, he confessed to wanting to feel degraded, without, however, revealing to her his flagellation syndrome that led him to have himself whipped by a service colleague during at least the last 12 years of his life. Clearly, the Charlotte who was more than 30 years older than he had become an important person in his life, worthy of discussing his most intimate feelings with, and even an excellent correspondent about artistic matters, for instance his preference for the heroic **Augustus John** portrait of himself over that by **Orpen** (perhaps because the Orpen portrait shrewdly reveals a lot about his inner character). Their relationship grew close enough to cause jealousy on the part of George Bernard, but both he and his wife were devastated by Lawrence's death. See **Stanley Weintraub**'s *Private Shaw and Public Shaw* (1963); J. M. and Nicole Wilson's edition of the Lawrence-Shaw correspondence; and J. Dunbar's *Mrs. G.B.S.: A Portrait* for more information.

Shaw, George Bernard (1856–1950)

G.B.S. met Lawrence in 1922 at the same time that his wife **Charlotte Shaw** did. While she became an emotional support for Lawrence, G.B.S. offered him wise literary advice and even copyediting of *Seven Pillars of Wisdom.* As related in a volume of Lawrence-Shaw correspondence edited by **J.** and N. **Wilson,** Shaw's work on that book included correction of Lawrence's punctuation and the recommendation that the introductory chapter be dropped, among other things. The fact that the introduction has been added to most recent editions shows the limitations of Shaw's intervention, but his lively dialog with Lawrence about literary, creative, and practical publishing matters, as well as other artistic concerns, makes for wonderful reading. This friendship between a quirky amateur writer of genius lacking self-confidence and a brilliant, hardened professional is one of the twentieth century's important literary associations, and it was cut off only by Lawrence's accidental death in 1935. Shaw left a memoir in **A. W. Lawrence**'s *T. E. Lawrence by His Friends.* **Stanley Weintraub**'s *Public Shaw and Private Shaw* offers further insight into the relationship. Weintraub's title reflects the fact that Lawrence changed his name to **Ross** and then **Shaw** in the 1920s when he was serving in the Tank Corps and the **Royal Air Force.** Shaw was so intrigued by Lawrence that he based the character Pvt. Napoleon Alexander Trotsky Meek in his play of 1934, *Too True to Be Good,* on Lawrence. The part was acted by **Walter Hudd** in the first performances.

Shaw, T. E.

Pseudonym of T. E. Lawrence, adopted in 1923 when Lawrence went to enlist in the Tank Corps. He had been using **John Hume Ross** when in the **Royal Air Force** in 1922–23. Lawrence claimed that he had adopted Shaw at random from the *Army List* after an officer in the War Office required him to take a new name, but given his close association with **G. B. Shaw** and particularly with his wife **Charlotte,** he may indeed have felt like a son to them, and his adopted family name may reflect

that. His full Tank Corps identification was 7875698 Private T. E. Shaw. Because his father had changed his own family name from Chapman to Lawrence, Lawrence seems to have felt little anxiety about changing the name, too, whenever it suited him to do so.

Sheikh Saad

Town on the Pilgrim Road and near the **Hejaz Railway,** about 20 miles northwest of **Deraa,** through which the Turkish Fourth Army retreated in September 1918 thinking themselves safe but where Lawrence and his men, who had arrived earlier, ambushed them, as related in chapters 116 and 117 of *Seven Pillars of Wisdom.* The villagers had to be prevented from killing the captured Turks because they were incensed over the Turkish massacre of civilians in **Tafas.**

Sherarat Tribe

Beduin tribe of what is now central Jordan. Lawrence passed through their territory, which encompasses the area south of **Maan,** during the northern loop of his raid on **Akaba** in June 1917. They were part of **Feisal**'s coalition of tribes and helped in making raids on the **Hejaz Railway.**

Shobek

Arabic name for the locale of the former Crusader fort called Monreale, about 15 miles northeast of **Petra.** Here the Turks had a governor, provisions, and about 180 men as well as local support, but in January 1918 **Auda, Sharif Nasir,** and the **Howeitat** succeeded in capturing the position, as related in chapter 84 of *Seven Pillars of Wisdom.* In September 1918 the Turks attacked the town but **Capt. H. S. Hornby** successfully defended it against them (chapter 107).

Short Note on the Design and Issue of Postage Stamps Prepared by the Survey of Egypt for His Highness Hussein, Emir and Sherif of Mecca and King of the Hejaz, A

This brief pamphlet, an illustration of which can be seen on p. 67 of **Jeremy Wilson**'s *T. E. Lawrence,* was intended to explain how and why a new set of stamps for the hoped-for sharifian state in Arabia was designed. Published by the Survey of Egypt in 1918, it shows the new stamps that had been designed by the survey and the **Arab Bureau** under the specific direction of Lawrence and **Sir Ronald Storrs** in 1916. Lawrence refers to these stamps in chapter 16 of *Seven Pillars of Wisdom.* In a letter of July 22, 1916, in **M. R. Lawrence**'s *Home Letters* (p. 328), Lawrence complains that the designs for the stamps cannot include fine detail because they are not engraved but that he is planning to have flavored gum on the stamp backs. He encloses stamps for his brothers and predicts that they will be valuable one day, an accurate prediction because they are so rare.

Shukri Pasha el Ayoubi

One of the Damascene notables tortured by **Jemal Pasha** in 1916 after the **Arab Revolt** was declared by **Sharif Hussein** because Jemal suspected him of participation in the revolt. After the capture of Damascus by the Arab forces in October 1918, Lawrence appointed Shukri, who had served as **Ali Riza Pasha**'s assistant on **Feisal**'s Damascus committee, as acting military governor, as reported in chapter 120 of *Seven Pillars of Wisdom.* Shukri raised the flag of **Feisal**'s movement in **Beirut** on October 3, 1918, but this caused trouble with the French, who aimed to con-

trol **Lebanon** and **Syria** after the war, and **General Allenby** ordered the flag removed. See **G. Antonius,** *The Arab Awakening.*

Simpson, Colin (born 1931)

Sunday Times journalist; with **Phillip Knightley,** coauthor of *The Secret Lives of Lawrence of Arabia* (1969), which first told the story of Lawrence's postwar flagellation syndrome and also accused Lawrence of imperialism.

Sims, Fl. Lt. Reginald G. (1885–1972)

Sims was a **Royal Air Force** equipment officer stationed at **Bridlington** and made notes about his friendship with Lawrence starting in late 1934. The first edition of these notes was entitled *The Doings of T. E.* and was privately printed in 1937, but by 1994 this had become *The Sayings and Doings of T. E. Lawrence* and was published by Fleece Press, with Leo John De Freitas as the coauthor. In February 1935 Sims shot several photos of Lawrence; these are posted on the telstudies.org Web site. Sims contributed an article to **A. W. Lawrence**'s *T. E. Lawrence by His Friends,* especially detailing Lawrence's friendly relations with Sims's wife and child.

Sinai Peninsula, Military Report on the

In November 1914, when Lawrence was working at the **Geographical Section** of the War Office in **London,** he was assigned the task of writing a military report on the Sinai peninsula. Because he had participated in the Wilderness of Zin survey in the northern Sinai desert and had just written *The Wilderness of Zin,* he was at least partially equipped to do a military report about the peninsula. The problem was that he had covered only a small part of the northern area of the peninsula himself and the report had to be about a much greater area of the peninsula, going as far as the **Suez Canal.** The resulting 190-page book, however, was ready in one month, and Lawrence complained that he had been forced to write two books instead of one about the Sinai. See **J. M. Wilson,** *Lawrence of Arabia,* pp. 153–54.

Sirhan, Wadi

An often-traveled dry riverbed and chain of wells extending from **Jauf,** in the **Nefud Desert,** about 250 miles northwest. Lawrence and the Arab forces traveled some distance up this wadi on the way to the attack on **Akaba** in June 1917.

Smith, Mrs. Clare Sydney (died 1962)

Wife of **Wing Comdr. Sydney Smith** of **R.A.F. Cattewater** (later **R.A.F. Mount Batten**) and the author of *The Golden Reign: The Story of My Friendship with Lawrence of Arabia* (1940). In this memoir, Mrs. Smith details the couple's friendship with him from the time Lawrence literally had knocked her off her feet at her sister's **London** apartment, to which her husband had brought Lawrence from Plymouth to evade the press when he arrived from **India,** through the period from March 1929 to 1931 when Lawrence served at the base. The book is named with Lawrence's own phrase for this period of his life, which he enjoyed greatly.

Smith, Wing Comdr. Sydney (1921–62)

Lawrence's commanding officer at **R.A.F. Cattewater,** later **R.A.F. Mount Batten.** In a letter of April 16, 1929, to R.A.F.

Comdr. **Sir Hugh Trenchard** (Brown, *Selected Letters,* p. 415), Lawrence praises Smith. He first met Smith at the **Cairo Conference** of 1921, and it was Smith who was delegated to secret him off the **SS** *Rajputana* in Plymouth harbor after the conclusion of his service in **India,** thereby evading the press. Lawrence worked under Smith on the **Schneider Trophy Race,** performed heroic rescue operations during an air boat crash at the base, and won the affection of the men. He and Smith were jointly given a Biscayne Baby speedboat, which they named the *Biscuit,* and enjoyed many rides on it together with Smith's wife. Smith was, however, transferred in late 1931, around which time Lawrence also was assigned (originally by Smith) to the **Hubert Scott-Paine** shipyard at **Hythe,** Southampton, to help develop fast boats.

Smuts, Gen. Jan Christiaan (1870–1950)

Born in the Cape Province of South Africa and educated at Cambridge, Smuts was an excellent guerrilla fighter on the Boer side in 1899 during the first Boer War, became South African defense minister under Prime Minister Louis Botha in 1910, and worked to protect the country from the Germans at the beginning of **World War I.** He then served as head of the Anglo–South African forces in German East Africa, fighting against German **Gen. Paul E. von Lettow-Vorbeck** until January 1917, when he joined the British **War Cabinet** in **London.** In February 1918, he came to **General Allenby**'s headquarters on behalf of the War Cabinet and concluded that the **Palestine** campaign should take precedence over operations in **Mesopotamia,** thus paving the way for Allenby's victory. He participated in the **Peace Conference** in 1919. **George Bernard Shaw** allegedly told the straightlaced Smuts that every schoolgirl should read *Seven Pillars of Wisdom.* Smuts served as prime minister of South Africa from 1919 to 1924, as a British commander and adviser to **Churchill** during World War II, and prime minister of South Africa again from 1939 to 1948.

South Hill

The name of the 173-acre manor of Lawrence's father, originally named Thomas Chapman. It is near Delvin, in **County Westmeath, Ireland.** Because of his father's elopement and adultery, Lawrence and his brothers never shared in the family lands in Ireland, which gave Lawrence a lifelong feeling of aristocratic disinheritance, which has been claimed as one of his motivations for working with Arab sheikhs to help them regain what he saw as their patrimony. See Kathryn Tidrick, *Heart-Beguiling Araby.*

Spencer, Gilbert (1893–1979)

Painter. As noted in V. M. Thompson's *"Not a Suitable Hobby for an Airman"— T. E. Lawrence as Publisher,* Spencer first saw Lawrence in Arab dress at Romani, **Egypt,** where Spencer was serving. Lawrence subsequently saw one of Spencer's paintings in 1923 and asked him to sketch **Lieutenant Junor,** a pilot mentioned from chapter 107 onward in *Seven Pillars of Wisdom.* Spencer relates in his *Memoirs of a Painter* that he did not think the pencil sketch a good one. It remains his only contribution to the 1926 subscriber's edition of *Seven Pillars of Wisdom.* Gilbert was the brother of more famous artist Stanley Spencer, whom Lawrence also knew. See **J. M. Wilson**'s *T. E. Lawrence* (p. 110) for a reproduction of this sketch.

Spenser, Edmund (1552?–99)

Poet of *The Faerie Queene,* which, according to a letter Lawrence wrote (Garnett,

Letters, p. 832) to **Ernest Altounyan** on December 9, 1934, he had read many times until the year 1916. Lawrence criticized the poem for moving too fast.

Spinoza, Baruch (1632–77)

Important philosopher. Lawrence mentions him in chapter 63 of *Seven Pillars of Wisdom* as the exponent of a cold, intellectual conception of God that did not permit God to love people in return for their love; undoubtedly he was thinking of Spinoza's comment that just because a man loves God he mustn't expect God to love him. Lawrence states there that he took this conception to be characteristic of all Semitic religiosity until an old man in the **Wadi Rumm,** with his statement that God is love, convinced him otherwise. As his philosophical positions in *Seven Pillars of Wisdom* and **The Mint** reveal, Lawrence was himself in the line of philosophers running from **Bernardino Telesio** to Spinoza to F. H. Bradley, as Stephen Tabachnick points out in his introduction to *The T. E. Lawrence Puzzle. See also* **James, William; Neutral Monism; Russell, Bertrand.**

Spurr, Edward

Engineer and pioneer in boat design. In 1938, Spurr produced an aerofoil prototype speedboat named Empire Day and inscribed "To L. of A.: a compte" (To Lawrence of Arabia: on account). Spurr had met Lawrence in late 1934 or early 1935, but there is disagreement about the extent of Lawrence's collaboration, if any, on the Empire Day design. See H. F. King, "Another Lawrence," *Flight International* (February 1966), and **J. M. Wilson,** *Lawrence of Arabia,* pp. 1153–54.

St. Malo

French resort town in northwest **France** where Lawrence and two brothers took some private gymnastics lessons when his parents lived nearby in **Dinard** from 1891 to 1893.

St. Nicholas' Church

See **Moreton, Dorset**

Stamps

See Short Note on the Design and Issue of Postage Stamps

Stark, Dame Freya (1893–1993)

English traveler, linguist, writer, and photographer. Stark studied Arabic after **World War I,** and from 1927 she traveled extensively in the Middle East, where she also learned Persian and Turkish, among other languages. During World War II, she was asked to propagandize among the Arabs for the Allied cause and did so, once again traveling extensively for that purpose. She then authored some 20 volumes, including *Perseus in the Wind* (1948), a collection of essays on various topics. In a letter to **Sydney Cockerell** of November 28, 1934 (Orlans, *Lawrence of Arabia, Strange Man of Letters,* p. 228), Lawrence praises her ability to draw character in *The Valleys of the Assassins* (1934) but criticizes her landscape descriptions as dull. He also praises her spirit of exploration, for she, like him, **Burton, Doughty,** and **Gertrude Bell,** among others, is clearly in the Anglo-Arabian travel tradition.

Steed, Henry Wickham (1871–1956)

Editor of *The Times* and author. Steed was involved in the talks at the 1919 **Peace Conference** around **President Woodrow Wilson**'s idea of sending an Allied committee to study the question of how **Syria** should be governed after the war. Steed stated that Lawrence tried to urge **Feisal** to meet with the French at the conference instead and to work out an agreement with them. Steed later failed to print part of a letter in which Lawrence urged the British government to live up to its promise of self-government in Syria for the Arabs under Feisal. Steed also editorialized that the British and French should cooperate in Syria, leaving the Arabs out, as **John Mack** has pointed out in *A Prince of Our Disorder* (p. 279).

Stewart, Desmond (born 1924)

Author of a skeptical biography, *T. E. Lawrence* (1977), in which he speculated that the **Deraa incident** was an invention of Lawrence's to hide the alleged fact that he had sexual relations with **Sharif Ali** at **Azrak.** According to Stewart's interpretation, Sharif Ali, not **Dahoum,** was the "S. A." of the *Seven Pillars of Wisdom* introductory poem. He also charged that Lawrence was murdered by British security services.

Stirling, Col. Walter F. (1880–1958)

Member of Military Intelligence in **Cairo** and author of the memoir *Safety Last* (1953), which includes several passages about Lawrence. In chapter 98 of *Seven Pillars of Wisdom,* Lawrence praises Stirling's skill as a staff officer and mentions his knowledge of horses as an asset when working with **Feisal.** Early in the war, Stirling (aided by other officers) succeeded in establishing an intelligence group utilizing the nuns at the Santa Katarina monastery in Sinai. It was to Stirling that—as first recounted in **Knightley** and **Simpson**'s *The Secret Lives of Lawrence of Arabia*— Lawrence reported in 1919, contrary to what he wrote in *Seven Pillars of Wisdom,* that the bey at **Deraa** *did* recognize him, owing to **Abd el Kader**'s description. He also told Stirling in that report that he resisted the bey's pederasty and that the bey had hushed up both Lawrence's capture and his escape. *See* **Deraa Incident.**

Stokes Gun

A British light trench mortar, designed in 1915 by Sir Wilfred Stokes and available in three-inch, four-inch, and eventually six-inch versions. The three-inch version could hurl a 10-pound shell 1,250 yards. In chapter 60 of *Seven Pillars of Wisdom,* Lawrence relates that he brought an English sergeant-instructor named Brook from the army school at Zeitun, **Egypt,** to teach **Feisal**'s forces to use the weapon. He was soon renamed "Stokes" after the subject he taught. The mortar was very successful in all theaters of the war and proved its worth in the attack on a train near **Mudowwara** station, as related in chapter 66, among other engagements. See W. H. Brook's essay in **A. W. Lawrence**'s *T. E. Lawrence by His Friends* and P. Haythornthwaite, *The World War One Source Book.*

Storrs, Sir Ronald (1881–1955)

A member of the Egyptian government staff from 1904 and oriental secretary of the British Agency in **Cairo** from 1909; served under British agent and consul-general of Egypt **H. H. Kitchener** from 1911. Storrs was involved in British support of the **Arab Revolt** through contact in Cairo with **Emir Abdullah** in early 1914. In chapter 6 of *Seven Pillars of Wisdom,* Lawrence describes Storrs as brilliant, cultured, insufficiently austere, and the most important of the pro-sharifian officials in Cairo. Storrs accompanied Lawrence on Lawrence's first trip to Arabia, discussing Debussy and Wagner with **Abdul Aziz el Masri** in German, French, and Arabic. In 1917, he became the British governor of **Jerusalem** and remained so until 1926, when he became governor of Cyprus until 1932. He was the governor of Northern Rhodesia from 1932 to 1934. In **A. W. Lawrence**'s *T. E. Lawrence by His Friends,* Storrs left a memoir affirming Lawrence's powerful capacity for diplomacy, intellectual undertakings, and friendship. And in Storrs's memoir *Orientations,* he affirms the accuracy of Lawrence's account of their conversation on the way to **Jidda** while also acknowledging that Lawrence has heightened it artistically.

Sturly

See **Custot, Pierre**

Sudan

During Lawrence's period in the Middle East and from the late nineteenth century, this country, lying immediately south of **Egypt,** was known as the Anglo-Egyptian Sudan and was governed by **Sir Reginald Wingate,** British governor-general and sirdar, or commander-in-chief, of the Egyptian army, which consisted of approximately 14,000 native troops and one British infantry battalion. The Turks incited a rebellion in Darfur that was put down in 1916, and tribal unrest also was suppressed by the British in 1916–17. In chapter 6 of *Seven Pillars of Wisdom,* Lawrence reports that Wingate always had supported the **Arab Revolt** politically, and in chapter 13 he mentions machine guns and troops sent to the Arab forces from Egypt by Wingate. In a letter to his mother of November 18, 1916, in the **Brown** collection

(p. 90), Lawrence mentions that he was in **Khartoum** during November 7–11 to report to Wingate after his exploratory trip to Arabia. In chapter 16 of *Seven Pillars of Wisdom,* Lawrence explains that Wingate was cheered by Lawrence's positive view of the revolt. Wingate replaced **Sir Henry McMahon** as high commissioner of Egypt and served in that capacity from 1917 to 1919.

Suez

Port on the **Suez Canal** from which Lawrence, with **Ronald Storrs,** embarked in October 1916 on the ship *Lama* for his exploratory trip to assess the **Arab Revolt.**

Suez Canal

Created by French engineer Ferdinand de Lesseps in 1859–69 to link the Mediterranean Sea and **Red Sea,** the 100-mile-long canal in Lawrence's time was seen as a vital necessity by the British for shortening the route from England to the Far East and therefore for keeping **India** under control. The British therefore protected the canal from 1915 with about 30,000 troops. The Turks, in the form of **Jemal Pasha**'s and **Col. Kress von Kressenstein**'s Suez Expeditionary Force of about 25,000 soldiers, attempted an attack on the canal on February 3, 1915, but were repelled because British aircraft warned the defenders in advance. The Turks lost about 1,400 men to the British side's 150, and the attacking force arrived back in **Beersheba,** about 150 miles north of the canal, in April 1915. Jemal lost face because of the failure of this raid, which, however, kept the British worried for the remainder of the war. Indeed the Turks under the leadership of von Kressenstein attempted a second attack in April 1916 with a force of 3,500, which scored a tactical success at Katia in the Sinai desert but was strongly repulsed at Romani in late July. Romani is 25 miles

from the Canal, and the Turks never again tried to attack it after their failure at Romani. See **A. P. Wavell,** *The Palestine Campaigns,* and **Von Kressenstein,** *War in the Desert,* for more information about the Sinai raids. In chapter 5 of *Seven Pillars of Wisdom,* Lawrence comments that in the period before the **Arab Revolt** began, **Feisal** told the Turks that he was raising troops in order to help them attack the canal, when in fact he was raising troops to attack the Turks. In chapter 48, Lawrence also makes the point that one reason he wanted to capture **Akaba** was that by 1917 the British had moved their line northward to Beersheba and **Gaza** and that, therefore, Turkish troops operating in Akaba could still pose a threat to the canal unless they were removed.

Suva, HMS

Captained by **William Boyle,** later admiral of the fleet, this is the 2,229-ton boarding steamer, armed with three 4.7-inch guns, that took Lawrence from **Yenbo** to **Jidda** so that he could return to **Egypt** to report on the prospects of the **Arab Revolt** after his first trip to Arabia in October 1916. The *Suva* also was one of five British vessels that took part in the Anglo-Arab defense of Yenbo in January 1917 and that, by simply shining their floodlights on the plain in and around the town, deterred the Turks from attacking, as reported in chapter 20 of *Seven Pillars of Wisdom.* Lawrence also mentions there that he rested on the ship after this encounter. See Boyle's *My Naval Life 1886–1941* and Comdr. Charles Parnell's "Lawrence of Arabia's Debt to Seapower," U.S. Naval Institute *Proceedings,* 105 (August 1979): 75–83.

Swann, Air Vice Marshal Sir Oliver (1878–1948)

Member of the Air Council for Personnel who was ordered by **Sir Hugh Trenchard,** commander of the **Royal Air Force,** to handle Lawrence's first enlistment as an airman under a cloak of secrecy in 1922. The Garnett *Letters* (pp. 363–64) include one from Lawrence to Swann of September 1, 1922, praising the personnel in the air force. Among his achievements, Swann was responsible for putting in place, in 1916, training in coordination between pilots and observers on ships.

Sykes, Sir Mark (1879–1919)

Middle East traveler; member of the South African bar; honorary attaché for the British government, Constantinople; Conservative member of parliament for Hull (from 1911); and Middle East adviser to the **War Cabinet.** A member of the de Bunsen Committee, set up by the War Cabinet to strategize about the British role in the Turkish-controlled areas, the colorful Sykes was sent in 1915 on an exploratory mission in the Middle East. On the basis of his knowledge, he was delegated to negotiate what subsequently became known as the **Sykes-Picot Agreement** with French envoy **Georges-Picot.** In chapter 6 of *Seven Pillars of Wisdom,* Lawrence states that Sykes went for quick rather than deep solutions and that at the **Peace Conference** in **Paris** Sykes admitted that he had been wrong to agree to French control of **Syria.** See R. Adelson, *Mark Sykes: Portrait of an Amateur.*

Sykes-Picot Agreement

An agreement of 1916, based on an exchange of notes between the British, French, and Russian governments relating to the situation that would obtain among the dominions of Turkey's empire in the event of a Turkish defeat. The document was negotiated between **Sir Mark Sykes** and **Charles François Georges-Picot** from November 1915 to February 1916 and in-

cluded the following provisions for zones of influence and direct control: (1) The Arabian peninsula would become independent, while **Palestine** west of the Jordan River would be run by an international regime except for the Haifa/Acre area, which would be governed directly by Britain. (2) The British sphere of influence would comprise the **Negev Desert,** an area east of the Jordan River, and central **Mesopotamia,** but Basra and Baghdad provinces would be under direct British control. (3) The French area of influence would include Damascus, **Homs, Hama,** and **Aleppo** and the **Mosul** district, while Cilicia in Asia Minor and the whole coast of **Syria** west of the cities named above were to be ruled directly by the French. The zones of influence of both Britain and **France** would be allowed to harbor semi-independent Arab states for which the colonial powers would supply advisers. Russia would annex Trebizond, **Erzurum,** Lake Van, and Bitlis in Anatolia. However, as explained by Lawrence in chapter 101 of *Seven Pillars of Wisdom,* in November 1917 the Bolsheviks revealed the agreement to the world, and it was then used by **Jemal Pasha** to tell the Arabs that they should not fight for Britain and France, who would betray them after the war instead of granting them independence. Lawrence says that he had luckily revealed the treaty to **Feisal** early on so the Bolshevik revelation was not a surprise to him. But the existence of the **McMahon-Hussein Correspondence,** which seemed to promise the Arabs independence, clashed with the Sykes-Picot understandings, leaving Lawrence in a perpetually embarrassing position, as he explains in chapter 47. Lawrence's plan, therefore, was for the Arabs to prove so useful to the English in the war that they would have to allow the Arabs to achieve independence in Syria despite the Sykes-Picot Agreement. The Sykes-Picot Agreement also seemed to contradict the **Balfour Decla-**

ration, in which Britain promised the Jews a national home in Palestine. Lawrence felt, however, as a famous footnote in that chapter states, that because the Arabs or at least the Hussein family (owing to the work of **Cairo Conference** of 1921) were ultimately given a measure of independence in **Iraq** and in **Transjordan,** England was extricated from part of the embarrassing contradiction between offering the Arabs independence and not offering it. In any case, the original Sykes-Picot understandings were modified by a postwar League of Nations mandatory system and never came into effect. Britain and France became de facto but temporary rather than permanent rulers of Palestine and Syria, respectively. The mandatory system did not work very well in that Britain was expelled from Palestine by Jewish resistance in 1947 and France from Syria by Arab, British, and Russian pressure in 1946. Turkey always retained control of Cilicia, and France ultimately ceded her Sykes-Picot right to a sphere of influence in the Mosul area. The Sykes-Picot Agreement, then, represented a snapshot of the interests of the great powers in the Middle East as they saw them in 1916 and paved the way for the postwar partition of the area but remained only an agreement on paper. **G. Antonius,** *The Arab Awakening,* contains the text of the Sykes-Picot Agreement. See also D. Fromkin, *A Peace to End All Peace,* and **E. Kedourie,** *In the Anglo-Arab Labyrinth.*

Syria

Lawrence's view of Syria is most clearly expressed in "Syria—the Raw Material" (**Arab Bulletin,** March 12, 1917) and in chapters 2, 58, and 59 of *Seven Pillars of Wisdom.* In his *Arab Bulletin* piece, a detailed analysis of the different population groups and towns in Syria and their views

of one another, he states that Syrian groups do not have a sense of one national identity. He suggests, however, that because of the discontent of many groups with the Ottoman government, they might be ready to support a new ruling element from outside Syria. Such a new element must be Sunni in religion, Arabic-speaking, and claiming to revive the past glories of the Abbasid or Ayubid dynasties. In this description, he of course refers to the **Hashemites** without naming them. In *Seven Pillars of Wisdom,* he repeats much of this analysis, which clearly derives from the *Arab Bulletin* piece, but does so for the most part in more elegant prose and openly names **Feisal** as a candidate who would fit all of the necessary conditions for a Syrian ruler. In the event, Feisal was installed by the British in October 1918 and proceeded to build an Arab government. In July 1919 the General Syrian Congress declared the territory's independence, and in March 1920 it installed Feisal as king. However these declarations were ignored by the great powers intent upon implementing the **Sykes-Picot Agreement,** and in April 1920 the mandate over Syria was awarded to **France** at the **San Remo Conference.** French forces under **General Gouraud** defeated Feisal's army at the **Battle of Meissaloun** and entered Damascus on July 25, 1920. Feisal was forced into exile on July 28 and eventually was placed by the British on the throne of **Iraq.** The French ruled Syria until mid-April 1946, when they were forced to withdraw their troops under British, American, Russian, and Arab pressure. April 17 is designated Withdrawal Day and is a national holiday in Syria. See **G. Antonius,** *The Arab Awakening,* the appendices of which include the texts of important relevant documents; P. Hitti, *History of Syria Including Lebanon and Palestine;* and Shimoni and Levine, *Political Dictionary of the Middle East in the Twentieth Century.*

T

T. E. Lawrence by His Friends

A collection of original and laudatory biographical essays by approximately 80 of Lawrence's friends and relatives, published in 1937 by **Jonathan Cape** and edited by Lawrence's brother **A. W. Lawrence.** All periods of his life are represented, and among the authors from the war and diplomatic periods are **Lord Allenby, Jaafar Pasha, Ronald Storrs,** and **Winston Churchill. G. B. Shaw** and **E. M. Forster** are among those writing about Lawrence's literary contributions. Until the publication of S. E. Tabachnick's *The T. E. Lawrence Puzzle* in 1984, this was the only collection of essays on Lawrence. Given the eyewitness testimony of the writers, *T. E. Lawrence by His Friends* is of permanent value, so it is especially good that in 2002 Hazel K. Bell and the **T. E. Lawrence Society** published an index for the book. There are now two additional collections of articles devoted to Lawrence, one by **Jeffrey Meyers** and one by Charles Stang; these are listed in the bibliography to the present volume.

T. E. Lawrence Society, The

A British society founded in 1985 and currently numbering approximately 600 members based in the United Kingdom and around the world. It includes a large American membership. The society holds annual meetings and since 1991 has published *The Journal of the T. E. Lawrence Society.* The founding editor was **Jeremy Wilson,** and the journal is now edited by Philip Kerrigan. The society also maintains a collection of Lawrence material at the Oxford Central Public Library and may be contacted at http://www.telsociety.org. There are also regional American societies devoted to Lawrence.

T. E. Notes

A newsletter founded and edited from 1990 by noted Lawrence bookseller **Denis W. McDonnell** and Mary McDonnell and Janet A. Riesman and now edited by Suellen J. Miller and Edith and Elaine Steblicki. The publication, including back issues, may be accessed at http://www.denismcd.com/tenotes.htm.

Tafas

Village about 60 miles southwest of Damascus and the site of a massacre by a retreating Turkish lancer regiment under its commander Sharif Bey on September 27, 1918, according to chapter 117 of *Seven Pillars of Wisdom.* **Tallal,** who was the sheikh of the village, charged suicidally into the Turkish forces after viewing the results of the massacre. His death and those of the villagers led to a massacre of the Turks, including 200 captive soldiers, by the Arab forces, for which Lawrence takes full responsibility in that chapter. **Richard Aldington** has charged him with dereliction of duty as an officer and a desire to revenge his own torture by the Turks during the **Deraa incident** if indeed he did allow a massacre, while Lawrence's defenders, such as **John Mack** and **J. M. Wilson,** among others, insist that the picture is unclear and that Lawrence takes the responsibility for the massacre too heavily on his own shoulders alone. This issue remains a crux in historical accounts of Lawrence's life and of the campaign.

Tafas el Rashid

A member of the Hawazim Harb **Beduin** tribe who, with his son, guided Lawrence to **Feisal**'s camp at the request of **Emir Ali,** as related in chapters 10, 11, and 12 of *Seven Pillars of Wisdom.*

Tafileh, Battle of

On January 16, 1918, Arab forces under **Sharif Nasir** and **Nuri el Said** took the town of Tafileh, about 15 miles southeast of the **Dead Sea.** This was part of **Feisal's** attempt to help **Allenby** in **Palestine** by disrupting Turkish supply lines. On January 26, about 900 Turkish infantry, along with 100 cavalry, two howitzers, and 27 machine guns under **Fakhri Pasha,** attempted to retake the town but were defeated by the defending Arab forces of about 500 men, including regular troops commanded by **Jaafar Pasha el Askari,** under Lawrence's direction. The Turkish losses were about 300 dead and 250 captured, while the Arab forces lost only 65 men. The Arabs were then able to capture seven small enemy gunboats at the Dead Sea port of El Mezra on January 28. In chapters 85 and 86 of *Seven Pillars of Wisdom,* Lawrence details the Battle of Tafileh, admitting that his formal report on it

in the *Army Quarterly* for April 1921 was only a parody of a genuine report. This has left the actual course of the battle as recorded in *Seven Pillars of Wisdom,* too, subject to some doubt. Col. **A. P. Wavell,** in his *The Palestine Campaigns,* praises the report highly, and Lawrence received the Distinguished Service Order on the basis of this battle, but Lawrence's detractors, especially **Richard Aldington,** have disputed his report of the battle and the ultimate value of the battle itself because the Turks recaptured the town, now defended by **Emir Zeid,** in March 1918 when Lawrence was not present to supervise its defense. Lawrence claimed that Tafileh was no longer useful to the Arabs at that time. See **Liddell Hart,** *"T. E. Lawrence": In Arabia and After,* and also Pope and Wheal, *The Dictionary of the First World War.* As recounted in chapter 90 of *Seven Pillars of Wisdom,* it was also at Tafileh in February 1918 that Zeid told Lawrence that he had spent all of the money that Lawrence had set aside for a winter offensive, leading to Lawrence's only attempt to be completely relieved of his duties; but Allenby sent him back to the Arab forces.

Taif

Town about 30 miles southeast of **Mecca,** captured by **Emir Abdullah** in June 1916 at the start of the **Arab Revolt,** but the fortress there remained under Turkish control until it surrendered to Abdullah's forces on September 22.

Talat Pasha, Mehmet (1874–1921)

A member of the triumvirate, also consisting of **Enver Pasha** and **Jemal Pasha,** that ruled Turkey from 1913 to 1918; and grand vizier, or prime minister, 1916–1918, upon the resignation of Said Halim Pasha. Talat, at first a minor postal official in Salonika, was an active member of the **Young Turks' Committee of Union and Progress** during the revolution of 1908 against **Sultan Abdul-Hamid II.** He subsequently became a member of the Ottoman parliament and twice served as minister of the interior. He at first was reluctant to wage war on the side of Germany. He was placed in charge of internal order and food supplies and later was held primarily responsible for the massacres of the **Armenians** and for widespread famine within the empire, owing to corrupt mismanagement. He dealt with negotiations with the Germans during the war, and when the Turkish cabinet resigned on October 18 after the armistice and he faced arrest or worse from the Turkish populace, he fled to Germany on a German warship. He was assassinated by an Armenian while he lived in exile in Berlin. In chapter 4 of *Seven Pillars of Wisdom,* Lawrence presents the triumvirate, including Talat, as amoral, intelligent, and ruthless, and in chapter 9 Lawrence indicates that Talat was the first among the Turkish leadership to fear the possibility of revolt in the **Hejaz** and to try to stop it. In a letter of October 22, 1929, to **William Yale** in the **David Garnett** edition of his correspondence (pp. 670–73), Lawrence notes that while **Feisal** was carrying on secret peace negotiations with Jemal in 1918, England was secretly negotiating with Talat at the same time, so Feisal was not particularly blameworthy. See Pope and Wheal, *The Dictionary of the First World War,* and Shimoni and Levine, *Political Dictionary of the Middle East in the Twentieth Century.*

Tallal el Hareidhin

Sheikh of the village of **Tafas.** In chapter 79 of *Seven Pillars of Wisdom,* Lawrence describes his swaggering manner and how he guided Lawrence around the **Deraa** district on a reconnaissance trip. It was during this trip that on November 20, 1917, Law-

rence was captured by the Turks and subjected to the torture described in chapter 80. This event, known as the **Deraa incident,** occurred when Lawrence left Tallal, who was wanted and known by the Turks, outside the town and ventured into it himself to reconnoiter it. Tallal accompanied Lawrence on several missions and supported the Arab forces with reinforcements. His final moment, however, came when on September 27, 1918, he suicidally charged into a group of retreating Turkish soldiers who had participated in a massacre at Tafas and was killed. The massacre and his dying prompted a massacre of the Turkish forces by the Arabs with, according to chapter 117 of *Seven Pillars of Wisdom,* the approval of Lawrence himself. Detractors have taxed Lawrence with this massacre, while his defenders have claimed that he took responsibility for it without however having caused or participated in it. Tallal is treated as a heroic figure in that chapter and remains one of the most memorable minor characters in the book, given the length of his association with Lawrence and his tragic end.

Tank Corps Training Centre, Bovington

After being discharged from the **Royal Air Force,** Lawrence served in the Tank Corps at Bovington Camp in Dorset from March 12, 1923, to August 1925, when he was allowed to reenter the R.A.F. Upon joining the Tanks, he used the name **T. E. Shaw** and retained it for the duration of his tank service. At Bovington, Lawrence was deeply unhappy because his true love was the air force, and he could not fully respect the men in his barracks. However, he was not far from **Thomas Hardy**'s residence and visited him on his motorcycle, which was also a source of pleasure. He made some friends, including Cpl. **Alec Dixon,** and was assigned to the quartermaster's storehouse after basic training. During this period, he bought **Clouds Hill,** his cottage, translated *Le Gigantesque* by **Adrian le Corbeau,** gave up on translating **Pierre Custot**'s *Sturly,* and worked on the writing and publication of the 1926 subscriber's edition of *Seven Pillars of Wisdom.*

Target Launches

Boats used as targets during **Royal Air Force** bombing practice. According to **J. M Wilson** in his *Lawrence of Arabia,* these were based on the 200 Class boats on which Lawrence worked during the last phase of his career in the R.A.F. at **Hythe** and were armor-plated in order to withstand the impact of 8.5-pound practice bombs that would be dropped from 10,000 feet. Along with **Hubert Scott-Paine, Fl. Lt. Beaufort-Greenwood,** and others, Lawrence participated in the discussions concerning the boats' design.

Technical Writing

Lawrence was a technical writer all his life, beginning with descriptions of castles visited during his summers in **France** and the Middle East, continuing with his articles about strategy and how to bomb trains, and ending with his technical manual on a **Royal Air Force** seaplane tender. Lawrence's excellence as a technical writer depends upon his precision and his colorful language, which makes mines, boats, and planes come alive; this is especially evident in his article **"Demolitions under Fire."** He was an equally excellent illustrator, and his drawings in his thesis on Crusader castles, for instance, are superb. Like *Seven Pillars of Wisdom,* most of his technical productions were exemplary pieces of writing in their genre, and he was quite proud of them. See Rodelle Weintraub, "T. E. Lawrence: Technical Writer," in *The T. E. Lawrence Puzzle,* edited by Tabachnick. *See* **"The Influence of the Crusades on European Military Architecture—To the End of the XIIth Century."**

Telesio, Bernardino (1508–88)

Renaissance philosopher. Known also as Telesius and mentioned as such in chapter 80 of *Seven Pillars of Wisdom,* where Lawrence describes the aftermath of his torture during the **Deraa incident.** As Lawrence claims in that chapter, Telesio thinks that there are two souls in man, one that is related to the body and another totally immaterial and concerned only with abstract and spiritual things. Lawrence uses Telesio's theory to show that the self is indeed divided, and he goes beyond Telesio to claim that if these divisions are pressed to the limit the self will break into separate entities conversing with one another, as happened to him after **Deraa.** Yet Telesio tried to reconcile the physical and spiritual realms in humans, and Lawrence sometimes feels that he is able to achieve wholeness of mind and body, as advocated by Oxford philosopher F. H. Bradley, for instance during frenzied moments of action. *See also* **James, William; Neutral Monism; Russell, Bertrand;** and **Spinoza, Baruch.**

Tell el Shehab Bridge

A bridge over the steep gorge of the **Yarmuk Valley.** Lawrence intended to blow it up on November 6, 1917, in order to disrupt Turkish supply lines and communications between **Syria** and **Palestine,** but after riding 80 miles in 13 hours at night, one of his men dropped his rifle, and the bridge's sentry opened fire, leading to the panicked departure of the **Serahin** tribesmen accompanying Lawrence, and their throwing away of the explosives, and thus to the complete failure of the expedition, as related in chapter 76 of *Seven Pillars of Wisdom.*

Templars

Also known as Knights Templars, this was a military and religious order begun during the Crusades and originally based in **Jerusalem.** Directly responsible only to the pope, the order was important especially during fighting in Gaza in 1244 as well as in many other struggles involving the Latin Kingdom. After the fall of the Latin Kingdom to the Muslims, the order retreated to Cyprus, transforming itself from a military group to a financial one, responsible for handling money throughout Europe. The order ended by 1314 when both the king of **France** and the pope united to seize its assets and power. Lawrence's interest in this order came about because of his study of the Crusader castles, and he criticized the Templars for allegedly borrowing designs from the Byzantines that he considered inferior to the French models supposedly used by the Hospitallers, another Crusader order. Thus the Templars' Chastel Pelèrin (at **Athlit**) he considered a foolish design. *See* **"The Influence of the Crusades on European Military Architecture—To the End of the XIIth Century."** See also Robin Fedden, *Crusader Castles.*

Tennyson, Alfred Lord (1809–92)

Great Victorian poet and one of Lawrence's favorite writers. In a letter of December 14, 1925 (Garnett, *Letters,* p. 487), Lawrence quotes the poet's "Mariana." This shows his continued enthusiasm for Tennyson's work, which can already be seen in a letter of August 4, 1906, to his mother (Brown, *Selected Letters,* p. 7), where he quotes from *Idylls of the King,* albeit mistakenly. In his *Portrait of T. E.*

Lawrence, **Vyvyan Richards** points to Lawrence's particular liking for Tennyson's "Dream of Fair Women" and "The Palace of Art" during his Oxford days.

Tewfik Bey

Keeper of the stores at **Yenbo** for **Feisal.** His petty argument about authority over the stores is detailed in chapter 23 of *Seven Pillars of Wisdom.*

Thesiger, Sir Wilfred (1910–2003)

British traveler and travel writer. Thesiger, the author of *Arabian Sands* (1959), *The Marsh Arabs* (1964), *Desert, Marsh and Mountain* (1979), *The Life of My Choice* (1988), and other narratives of his travels in the Middle East and in Africa, is the last exemplar of the Anglo-Arabian travel tradition to which *Seven Pillars of Wisdom* also belongs. Born in Addis Ababa, Ethiopia, he made a career of wandering the last unexplored portions of the earth, with particular reference to the Middle East, and won numerous awards for doing so. He praised the Arabs, particularly the **Beduin,** above all other peoples for their austerity, found spirituality in the desert, and lived by an aristocratic hunter's and warrior's code. While he was influenced by Lawrence and mentions him several times in *Arabian Sands,* unlike Thesiger Lawrence did not hunt, was repelled by fighting, and rejected the exaltation of one ethnic group or nationality over others. In that sense, the Lawrence who wrote long before Thesiger did is our contemporary, while Thesiger, although a more recent writer, often seems an anachronism, as Stephen Tabachnick points out in "Wilfred Thesiger: The Man Who Would Be Last," *Contention* 2:1 (fall 1992): 181–96. See also Michael Asher, *Thesiger: A Biography.*

Lawrence and journalist Lowell Thomas in Akaba in 1918. Photographer: Harry Chase. Courtesy of Corbis.

Thomas, Bertram Sidney (1892–1950)

British diplomat and explorer. After fighting in **Mesopotamia** in **World War I,** Thomas served in the Middle East as assistant British representative in **Transjordan** from 1922 to 1924 and in numerous other posts. In *The Empty Quarter* he records his exploration of the **Rub al Khali** desert in Saudi Arabia; in February 1931 he became the first European to cross this desert. Thomas considered Lawrence a friend to whom he turned for editorial reading of his book. Although Thomas's feat obviated Lawrence's own plan to use an airship to cross that desert, Lawrence liked Thomas's book, as he states in his introduction to it, but in a letter of 1933 (Garnett, *Letters,* p. 768) Lawrence indicates that Thomas was only an excellent explorer, not an excellent writer.

Thomas, Lowell J. (1892–1981)

American journalist and publicist. Thomas was a Princeton University lecturer who gave up his position to take part in Lord Beaverbrook's campaign to glorify Britain's role in **World War I.** Thomas is considered the man (outside of Lawrence himself) most responsible for Lawrence's fame because of his postwar multimedia show about Lawrence, which was seen by millions of people in New York and **London** over the course of four years. Consisting of slides, music, and even incense and entitled "With **Allenby** in **Palestine** and Lawrence in Arabia," the show presented Lawrence as modest, brave, brilliant, and completely dedicated to Arab independence and British victory. The message went down well with a public fed up with four horrible years of slaughter on the western front and eager for romance, heroism, and a reaffirmation of their own principles. Lawrence often condemned the show to his friends, but from Thomas's memoir in **A. W. Lawrence**'s essay collection *T. E. Lawrence by His Friends,* it appears that Lawrence enjoyed posing for the photographs of Thomas's photographer, **Harry Chase,** and was a willing collaborator with Thomas in his own myth. He visited the show itself several times, incognito. Thomas went on to write the first biography, *With Lawrence in Arabia* (1924), in which he portrayed Lawrence as a hero of epic proportions—a modest archaeologist who was able to don Beduin robes and lead the tribes to victory. This exaggerated portrait was to become the target of later debunkers such as **Richard Aldington,** who often attack Thomas's mythical image rather than Lawrence himself. But Thomas honestly saw Lawrence exactly this way and in any case he was quick to understand that this story had the ingredients for an enormous popular success. In fact, it is one of the great publicity successes of all time, and Thomas became famous because of it. He went on to write some 30 books and to become a household name. To the end of his life, Thomas insisted that Lawrence was the most remarkable person that he had met in a lifetime of travels. But he himself was amazed at the size and scope of the interest in Lawrence's story that he was able to arouse.

Thomson, Baron Christopher Birdwood (1875–1930)

Brigadier general, Labour secretary of state for air, and author of *Three Generals on War* (1922), which Lawrence in a letter of July 29, 1929, to **Ernest Thurtle** (Garnett, *Letters,* pp. 668–69) criticized as a poor book. During the **Schneider Trophy Race,** Thomson saw Lawrence, a simple airman, speaking as if an on equal basis to several distinguished persons and was offended. He was killed in a crash of an R.101 airship. Lawrence in a letter of October 25, 1930, to Thurtle (Garnett, *Letters,* pp. 704–5) commented that Thomson was not a good air minister.

Thurtle, Ernest (1884–1954)

Labour member of parliament from 1923 and author of the pamphlet "Shootings at Dawn: The Death Penalty at Work" (1924). Thurtle, who was wounded during **World War I** and related through marriage to the pacifist member of parliament George Lansbury, became an ardent opponent of the death penalty for military desertion and cowardice. In 1930, after great struggle against such foes as **Edmund Allenby,** he succeeded in getting the British government to outlaw the practice. Lawrence supported this cause as well because he himself had run quickly from danger as he stated in a letter to Thurtle of June 26, 1929 (Garnett, *Letters,* pp. 660–61). In this and several other letters from 1929 to 1935, Lawrence urged Thurtle to allow Leon Trotsky to visit England and offered his opinion about many service-related matters.

Tigris River

This waterway flows for 1,150 miles. It begins in the Taurus Mountains in Turkey, continues southeast through **Iraq** to join the Euphrates River, and then becomes the Shatt el Arab, which flows into the Persian Gulf.

Times, The

In the prewar period, Lawrence wrote to *The Times* on August 9, 1911, complaining of destruction of Syrian archaeological sites by the Turks; this letter may be read in **Jeremy Wilson**'s *Lawrence of Arabia* (pp. 92–93). Wilson comments that this was Lawrence's first published piece of writing outside of school magazines. In the immediate postwar period, Lawrence wrote important political articles for *The Times* that appeared on October 10, 1918, October 17, 1918, November 27–28, 1918, September 11, 1919, May 30, 1920 (*Sunday Times*), August 7, 1920, August 11, 1920, and August 22, 1920 (*Sunday Times*). He wrote letters to the editor to try to influence the political situation in the Middle East. In one of these, dated September 8, 1919 (Garnett, *Letters,* pp. 281–82), he lays out the British undertakings to the Arabs contained in the **McMahon-Hussein Correspondence,** the **Sykes-Picot Agreement,** the British statement to the seven Syrians of Cairo of June 11, 1917, and the **Anglo-French Declaration** of November 9, 1918, in order to show that there are no contradictions between them. In another letter, of July 22, 1920, he criticizes the British government's position in **Mesopotamia,** then in rebellion against British rule. Lawrence's *Times* articles and letters are available in **Stanley** and Rodelle **Weintraub,** editors, *Evolution of a Revolt.* Many articles and reviews concerning Lawrence and his military, political, literary, and mechanical work, as well as discussion of his alleged spying in Afghanistan, have appeared in the newspaper from the middle 1920s to the present day.

Tolstoy, Count Leo (1828–1910)

Great Russian novelist whose *War and Peace* Lawrence revered, as he made clear on February 20, 1924, to **E. M. Forster** (Garnett, *Letters,* p. 456). And on December 1, 1927, he wrote **Edward Garnett** that it was one of the great books of the world, the other four being **Dostoyevsky**'s *Brothers Karamazov,* **Melville**'s *Moby Dick,* Rabelais's, and Cervantes's *Don Quixote* (Garnett, *Letters,* p. 548). However, in a letter to Edward Garnett of August 23, 1922, he claims that Tolstoy is not a great stylist (Garnett, *Letters,* p. 359), but it is important to remember that he read his work in the bland Constance Garnett translation, the only one available in England at that time. Lawrence felt that Dostoyevsky, while the greatest Russian writer, never achieved an epic like *War and Peace.* In writing *Seven Pillars of Wisdom,* Lawrence was competing with all of these writers as well as with **Nietzsche,** and many academic critics, including Stephen Tabachnick, **Jeffrey Meyers,** and **Stanley** and Rodelle **Weintraub,** feel that he matched them in several important respects.

Tomlinson, Henry Major (1873–1958)

Journalist, novelist, and essayist fascinated by the tropics, **London,** and antiwar topics. In a letter of February 19, 1930, to A. S. Frere-Reeves, Lawrence praises Tomlinson highly for his nature writing, and in "Mixed Biscuits," a review of Tomlinson, **Hudson,** Gerhardi, Machen, and Baring that appeared in *The Spectator* for August 20, 1927, Lawrence praises Tomlinson's *The Sea and the Jungle* (1912) as a classic but finds it over-written. Like his other reviews, Lawrence published this one under the pseudonym "C. D." for **Colin Dale.** This letter and review by Lawrence are available, along with many other letters and reviews, in Harold Orlans's compendium, *Lawrence of Arabia, Strange Man of Letters.*

Townshend, Gen. Charles Vere Ferrers (1861–1924)

General forced to surrender at **Kut-al-Amara** by Turkish forces in the largest **World War I** British defeat in the Middle

East outside of **Gallipoli,** which preceded it. While he succeeded in defending Chitral in **India** before coming to the Middle East, his ill-fated march on Baghdad revealed impetuousness when he pushed on up the **Tigris River** without awaiting reinforcements. In addition, after the defeat he lived in luxury in a grand hotel in Constantinople while his men suffered great privation. At first proclaimed a hero upon his return to England after the war, he was denied any further military employment. Some have blamed Townshend's commander, Gen. Sir John Nixon, for demanding that Townshend continue to advance, and the War Office in **London** for being insufficiently aware of the situation. Lawrence was dispatched from **Cairo** with **Aubrey Herbert** to bribe the Turkish commander **Khalil Pasha** to release Townshend's army (although Lawrence never felt this mission had much chance of success). The attempt failed, and Lawrence wrote a scathing report, "Intelligence. I.E.F. 'D'," on the British military and political government in Mesopotamia; this is reprinted in **Jeremy Wilson,** *Lawrence of Arabia* (pp. 949–59). In chapter 6 of *Seven Pillars of Wisdom,* Lawrence offers a plan by which Kut might have been saved, and while acknowledging that blunders had been made by the British at Kut, he also notes that Townshend's defense was strong and refrains from overtly blaming him for the disaster. See Townshend's *My Campaign in Mesopotamia,* and F. J. Moberly, *The Campaign in Mesopotamia 1914–1918.*

Transjordan

The territory east of the Jordan River from which the modern state of Jordan was principally formed. It was originally part of the Turkish province of Damascus before **World War I** and then part of the British mandatory area of **Palestine** after the war. At the **Cairo Conference** of 1921 the Brit-

ish decided to separate it from Palestine, which had been set aside in 1917 for a Jewish National Home by the **Balfour Declaration,** and to allow **Abdullah ibn Hussein,** who had already set up his rule there, to continue to rule it; this was regarded as a betrayal by the Zionists. Transjordan remained a mandatory territory and subject to the British high commissioner in **Jerusalem** and a British resident in **Amman.** During the last three months of 1921, Lawrence, then a member of the **Colonial Office,** served as British representative in Transjordan, helping Abdullah consolidate his rule. In 1946, the country was granted independence, and in 1948 it assumed the name Jordan and included not only territory on the East Bank of the Jordan River, but on the West Bank as well. It lost the West Bank, however, as a result of the 1967 Six-Day War with Israel.

Translation

In his article in **A. W. Lawrence**'s *T. E. Lawrence by His Friends,* publisher **Jonathan Cape** recalls Lawrence's request to translate from the French in 1923 for some extra money. Cape first suggested **Mardrus**'s version of the *Arabian Nights* but was unable to secure copyright privileges. He then sent **Adrien le Corbeau**'s *Le Gigantesque,* or *The Forest Giant,* and Lawrence succeeded in translating it in a few months. This translation is perhaps no more distinguished than the book itself, about a giant redwood, but it shows an excellent grasp of contemporary French. (For this, see **Maurice Larés,** *T. E. Lawrence, la France et les Français.*) He was unable to complete **Pierre Custot**'s *Sturly* and dropped the idea of translating **Gustave Flaubert**'s *Salammbô,* which had been suggested by Cape. Lawrence's most important translation, however, was not from the French but from the Greek—**Homer**'s *Odyssey.* Partially while serving in **Kara-**

chi, Lawrence produced what is widely regarded as one of the finest prose translations of that work. It was praised by scholar **Maurice Bowra** in an introduction to the **Oxford University** Press edition, and Maren Cohn showed that Lawrence's translation reflects his personality in often subtle ways (see her "Reflexive Heroes" and, with Stephanie Nelson, "Lawrence's *Odyssey,*" in Charles Stang, editor, *The Waking Dream of T. E. Lawrence*). Lawrence's gifts as a literary translator can be seen as a facet of his excellent historical grounding, his fine grasp of French and Greek, his war experience, and his writing ability. By his own admission in chapter 40 of *Seven Pillars of Wisdom,* his spoken Arabic was ungrammatical and combined the colloquial and the literary language from different parts of the Arab world, and so was far from perfect. Yet he was able to translate *Two Arabic Folk Tales* (1937), which **Philip O'Brien** in his *T. E. Lawrence: A Bibliography* speculates was probably done as an exercise during Lawrence's prewar **Carchemish** period.

Tremadoc, Wales

According to **John Mack,** Lawrence was born on August 16, 1888, in a rented cottage called Gorphwyspha or "place of rest" in Carnarvon County, Tremadoc Parish, Wales, to which his parents had moved after leaving **Ireland. Liddell-Hart** points out that the county resembles an arm pointing into the Irish Sea, with the village of Tremadoc located at the angle where the land begins to meet the sea. The Lawrences lived in Tremadoc for about a year, and then moved to **Kirkcudbright,** Scotland.

Trenchard, Air Marshal Sir Hugh, 1st Viscount (1873–1956)

Air Marshal responsible for the development of the **Royal Air Force** into a third branch of service equal with the army and navy. After stints in **India,** the Boer War, and in the South Nigerian Regiment, Trenchard became commander of the entire Royal Flying Corps (precursor of the R.A.F.) in **France** during **World War I.** After the war, in January 1918, he became air chief of staff of the R.A.F. and by 1927 was appointed first marshal. Lawrence first met Trenchard in 1920 when he discussed the use of air power to control **Mesopotamia** with Lawrence, then a member of the **Colonial Office.** Lawrence was then able to use this acquaintance when in January 1922 he asked Trenchard for permission to join the R.A.F. in the ranks, which was approved. Thereafter, their relationship was sometimes strained, although Lawrence respected Trenchard for having built the air force and Trenchard respected Lawrence's wartime achievements. Lawrence would detail small problems needing correction in personal letters to Trenchard, and once even gave away Trenchard's identity when he, incognito, was trying to inspect a base on which Lawrence was serving. For his part, Trenchard had to order Lawrence's transfer from India when apocryphal stories about spying began to spread and had to take many measures to deal with the resultant publicity. Also, he had to face the dislike of junior officers for Lawrence when they feared that he would criticize them. But he continued to respect Lawrence. Trenchard became Metropolitan Police commissioner of **London** in 1931 after retiring from the R.A.F. just a few years before Lawrence did. See Andrew Boyle, *Trenchard.*

Tuke, Henry Scott (1858–1929)

Painter and full member of the Royal Academy from 1914. Tuke was best known for his paintings of Falmouth Bay, which he created from his boat-studio. His *Portrait of a Young Soldier* was among Lawrence's possessions at the time of his death, and there is speculation that it uses Lawrence as a model, but this is not proven. The date of the picture seems to be 1922, but Lawrence would have been 34 at that time and not the approximately 18-year-old depicted in the painting. However, the young soldier undressing to go swimming does bear a resemblance to Lawrence, and Tuke may have speculatively painted a younger Lawrence if he was indeed the model. See **Jeremy Wilson**'s *T. E. Lawrence,* p. 228, for a color copy of the picture.

Turkey, War Aims of

Toward the end of the nineteenth century, the Turkish Empire was referred to as "the sick man of Europe" because of its perceived weakness. Plagued by constant rebellions by its numerous and completely diverse subject peoples, aggressive designs by neighboring powers, and a repressive and often incompetent ruling class, the empire continually lost ground: Crete became independent in 1910, land in north Africa and Mediterranean islands was lost in the Italo-Turkish War of 1911–12, and almost all of Turkey's European possessions were lost after the First Balkan War (1912–1913). The **Young Turks** tried to stop this trend by allying themselves with Germany, which was also an enemy of Turkey's traditional enemy **Russia.** Germany had been engaged in many construction and aid projects in Turkey before the war, including the **Hejaz Railway.** Turkey's rulers hoped through this alliance and the war itself to maintain the empire, eliminate the humiliating Capitulations under which foreigners were not subject to Ottoman law, and even to force Britain out of **Egypt.** In the event, Turkey was forced to sign the armistice of Mudros on October 30, 1918, and, as a result of the **Treaty of Sèvres** of August 10, 1920, and the **Treaty of Lausanne** of 1923, it was deprived of

all its imperial possessions and reduced to its present size. Turkey's participation in **World War I,** therefore, can be seen as the country's final, failed attempt to maintain its position as an imperial power.

Turki

A member of **Sharif Ali**'s entourage who rushed out to help Lawrence when he fell during a train demolition near kilometer 172 of the **Hejaz Railway,** as related in chapter 78 of *Seven Pillars of Wisdom.*

Turkish Army

In *Seven Pillars of Wisdom,* Lawrence portrays the Turkish army as incompetent, brutal, and weak. One or more of these qualities is embodied, for instance, in the bey at **Deraa,** who tortures and sexually assaults Lawrence; in Lawrence's portrayal of a member of the ruling triumvirate, **Jemal Pasha,** who is linked to hangings and massacres; and in his presentation of **Fakhri Pasha,** the commander of the Turkish Twelfth Army at **Medina,** who is implicated by Lawrence in Armenian massacres. The Turks are said by Lawrence to be more brutal than the Arabs because of their willingness to attack civilians. The Turkish atrocities at **Tafas** are given as an example of this. The Turkish military hospital at Damascus, with its rotting corpses and wounded men left to die, is an example of the Turks' indifference to the fate of their own men in Lawrence's portrayal. Except for the German commanders, such as **Gen. Erich von Falkenhayn,** and the German machine gunners at Tafas who kept their formation and fended off Arab attacks, there is very little praise of the Turkish army in Lawrence's account. This has led several writers to accuse him of bias. While it is true that the ruling triumvirate of **Jemal Pasha, Enver Pasha, and Talat Pasha** were indeed deeply implicated in the massacres of **Armenians** and the suppression of Arab nationalism, the Turkish army itself seems to have been more competent than Lawrence portrays it. While it had been completely defeated in the Balkan Wars of 1912–1913, the Turkish army had made improvements under the tutelage of German Gen. **Liman von Sanders** and was thus able to make a good showing for itself in several important engagements during **World War I.** In addition to **Gallipoli** (where **Mustapha Kemal Pasha** proved his leadership) and **Kut,** which were major Turkish victories over the British, the two **battles at Gaza** until **Allenby**'s breakthrough in **Beersheba** in 1917 were Turkish successes. Moreover, under the leadership of **Jemal Pasha** and **Col. Kress von Kressenstein,** 25,000 Turks managed to assault (albeit unsuccessfully) the **Suez Canal** zone early in the war, traversing the Sinai desert to do so. Von Kressenstein mounted a second attack in April 1916 with 3,500 men and won the first Battle of Romani, in Sinai, but was forced to withdraw to El Arish, even though his force had grown to 16,000 men, after a severe loss at the second Battle of Romani. It must be remembered that when the British did finally break through and win in **Palestine,** under **General Allenby,** the Turks were completely outnumbered and outgunned by a factor of three to one, with only 36,000 men on the Turkish side to approximately 100,000 on the Allied side in the last year of the war. **A. P. Wavell,** in his *The Palestine Campaigns* (1928), remarks that the Turkish soldier, while enduring and courageous, was lacking in the education that facilitates modern military operations and that his army's equipment was insufficient in numbers and entirely out of date. He confirms Lawrence's portrait of Jemal Pasha as lacking in military ability and morality, but finds the commander of the Fourth Army **Jemal Kuchuk,** an excellent soldier. Moreover, he praises **Fakhri** (or Fakhreddin) **Pasha** for his defense of **Medina,** which held throughout the **Arab Revolt.** At the end of his *Five Years in Turkey,* Liman von Sanders claims that the failure of Turkey in the war was largely due to economic factors and that both the Turkish and German governments had expected Turkey to do too much, including the defense of far-flung borders and conducting attacks against additional territories, with too few means. His first inspection showed that Turkish soldiers were poorly clothed, officers unpaid, and hospital conditions lacking. While the German military mission was able to make headway against some of these problems, they could not all be remedied. Von Sanders feels, therefore, that both countries' governments suffered from illusions about what was possible. Lawrence's portrait of the enemy army in *Seven Pillars of Wisdom,* while emphasizing its failures, does not take fully into account its lack of men, materiel, and education. Given its impoverished and overextended situation, the Turkish army did not, perhaps, do badly against an enemy greatly superior in resources.

Turkish Army Handbook

*See **Handbook of the Turkish Army 1916***

"Twenty-Seven Articles"

An important set of guidelines, published in the *Arab Bulletin* for August 20, 1917, written by Lawrence and intended to teach British personnel how to work with the **Beduin.** This includes advice on how to influence Arab leaders without being noticed, when to wear Arab dress, what to wear, and how to deal with religious issues, among other matters. Perhaps the most important lessons Lawrence wishes to pass on are that constant study of the Arabs and a constant search for the true reasons for their behavior are indispensable. He also warns against the mental dangers of overly deep involvement in the Arab disguise—what he calls in the first chapter of *Seven Pillars of Wisdom* the madness that can come from seeing with the perspective of Arab and British cultures at once. The "Twenty-Seven Articles" are available in an appendix in **John Mack,** *A Prince of Our Disorder.*

"200 Class Seaplane Tender—Provisional Issue of Notes"

An instruction manual written in 1932 by Lawrence for the fast 37½-foot boats built by the **British Power Boat Company,** which were meant to service seaplanes and for rescue operations. In "T. E. Lawrence: Technical Writer" in *The T. E. Lawrence Puzzle* (edited by Tabachnick), Rodelle Weintraub finds this manual ideal in terms of its focus on the appropriate audience. Because the boat design was quickly superceded, the manual was never published; however, some extracts from it are available in *The Essential T. E. Lawrence,* edited by **David Garnett.**

U

Um Keis

Town in **Syria** on the site of the ancient city of **Gadara**.

Umari, Subhi el (1898–circa 1990)

Author of *Lawrence Kama Araftuhu* [*Lawrence as I Knew Him*], a memoir published in **Beirut** in 1969, which throws doubt on some of Lawrence's assertions in *Seven Pillars of Wisdom,* including Lawrence's claim of having made a journey behind Turkish lines into **Syria** in June 1917, his role in instructing the Arabs in demolitions, and his presence in **Tafas** after the Turkish massacre there. El Umari, formerly a Syrian officer, joined **Feisal**'s forces in October 1917.

Umtaiye

A ruined Roman fortress town 15 miles south of **Deraa** in what is now Jordan, which served as a forward base for the Arab armies in September 1918. For Lawrence, the value of Umtaiye as a base was that it was equidistant from Deraa, Jebel Druse, and the Rualla Desert, was placed well for control of Deraa's three railway lines, and had excellent supplies of water and pasture, as he states in chapter 111 of *Seven Pillars of Wisdom;* its weakness, however, was that it was vulnerable to air attack, as he writes in chapter 113. According to machine gunner **Tom Beaumont,** it was at Umtaiye in September 1918 that Lawrence told him that his beloved servant **Dahoum,** also known as Salim Achmed or "S. A.," was dying of typhoid. See **Knightley** and **Simpson,** *The Secret Lives of Lawrence of Arabia,* for a full discussion of Beaumont's testimony and the S. A. question.

United States

Although Lawrence never visited the United States, his attitude about it was positive, as he wrote to **Henry Williamson** (P. Wilson, editor, *Correspondence with Henry Williamson,* p. 105). The possible reasons that he never succumbed to fashionable European-style anti-Americanism are that he had excellent relations with American publisher **Frank Doubleday** and, for the most part, with publicist **Lowell Thomas,** and that he greatly admired American writers **Herman Melville** and Walt Whitman (Garnett, *Letters,* p. 467) as well as President Woodrow Wilson's stance at the 1919 **Peace Conference** in **Paris.** Joel Hodson, in his *Lawrence of Arabia and American Culture,* points out the major role that Americans had in shaping the Lawrence legend and the enthusiastic reception that Lawrence has received in America. Indeed, the first doctoral dissertations on Lawrence's career were written in American universities.

Uxbridge, R.A.F. Training Depot

The training base where Lawrence served from August 30, 1922, when he joined the **Royal Air Force** under the name **John Hume Ross** until November 8 when he was he was transferred to the R.A.F. School of Photography at **Farnborough.** Parts 1 and 2 of *The Mint* detail his degrading (and self-imposed) experience of basic training at Uxbridge as an "erk" or recruit. While he found some commonality with the men regarding their ill-treatment by noncommissioned and regular officers, he did not, at least during this period of his R.A.F. service, achieve genuine integration, which is not surprising—given the fact that he had been a colonel during **World War I,** had served in high governmental positions, and was an intellectual who read voraciously and was in the process of writing *Seven Pillars of Wisdom.* During his Uxbridge service, he was 352087 A/c Ross. Lawrence was discharged from Farnborough, and the R.A.F. itself, in January 1923 when his identity became widely known and the resulting publicity became distracting.

V

Vickery, Maj. Charles (1881–1951)

One of **Col. Stewart Newcombe**'s staff officers, who joined Lawrence and the Arab forces in January 1917. As Lawrence tells us in chapter 23 of *Seven Pillars of Wisdom,* Vickery was a gunner with 10 years of service in the **Sudan** and with a good knowledge of Arabic. As we also learn there, Vickery thought Lawrence a speculative visionary and braggart. For his part, Lawrence felt that Vickery, who with **Boyle** had directed the successful battle for **Wejh,** handled the Arab soldiers too much like regular troops and did not worry sufficiently about casualties, as he tells us in chapter 27. Shortly after that battle, Vickery was transferred to **France.**

Victoria Cross

One of the highest British awards for deeds of valor. In *T. E. Lawrence to His Biographers Robert Graves & Liddell Hart* (p. 1:92), Lawrence says that he was nominated for this medal by **Sir Reginald Wingate,** high commissioner of **Egypt,** for the capture of **Akaba** but did not receive it because he performed no outstanding individual acts of bravery during the campaign. In the event, Lawrence received a Companion of the Order of the Bath and was promoted to major. It appears, however, that the Order of the Bath was given for his secret northern ride of June 1917 behind Turkish lines in **Syria** rather than for Akaba and that he did not receive the Victoria Cross because no British officer witnessed his actions during that ride. Lawrence never expressed appreciation for this or any other medal; an apocryphal story has it that he later hung the Order of the Bath and a French medal on the neck of a dog. See **J. M. Wilson,** *Lawrence of Arabia,* pp. 424–25.

Viollet le Duc, Eugene Emmanuel (1814–79)

French architect, forerunner of Antonio Gaudi and Victor Horta and other art nouveau practitioners, who wrote the *Dictionnaire raisonné de l'architecture francais du XI au XV siecle* (*Dictionary of French Architecture from the 11th to the 15th Century*) as well as a dictionary of French furniture. In *To His Biographers Robert Graves & Liddell Hart,* Lawrence says that he studied le Duc's work on siege maneuvers, and in a letter of June 8, 1911 (Garnett, *Letters,* p.110), he proposes a theory about how the outwork at **Chateau Gaillard** was breached that contradicts le Duc's.

Von Falkenhayn, Gen. Erich (1861–1922)

Chief of the Great General Staff 1914–1916 but relieved after the Battle of Ver-

General von Falkenhayn, sent in 1917 to advise the Turkish army, being shown around the Mosque of Omar in Jerusalem by Jemal Pasha. Courtesy of the Australian War Memorial.

A German photograph of Col. Kress von Kressenstein and his staff at Huj, northeast of Gaza, Palestine, in 1917. Von Kressenstein is the sixth figure from the right, holding a cane. Courtesy of the Australian War Memorial.

Gen. Otto Liman von Sanders confers with some German and Turkish officers near Haifa in June 1918. Courtesy of the Australian War Memorial.

dun. He then proceeded to conduct a brilliant campaign in Rumania. In 1917, he was sent to lead the Turkish **Yildirim** force to reconquer Baghdad from the British but was unable to undertake that task, or to hold back **Allenby** in **Palestine.** He was replaced by **Gen. Liman von Sanders** in February 1918 and spent the remainder of the war in relative obscurity in Lithuania. Lawrence briefly mentions him in chapters 60 and 82 of *Seven Pillars of Wisdom,* always with respect. See P. Haythornthwaite, *The World War One Source Book.*

Von Kressenstein, Col. Friedrich Freiherr Kress (1870–1948)

German artillery officer and adviser to **Jemal Pasha.** He planned and led two unsuccessful attacks on the British in the Sinai peninsula in 1915 and 1916 and di-

rected the successful Turkish defenses during the first two **Battles of Gaza,** but he was replaced by **von Falkenhayn** in November 1917 after **Allenby**'s successful breakthrough in **Beersheba** and Gaza in October–November 1917. Von Kressenstein subsequently commanded the Turkish Eighth Army in **Palestine** until the summer of 1918, at which time he was transferred to the Caucasus. He is the author of *War in the Desert.*

Von Lettow-Vorbeck, Gen. Paul E. (1870–1964)

Outstanding German guerrilla leader of **World War I.** With a force ranging from 1,400 to 11,000 men, von Lettow-Vorbeck kept tens of thousands of British and colonial troops occupied in German East Africa throughout the war and surrendered undefeated when Germany capitulated in

1918. One of his antagonists was **Richard Meinertzhagen,** who later became **Allenby**'s intelligence chief and from whom Lawrence might have learned of von Lettow-Vorbeck's methods, although Lawrence does not mention him in his letters or elsewhere. See von Lettow-Vorbeck's *My Reminiscences of East Africa* (English edition, 1920).

Von Sanders, Lt. Gen. Otto Liman (1855–1929)

In August 1913, Liman von Sanders was appointed director of the German military mission to Turkey, and in January 1914 he became the inspector-general of the Turkish army. In these roles, his task was to prepare the Turkish army for war. In August 1914, von Sanders was made commander of the Turkish First Army in the Bosporus, and in March 1915 he was given the command of the Turkish Fifth Army at **Gallipoli.** While he is criticized for having miscalculated some of the British landing places, he is given the major credit for containing Sir Ian Hamilton's attempt to land British forces at Suvla and even for masterminding the British defeat in this campaign. In February 1918, however, he found himself facing a much larger British army as commander of a Turko-German force on the **Palestine** front, and during the **Battle of Megiddo** in September 1918, von Sanders was almost captured at his headquarters in Nazareth. In February 1919, after the war was over, he briefly was arrested by the British as he tried to arrange for the passage of German soldiers from Turkey and announced his resignation soon after his release. His *Five Years in Turkey* (1920; English translation 1927) is one of the primary sources for German-Turkish strategy during the war and a model of professional writing.

W

Wahabism

A puritanical Islamic doctrine, begun and held by a sect largely based in Arabia and named after its founder, Mohammed ibn Abd el Wahhab (1703–87). It insists on strict adherence to the rituals of **Islam** and public morality, eschews mysticism and liberal interpretation of the Koran, and does not shy away from the use of force to enforce its doctrines. In 1813 the Turks, represented by the Egyptian Mohammed Ali, crushed the Wahabis, who were seen to be a threat to Turkish rule of Arabia, and in 1818 Ibrahim Pasha again did this, yet Wahabism survived. The House of Saud has always been strongly Wahabi and has spread Wahabism by setting up schools around the world. Lawrence and the British found the Hussein family attractive as rulers in Arabia and elsewhere during the **World War I** period because the family, although the official guardians of **Mecca,** had little use for religious strictness of the Wahabi variety; but in 1924 **Ibn Saud** drove **Sharif Hussein** and his sons into exile. In a letter of May 1, 1928, to **Sir Hugh Trenchard** (Garnett, *Letters,* pp. 598–600) Lawrence bluntly states that religious ideas have become fanaticism in the case of the Wahabis. Lawrence claims in *Seven Pillars of Wisdom* that there was relatively little religious fervor to be found in Feisal's army, and he undoubtedly had the Wahabi Ibn Saud in mind as a comparison with the Hashemites when he wrote this. During World War I, however, Ibn Saud deserted the Turks, whom he had originally pledged to support, and came over to the side of the British, carrying out some minimal anti-Turkish actions. See C. Glassé, *The Concise Encyclopedia of Islam,* for more information.

Walker, Sir Emery (1851–1933)

Typographer, engraver, and collaborator with **William Morris** on the Kelmscott Press and founder of the Doves Press. Walker's 1932 edition of Lawrence's translation of **Homer**'s *Odyssey,* coproduced with **Bruce Rogers** and **Wilfred Merton,** is considered one of the most beautiful twentieth-century books. See Dorothy A. Harrop, *Sir Emery Walker 1851–1933.*

Walpole, Sir Hugh (1884–1941)

Writer, author of the multi-volume Cumberland family saga. Lawrence wrote to **Henry Williamson** on December 11, 1934 (Garnett, *Letters,* p. 834), that he considered Walpole a second-rate writer.

War Cabinet

British government committee charged with the planning and conduct of **World War I.** At first, in November 1914, a War Council consisting of Asquith, **Kitchener,** and **Winston Churchill** was formed from the Committee of Imperial Defence; this in turn gave way in November 1915 to a War Committee consisting of Asquith, **Lloyd George,** Bonar Law, Lord Arthur Balfour, and Reginald McKenna. After the resignation of Asquith as prime minister in 1916, the new Prime Minister, David Lloyd George, built the War Cabinet, consisting of himself, **Lord Curzon,** Lord Milner, and Arthur Henderson, and also Bonar Law and later **Jan Smuts** of South Africa. This group was responsible for the policies controlling British conduct of the war until its end.

Wassmuss, Wilhelm (1880–1935)

German agent in Persia, often compared to Lawrence, who, however, does not mention him. Wassmuss began as German consul in Shiraz in 1915 and then moved to the Persian Gulf region, where he encouraged attacks on the British by the local population. He also encouraged one of his local allies to hold the British consul in Shiraz hostage, along with six others. He caused enormous trouble for the British, but in 1915 while fleeing them he left behind a code book, which helped the British break the German codes. Wassmuss managed to remain uncaptured until March 1919, well after the war. An idealist at heart, he returned to Persia in 1924 to teach new agricultural methods at his own model farm. However, he was undermined at every turn by jealousy and rivalry among his own supporters, and the farm failed. He returned to Germany in 1931 a broken man, and died there in 1935. See

Christopher Sykes, *Wassmuss—"The German Lawrence."*

Wavell, Field Marshal Lord Sir Archibald P. (1883–1950)

Wavell served in **France** and the Caucasus before joining the **Egyptian Expeditionary Force** as a brevet lieutenant colonel and served in **Egypt** from 1917 to 1920. Lawrence sent him a copy of the 1922 Oxford text of *Seven Pillars of Wisdom* to read in 1923, and Wavell wrote him appreciatively about the book (Garnett, *Letters,* p. 422). Wavell's *The Palestine Campaigns* (1928) is one of the best books on the British role in that area in **World War I.** In it, Wavell praises Lawrence's part in the **Arab Revolt** and claims that the revolt was highly valuable as it diverted Turkish forces from the **Palestine** front and protected the British army's right flank as it advanced through Palestine. However, he disagrees with Lawrence's account of the **fall of Damascus** and feels that Lawrence has not been fair to **General Chauvel.** In a letter of September 2, 1928, to Wavell (Garnett, *Letters,* pp. 575–76), Lawrence praised the parts of the book devoted to himself but said that he had not yet read the whole book. Wavell also wrote *Allenby* (1940) and *Allenby in Egypt* (1943), among other works. In 1937–38 he was the commander of British troops in Palestine and **Transjordan** and served as commander-in-chief of the British forces in the Middle East from 1939 to 1941. During that time, he defeated the Italian forces under Marshall Graziani but was himself defeated by German Gen. Erwin Rommel. Wavell went on to several prestigious positions, including commander-in-chief in **India,** and won numerous honors. The influence of the Palestine campaign and of Lawrence's campaign on Wavell's thinking was very strong.

Weintraub, Stanley (born 1929)

English professor and prolific writer. A pioneering Lawrence scholar who wrote *Private Shaw and Public Shaw* (1958) about Lawrence's relationship with **G. B. Shaw** and who, with his wife Rodelle, edited a volume of Lawrence's early postwar writings and coauthored *Lawrence of Arabia: The Literary Impulse* (1975). Weintraub taught at Pennsylvania State University for most of his career.

Weizmann, Dr. Chaim (1874–1952)

Chemist, Zionist leader, and first president of Israel. Born in Russia, in 1904 Weizmann moved to England, where he played an influential role in the development of the **Balfour Declaration.** A brilliant scientist, Weizmann headed the Royal Navy's research laboratory from 1916 to 1919, and one story has it that the declaration came about in part as a repayment for Weizmann's discovery of a method to synthesize an important gunpowder ingredient—acetone—at a time when England was having difficulty importing it. At the **Peace Conference,** on January 3, 1919, Lawrence brought Weizmann and **Feisal** together and helped persuade them to sign the first treaty of cooperation between the Zionist movement and Arab nationalism, which Lawrence himself had drawn up. The document may be seen in **George Antonius**'s *The Arab Awakening,* Appendix F. Weizmann regarded Lawrence as a friend of **Zionism** and his personal friend, and indeed, Lawrence defended him in no uncertain terms to the Anglican bishop of **Jerusalem** in a striking letter (Garnett, *Letters,* pp. 342–44). Weizmann's *Trial and Error* (1949) contains references to Lawrence, and he contributed a memoir to **A. W. Lawrence**'s *T. E. Lawrence by His Friends.*

Wejh

Red Sea Arabian port, about 175 miles north of **Yenbo.** The capture of Wejh in January 1917 gave the Arabs the initiative, isolated the Turkish garrison at **Medina,** and brought the war in the **Hejaz** to a successful conclusion. From that point on, the British decided to raise a regular Arab force for fighting in the north. Previously there had been a debate about whether or not British and French troops should take part in the campaign, which the French representative **Colonel Brémond** had wished and Lawrence opposed; after the capture of Wejh this was no longer an issue. In chapter 21 of *Seven Pillars of Wisdom,* Lawrence discusses his advice to **Feisal** to proceed to Wejh. Chapters 21–26 describe the preparations for and capture of Wejh. Lawrence had planned a combined sea and land assault, but in the event the battle was decided before Lawrence and the main body of the Arab forces could arrive by land. Instead, the 200 Turkish soldiers in the town were overwhelmed by the troopship *Hardinge*'s guns and some 200 British sailors and an Arab landing party of 400 under **Maj. Charles Vickery.** The Turkish defenses on the north side of the town were weak, and that is where the *Hardinge*'s **Captain Boyle** and Major Vickery attacked, capturing each small defensive position in turn. Boyle used seaplanes and the light cruiser *Fox* to focus his ship's fire, and Vickery placed a heliograph on the shore with which to send messages to Boyle. The fighting, which began on the morning of January 23, 1917, took a total of 36 hours. The fighting ended when the *Fox* was ordered to shell a mosque in which the last Turkish resistance was based, and 15 Turkish troops stumbled out. The town, which was occupied in large part by Egyptian traders who preferred the Turks to the British and Arabs, was largely in ruins, having been both shelled from the sea and looted during the battle. As a result of this battle, the northern Red Sea with the exception of **Akaba** was cleared of the Turks, and it was from Wejh that Lawrence and the Arab forces later began their march on that city, which ended with its capture. See Charles R. Parnell, "Lawrence of Arabia's Debt to Seapower," U.S. Naval Institute *Proceedings* (August 1979), pp. 75–83; Pope and Wheal, *The Dictionary of the First World War;* and **A. P. Wavell**, *The Palestine Campaigns.*

Wells, H. G. (1866–1946)

Science fiction and popular author of *the Time Machine* (1895) and *War of the Worlds* (1898). Wells praised *Seven Pillars of Wisdom,* which he read in 1924, before the 1926 subscriber's edition was published. His praise probably helped Lawrence gain subscribers (Garnett, *Letters,* p. 465), and he also invited Lawrence to visit him. In his turn, Lawrence published a review of Wells's short stories praising their individuality, and Wells told **Francis Yeats-Brown,** the *Spectator* editor who commissioned the review, that it was one of the most interesting that he had seen. The review appeared in that magazine for February 1928, was republished in *Men in Print,* and is now available in Harold Orlans's *Lawrence of Arabia, Strange Man of Letters.*

Wemyss, Adm. Sir Rosslyn (1864–1933)

Naval commander. Wemyss began **World War I** in command of a cruiser squadron in 1914 and from February 1915 was given the task of preparing Mudros harbor for operations in the Dardanelles. From there he commanded a battle squadron off the **Gallipoli** coast, and then from January 1916 he headed the Egyptian Squadron, which supported the **Palestine** campaign, in part by devising anti-submarine mea-

sures. In chapter 16 of *Seven Pillars of Wisdom,* Lawrence states that Wemyss strongly supported the **Arab Revolt** from its inception. Among many other acts of support, he sent his flagship, the *Euryalus,* to **Akaba** as a guardship when the city was captured by Lawrence. In 1917 he became deputy to the naval minister in **London,** and in December 1917 he became first sea lord, the senior naval officer. He represented the navy at the **Peace Conference** and resigned in November 1919. A portrait of Wemyss by **Sir William Orpen** can be seen on p. 72 of **J. M. Wilson**'s *T. E. Lawrence.* See Pope and Wheal, *The Dictionary of the First World War.*

Westminster Press

The commercial typesetting company in **London** that set up the galley proofs of the 1926 subscriber's edition of *Seven Pillars of Wisdom.*

Whittingham and Griggs

Properly, Charles Whittingham and Griggs, Ltd. The **London** printing company responsible for the color lithographs in the 1926 subscriber's edition of *Seven Pillars of Wisdom.*

Wilderness of Zin, The

An important archaeological report, co-authored by Lawrence and **C. Leonard Woolley,** and published by the **Palestine Exploration Fund** in 1915. In December 1913, Lawrence and Woolley were called from their research site at **Carchemish, Syria,** to join then-Capt. **Stewart Newcombe** in **Beersheba,** then **Palestine,** for a six-week survey of the Sinai and **Negev** deserts. This survey was really military in nature, because Newcombe's military engineering team was involved in mapping Turkish defenses here at the edge of Palestine, only about 100 miles from the **Suez Canal,** which the British government was greatly concerned with defending, and Lawrence and Woolley were along to give the survey archaeological cover and credibility. In the fall of 1914, long after the survey was over and the war had begun, the British government pressed Lawrence, now working in the **Geographical Section** of the general staff in **London,** and Woolley quickly to revise and publish the book so as to make the survey seem like a legitimate archeological exercise. Because of the quality of Lawrence's and Woolley's work, this rushed book, designed to mask a military spying mission, remains of permanent importance in biblical studies. It correctly proposed Ain el Qudeirat in northern Sinai, instead of the previously proposed Ain Kadeis, as the site of the biblical Kadesh-Barnea, where the Hebrews sojourned and from which Moses sent spies out to Canaan (Deut. 1:2, 19, 2:1; Numb. 13:3–21). The book's preface says that Lawrence was responsible for most of chapter IV, in which this information is found. But as Lawrence wrote in his introduction to the book, he and Woolley consulted on all aspects even though they each investigated different areas of the desert, so no idea or sentence can be assigned to Lawrence or to Woolley with certainty. In addition to this important site identification, Lawrence and Woolley were the first to recognize the earthenware pottery known as Negev pottery, and they also added to our knowledge of the **Nabataeans,** the group of desert dwellers who flourished from the fourth century B.C.E., building a string of cities famous for their water control systems, until they were annexed by the Romans in 106 C.E. The book has one of the best plans ever made of the formerly Nabataean Byzantine city of Shivta. Lawrence and Woolley also demonstrated—on the basis of rings in cisterns, the lack of wood in the Byzantine dwellings, the presence of Byzantine storerooms, and the use

of terrace gardening from the Byzantine times, among other things—that the weather in the Negev remained the same as it had been in Byzantine days. The book has been published in several editions, and until Professor Nelson Glueck's *Rivers in the Desert* appeared more than 40 years later, it was the primary authority on the Nabataean and Byzantine ruins in the northern Sinai and southern Negev Desert. There were also military consequences of the survey and of Lawrence's travels during it. Beersheba, from which the team first set out, was to become the first town in Palestine captured by the British during **World War I** (in 1917 under **General Allenby),** while **Akaba,** now in Jordan, which Lawrence first visited during this Wilderness of Zin survey, was captured by him during the **Arab Revolt.** An edition of *The Wilderness of Zin* was published by Stacey International in 2003. See Stephen E. Tabachnick, "Lawrence of Arabia as Archaeologist," *Biblical Archaeology Review* (Sept.–Oct. 1997): 40–47, 70–71.

Williamson, Henry (1895–1977)

Author of nature writings and several novels, including *Tarka the Otter,* about which Lawrence, then in **Karachi,** wrote a 5,000-word letter to **Edward Garnett,** commenting on its style (see Peter Wilson, editor, *T. E. Lawrence: Correspondence with Henry Williamson,* pp. 13–33). This letter was passed on to Williamson by Garnett, and a friendship began. The Williamson-Lawrence correspondence, however, shows that the friendship was more on Williamson's side than on Lawrence's, although Lawrence undoubtedly enjoyed exchanging literary views with Williamson. However, Williamson's affinity for the English fascist Oswald Mosley and for Adolf Hitler were alien to Lawrence, as Williamson told **John Mack** in 1965. Lawrence died in a motorcycle accident when on his way back from sending a telegram agreeing to a meeting with Williamson at **Clouds Hill.** Williamson told Mack that, if this meeting had taken place, he intended to use it to discuss arranging a meeting between Lawrence and Hitler.

Wilson, Sir Arnold Talbot (1884–1940)

Army officer in Persia, 1907–14; political officer with the British Expeditionary Forces in **Mesopotamia,** 1914–18; acting civil commissioner in the Persian Gulf, 1918–20, in the absence of **Sir Percy Cox;** and author of *Mesopotamia 1917–1920: A Clash of Loyalties* (1931), an apologia for his role in the Middle East. Wilson, while an able administrator, was blamed for the serious insurrection against the British in Mesopotamia in 1920. Lawrence strongly criticizes Wilson's government in "France, Britain, and the Arabs" (*Observer,* August 8, 1920), and his criticism of British rule over Mesopotamia also appears in the introduction to *Seven Pillars of Wisdom.* Wilson was recalled to London, worked for the Anglo-Persian Oil Company, and later became a Conservative member of parliament. He was shot down in World War II when serving voluntarily with the **Royal Air Force.**

Wilson, Col. Cyril E. (1873–1938)

Wilson was sent in August 1916 by **Sir Reginald Wingate** to serve as representative to **Sharif Hussein** and **Feisal** in **Jidda.** Wilson recommended that a British army brigade be sent to support the **Arab Revolt,** which he considered in danger of disintegration. This recommendation, however, was never acted upon, in part because Lawrence in a memorandum to the Egyptian government disputed it. However, Wilson succeeded in getting Feisal sup-

plied with a battery of mountain guns and Maxim machine guns and gunners from the Egyptian army, as Lawrence tells us in chapter 13 of *Seven Pillars of Wisdom.* In chapter 36, he praises Wilson for his honesty. Wilson at first saw Lawrence negatively but by May 1917 praised him in an official report. In a letter of March 30, 1933, to **Eric Kennington** (Garnett, *Letters,* p. 406), Lawrence expresses pleasure that Kennington has painted Wilson for the 1926 subscriber's edition of *Seven Pillars of Wisdom* and sees him as a narrow but honest and straightforward colonial official.

Wilson, Jeremy Michael (born 1944)

By trade a senior copyeditor, and educated at **Oxford** and the London School of Economics, Jeremy Wilson is one of the leading Lawrence scholars around the turn of the twentieth century. His most important works, *Lawrence of Arabia: The Authorized Biography of T. E. Lawrence* (1990), an edition of the 1922 Oxford text of *Seven Pillars of Wisdom,* and an ongoing series of volumes of Lawrence's correspondence, are permanent and fundamental contributions to the field. Moreover, the latter two works have been produced by Wilson himself under his Castle Hill Press imprint and uphold the highest standards of bookmaking, thus following Lawrence's own interest in fine printing. Wilson also began the journal of the **T. E. Lawrence Society** and created a Web site devoted to Lawrence. He also contributed an excellent centenary exhibition catalog of Lawrence material, *T. E. Lawrence* (1988), an edition of Lawrence's poetry anthology ***Minorities,*** and introductions to Lawrence's ***The Mint*** and to his ***Odyssey*** translation, among other works. Wilson's strength is his precision and desire to establish facts on the basis of documentation. He is far more a historian than a literary critic, and he does not usually venture into aesthetic criticism of Lawrence's works. He is also an avid partisan of Lawrence who sometimes fudges problematic areas of Lawrence's life and career. For a critique of his Lawrence biography, see S. Tabachnick's review in *English Literature in Transition: 1880–1920* 35:1 (1992): 89–93 and chapter 8 of Fred Crawford's *Richard Aldington and Lawrence of Arabia,* in which Crawford defends **Aldington** against Wilson's charges, criticizing Wilson's biography as he does so.

Wilson, Thomas Woodrow (1856–1924)

Twenty-eighth president of the United States (1913–21). Wilson had Congress declare war on April 2, 1917, and was an active participant in the **Peace Conference** of 1919 and an ardent advocate of self-determination. Point Twelve of his famous "Fourteen Points" declared that the non-Turkish groups in the former Ottoman Empire should be given a chance at autonomous rule. Lawrence had hopes that Wilson would be able to achieve that for the Arabs but was disappointed when the conference failed to adopt Wilson's views. According to a letter of January 30, 1919, to his mother (Brown, *Selected Letters,* p. 162), he seems to have met Wilson at the conference.

Wingate, Gen. Sir Reginald (1861–1953)

Governor-general of the **Sudan;** sirdar, or commander-in-chief, of the Egyptian army, 1899–1916; and high commissioner of **Egypt,** December 1916–19, after the departure of **Sir Henry McMahon.** He was made a baron in 1920. The Egyptian army commander was based in the Sudan because the army, consisting of around 18,000 men, was largely needed to main-

tain order there, in addition to its duties of maintaining order in Egypt and defending the **Suez Canal,** because of constant brigandage and unrest. Lawrence tells us in chapters 6 and 16 of *Seven Pillars of Wisdom* that Wingate was an early supporter of the **Arab Revolt** and in 1916 became General Office Commanding (G.O.C.) **Hejaz** Operations, in reality a small support force of officers, instructors, and quartermasters, while McMahon continued to be responsible for the political side of the revolt. Lawrence enjoyed staying at Wingate's palace in Khartoum, where he read **Malory**'s *Morte d'Arthur* in between discussions with Wingate about the revolt. But Lawrence felt that **Colonel Brémond** would convince Wingate to send British and French soldiers to the Hejaz, and he successfully acted to head off that possibility by convincing **Clayton** and McMahon that Arab irregulars could succeed with British assistance and supplies rather than troops. Later on, Wingate was convinced to allow **Feisal**'s forces to come under **Allenby**'s command, as Lawrence explains in chapter 57 of *Seven Pillars of Wisdom.* See M. W. Daly, *The Sirdar: Sir Reginald Wingate and the British Empire in the Middle East.*

Winterton, Lord Edward Turnour, 6th Earl (born 1883)

Officer during the **Arab Revolt,** undersecretary of state for India (1922–24; 1924–29) and member of parliament for many years. In chapter 107 of *Seven Pillars of Wisdom,* Lawrence tells us that Winterton was an experienced officer from the **Imperial Camel Corps** now serving with the Arab forces. **Malcolm Brown** (*Selected Letters,* p. 290) notes that it was at Winterton's house in 1921 that Winterton, Lawrence, Lord Harlech, and Lord Moyne convinced **Feisal** to accept the throne of **Iraq** after having been expelled from **Syria** by the French.

Women

There are three main aspects involved in Lawrence's attitudes toward women. First, his attitudes are bound up with his relationship with his mother. Dominating, guilt-driven because of her adultery, and religiously inflexible, she seems to have put Lawrence off normal relationships with women his age. Although **Janet Laurie** claimed later in life that Lawrence had proposed to her when a young man, most authorities do not accept this story, and it seems that the atmosphere in the Lawrence home was uncongenial to girlfriends. Second, there is the question of Lawrence's possible homosexuality, as well as his postwar flagellation syndrome, and his admission to **Robert Graves** and others that he had never had the experience of sexual intercourse. Third, there is the factual evidence that he did not marry or even go out with girls and that he expressed unusual ideas about them in his works—seeing them as anything but objects of sexual desire or as subjects for love. He liked the **Royal Air Force** in part because in his view women and machinery did not mix, and he felt that he would therefore be free of women in the R.A.F. But all of this did not preclude women friends, especially married women, with some of whom he became quite close. Of these, **Charlotte Shaw** is the most important, judging from their correspondence; she played the role of comforter and surrogate, but unthreatening, mother, and it was in a letter to her that he confessed to having been raped at **Deraa. Clare Sydney Smith,** the wife of the commander of the **Mount Batten R.A.F.** station, also provided some of the comforts of home for Lawrence. Her *Golden Reign* is a memoir of this period. Lawrence also enjoyed speaking to his Arabic teacher, **Fareeda el Akle,** and to traveler and intelligence agent **Gertrude Bell.** These sexless, appreciative, vaguely mothering relationships seem to have satisfied both Lawrence and the women participating in them. It should be noted that many of those most fascinated by Lawrence have been women, such as the Argentinian critic **Victoria Ocampo** and biographer Flora Armitage, and that the membership in the T. E. Lawrence societies in England and the United States includes many women.

Woolf, Leonard S. (1880–1969)

Critic, codirector of the Hogarth Press with his wife **Virginia Woolf.** In a review of *Revolt in the Desert* in *The Nation and Athenaeum* (March 19, 1927), Woolf compared Lawrence's and **Doughty**'s styles, eliciting a long comment from Lawrence to a friend that his style really did not have much in common with Doughty's, although he had expected such comparisons.

Woolf, Virginia (1882–1941)

Novelist, wife of **Leonard Woolf.** In a letter to **E. M. Forster** of October 27, 1927 (Brown, *Selected Letters,* pp. 351–52), Lawrence criticizes her article on Forster that appeared in the *Saturday Review of Literature* for December 17, 1927. **Brown** comments that Lawrence had seen the review in draft before it was published. In the letter, Lawrence also praises the Woolf article for some good points.

Woolley, Sir Charles Leonard (1888–1960)

Noted archaeologist, author of the memoirs *Dead Towns and Living Men* (1920) and *As I Seem to Remember* (1962) and many professional works. Woolley, assistant keeper of the **Ashmolean Museum** under **D. G. Hogarth,** knew Lawrence slightly when he was a schoolboy, worked with Lawrence at Hogarth's dig at **Carchemish, Syria,** from 1911 to 1914, and participated with him in the **Wilderness of Zin** survey in early 1914 and then in a spying mission concerning the railway that the **Germans** were building through the Amanus Mountains for the Turks. The result of the survey was the book Woolley coauthored with Lawrence, *The Wilderness of Zin,* which remains important in biblical studies to this day, and the result of the spying mission was that the pair got all of the railway plans from a disgruntled Italian engineer. Like Lawrence, Woolley worked for British Intelligence in **Egypt** during **World War I** but was captured and interned in a Turkish prisoner-of-war camp from 1916 to 1918. He returned to Carchemish after the war and also worked in Egypt. In 1922 he was appointed head of the project that would give him permanent, worldwide fame, namely the excavation of the Sumerian city of Ur, which was wildly successful in unearthing exciting finds; his book *Ur of the Chaldees* (1929) became a best seller. Two subsequent excavations in Turkey were also very successful. Woolley's view of Lawrence, expressed in his essay in *T. E. Lawrence by His Friends,* was that Lawrence was a brilliant but erratic archaeologist, a very good foreman at Carchemish, and was prejudiced toward the **Beduin** and against town Arabs. Even at that time, according to Woolley, Lawrence had a passion for **Syria** and accordingly disliked the Turks and French policy in the Middle East. According to Woolley, Lawrence's relationship with **Dahoum** was questioned by the local Arabs, and although he denied that Lawrence was an overt homosexual, he seems to imply homosexuality in Lawrence's nature. He also felt that Lawrence enjoyed shocking people and liked practical jokes directed against others but could not abide being made fun of himself. He notes that Lawrence enjoyed dressing up in dandyish clothes but was unprepossessing physically. Woolley felt that there was an essential immaturity in Lawrence along with

courage and high intelligence. After the war, Lawrence and Woolley did not correspond much, and there seems to have been distance between the two men. Yet *The Wilderness of Zin* has left a permanently valuable monument to their collaboration. See H.V.F. Winstone, *Woolley of Ur: The Life of Sir Leonard Woolley.*

World War I

The Middle Eastern aspect of this war included actions around Turkey itself, particularly the **Gallipoli** landings and Russo-Turkish battles; actions in north Africa, especially the campaign against the **Senussi** in Libya; actions in the Arabian peninsula, particularly the **Arab Revolt;** actions in **Palestine** and the Sinai peninsula, including two failed Turkish raids on the **Suez Canal;** and actions in **Mesopotamia,** including the capture of 10,000 British soldiers at **Kut-al-Amara** by the Turks and the capture of Baghdad by the British. While these actions cannot be compared in scope to the major campaigns in Western Europe, the British losses at Gallipoli and Kut were significant, while **General Allenby**'s defeat of the Turks in Palestine, like the Turks' loss of Baghdad, was important for Western morale and for the ultimate defeat of Germany, which was allied with Turkey. The campaigns in the east also had a great deal of color, including exciting cavalry charges, such as that at **Beersheba,** Palestine, in October 1917, the use of **Beduin** forces during the **Arab Revolt** under Lawrence, the brilliant use of diversion at Beersheba by British Intelligence chief **Richard Meinertzhagen,** and Allenby's strategic vision, including a further brilliant use of deceptive tactics preceding his final offensive in fall 1918. The overall pattern was British setback and loss at Gallipoli, Kut, and Gaza and a slow start to the Arab Revolt in the **Hejaz** early in the war, followed by the ascension of Allenby and General Maude's advance to **Bagh-**

dad, as well as the success of the Arabs in capturing **Akaba.** In fairness to the Turks and the German officers working with them, the major reason for the British successes was that the Turko-German forces were greatly outnumbered in terms of men and materiel. Allenby, for instance, was able to bring three times as many British as Turkish forces to bear, with the almost inevitable result that the Turks were forced into retreat after retreat. The war in the Middle East lasted for a full four years, testimony to the fight that the Turks and their German officers and assistants waged. Lawrence's strategic theories were one of the outstanding contributions of the Middle Eastern theater to the practice of future wars, while Allenby's use of concentrated force and mobility were precursors of the German Blitzkrieg tactics of World War II. See **K. Morsey,** "T. E. Lawrence: Strategist," in *The T. E. Lawrence Puzzle,* edited by Tabachnick, pp. 185–203; **A. P. Wavell,** *The Palestine Campaigns;* MacMunn and Falls, *Military Operations, Egypt and Palestine;* F. J. Moberly, *The Campaign in Mesopotamia 1914–18;* P. Haythornthwaite, *The World War One Source Book;* Pope and Wheal, *The Dictionary of the First World War;* **Liman von Sanders,** *Five Years in Turkey.*

The World's Work

A magazine of current affairs founded in New York by Walter Hines Page (1855–1918), an outstanding journalist and advocate of the English Speaking Union, and published by Doubleday, Page and Company, in which he was a partner. It ran from November 1900 through July 1932 and included 61 numbers in all. Lawrence published seven articles in this journal: "With Feisal at Court and Afield" (July 1921): 277–88; "Arabian Nights and Days" (August 1921): 381–86, (September 1921): 516–20; "Adventures in Arabia's Deliverance" (October 1921): 617–21; "Fomenting Revolt in Arabia" (February 1927): 369–92; "Dynamiting Turks" (March 1927): 513–33; "With Lawrence's Guerrillas" (April 1927): 643–63; and "The Conquest of Damascus" (May 1927): 36–53. **J. M. Wilson** points out in his biography that Lawrence gave the first four pieces, all from an early manuscript version of *Seven Pillars of Wisdom,* to **Robert Graves,** then in need of money, and that Graves is the one who sold them to the magazine. The three pieces from 1927 were a serialization of *Revolt in the Desert,* which was published in that year. All seven pieces are included as passages in *Seven Pillars of Wisdom,* sometimes in revised form.

Wuld Ali Tribe

A **Beduin** tribe from the area about 100 miles east of **Wejh.** In November 1917, immediately following Lawrence's escape from **Deraa,** a raiding party of Wuld Ali tribesmen let Lawrence and his companions go without robbing them when they found out who they were, as recounted in chapter 80 of *Seven Pillars of Wisdom.*

Y

Yale, Prof. William (1887–1975)

American engineer and Middle East expert. Yale, who had worked in Panama in 1907 and received his Ph.D. in 1910, was sent to the Middle East in 1913 by Standard Oil to prospect for oil. In 1917, he was appointed special agent in **Cairo** by the State Department and in 1918 as a military observer with the rank of captain to **General Allenby**'s campaign in **Palestine.** In 1919, he was appointed to the **King-Crane Commission,** which was sent to the **Peace Conference** in **Paris** by President **Woodrow Wilson.** At the conference, Yale spoke to Lawrence and recorded the conversation in his notebook. Lawrence opposed the British government in **Mesopotamia,** which ran along Anglo-Indian colonial lines. According to Yale, Lawrence also liked Yale's ideas about having the United States help mediate between the Arabs, **France,** and Britain concerning postwar rule in **Syria** (see the Garnett edition of the *Letters,* pp. 282–88). After this period, Yale became a professor of history at the University of New Hampshire and Boston University, except for the period from 1942 to 1945, when he was a State Department expert on **Palestine.** He is the author of *The Near East: A Modern History* (1958).

Yarmuk Valley Bridges

The Yarmuk River, a tributary of the Jordan River, flows on an east-west axis approximately 49 miles, forming part of the boundary between **Syria** and what is now Jordan. A series of Turkish railroad bridges spanned the river over deep gorges, so that trains could travel between **Palestine** and Damascus. In chapter 70 of *Seven Pillars of Wisdom,* Lawrence relates how he devised a plan to travel from **Akaba** to cut the westernmost bridge, near Um Keis, or ancient **Gadara.** On November 8, 1917, he arrived at the **Tell el Shehab bridge** after traveling some 420 miles, only to have one of his men drop his rifle, setting up a storm among the Turkish guards of the bridge, as related in chapter 76. Lawrence, sick with failure, was unable to keep his word to **Allenby** that he would hamper the Turks by cutting this important bridge before Allenby's offensive. Cutting the bridge would have deprived the Turkish Seventh and Eighth armies in Palestine of supplies and also cut off one possible avenue of their escape; but owing to Lawrence's failure, it was not to be. In any event, Allenby's offensive took place only almost a year later.

Yeats, William Butler (1865–1939)

Important Anglo-Irish poet and president of the Irish Academy of Letters. In that capacity, Yeats wrote Lawrence in 1932 informing him that he had been nominated to the academy by virtue of his being the son of an Irishman. Yeats's letter praises Lawrence as one of his heroes, notable for both intellect and bravery. Lawrence's acceptance of the nomination was conveyed by **Mrs. Charlotte Shaw** under his new adopted name of Shaw. (The relevant two letters from Yeats are in *Letters to T. E. Lawrence,* edited by **A. W. Lawrence.** The letters from Lawrence to and about Yeats can be seen in the Garnett *Letters.*) Around 1920, Lawrence did not think much of Yeats's poetry, but by 1931 he considered him an important poet. He mentioned in his letter of October 12, 1932, thanking Yeats for his nomination, that he had once seen Yeats in Oxford. Lawrence was a lover of poetry all of his life and eagerly followed the new directions in verse, sometimes understanding and accepting them and sometimes not. His growing appreciation of Yeats shows his own growth as a reader.

Yeats-Brown, Francis (1886–1944)

British officer and writer. Best known for his autobiography, *Lives of a Bengal Lancer* (1930), Yeats-Brown wrote a number of books about **India** and yoga and served as the literary editor at *The Spectator.* In that capacity, he sent Lawrence several books to review in 1927, which

Lawrence did, under the pseudonym "C. D.," or **Colin Dale.**

Yemen

In 1914, by agreement, the Ottomans controlled the government in Yemen, while a Shiite imam controlled the countryside; this followed many anti-Ottoman outbreaks prior to 1914. When **World War I** erupted, however, an Ottoman force of 14,000 largely Syrian soldiers under Ali Said Pasha was determined to hold Yemen in order to shore up control over the holy cities in the **Hejaz** as well. The Germans also planned to set up a radio transmitter there in order to contact **Gen. Paul E. von Lettow-Vorbeck,** who was running a guerrilla campaign against British forces in German East Africa, but their plans came to naught when the boat in which the Germans were sailing was sunk. Some German sailors from the destroyer *Emden,* sunk off the East Indies, made it to Yemen and bolstered the Ottomans, as did other German sailors from the port of Massawa in Ethiopia. A British naval bombardment in November 1914 of a Yemeni port on the **Red Sea** opened hostilities, and Ali Said Pasha moved to block off Aden, then protected by a small British force. In 1915 a force under Ali Pasha advanced to the port of Aden but was beaten back and remained stalemated around Aden until the end of the war, when he surrendered but entered Aden with approximately 2,500 troops as a hero. See David Nicolle and Richard Hook, *Lawrence and the Arab Revolts,* for further information.

Yenbo

Port on the coast of Arabia, about 200 miles north of **Jidda,** which was captured by the **Royal Navy** in July 1916 and subsequently used as a base by **Feisal**'s forces. There they were instructed by **Garland** in explosives in order to attack the **Hejaz Railway,** as explained by Lawrence in chapter 17 of *Seven Pillars of Wisdom.* Yenbo was also an important supply base for the Arab forces, having been supported by the British.

Yildirim

Planned as a lightning *(yildirim)* strike unit of the Turkish army in June 1917 by an order of **Enver Pasha,** the Yildirim consisted of Turkish divisions formed at **Aleppo, Syria,** from the Third and Fifteenth Army Corps, which had previously been in action against **Russia** and Rumania. These units were combined with battalions of the German Pasha II, or Asia Corps. The headquarters staff was largely German rather than Turkish, and the Yildirim was commanded by **General von Falkenhayn.** The original plan was for the Yildirim to recapture Baghdad from the British. In the event, the Yildirim force was used belatedly in the failed defense of **Jerusalem** after **Allenby**'s offensive and never was utilized as an effective fighting force. See **A. P. Wavell,** *The Palestine Campaigns;* **Liman von Sanders,** *Five Years in Turkey;* and Pope and Wheal, *The Dictionary of the First World War.*

Young, Maj. Sir Hubert W. (1885–1950)

Staff officer from the Mesopotamian army assigned to the Arab forces. Young first met Lawrence at **Carchemish** in 1913 and greatly enjoyed his visit. He met Lawrence again in May 1916, when Lawrence was sent to bribe the Turkish commander, **Khalil Pasha,** to release the British force

under **General Townshend** that he had surrounded at **Kut-al-Amara.** Young resented Lawrence's criticism of the British army in **Mesopotamia.** Later, when he came to serve with Lawrence in the Arab theater, he felt that Lawrence did not sufficiently respect the regular army, but he also admitted that no one else could have filled Lawrence's role as he did. Young also served with Lawrence in the **Colonial Office** under **Winston Churchill.** His memoir, *The Independent Arab* (1933), is an important source for the **World War I** and interwar period in the Middle East. Lawrence was appreciative of Young's role, which he praises in chapter 94 and elsewhere in *Seven Pillars of Wisdom.*

Young Turks

A revolutionary secret society composed largely of Ottoman officers who in 1908 revolted against **Sultan Abdul-Hamid II** and in 1909 forced his deposition. This society and its larger political party, which included other such formerly secret societies, the **Committee of Union and Progress (CUP),** ran the government (except for a six-month period when it was led by the Liberal Union) until the defeat of Turkey in 1918 by the Allied powers. During the reign of this party, and under the direction of its ruling **World War I** triumvirate of **Enver Pasha, Talat Pasha,** and **Jemal Pasha,** Turkey lost all of her European possessions and all of her Arab ones. Instead of promoting decentralization, the party insisted upon **Pan-Turanism,** or the spread of the Turkish language and the suppression of nationalism among the empire's peoples. This harsh policy accounted for the Arabs' defection and the strength of the **Arab Revolt.** While the loss of the empire was certainly a failure, the CUP did manage some reforms, including secularism, at least outward respect for parliamentarianism, and freedom of expression, which later paved the way for **Mustapha Kemal Pasha**'s modernization of the Turkish state. Lawrence discusses these trends in chapter 4 of *Seven Pillars of Wisdom,* in which he stresses the Young Turks' surprise at the forces of nationalism that their revolution against the sultan had let loose and their attempt to suppress them through Pan-Turanist policies.

Z

Zeid ibn Hussein, Emir (1896–1972)

The youngest of **Sheikh Hussein**'s four sons, born of a Turkish mother and, so, a half-brother to the other sons. According to *Arabian Personalities of the Early Twentieth Century* (edited by Bidwell), Zeid was the least important of the sons, being less intense and fond of games and tricks. He was, however, designated to meet a British delegation in **Hejaz** just before the **Arab Revolt** took place and served as his father's representative at **Jidda.** In *Seven Pillars of Wisdom,* he is noted for having squandered 24,000 pounds sterling in gold entrusted to him by Lawrence for a spring offensive, by giving it to villagers and **Beduin** tribesmen, as related in chapter 90. This resulted in Lawrence's only genuine attempt to quit his role as adviser to the Arabs entirely. Lawrence was distressed particularly because he liked Zeid and respected his fighting spirit at the battle of **Tafileh,** as recounted in chapter 86. After the war, Zeid studied at Oxford and was acting regent in **Iraq** when **Feisal** was ill. In 1958, he was serving as ambassador in **London** when General Qasim overthrew the **Hashemites** in Iraq. Zeid died in exile in **France** in 1972.

Zionism

The modern Jewish nationalist movement, founded by Theodore Herzl with the publication of his pamphlet *The Jewish State* in 1896, but traceable to earlier Eastern European writers such as Moses Hess and Yehuda Pinsker. A reaction to Jewish landlessness and vulnerability in Europe, Zionism achieved success when in 1917 the British government, eager for Jewish support during **World War I,** issued the **Balfour Declaration** favoring a home for the Jews in **Palestine.** Because he is called Lawrence of Arabia, some people are not aware that Lawrence was in favor of Zionism as well as of Arab nationalism. He felt that the two movements could coexist and would be mutually beneficial. In *Seven Pillars of Wisdom,* he refers to Zionism positively, in chapter 3 and chapter 59, and also questions British promises to the Jews in chapter 101. Before the war, he praised Jewish colonies in Palestine (Garnett, *Letters,* p. 74), and in 1922, he defended **Chaim Weizmann,** the head of the Zionist movement, from attack by the Anglican bishop of Jerusalem (*Letters,* p. 343). In January 1919, Lawrence was instrumental in bringing Weizmann and **Feisal** together to sign an agreement of cooperation, the full text of which can be found in the appendix to **George Antonius**'s *The Arab Awakening.* In **A. W. Lawrence**'s *T. E. Lawrence by His Friends,* Weizmann writes that he considered Lawrence a friend. If Zionists have any quarrel with Lawrence, it is over his acquiescence, at the **Cairo Conference** of 1921, in the detachment of **Transjordan** from the Palestine mandate; this greatly reduced the area of Palestine that the Balfour Declaration had assigned to the Jews. But he did not originate this policy, and it seems that at the conference the British as a group merely acquiesced in a *fait accompli,* that is, the **Emir Abdullah ibn Hussein**'s seizure of Transjordan and his setting up of his rule there.

List of Entries by Subject

5. Diplomacy, 1919–22

6. In the R.A.F. and After 1922–35

7. *Personal Life, Tastes, and Beliefs*

8. *His Literary and Publishing Career*

9. The Legend: Its Creators and
   Interpreters

Bibliography

This bibliography contains full publication information for all of the books that have been referred to in this encyclopedia. Article author, title, and publication information is given only within the entries themselves. Philip O'Brien's *T. E. Lawrence: A Bibliography,* 2nd ed. (New Castle, Del.: Oak Knoll, 2000) is the primary listing of works by and about Lawrence through 1999. The American newsletter *T. E. Notes* and the British *Journal of the T. E. Lawrence Society,* which can be accessed via J. M. Wilson's Web sites http://lawrenceofarabia.info/ and http://telstudies.org, should be consulted for current research.

Major Works by T. E. Lawrence

With C. Leonard Woolley, D. G. Hogarth, and P.L.O. Guy. *Carchemish: Report on the Excavations at Djerabis on Behalf of the British Museum.* 3 vols. London: British Museum, 1914, 1921, 1952.

Crusader Castles. Introduction by Denys Pringle. Oxford: Clarendon Press, 1988. Originally published in a two-volume edition by Golden Cockerel Press in 1936.

The Diary of T. E. Lawrence MCMXI. London: Corvinus Press, 1937.

The Essential T. E. Lawrence. Edited by David Garnett. New York: Viking, 1939.

Evolution of a Revolt: Early Postwar Writings of T. E. Lawrence. Edited by Stanley and Rodelle Weintraub. University Park: Pennsylvania State University Press, 1968.

The Home Letters of T. E. Lawrence and His Brothers. Edited by M. R. Lawrence. Oxford: Basil Blackwell, 1954.

Lawrence of Arabia, Strange Man of Letters: The Literary Criticism and Correspondence of T. E. Lawrence. Edited by Harold Orlans. Rutherford, N.J.: Fairleigh Dickinson University Press, 1993.

The Letters of T. E. Lawrence. Edited by David Garnett. London: Jonathan Cape, 1938.

Letters from T. E. Shaw to Bruce Rogers. Edited by Bruce Rogers. [New York]: Press of W. E. Rudge, 1933.

Minorities. Edited by J. M. Wilson. Preface by C. Day Lewis. London: Jonathan Cape, 1971.

The Mint. Note by A. W. Lawrence. London: Jonathan Cape, 1988. Originally published in 1955.

More Letters from T. E. Shaw to Bruce Rogers. Edited by Bruce Rogers. [New York]: Privately printed, 1936.

[T. E. Shaw, translator.] *The Odyssey of Homer.* Introduction by Sir Maurice Bowra. London: Oxford University Press, 1955.

Oriental Assembly. Edited by A. W. Lawrence. New York: Dutton, 1940.

Revolt in the Desert. New York: George Doran, 1927.

Secret Despatches from Arabia. Foreword by A. W. Lawrence. London: Golden Cockerel Press, 1939.

Seven Pillars of Wisdom: The Complete 1922 Text. 2 vols. Edited by J. M. Wilson. Fordingbridge, Hampshire: Castle Hill Press, 1997.

Seven Pillars of Wisdom: A Triumph. Harmondsworth: Penguin, 1987.

Shaw-Ede: T. E. Lawrence's Letters to H. S. Ede 1927–1935. London: Golden Cockerel, 1942.

T. E. Lawrence: Correspondence with Bernard and Charlotte Shaw, 1922–26. Edited by J. M. Wilson and Nicolle Wilson. Fordingbridge, Hampshire: Castle Hill Press, 2000.

T. E. Lawrence: Correspondence with Henry Williamson. Edited by Peter Wilson. Fordingbridge, Hampshire: Castle Hill Press, 2000.

T. E. Lawrence: The Selected Letters. Edited by Malcolm Brown. New York: W. W. Norton, 1989.

T. E. Lawrence: Letters to E. T. Leeds. Edited by J. M. Wilson. Andoversford: Whittington Press, 1988.

T. E. Lawrence to His Biographers Robert Graves & Liddell Hart. Edited by Robert Graves and

Basil Liddell Hart. London: Cassell, 1963. Originally published in 1938.

With C. Leonard Woolley. *The Wilderness of Zin*. London: Palestine Exploration Fund, 1915.

Works about Lawrence

Aldington, Richard. *Lawrence of Arabia: A Biographical Enquiry*. London: Collins, 1955.

Allen, Malcolm. *The Medievalism of Lawrence of Arabia*. University Park: Pennsylvania State University Press, 1991.

Altounyan, E.H.R. *Ornament of Honour*. Cambridge: Cambridge University Press, 1937.

Asher, Michael. *Lawrence: The Uncrowned King of Arabia*. Woodstock, New York: Overlook, 1999.

———. *Thesiger: A Biography*. New York: Viking, 1994.

Béraud-Villars, Jean. *T. E. Lawrence, or The Search for the Absolute*. Translated by Peter Dawnay. London: Sidgwick and Jackson, 1958.

Blackmore, Charles. *In the Footsteps of Lawrence of Arabia*. London: Harrap, 1986.

Caton, Stephen C. *Lawrence of Arabia: A Film's Anthropology*. Berkeley and London: University of California Press, 1999.

Crawford, Fred D. *Richard Aldington and Lawrence of Arabia: A Cautionary Tale*. Carbondale: Southern Illinois University Press, 1998.

Graves, Robert. *Lawrence and the Arabian Adventure*. New York: Doubleday, Doran, 1928.

Grosvenor, Charles. *An Iconography: The Portraits of T. E. Lawrence*. Hillsdale, N.J.: Otterbein, 1988.

Guillaume, Renée, and André Guillaume. *An Introduction and Notes: T. E. Lawrence's "Seven Pillars of Wisdom."* Translated by Hilary Mandleberg. Oxshott, Surrey: Tabard Press, 1998.

Hodson, Joel C. *Lawrence of Arabia and American Culture: The Making of a Transatlantic Legend*. Wesport, Conn.: Greenwood, 1995.

Hyde, H. Montgomery. *Solitary in the Ranks: Lawrence of Arabia as Airman and Private Soldier*. London: Constable, 1977.

James, Lawrence. *The Golden Warrior: The Life and Legend of Lawrence of Arabia*. New York: Paragon House, 1993.

Knight, Ronald D. *T. E. Lawrence and the Max Gate Circle*. Weymouth, Dorset: Bat and Ball Press, 1988.

Knightley, Phillip, and Colin Simpson. *The Secret Lives of Lawrence of Arabia*. New York: McGraw-Hill, 1970.

Knowles, Pat, and Robert Hunt. *Clouds Hill, Dorset "An handful with quietness."* Weymouth, Dorset: E.V.G. Hunt, 1994.

Larés, Maurice Jean-Marie. *T. E. Lawrence avant l'Arabie 1888–1914*. Paris: L'Harmattan, 2002.

———. *T. E. Lawrence, la France et les Français*. Paris: Publications de la Sorbonne, 1980.

Lawrence, A. W., ed. *Letters to T. E. Lawrence*. London: Jonathan Cape, 1962.

———. *T. E. Lawrence by His Friends*. New York: Doubleday, Doran, 1937.

Liddell Hart, Basil. *"T. E. Lawrence": In Arabia and After*. London: Jonathan Cape, 1934.

Lockman, J. N. *Parallel Captures?: Lord Jim and Lawrence of Arabia*. Whitmore Lake, Mich.: Falcon, 1997.

———. *Scattered Tracks on the Lawrence Trail*. Whitmore Lake, Mich.: Falcon, 1996.

Mack, John E. *A Prince of Our Disorder: The Life of T. E. Lawrence*. London: Weidenfeld and Nicolson, 1976.

Marriott, Paul. *Oxford's Legendary Son: The Young Lawrence of Arabia, 1888–1910*. Oxford: Paul Marriott, 1977.

Marriott, Paul, and Yvonne Argent. *The Last Days of T. E. Lawrence: A Leaf in the Wind*. Brighton: Alpha, 1996.

Meyers, Jeffrey. *The Wounded Spirit: A Study of "Seven Pillars of Wisdom."* 2nd ed. New York: St. Martin's, 1989.

Meyers, Jeffrey, ed. *T. E. Lawrence: Soldier, Writer, Legend*. New York: St. Martin's, 1989.

Morris, L. Robert, and Lawrence Raskin. *Lawrence of Arabia: The Thirtieth Anniversary Pictorial History*. New York: Doubleday, 1992.

Morsey, Konrad. *T. E. Lawrence und der arabische Aufstand 1916–18*. Osnabruck: Biblio-Verlag, 1976.

Mousa, Suleiman. *T. E. Lawrence: An Arab View*. Translated by Albert Boutros. New York: Oxford University Press, 1966.

Nutting, Anthony. *Lawrence of Arabia: The Man and the Motive*. London: Hollis & Carter, 1961.

O'Donnell, Thomas J. *The Confessions of T. E. Lawrence: The Romantic Hero's Presentation of Self*. Athens: Ohio State University Press, 1979.

Orgill, Douglas, *Lawrence*. New York: Ballantine, 1973.

Orlans, Harold. *T. E. Lawrence: Biography of a Broken Hero*. Jefferson, North Carolina: McFarland, 2002.

Rattigan, Terence. *Ross: A Dramatic Portrait*. London: Hamish Hamilton, 1960.

Richards, Vyvyan. *A Portrait of T. E. Lawrence: The Lawrence of the Seven Pillars of Wisdom*. London: Jonathan Cape, 1936.

Smith, Clare Sydney. *The Golden Reign: The Story of My Friendship with "Lawrence of Arabia."* London: Cassell, 1949.

Stang, Charles M., ed. *The Waking Dream of T. E. Lawrence: Essays on His Life, Literature and Legacy.* Houndmills: Palgrave, 2002.

Stewart, Desmond. *T. E. Lawrence.* London: Hamish Hamilton, 1977.

Tabachnick, Stephen E. *T. E. Lawrence.* Rev. ed. New York: Twayne, 1997. Originally published in 1978.

Tabachnick, Stephen E., ed. *The T. E. Lawrence Puzzle.* Athens: University of Georgia Press, 1984.

Tabachnick, Stephen E., and Christopher Matheson. *Images of Lawrence.* London: Jonathan Cape, 1988.

Thompson, Valerie. *"Not a Suitable Hobby for an Airman"—T. E. Lawrence as Publisher.* Long Hanborough, Oxford: Orchard Books, 1986.

Weintraub, Stanley. *Private Shaw and Public Shaw.* New York: George Brazillier, 1963.

Williamson, Henry. *Genius of Friendship, "T. E. Lawrence."* London: Faber and Faber, 1941.

Wilson, Jeremy. *Lawrence of Arabia: The Authorized Biography of T. E. Lawrence.* New York: Atheneum, 1990.

———. *T. E. Lawrence, Lawrence of Arabia.* London: National Portrait Gallery, 1988.

Wolfe, Daniel. *T. E. Lawrence.* Lives of Gay Men and Lesbians, ed. Martin Duberman. New York: Chelsea House, 1995.

Works about Related Topics, or with Sections on Lawrence

Aaronsohn, Alexander. *With the Turks in Palestine.* Boston: Houghton Mifflin, 1916.

Adam, Colin Forbes. *The Life of Lord Lloyd.* London: Macmillan, 1948.

Adelson, Roger. *Mark Sykes: Portrait of an Amateur.* London: Jonathan Cape, 1975.

Ahmad, Feroz. *The Young Turks: The Committee of Union and Progress in Turkish Politics, 1908–1914.* Oxford: Oxford University Press, 1969.

Aldington, Richard. *Letters to Alan Bird from Richard Aldington 1949–1962.* Edited by Miriam Benkovitz. New York: New York Public Library, 1975.

Allan, Mea. *Palgrave of Arabia: The Life of William Gifford Palgrave, 1826–88.* London: Macmillan, 1972.

Antonius, George. *The Arab Awakening.* London: Hamish Hamilton, 1938.

Armstrong, Harold C. *The Grey Wolf: The Life of Kemal Ataturk.* New York: Putnam, 1933.

Asprey, Robert. *War in the Shadows: The Guerrilla in History.* 2 vols. Garden City, N.Y.: Doubleday, 1975.

Baker, Randall. *King Husain and the Kingdom of Hejaz.* Cambridge: Oleander, 1979.

Bang, Anne K. *The Idrisi State in Asir, 1906–1934.* Bergen, Norway: University of Bergen, 1996.

Barker, A. J. *The Neglected War: Mesopotamia, 1914–1918.* London: Faber, 1967.

Barrow, Gen. Sir George. *The Fire of Life.* London and New York: Hutchinson, 1942.

Bidwell, Robin, ed. *Arabian Personalities of the Early Twentieth Century.* Arabia Past & Present, No. 19. Cambridge: Oleander Press, 1986. First published in 1917.

Blackmur, R. P. *The Expense of Greatness.* New York: Arrow, 1940.

Blunt, Wilfrid. *Cockerell: Sydney Carlyle Cockerell, Friend of Ruskin and William Morris and Director of the Fitzwilliam Museum, Cambridge.* London: Hamilton, 1964.

Boase, T.S.R. *Castles and Churches of the Crusading Kingdom.* London: Oxford University Press, 1967.

Boyle, Andrew. *Trenchard.* London: Collins, 1962.

Boyle, William. *My Naval Life 1886–1941.* London: Hutchinson, 1942.

Braddon, Russell. *The Siege.* New York: Viking, 1970.

Bray, N.N.E. *A Paladin of Arabia: The Life of Brevet Lieut.-Colonel G. E. Leachman, C.I.E., D.S.O., of the Royal Sussex Regiment.* London: J. Heritage and Unicorn, 1936.

Brémond, Edouard. *Le Hedjaz dans la Guerre Mondial.* Paris: Payot, 1931.

Brodie, Fawn. *The Devil Drives: A Life of Sir Richard F. Burton.* London: Eyre and Spottiswoode, 1967.

Buchan, John. *Pilgrim's Way: An Essay in Recollection.* Boston: Houghton Mifflin, 1940.

Burns, Ross. *Monuments of Syria: An Historical Guide.* London and New York: I. B. Tauris, 1999.

Busch, Briton Cooper. *Britain, India, and the Arabs, 1914–1921.* Berkeley: University of California Press, 1971.

Capstick, Peter. *Warrior: The Legend of Colonel Richard Meinertzhagen.* New York: St. Martin's, 1998.

Cocker, Mark. *Richard Meinertzhagen: Soldier, Scientist, Spy.* London: Secker and Warburg, 1989.

Daly, M. W. *The Sirdar: Sir Reginald Wingate and the British Empire in the Middle East.* Philadelphia: American Philosophical Society, 1997.

Danchev, Alex. *Alchemists of War: The Life of Basil Liddell Hart.* London: Weidenfeld and Nicolson, 1998.

Dawson, Graham. *Soldier Heroes: British Adventure, Empire and the Imagining of Masculinities.* London: Routledge, 1994.

Desmond, Kevin, and Leo Villa. *The World Water Speed Record*. London: Batsford, 1976.

Dixon, Alec. *Tinned Soldier: A Personal Record 1919–1926*. London: Jonathan Cape, 1941.

Djemal Pasha. *Memories of a Turkish Statesman, 1913–1919*. London: Hutchinson, 1922.

Doughty, Charles M. *Travels in Arabia Deserta*. 2 vols. New York: Dover, 1979.

Dunbar, Janet. *Mrs. G.B.S.: A Portrait*. New York: Harper and Row, 1963.

Elgood, Percival G. *Egypt and the Army*. London: Oxford University Press, 1924.

Engle, Anita. *The NILI Spies*. London: Hogarth Press, 1959.

Facey, William, ed. *A Soldier's Story: From Ottoman Rule to Independent Iraq—The Memoirs of Jafar Pasha al-Askari*. London: Arabian Publishers, 2003.

Falls, Cyril. *Armageddon 1918*. London: Weidenfeld and Nicolson, 1964.

Fedden, Robin. *Crusader Castles*. London: Art and Technics, 1950.

Forster, E. M. *Abinger Harvest*. New York: Harcourt Brace Jovanovich, 1964. Originally published in 1936.

———. *Two Cheers for Democracy*. New York: Harcourt, Brace, 1951.

Freulich, Roman. *Soldiers in Judea*. New York: Herzl Press, 1964.

Fromkin, David. *A Peace to End All Peace: Creating the Modern Middle East 1914–1922*. New York: Avon, 1989.

Garstang, John. *The Hittite Empire*. London: Hutchnson, 1941.

Gilbert, Bentley. *David Lloyd George: A Political Life*. Columbus: Ohio State University Press, 1987.

Gilbert, Martin. *Winston S. Churchill*. Vol. 3; vol. 4; comp. vol. IV, pt. 3. Boston: Houghton Mifflin, 1971, 1975, 1978.

Glassé, Cyril. *The Concise Encyclopedia of Islam*. San Francisco: Harper, 1989.

Glueck, Nelson. *Rivers in the Desert: A History of the Negev*. New York: Farrar, Straus, 1959.

Graves, Philip. *The Life of Sir Percy Cox*. London: Hutchinson, 1941.

[Graves, Philip, with T. E. Lawrence]. *Handbook of the Turkish Army 1916*. 8th prov. ed. London: Imperial War Museum; Nashville: Battery Press; Skokie: Articles of War, 1996. Originally published in 1916.

Graves, Richard Perceval. *Robert Graves, 1895–1926*. London: Weidenfeld and Nicolson, 1986.

Gullett, H. S. *The Australian Imperial Force in Sinai and Palestine, 1914–1918*. Sydney: Angles and Robertson, 1923.

Gurney, O. R. *The Hittites*. London and Baltimore: Penguin, 1952.

Hammond, Philip. *The Nabataeans: Their History, Culture, and Archaeology*. Gothenburg, Sweden: P. Åström, 1973.

Hankey, Maurice. *The Supreme Command 1914–1918*. London: Allen and Unwin, 1961.

Harrop, Dorothy A. *Sir Emery Walker 1881–1933*. London: Nine Elms, 1986.

Haythornthwaite, Philip J. *The World War One Source Book*. London: Arms and Armour Press, 1996.

Hitti, Philip K. *History of Syria Including Lebanon and Palestine*. New York: Macmillan, 1951.

Hogarth, D. G., et al., eds. *The Arab Bulletin: Bulletin of the Arab Bureau in Cairo 1916–1919*. 4 vols. Introduction and notes by Robin Bidwell. Gerrards Cross, Buckinghamshire: Archive Editions, 1986.

———. *The Life of Charles M. Doughty*. London: Oxford University Press, 1928.

Howard, H. C. *The King-Crane Commission*. Beirut: Khayats, 1963.

Howarth, David. *The Desert King: Ibn Saud and His Arabia*. New York: McGraw-Hill, 1964.

Hughes, Matthew. *Allenby and British Strategy in the Middle East, 1917–1919*. London: Frank Cass, 1999.

Jarvis, C. S. *Arab Command: The Biography of Lieutenant-Colonel F. G. Peake Pasha*. London: Hutchinson, 1942.

———. *Three Deserts*. London: J. Murray, 1936.

Jerrold, Walter. *Earl Kitchener of Khartoum: The Story of His Life*. London: J. Johnson, 1916.

Karsh, Efraim, and Inari Karsh. *Empires of the Sand: The Struggle for Mastery in the Middle East 1789–1923*. Cambridge: Harvard University Press, 1999.

Kedourie, Elie. *The Chatham House Version and Other Middle-Eastern Studies*. New York: Praeger, 1970.

———. *In the Anglo-Arab Labyrinth: The McMahon-Husayn Correspondence and Its Interpretations 1914–1939*. Cambridge: Cambridge University Press, 1976.

Khoury, Philip. *Syria and the French Mandate*. Princeton, N.J.: Princeton University Press, 1987.

———. *Urban Notables and Arab Nationalism: The Politics of Damascus 1860–1920*. Cambridge: Cambridge University Press, 1983.

Kiernan, R. H. *The Unveiling of Arabia*. London: Harrap, 1937.

Kirkbride, Sir Alec S. *An Awakening: The Arab Campaign 1917–1918*. London: University Press of Arabia, 1971.

———. *A Crackle of Thorns: Experiences in the Middle East*. London: J. Murray, 1956.

Klieman, Aaron S. *Foundations of British Policy in the Arab World: The Cairo Conference of 1921.* Baltimore: Johns Hopkins, 1970.

Larcher, Maurice, trans. and ed. *The Turkish War in the World War.* Washington, D.C.: Army War College, 1931.

Lloyd, John. *Aircraft of World War I.* London: Ian Allen, 1957.

Lockman, J. N. [Jon Loken]. *Meinertzhagen's Diary Ruse: False Entries on T. E. Lawrence.* Grand Rapids, Mich.: Cornerstone, 1995.

Lord, John. *Duty, Honor, Empire: The Life and Times of Col. Richard Meinertzhagen.* New York: Random House, 1970.

MacMunn, George, and Cyril Falls, eds. *Military Operations, Egypt and Palestine.* 2 vols. London: His Majesty's Stationery Office, 1928.

Magnus, Philip Montefiore. *Kitchener: Portrait of an Imperialist.* New York: Dutton, 1959.

Marwil, Jonathan. *Frederic Manning: An Unfinished Life.* Durham, N.C.: Duke University Press, 1988.

McCormick, Donald. *The Mask of Merlin: A Critical Biography of David Lloyd George.* New York: Holt, Rinehart, 1964.

Meinertzhagen, Richard. *Middle East Diary, 1917–1956.* London: Cresset Press, 1959.

Meyers, Jeffrey. *The Enemy: A Biography of Wyndham Lewis.* London: Routledge, 1982.

Millar, Ronald W. *Kut: The Death of an Army.* London: Secker and Warburg, 1969.

Moberly, F. J. *The Campaign in Mesopotamia 1914–1918.* London: H.M.S.O., 1923–1927.

Monroe, Elizabeth. *Philby of Arabia.* London: Faber, 1973.

Moorehead, Alan. *Gallipoli.* New York: Harper, 1956.

Moorey, P.R.S. *Cemeteries of the First Millenium B.C. at Deve Hüyük, near Carchemish, Salvaged by T. E. Lawrence and C. L. Woolley in 1913.* Oxford: British Archaeological Reports, 1980.

Morgenthau, Hans. *Secrets of the Bosphorus.* London: Hutchinson, 1918.

Negev, Avraham, ed. *The Archaeological Encyclopedia of the Holy Land.* Nashville: Thomas Nelson, 1986.

Nicolle, David, and Richard Hook. *Lawrence and the Arab Revolts: Warfare and Soldiers in the Middle East 1914–18.* London: Osprey, 1989.

Nicolle, David, and Raffaele Ruggieri. *The Ottoman Army 1914–18.* London: Osprey, 1996.

Ochsenwald, William. *The Hijaz Railroad.* Charlottesville: University Press of Virginia, 1980.

Perrett, Bryan. *Megiddo 1918: Lawrence, Allenby, and the March on Damascus.* Westport, Conn.: Praeger, 2004.

Philby, H. St. John. *Sa'udi Arabia.* New York: F. A. Praeger, 1955.

———. *Arabia of the Wahhabis.* New York: Arno Press, 1973.

Pirie-Gordon, H., ed. *A Brief Record of the Advance of the Egyptian Expeditionary Force under the Command of General Sir Edmund H. H. Allenby, July 1917 to October 1918.* London: H.M.S.O., 1919.

Pope, Stephen, and Elizabeth-Anne Wheal. *The Dictionary of the First World War.* New York: St. Martin's Press, 1995.

Porter, Denis. *Haunted Journeys: Desire and Transgression in European Travel Writing.* Princeton, N.J.: Princeton University Press, 1991.

Pritchett, V. S. *Books in General.* London: Chatto and Windus, 1953.

Rance, Adrian. *Fast Boats and Flying Boats: A Biography of Hubert Scott-Paine, Solent Marine and Aviation Pioneer.* Southampton: Ensign, 1989.

Rich, Barbara [Laura Riding and Robert Graves]. *No Decency Left.* London: Jonathan Cape, 1932.

Rolls, Sam Cottingham. *Steel Chariots in the Desert: The Story of an Armoured-Car Driver with the Duke of Westminster in Libya and in Arabia with T. E. Lawrence.* London: Jonathan Cape, 1937.

Rutherford, Andrew. *The Literature of War: Studies in Heroic Virtue.* Basingstoke, Macmillan, 1989.

Said, Edward. *Orientalism.* New York: Pantheon, 1978.

Savage, Raymond. *Allenby of Armageddon: A Record of the Career of Field-Marshal Viscount Allenby.* London: Hoddern and Stoughton, 1925.

Sayce, A. H. *David George Hogarth, 1862–1927.* London: Humphrey Milford, 1928.

Sharpe, Michael. *Biplanes, Triplanes, and Seaplanes.* London: Brown Books, 2000.

Sheffy, Yigal. *British Military Intelligence in the Palestine Campaign, 1914–1918.* London: Frank Cass, 1998.

Shimoni, Yaacov, and Evyatar Levine, eds. *Political Dictionary of the Middle East in the Twentieth Century.* London: Weidenfeld and Nicolson, 1972.

Shotwell, James T. *At the Peace Conference.* New York: Macmillan, 1937.

Silberman, Neil Asher. *Digging for God and Country: Exploration, Archeology, and the Secret Struggle for the Holy Land, 1799–1917.* New York: Knopf, 1982.

Silverman, Kaja. *Male Subjectivity at the Margins.* New York: Routledge, 1992.

Stirling, Walter. *Safety Last.* With a foreword by Siegfried Sasson and an epilogue by Lord Kinross. London: Hollis and Carter, 1953.

Storrs, Sir Ronald. *Orientations.* London: Nicholson and Watson, 1943.

Sutherland, L. W. *Aces and Kings.* London: J. Hamilton, 1936.

Sykes, Christopher. *Wassmuss: "The German Lawrence."* New York: Longmans, Green, 1936.

Tabachnick, Stephen E. *Charles Doughty.* Boston: Twayne, 1981.

———, ed. *Explorations in Doughty's "Arabia Deserta."* Athens: University of Georgia Press, 1987.

Tauber, Eliezer. *The Arab Movements in World War I.* London: Frank Cass, 1993.

Taylor, Andrew. *God's Fugitive: The Life of C. M. Doughty.* New York: Dorset, 1999.

Taylor, John, and Fred Jane. *Jane's Fighting Aircraft of World War I.* Foreword by John W. R. Taylor. London: Studio Editions, 1990.

Thomas, Bertram. *Arabia Felix: Across the "Empty Quarter" of Arabia.* With a foreword by T. E. Lawrence and an afterword by Sir Arthur Keith. New York: Charles Scribner, 1932.

Thomas, Lowell. *Adventures among Immortals: Percy Burton—Impresario.* New York: Dodd, Mead, 1937.

Tidrick, Kathryn. *Heart-Beguiling Araby.* Cambridge: Cambridge University Press, 1981.

Townshend, Sir Charles Vere Ferrers. *My Campaign in Mesopotamia.* London: Butterworth, 1920.

Trumpener, Ulrich. *Germany and the Ottoman Empire, 1914–1918.* Princeton, N.J.: Princeton University Press, 1968.

Verrier, Anthony, ed. *Agents of Empire: Anglo-Zionist Intelligence Operations 1915–1919; Brigadier Walter Gribbon, Aaron Aaronsohn and the NILI Ring.* London: Brassey's, 1995.

Von Lettow-Vorbeck, Paul E. *My Reminiscences of East Africa.* London: Hurst and Blackett, 1920.

Von Kressenstein, Friedrich Freiherr. *War in the Desert.* Washington: Historical Section, Army War College, 1936.

Von Sanders, Liman. *Five Years in Turkey.* Annapolis, Md.: United States Naval Institute, 1927.

Wallach, Janet. *Desert Queen: The Extraordinary Life of Gertrude Bell, Adventurer, Adviser to Kings, Ally of Lawrence of Arabia.* New York: Anchor, 1999.

Wavell, Archibald. *Allenby: A Study in Greatness.* New York: Oxford University Press, 1941.

———. *The Palestine Campaigns.* London: Constable, 1928.

Weldon, Lewen Francis Barrington. *"Hard Lying": Eastern Mediterranean, 1914–1919.* London: Jenkins, 1925.

Westrate, Bruce. *The Arab Bureau: British Policy in the Middle East, 1916–1920.* University Park: Pennsylvania State University Press, 1992.

White, B. T. *Tanks and Other Armored Fighting Vehicles, 1900 to 1918.* New York: Macmillan, 1970.

Wilson, Arnold Talbot. *Loyalties: Mesopotamia 1914–1917: A Personal and Historical Record.* New York: Greenwood, 1969.

Wilson, Colin. *The Outsider.* Boston: Houghton Mifflin, 1956.

Winstone, Harry Victor Frederick. *Captain Shakespear: A Portrait.* New York: Quartet, 1978.

———. *The Illicit Adventure: The Story of Political and Military Intelligence in the Middle East from 1898 to 1926.* London: Jonathan Cape, 1982.

———. *Leachman: "OC Desert": The Life of Lieutenant-Colonel Gerard Leachman, D.S.O.* London: Quartet, 1982.

———. *Woolley of Ur: The Life of Sir Leonard Woolley.* London: Secker and Warburg, 1990.

Winterton, Edward Turnour. *Fifty Tumultuous Years.* London: Hutchinson, 1955.

Woolley, C. Leonard. *As I Seem to Remember.* London: Allen and Unwin, 1962.

———. *Dead Towns and Living Men: Being Pages from an Antiquary's Notebook.* London: Lutterworth Press, 1954. Originally published in 1929.

Yapp, M. E. *The Making of the Modern Near East 1792–1923.* London and New York: Longman, 1987.

Young, Hubert. *The Independent Arab.* London: John Murray, 1933.

Zurcher, Erik Jan. *The Unionist Factor: The Role of the Committee of Union and Progress in the Turkish National Movement, 1905–1926.* Leiden: E. J. Brill, 1984.

Index

Page numbers in **bold** refer to main entries.

About the Author

STEPHEN E. TABACHNICK is Professor and Chair of English at the University of Memphis. He specializes in British literature from 1880 to 1940 and is also interested in biography, autobiography, and poetry. His previous books include *Fiercer Than Tigers: The Life and Works of Rex Warner* (2002), *T. E. Lawrence* (1978, 1997), *Images of Lawrence* (1988), *Explorations in Doughty's Arabia Deserta* (1987), and *Charles Doughty* (1981).